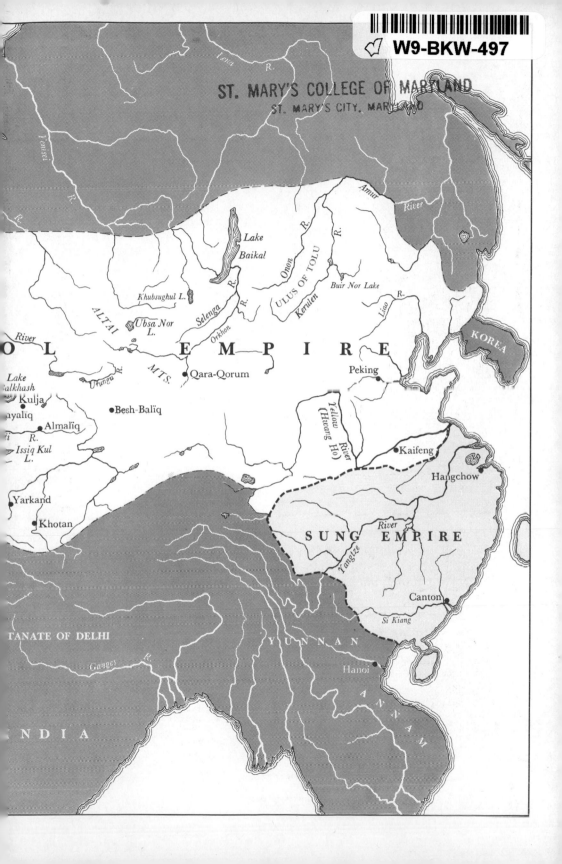

Lena R.

Yenisei

R.

Amur River

Lake Baikal

Onon R.

ULUS OF TOLU

Kerulen

Buir Nor Lake

R.

Liao R.

KOREA

Khubsughul L.

Selenga R.

ALTAI

Ubsa Nor L.

Orkhon

O L   E M P I R E

River

Urunga R.

M T S.

Qara-Qorum

Peking

Lake Balkhash

Kulja

ayaliq

Besh-Baliq

Yellow River (Hoang Ho)

Almalïq

R.

Issiq Kul L.

Kaifeng

Hangchow

Yarkand

Khotan

S U N G   E M P I R E

River

Yangtze

TANATE OF DELHI

Canton

Y U N N A N

Ganges R.

Hanoi

Si Kiang

N D I A

A N N A M

The Successors of Genghis Khan

Persian Heritage Series

The Successors of Genghis Khan

TRANSLATED FROM THE PERSIAN OF
RASHĪD AL-DĪN
BY
JOHN ANDREW BOYLE

NEW YORK AND LONDON
COLUMBIA UNIVERSITY PRESS
1971

John Andrew Boyle
is Head of the Department of Persian Studies
at the University of Manchester
in England

Copyright © 1971 Columbia University Press
International Standard Book Number: 0-231-03351-6
Library of Congress Catalog Card Number: 70-135987
Printed in the United States of America

TO THE MEMORY OF
VLADIMIR FEDOROVICH MINORSKY
(1877–1966)
WHOSE SCHOLARSHIP,
LIKE RASHĪD AL-DĪN'S *HISTORY*,
EMBRACED THE WHOLE CONTINENT
OF EURASIA

This is the first of a projected four-volume series which aims at a complete translation of the first section of Rashīd-al Dīn's great world history. This section, which deals with the Turkish and Mongol tribes, Genghis Khan and his ancestors, the successors of Genghis Khan, and finally the Ilkhans of Persia, is the most original section of Rashīd-al-Dīn's unique achievement. It is based on first-hand information and native sources, much of which is now lost.

The second section of Rashīd al-Dīn's history represents the author's successful attempt at writing for the first time a universal history. Beginning with Adam and the Patriarchs, this section "recounts the history of the pre-Islamic kings of Persia; of Muhammad and the Caliphate down to its extinction by the Mongols in 1258; of the post-Muhammadan dynasties of Persia; of Oghuz and his descendants, the Turks, of the Chinese; of the Jews; of the Franks and their Emperors and Popes; and of the Indians, with a detailed account of Buddha and Buddhism."

The translation of the above section will follow the translation of the first in the *Persian Heritage Series*.

The Persian Heritage Series is published under the joint auspices of UNESCO and the Royal Institute of Publication and Translation of Iran, affiliated with the Pahlavi Foundation. The Series owes its foundation to an initiative of H.M. the Shahanshah of Iran, and enjoys his continuing encouragement and support. The Series aims at making the best of Persian classics available in the major Western languages. The translations in this Series are intended not only to satisfy the needs of the students of Persian history and culture but also to respond to the demands of the intelligent reader who seeks to broaden his intellectual and artistic horizons through an acquaintance with the major world literatures.

EHSAN YAR-SHATER

The present work was planned as a supplement to my translation of the *History of the World-Conqueror* of Juvainī, which breaks off in the reign of the Great Khan Möngke (1251–1259); this section of the *Jāmiʿ al-Tawārīkh* of Rashīd al-Dīn carries the history of the Mongol Empire down to the reign of Möngke's great nephew Temür Öljeitü (1294–1307). As the basis of my translation I have used the text established by Edgar Blochet and published in the Gibb Memorial Series in 1911. The Russian translation by Y. P. Verkhovsky (1960) is made from an as yet unpublished text based upon two ancient manuscripts unknown to Blochet: one in the State Public Library in Tashkent, undated but apparently going back to the beginning of the 14th century, and one in the Topkapī Sarayī Library in Istanbul, dated 1317, that is, one year before Rashīd al-Dīn's death. This text is in some respects fuller than Blochet's, containing, for example, details about the Great Khan Ögedei's burial which are absent from the latter text. Such passages have been incorporated in the footnotes in translations made from Verkhovsky's Russian version. The chief importance of Verkhovsky's text lies, however, in the better preservation of Turkish and Mongol personal and geographical names, which tend to become corrupted in the later manuscripts on which Blochet's text is based. Verkhovsky has not always adopted these readings, but they are meticulously recorded in his apparatus, which has in consequence been of great assistance in solving the onomastic problems Rashīd al-Dīn's work presents in such profusion.

Many of these problems have of course been long since solved in Louis Hambis's translation of Chapter CVII of the *Yüan shih*, with supplementary notes by Paul Pelliot. The copious genealogical data in that work—derived not only from the Chinese sources but also from Rashīd al-Dīn—have rendered it unnecessary to reproduce here the tables included in Verkhovsky's but not in Blochet's text. Instead, I have supplied briefer tables, containing only the rulers of the various dynasties (see pp. 342–45). The appearance in 1963–1967 of the first three volumes of Gerhard Doerfer's monumental work, *Türkische und mongolische Elemente im Neupersischen*, has rendered it equally unnecessary to provide a detailed commentary on the Turkish and Mongol words and expressions in which the *Jāmiʿ al-Tawārīkh* abounds. For fuller information on these terms the reader is referred to Doerfer's volumes, while such Turkish and Mongol words as are retained in the English text are explained in the Glossary (see pp. 339–41), which likewise includes a number of Islamic terms of Persian and Arabic origin. No work has been of greater assistance in my researches than Pelliot's posthumous *Notes on Marco Polo*, in which frequent references are made to Blochet's text of Rashīd al-Dīn and much new light is thrown upon the historical and geographical problems common to the two authors. On such problems I have been able once again, as with my earlier translation, to consult Professor Francis W. Cleaves, Professor of Far Eastern Languages in Harvard University; I also received much help from Dr. Igor de Rachewiltz, Senior Fellow in the Department of Far Eastern History of the Australian National University, Canberra, who kindly interpreted for me several passages from the *Yüan shih*. I am deeply grateful to these two scholars for giving me access to a source which is still for the most part a closed book to all but Sinologists.

Arabic and Persian names are spelled in the translation in accordance with the system of the Royal Asiatic Society; Turkish and Mongol names, on the other hand, are spelled as far as possible in accordance with the phonetic laws of those languages with their more complicated vowel system: *ö* and *ü* are pronounced as in German (French *eu* and *u*) and *i* as the Russian *ы* (Polish *y*). Rashīd al-Dīn's spelling of Chinese names and terms, reflecting as it does the Mongol pronunciation of 13th-century Mandarin, is retained in the text, but the Wade-Giles orthography is adopted in the footnotes except for modern place-names, which appear in the more familiar Post Office transcriptions, for example, Siangyang rather than Hsiang-yang and Fukien rather than Fu-chien. Corrupt spellings are indicated in the footnotes by the same alphabet of capital letters as in the *History of the World-Conqueror*. As in that work, Arabic phrases and passages in the original are indicated by the use of italics.

In abridging the titles of works of references, I have in general had recourse to one or the other of two systems: either the author's name is followed by the year in which the book or article was published, for example, Cleaves 1952, Jahn 1969, or, especially in the case of works very frequently cited, an abbreviated form of the title is adopted, for example, *Campagnes*, *Horde d'Or*. A list of these bibliographical abbreviations will be found in the Appendix (pp. 333–38).

Rashīd al-Dīn follows his Mongol authorities in dating events by the twelve-year Animal Cycle, though for the most part giving the equivalent year according to the Muslim calendar. I have in all cases supplied the corresponding Julian year in the footnotes but have thought it useful to provide in the Appendix (p. 346) a table showing the years of the Animal Cycle corresponding to A.D. 1168–1371. It should be noted that the correspondence is only approximate, the Animal Cycle years beginning at the entry of the sun into 15° Aquarius, which at that time was on or about 27th January (now 4th February).

In conclusion, I should like to record my thanks to the Leverhulme Trust for awarding me a grant toward the preparation of the *Successors of Genghis Khan*; to Professor Ehsan Yar-Shater, Chairman of the Department of Middle Eastern languages and Cultures at Columbia University, New York, for accepting the book for inclusion in the Persian Heritage Series; to Professor Abbas Zaryab of the University of Tehran for revising the translation in accordance with the requirements of UNESCO; to Mr. Bernard Gronert, Executive Editor of the Columbia University Press, and Mrs. Barbara-Jo Kawash, the editor assigned to my manuscript, for their help and guidance during the process of publication; and to my friends Professor Charles F. Beckingham, Head of the Department of the Near and Middle East in the School of Oriental and African Studies, and Professor Thomas M. Johnstone, Professor of Arabic in the University of London, for their assistance with the proof-reading.

Manchester, December 1970   JOHN A. BOYLE

CONTENTS

Introduction

Rashīd al-Dīn Faḍl Allāh, often referred to by his contemporaries simply as Rashīd Ṭabīb ("Rashīd the Physician"), was born *ca.* 1247 in Hamadan, the Ecbatana of the Ancients. Concerning the period of his youth and early manhood, we possess no information whatsoever. The son of a Jewish apothecary, he became a convert to Islam at the age of thirty, having previously, it must be assumed, been a loyal member of the Jewish community of his native town, then an important center of Jewish culture and the seat of a well-organized *yeshivah*, or Rabbinical college, circumstances which account for his familiarity with the customs and traditions of Judaism and his knowledge of the Hebrew language.[1] His conversion may well have coincided with his entry into the service of the Il-Khan Abaqa (1265–1281), the second Mongol ruler of Iran, in the capacity of a physician, and he is perhaps to be identified with the Jew called Rashīd al-Daula (a variant form of his name), who, according to the continuator of Barhebraeus,[2] was appointed steward to the Il-Khan Geikhatu (1291–1295) "to prepare food which was suitable . . . , of every kind, which might be demanded, and wheresoever it might be demanded." At the time of the economic upheaval which preceded the experimental introduction of *ch'ao*, or Chinese paper currency, when, we are told, not even a single sheep could be procured for the Il-Khan's table, Rashīd al-Daula "stood up strongly in this matter and he spent a large sum of his own money, and he bought myriads of sheep and oxen, and he appointed butchers and cooks, and he was ready in a most wonderful fashion on the condition that in every month of days silver should be collected for the *ṣāḥib-dīwān*, because the treasury was empty, and it was destitute of money, and not even the smallest coin was to be found therein. And he wrote letters and sent them to the various countries, but the Jew was unable to collect anything. And thus the whole of his possessions came to an end, and as he was unable to stand in (i.e. continue) a work such as he was doing, he left and fled."

[1] On the question of Rashīd al-Dīn's Jewish origins, see Spuler 1939, pp. 247–49, and Fischel 1953, pp. 15–18.

[2] Barhebraeus, p. 496.

3

If this Rashīd al-Daula is not the future statesman and historian, it is strange that a man of the latter's talents should have remained in total obscurity from his entry into Abaqa's service until his appearance, some 20 years later, in the spring of 1298, as a deputy to Ṣadr al-Dīn Zanjānī, the vizier of Abaqa's grandson Ghazan (1295–1304). Rashīd al-Dīn[3] himself recounts the circumstances which led to the execution of Ṣadr al-Dīn, perhaps the most perfidious and unprincipled of the Il-Khanid viziers. It emerges from the account that he already stood high in the Il-Khan's favor and was on terms of friendship with his commander-in-chief, the Mongol Qutlugh-Shāh. In the autumn of 1298, Saʿd al-Dīn Sāvajī was appointed Ṣadr al-Dīn's successor, with Rashīd al-Dīn as his associate. We next hear of Rashīd as accompanying Ghazan on his last expedition (1302–1303) against the Mamlūks: in March 1303, he played a prominent part in the negotiations which led to the surrender of Raḥbat al-Shām, the present-day Syrian town of Meyadin on the west bank of the Euphrates. It was during Ghazan's brief reign that he carried out the fiscal reforms which go under his master's name but of which Rashīd himself may well have been the real author, reforms intended to protect the sedentary population from the rapacity of the Mongol nomad aristocracy. It was now too that he was commissioned by Ghazan to write a history of the Mongols and their conquests, a work completed and expanded under Ghazan's successor Öljeitü (1304–1316) to form the *Jāmiʿ al-Tawārīkh* ("Complete Collection of Histories"), "a vast historical encyclopedia," in the words of Barthold,[4] "such as no single people, either in Asia or in Europe, possessed in the Middle Ages."

Rashīd enjoyed still greater favor under Öljeitü. He had become the owner of vast estates in every corner of the Il-Khan's realm: orchards and vineyards in Azerbaijan, date-palm plantations in southern Iraq, arable land in western Anatolia. The administration of the state had become almost a private monopoly of his family: of his fourteen sons, eight were governors of provinces, including the whole of western Iran, Georgia, Iraq, and the greater part of what is now Turkey. Immense sums were at his disposal for expenditure on public and private enterprises. In Öljeitü's new capital at Sulṭānīya he built a fine suburb with a magnificent mosque, a *madrasa*, and a hospital;

[3] See *CHI*, p. 385. [4] *Turkestan*, p. 46.

at Tabriz he founded a similar suburb called, after himself, the Rab'-i Rashīdī. On the transcription, binding, maps, and illustrations of his various writings, he is said to have laid out a sum of 60,000 *dīnārs*, the equivalent of £36,000 in British money.

In 1312 his colleague Sa'd al-Dīn fell from grace and was put to death, and for a brief while Rashīd al-Dīn was in danger of sharing his fate. A letter in the Hebrew script purporting to be written by Rashīd was discovered and laid before Öljeitü. In it the writer urged his correspondent, a Jewish protégé of one of the Mongol emirs, to administer poison to the Il-Khan. Rashīd al-Dīn was able to prove the letter a forgery and continued to enjoy Öljeitü's favor and confidence for the remainder of the latter's reign. A rift, however, soon developed with his new colleague, Tāj al-Dīn 'Alī-Shāh, and the Il-Khan sought to remedy matters by dividing his empire into two administrative spheres, Rashīd al-Dīn being responsible for central and southern Iran, while 'Alī-Shāh was placed in charge of north-western Iran, Mesopotamia, and Asia Minor. The antagonism between the two viziers persisted despite this segregation of their duties, and in 1317, in the reign of Öljeitü's son, Abū Sa'id (1316–1335), 'Alī-Shāh succeeded by his intrigues in securing his rival's dismissal. Persuaded against his will to re-enter the Il-Khan's service, Rashīd al-Dīn was attacked once again by 'Alī-Shāh and his party and accused of having poisoned Abū Sa'īd's father. According to the Mamlūk sources, he admitted having gone against the advice of Öljeitü's physicians and prescribed a purgative for his disorder, the symptoms of which do appear to have been consistent with metallic poisoning. On this admission he was cruelly put to death, his severed head, according to the same authorities, being taken to Tabriz and carried about the town for several days with cries of: "This is the head of the Jew who abused the name of God; may God's curse be upon him!" Rab'-i Rashīdī, the suburb of Tabriz which he had founded and given his name, was looted by the mob, and all his estates and property were confiscated, even his pious foundations being robbed of their endowments. His final resting-place, a mausoleum of his own construction, was destroyed less than a century later by Mīrān-Shāh, the mad son of Tīmūr, who caused Rashīd's body to be exhumed and re-interred in the Jewish cemetery.

The encyclopedist Ibn Ḥajar of Ascalon (d. 1449) reproduces what was undoubtedly the contemporary assessment of Rashīd al-Dīn: a Jewish apothecary's son turned Muslim who rose in the service of the Il-Khans to the rank of vizier; who championed and protected the followers of his adopted faith; who built fine public buildings in Tabriz; who, while merciless to his enemies, was generous in the extreme to the learned and the pious; and who wrote a rationalistic commentary on the Koran for which he was accused of *ilḥād*, that is, of belonging to the outcast sect of the Ismāʿīlīs, or Assassins.[5] To the *Jāmiʿ al-Tawārīkh*, the work on which his fame now rests, Ibn Ḥajar makes no reference whatsoever.

HIS WORKS

Rashīd al-Dīn himself has described the elaborate measures which he adopted to ensure the preservation of his writings and their transmission to posterity.[6] These measures included the translation into Arabic of all his Persian and into Persian of all his Arabic works, while a specified annual sum was allocated for the preparation of two complete transcripts, one in either language, "on the best Baghdad paper and in the finest and most legible writing," to be presented to one of the chief towns of the Muslim world. Despite these and other precautions, it was the opinion of Quatremère[7] that "we have lost the greater part of the works of this learned historian, and all the measures which he took have not had a more fortunate success than the precautions devised by the Emperor Tacitus to secure the preservation of his illustrious relative's writings." The passage of time has shown Quatremère to have been unduly pessimistic. A diligent search of the libraries of Persia, Turkey, and Central Asia has filled some of the lacunae, and it is too early to assume that any of the works still missing are irretrievably lost.

Of his theological writings reference has already been made to his commentary on the Koran, which bore the title *Miftāḥ al-Tafāsīr* ("Key to the Commentaries"). Neither this nor his *Favāʾid-i Sulṭānīya*

---

[5] Ibn Ḥajar, pp. 232–33.   [6] See Browne, pp. 77–79.

[7] Quoted by Browne, pp. 79–80.

("Royal Deductions"), based on a conversation with Öljeitü on religious and philosophical questions, nor his *As'ila u Ajviba* ("Question and Answers"), containing the author's correspondence with Muslim and even Byzantine scholars, has yet been published. His *Kitāb al-Aḥyā wa-'l-Āthār* ("Book of Animals and Monuments"), dealing with botany, agriculture, and architecture, is described by Browne as "unhappily lost." Several chapters of it were, however, published in Tehran in 1905 from a manuscript which may still be in existence. Finally, a work unknown to Quatremère, the *Mukātabāt-i Rashīdī*, the correspondence of Rashīd al-Dīn, mainly on political and financial matters, with his sons and other Il-Khanid officials, was published in 1947 by Professor Shafi of Lahore and has recently been translated into Russian.[8]

Of his *magnum opus*, the *Jāmiʻ al-Tawārīkh*, there appear to have been two versions, an earlier (1306–1307) consisting of three, and a later (*ca.* 1310) consisting of four volumes.[9] Volume I, the *Ta'rīkh-i Ghāzānī*, a history of the Mongols from their beginnings until the reign of Ghazan, has already been mentioned. In Volume II, commissioned by Ghazan's successor, Öljeitü, Rashīd al-Dīn was set the formidable task of compiling a general history of all the Eurasian peoples with whom the Mongols had come into contact. Beginning with Adam and the Patriarchs, the volume recounts the history of the pre-Islamic kings of Persia; of Muḥammad and the Caliphate down to its extinction by the Mongols in 1258; of the post-Muḥammadan dynasties of Persia; of Oghuz and his descendants, the Turks; of the Chinese; of the Jews; of the Franks and their Emperors and Popes; and of the Indians, with a detailed account of Buddha and Buddhism. Volume II is, in fact, the first universal history. "One can seek in vain," says Professor Jahn,[10] "both in the foregoing and in the following centuries for an equally bold and at the same time successful enterprise. This very first attempt to commit to paper a faithful account of the history of the world has not as yet been accorded the recognition it deserves as a unique achievement . . ." A history of Öljeitü from his birth until the year 706/1306–7 was originally prefixed to Volume II. A manuscript

---

[8] On Rashīd al-Dīn's nonhistorical works, see Togan 1962, pp. 60–63, and Jahn 1964, *passim*.

[9] See Jahn 1964, p. 119.   [10] Jahn 1965, p. x.

of this portion discovered by Professor A. Z. V. Togan in Meshed has since disappeared. The original Volume III, bearing the title *Ṣuwar al-Aqālīm* ("Forms of the Climes"), was a geographical compendium containing "not only a geographical and topographical description of the globe as it was then known . . . , but also an account of the system of highways in the Mongol Empire, with mention of the milestones erected at imperial command, and a list of postal stages."[11] No manuscript of this volume has yet come to light. On the other hand, Volume III of the second version (in which the *Ṣuwar al-Aqālīm* became Volume IV), bearing the title *Shuʿab-i Panjgāna* ("The Five Genealogies"), has survived in a unique manuscript, discovered by Professor Togan in 1927, in the Topkapı Sarayı Library in Istanbul. As its title indicates, it contains the genealogies of the ruling houses of five nations: the Arabs, Jews, Mongols, Franks, and Chinese.[12]

The text of Volume I, published piecemeal in various countries over a period of more than a century, is now available in its entirety. On the other hand, much of Volume II is still accessible only in manuscripts. The sections on Sultan Maḥmūd of Ghazna and the Seljuqs were published by the late Professor Ateş in 1957 and 1960, respectively, and that on the Ismāʿīlīs by Mr. Dabīr Siyāqī (1958), and again by Messrs. Dānish-Pazhūh and Mudarrisī (1960), whilst Professor Jahn has produced an edition and translation of the *History of the Franks* (1951), facsimiles of the Persian and Arabic text of the *History of India* (1965) and a translation and facsimile of the *History of Oghuz and the Turks* (1969). The remainder of the volume, as also Volume III, the *Shuʿab-i Panjgāna*, is as yet unpublished.

It is, of course, Volume II, with its concluding sections on the history of the various non-Muslim peoples, that gives the work its unique character as "the first universal history of Orient and Occident."[13] As a historical document, however, it is not to be compared with Volume I, the *Taʾrīkh-i Ghāzānī*, which, based as it largely is on native sources now lost, constitutes our chief authority on the origins of the Mongol peoples and the rise of the Mongol World Empire. This volume, according to the original arrangement, consisted of

---

[11] Jahn 1964, p. 120.
[12] On the *Shuʿab-i Panjgāna*, see Togan 1962, pp. 68–69, and Jahn 1963, pp. 198–99.
[13] Jahn 1965, p. x.

two sections of unequal length, of which the first and shorter contained the history of the different Turkish and Mongol tribes, their divisions, genealogies, legends, etc., in a preface and four chapters, whilst the second and very much larger section dealt with the history of Genghis Khan, his ancestors, and his successors, down to the Il-Khan Ghazan. A more convenient division into three separate volumes, first proposed by E. G. Browne in 1908, has been adopted by the Russians in their recent editions and translations of the Persian text. In accordance with this arrangement, Rashīd al-Dīn's original Volume I is sub-divided as follows:

> Volume I, Part 1: The Turkish and Mongol Tribes
> Volume I, Part 2: Genghis Khan and his Ancestors
> Volume II: The Successors of Genghis Khan
> Volume III: The Il-Khans of Persia

Besides the new Russian translations, there is also an older Russian version of Volume I of the text as thus divided, while the beginning of Volume III (the reign of Hülegü) was translated into French by Quatremère as long ago as 1836. In the present version of Volume II, Rashīd al-Dīn appears for the first time in English dress.[14]

The volume begins with the history of Ögedei, Genghis Khan's third son and first successor (1229–1241) as Great Khan. Next come accounts of Genghis Khan's other three sons: the eldest, Jochi (d. 1227), with the history of the Golden Horde, founded by his son Batu (1237–1256), down to the reign of Toqta (1291–1312); the second, Chaghatai, the eponymous founder (1227–1242) of the Chaghatai dynasty in Central Asia, with the history of that dynasty down to the reign of Du'a (1282–1307); and the youngest, Tolui (d. 1233), the father of two Great Khans, Möngke and Qubilai, and of Hülegü, the founder of the Il-Khanid dynasty of Persia. There follow the reigns of the Great Khans, successors to Ögedei: his son Güyük (1246–1248), his nephews Möngke (1251–1259) and Qubilai (1260–1294) and, finally, Qubilai's grandson, Temür Öljeitü (1294–1307). As in the case of Genghis Khan, the biography of each prince is divided into three parts: the first contains a list of his wives, sons, and descendants, the

---

[14] A French translation of the first 136 pages of Blochet's text (pp. 16–122 of the present translation) was found amongst the papers of the late Paul Pelliot.

9

second gives the details of his life and reign, and the third, in theory, consists of anecdotes illustrating the ruler's character, a selection of his *biligs*, or sayings, along with other miscellaneous information. But, in practice, this latter part is often absent, the rubric being followed in the manuscripts by a space left blank for the subsequent insertion of the relevant data. Part I, in the original manuscripts, included a portrait of the prince and a genealogical table of his descendants and Part II a picture of his enthronement; references to these and other illustrations are made in the present text. In Part II, in the case of the Great Khans only, the narrative is interrupted at intervals to give the names of the contemporary Chinese and Muslim rulers and also some account of contemporary events within the latter's territories. Here, too, there are sometimes blanks in the manuscripts where the name of a ruler had not been ascertainable at the time of writing.

The *Successors of Genghis Khan*, as the English title indicates, takes up the history of the Mongol Empire from the death of its founder. It recounts the campaigns in Russia and eastern Europe (1236–1242) which led to the establishment of the Golden Horde; it describes the conquest of southern China (1268–1279), which changed the House of Qubilai (better known to us as Kubla Khan) into the Chinese dynasty of the Yüan; and it breaks off in the reign of Qubilai's grandson Temür (1294–1307), still the nominal suzerain of territories extending westward from Korea to the Balkans. Only Hülegü's expedition to the West, the destruction of the Ismāʿīlīs (1256), the overthrow of the Caliphate (1258), and the long struggle with the Mamlūk rulers of Egypt (1259–1313) receive no mention, these events being recorded in the following volume on the Il-Khans of Persia. Here, in the *Successors of Genghis Khan*, we have, as in the *Travels of Marco Polo*, a survey of Asia under the *pax Mongolica*, but with this difference—that Rashīd al-Dīn had access to far more copious and authoritative sources of information than the Venetian, whose account of Qubilai's Empire, for all its amazing detail, is of necessity restricted to the evidence of his own eyes and ears.

The earliest parts of the *Jāmiʿ al-Tawārīkh* are based almost exclusively on a Mongolian chronicle called the *Altan Debter*, or "Golden Book," which, as Rashīd al-Dīn himself tells us, was preserved in the Il-Khan's treasury in the charge of certain high officers. It is unlikely that the historian had direct access to this work, which was regarded as sacred; its contents were probably expounded to him orally by Bolad Ching-sang, "Bolad the *chêng-hsiang* or Minister," the representative of the Great Khan at the Persian Court, and by Ghazan himself, who as an authority on the Mongol traditions was second only to Bolad. The original text of the *Golden Book* has not come down to us, but a Chinese version, the *Shêng-wu ch'in-chêng lu*, or "Description of the Personal Campaigns of the Holy Warrior (that is, Genghis Khan)," written at some time prior to 1285, is still extant, and the work was also utilized in the *Yüan shih*, the dynastic history of the Mongols compiled in 1369.[15] In his account of Genghis Khan's campaign in western Asia, Rashīd al-Dīn is for the most part content to reproduce, in a somewhat abridged form, the narrative of Juvainī, in his *Ta'rīkh-i Jahān-Gushā* ("History of the World Conqueror"),[16] but here too there are not infrequent interpolations from the Mongolian chronicle, and he even adopts its faulty chronology, in accordance with which the events of the campaign take place a year later than in reality. In the present volume, Juvainī continues, down to the reign of Möngke (1251–1259), to be Rashīd al-Dīn's main authority, but with considerable additional material from other sources. Thus the earlier historian's account of the invasion of eastern Europe (1241–1242) is repeated almost verbatim and is then followed, in a later chapter, by a much more detailed version of the same events, based, like the preceding description of the campaigns in Russia (1237–1240), on "rough Mongol records,"[17] as is evident from the orthography of the proper names. So too in recounting the final campaign against the Chin rulers of northern China (1231–1234), Rashīd al-Dīn combines data from Juvainī with information derived from Far East—Mongol and, to some extent, Chinese—sources. For the reigns of Qubilai and Temür he must have relied mainly upon the official correspondence of the Il-Khans, supplemented no doubt by the questioning of ambassadors and merchants arriving from eastern Asia. The Great Khan's representative, Bolad Chingsang, whom Rashīd had consulted on the early history of the Mongols, seems also to have been his chief authority on contemporary China.

[15] See Boyle 1962, p. 164.   [16] See *HWC* and Juvainī.
[17] Minorsky 1952, p. 223.

The accounts of Qubilai's campaigns are plainly based on Mongolian rather than Chinese sources. They lack the topographical and chronological precision of the *Yüan shih* and contain many obviously legendary or folkloristic elements. They are valuable none the less as illustrative of the Mongol point of view and add considerable detail and color to the somewhat laconic narrative of the Chinese chronicles. Thus we read in Rashīd al-Dīn that Qubilai, when crossing the Yangtse to lay siege to Wuchang in Hupeh, made use of a specially fashioned birch-bark talisman.[18] This resort to a shamanistic practice, designed apparently to placate the water spirits of the great river, is passed over in silence by the Chinese authorities; but we may well believe that the convert to Buddhism and the patron of Confucianism was still at heart a primitive animist. Again, the story of the twenty thousand criminals released from jail by the Great Khan's decree to take part in the conquest of the South[19] is too circumstantial not to have some foundation in fact. Many legends must have been woven around the long and famous siege (1268–1273) of Siangyang, and it is perhaps in some such popular tale that Gau Finjan (the historical Kao Ho-chang involved in the murder of the vizier Aḥmad of Fanākat, Polo's Bailo Acmat) is made to play a part in the final capture of the stronghold.[20] Rashīd al-Dīn is at least right in stating that the mangonels employed against the defenses were of Muslim manufacture. They can hardly have been constructed, as Marco Polo alleges, by Christian engineers under the supervision of his father, his uncle, and himself during the course of a siege which had not yet begun when the elder Polos left China after their first visit and had been over for 2 years before Marco himself first entered China![21] On the whole, however, Polo and Rashīd al-Dīn tend to corroborate and complement each other's statements, and between them the Venetian and the Persian provide a wonderfully vivid and detailed picture of Mongol China. It is perhaps these chapters of the *Successors of Genghis Khan* that will make the greatest appeal to the general reader.

To the historian, Rashīd al-Dīn's work is above all a repository of material on the history, legends, beliefs, and mode of life of the 12th- and 13th-century Mongols, material that has survived nowhere else in such

[18] See p. 248 and note 31. [19] See pp. 271–72.
[20] See pp. 288–91 and note 199. [21] See pp. 290–91 and note 204.

profusion. The earliest parts of the *Ta'rīkh-i Ghāzānī* are, as we have seen, based almost exclusively on native tradition. In the present volume, the data on the Golden Horde, on the rebellion of Qubilai's younger brother Arïq Böke,[22] and on the long-drawn-out struggle between Qubilai and Qaidu[23] are derived from similar written or oral sources. We learn here too how this material was preserved: how "it was the custom in those days to write down day by day every word that the ruler uttered," a special courtier being appointed for this purpose; how these *biligs* or sayings, often couched in "rhythmical and obscure language," were recited on festive occasions by such exalted persons as the Great Khan Ögedei and his brother Chaghatai;[24] and how Temür Öljeitü was chosen to succeed his grandfather Qubilai because he knew the *biligs* of Genghis Khan better than his rival and declaimed them "well and with a pure accent."[25] Of the *biligs* recorded in the *Successors of Genghis Khan*, we may quote the saying attributed to a grandson of Genghis Khan's youngest son Tolui, a man called Toq-Temür, who was "extremely brave and a very good archer":

In battle he rode a gray horse and used to say: "People choose bays and horses of other colors so that blood may not show on them and the enemy not be encouraged. As for me, I choose a gray horse, because just as red is the adornment of women, so the blood on a rider and his horse, which drips on to the man's clothes and the horse's limbs and can be seen from afar, is the adornment and decoration of men."[26]

Besides preserving the traditional lore of the Mongols and recording the history of their world empire, Rashīd al-Dīn was also the historian of his own country. Volume III of the *Ta'rīkh-i Ghāzānī* is our main source on the Il-Khanid period of Persian history and contains what Professor Petrushevsky has called a "priceless collection"[27] of Ghazan's *yarlïghs*, or decrees, on his fiscal reforms, of which Rashīd al-Dīn was an ardent supporter and perhaps the initiator. The fame of the statesman-historian rests, however, less on these solid achievements than on the attempt, in the second part of his work, to compile a general history of the whole Eurasian continent. His is certainly the credit of producing, 600 years before Wells' *Outline of History*, the first World History in the full sense ever written in any language.

[22] See pp. 248–65.   [24] See p. 155.   [26] P. 162.
[23] See pp. 22–24 and 266–69.   [25] See p. 321.   [27] Petrushevsky 1967, p. 8.

1

Beginning of the History of Ögetei Qa'an,

the Son of Chingiz-Khan:

History of Ögetei Qa'an,

which is in Three Parts

BEGINNING OF THE HISTORY OF
ÖGETEI[1] QA'AN,

THE SON OF CHINGIZ-KHAN[2]

History of Ögetei Qa'an, which is in Three Parts

Those stories which refer to him personally and concern his deeds and actions and sayings in respect to kingship, justice, and bounty, apart from what has been included in the histories of his father, brothers, and kinsmen, will now be related so that the reader may at once be apprised of them herefrom. And the reason for giving his history precedence over that of his brothers Jochi and Chaghatai, who were older than he,[3] is that he was the heir-apparent of Chingiz-Khan and the Qa'an of the time, and his reign followed that of Chingiz-Khan, so that it is in the order of the Khanate.

◆ PART I. An account of his lineage; a detailed account of his wives and of the branches into which his descendants have divided down to the present day; his portrait; and a genealogical table of his descendants.

◆ PART II. The [general] history of and [particular] anecdotes regarding his reign; a picture of his throne and wives and the princes and emirs on the occasion of his ascending the throne of the Khanate; an account of the battles he fought and the victories he gained.

◆ PART III. His praiseworthy character and morals; the excellent *biligs*,[4] parables and pronouncements which he uttered and promulgated; such events and happenings as occurred during his reign but have not been included in the two previous parts, the information having been acquired on separate occasions and at irregular intervals from various books and persons.

---

[1] Mo. Ögedei or Ögödei, the Occoday of Carpini. The Ögetei of the Muslim sources is apparently due to a misreading of the Uighur script, in which *d* and *t* are not distinguished. See Doerfer, I, No. 49 (pp. 167–69).

[2] There is no certain etymology of the first element in the title (Anglicized as Genghis Khan) bestowed upon the Mongol Temüjin. For the various theories, see Doerfer, I, No. 185 (pp. 312–15). The most widely accepted is that *chingiz* (*chinggis*) is a palatalized form of T. *tengiz*, "sea," and that the title in consequence means "Oceanic Khan," that is, "Universal Ruler."

[3] The precise ages of Ögedei's older brothers are not known. Ögedei himself was born in 1186.   [4] See Glossary.

PART I

OF THE HISTORY OF ÖGETEI QA'AN

An account of his lineage; an account of his wives;
a detailed account of the various branches
into which his sons and grandsons have divided down to the present day;
his portrait;
and a genealogical table of his descendants

Ögetei Qa'an was the third son of Chingiz-Khan and his wife Börte Fujin, who was the mother of his five[5] chief sons and five principal daughters. She belonged to the Qonqïrat tribe[6] and was the daughter of Dei Noyan:[7] an account of Ögetei's brothers and sisters has been given in the history of Chingiz-Khan.[8] Ögetei's name had originally been ———.[9] He did not like it, and afterward he was named Ögetei: the meaning of the word is "ascent to the top."[10] He was famous for his intelligence, ability, judgment, counsel, firmness, dignity, and justice; but he was pleasure loving and a wine-bibber, and Chingiz-Khan sometimes used to rebuke and admonish him on that account. And when Chingiz-Khan had tested the qualities of his sons and discovered for what employment each of them was fitted, he had some hesitation regarding the disposal of the throne and the Khanate, thinking now of Ögetei Qa'an and now of his youngest son, Tolui Khan. And although it has been the rule and custom of the Mongols from ancient times that the father's *yurt*[11] or original abode and house should be administered by the youngest son, he afterward said: "The

---

[5] A mistake for *four*: Jochi, Chaghatai, Ögetei, and Tolui.
[6] On the Qonqïrat (Qonggirat), or Onggirat, a tribe in the extreme east of Mongolia, see *Campagnes*, pp. 402–409.
[7] On Dei Noyan or Dei Sechen, see *Campagnes*, pp. 411–14.
[8] See Smirnova, pp. 68–70. [9] There is a blank in the MSS.
[10] Actually, Mo. *ögede* means "upward, uphill."
[11] See Glossary.

17

business of the throne and kingdom is a difficult business: let Ögetei administer it. But as for such things as my *yurt* and house and the property, treasures, and troops that I have gathered together, let these be all administered by Tolui." And whenever he consulted with his sons about this, they, seeing it to be their father's counsel, would all agree to it and support it. Finally, when a disease overtook him in the land of the Tangqut,[12] as has been mentioned,[13] he held a private meeting and made [Ögetei] his heir, settling the throne and the Khanate upon him. He also assigned a [special] path to each of his sons, saying: "Whoever has a desire for ————,[14] let him join Jochi, And whoever wishes to have a good knowledge of the *yosun*,[15] manners, and *biligs*, let him go to Chaghatai. And whoever has an inclination for generosity and liberality and seeks wealth and riches, let him approach Ögetei. And whoever wishes for valor, and fame, and the defeat of armies, and the capture of kingdoms, and world conquest, let him attend upon Tolui." He also had established his sons and the emirs and the army and, as has been set forth in his history, had given each of them his separate allotted share.

❧ ACCOUNT OF HIS WIVES AND CONCUBINES

Ögetei Qa'an had many wives and sixty concubines. But his chief wives, those who were well known, were four. His first wife, Boraqchin, was of the tribe of ————,[16] the daughter of ————;[17] she was the eldest. His second wife, Töregene, was of the tribe of the Uhaz-Merkit,[18] and in some accounts it is stated that she was the wife of Tayir-Usun,[19] the leader of the Uhaz-Merkit, and that when her husband was killed she was carried off and Ögetei Qa'an married her,

[12] The Tangut (in Chinese, Hsi Hsia) were a people of Tibetan origin, living in what is now Kansu and the Ordos Region of Inner Mongolia.

[13] Smirnova, pp. 232–33.

[14] There is a blank in the MSS, to be filled, according to the corresponding passage in Juvainī (*HWC*, p. 40), with a word or phrase meaning "hunting" or "the chase."

[15] See Glossary.   [16] Blank in the MSS.

[17] Blank in the MSS.

[18] On the various clans of the Merkit (a forest tribe in the region of the Lower Selenga along the southern shores of Lake Baikal), see *Campagnes*, pp. 273–78.

[19] For Dayir-Usun, see above, p. 16, note 1.

Tayir-Usun having previously given his daughter Qulan Khatun in marriage to Chingiz-Khan. According to one account, Töregene belonged to this tribe but was not the wife of Tayir-Usun.[20] This wife was of no great beauty but of a very masterful nature. As shall be mentioned in the history of Güyük Khan,[21] she reigned for awhile, and because she paid no attention to the testament of Chingiz-Khan and did not listen to the words of *aqa* and *ini*[22] she cast confusion amongst *aqa* and *ini* and the seed of Chingiz-Khan, as shall be related in the history of Güyük Khan.

☙ ACCOUNT OF THE SONS OF ÖGETEI QA'AN

Ögetei had seven sons. The mother of the five eldest was Töregene Khatun, and the two others were each of them born of a concubine. The names of those seven sons and their descendants, insofar as they are known, shall be set forth in detail [below],

First son—Güyük

His *yurt* was in the land of the Qobaq in a place called ——— ———, Emil, or ——— ———.[23] Although Ögetei Qa'an's heir apparent was his grandson Shiremün, yet after the death of Qa'an, Töregene Khatun and the sons of Ögetei Qa'an disobeyed [Ögetei's] command and elevated Güyük to the Khanate, despite the fact that all his life he had been afflicted with chronic diseases. His life will be described in detail in a separate history.[24] He had three sons, as follows:

---

[20] According to *SH*, p. 198, her first husband had been Qodu, the eldest son of Toqto'a, the ruler of the Uduyit-Merkit. According to the *Yüan shih* (*Papauté*, p. [193]), she was a Naiman.

[21] See below, p. 174.

[22] See Glossary.

[23] Güyük's apanage lay between the Qobaq (Kobuk) and Emil (Emel) in what is now Northern Sinkiang. See *Papauté*, pp. [206]–[207], note 2. The other names (BRY MNKRAQ and YWR SAWR) have not been identified. (The latter name is perhaps a corruption of *QWM SNKR, that is Qum-Sengir, on which see below, p. 121, note 95.)

[24] See below, pp. 174–88.

Khwāja Oghul. His mother was Oghul-Qaimish Khatun of the ———[25] tribe. He has no known children.

Naqu. He too was born of Oghul-Qaimish Khatun and had a son called Chabat. When Baraq entered Persia to attack Abaqa Khan [Qaidu] sent this Chabat with one thousand men, who were his private forces, to reinforce [Baraq]. He withdrew in anger before the battle, and when he came to Bukhārā, Beg-Temür, the son of Baraq, sent an army after him to capture him, but he fled with nine horsemen and came by way of the desert to Qaidu. He fell ill with fear and died of that illness.[26]

Hoqu. His mother was a concubine. It is said that he has a grandson, called Tökme, who disputed with Chapar, the son of Qaidu, and [who] refuses to obey [Chapar], saying, "The accession should go to me." His father's name [also] was Tökme.[27]

The stories of these three sons will be told in detail in the histories of Güyük Khan and Möngke Khan,[28] in the proper place, God willing.

Second son—Köten

Möngke Qa'an gave him a *yurt* in the land of the Tangqut and sent him thither with an army.[29] He had three sons,[30] as follows:

Möngetü. His mother was ———.[31]

Küyen. He was born of ———.[32] He had a son, Yesü-Buqa.

---

[25] Blank in the MSS. Elsewhere (Khetagurov, p. 116), Rashīd al-Dīn says that she was a Merkit. See also *Papauté*, p. [198] and note 2.

[26] See below pp. 140 and 152–53; also Arends, p. 76.

[27] See also below, p. 175, in the section on Güyük Khan. There Verkhovsky's text is in agreement with Blochet's, but here (Verkhovsky, pp. 10–11) he speaks of ten sons of Hoqu, of whom only eight are actually enumerated. The *Yüan shih* (*Chapitre CVII*, p. 86 and 87, note 6) mentions only one son T'u-lu (*Tu[q]lu[q]), prince of Nan-p'ing.

[28] So according to Khetagurov's text (p. 11). Blochet, whose MSS have blanks in this place, has supplied the names of Chaghatai Khan and Abaqa Khan (p. 5). On Khwāja and Naqu, see below, pp. 175, 204, and 207–14. Hoqu is mentioned only in the passage referred to in note 27.

[29] Köten (Ködön, Godon) had, in fact, already been appointed to this region during Güyük's reign. He was the first of the Mongols to establish relations with Tibetan lamaism. See Franke, V, pp. 331–32; also Schmidt, p. 111–13.

[30] Five, according to the *Yüan shih* (*Chapitre CVII*, p. 74).

[31] Blank in the MSS.   [32] Blank in the MSS.

Jibik-Temür. His mother was ———.[33] He had sons but their names are not known.

When the sons of Ögetei Qa'an and Güyük Khan plotted treason and treachery against Möngke Qa'an, because these sons of Köten had formerly been his friends and supporters, he did them no injury when he convicted those people of their crime and withdrew and distributed their armies; on the contrary, he confirmed them in the possession of the armies they had. And since the country of the Tangqut was their *yurt*, Qubilai Qa'an and his son Temür Qa'an maintained the seed of Köten there, and they are still as ever friends and supporters of the Qa'an and obedient to his command; their affairs are prosperous and well ordered under the shadow of the Qa'an's favor.

Third son—Köchü

This son had the appearance of being very intelligent and fortunate. Möngke Qa'an intended to make him his heir, but he died during [Möngke Qa'an's] lifetime. He had three sons, as follows:

Shiremün. His mother was ———[34] Khatun of the ———[35] tribe.

Boladchi. He was born of ———[36] Khatun of the ———[37] tribe and was in attendance on ———.[38]

Söse. His mother was ———[39] of the ———[40] tribe. He was in attendance on ———.[41]

When Köchü died, Möngke Qa'an, because of his friendship for his father, made much of Shiremün, his eldest son, [who was] exceedingly intelligent and clever; he brought him up in his *ordos* and used to say that he was his heir and successor. In the end [Shiremün] plotted treason and treachery against Möngke Qa'an and was convicted for his crime. When Möngke Qa'an sent his brother Qubilai Qa'an to Khitai,[42] Qubilai, having a friendship for this Shiremün, asked him of his brother and took him [Shiremün] with him. But

---

[33] Blank in the MSS.
[35] Blank in the MSS.
[37] Blank in the MSS.
[39] Blank in the MSS.
[41] Blank in the MSS.

[34] Blank in the MSS.
[36] Blank in the MSS.
[38] Blank in the MSS.
[40] Blank in the MSS.

[42] The medieval name for northern China, our Cathay, on which see *Polo I*, pp. 216 ff.

when Möngke Qa'an set out for Nangiyas,[43] and Qubilai Qa'an joined him, he did not trust Shiremün and ordered him to be thrown in the river.

Fourth son—Qarachar

It is said that this Qarachar had one son, whose name was Totaq, and their *yurt* was in ————.[44]

Fifth son—Qashi

Inasmuch as at the time he was born Chingiz-Khan had conquered the country of Qashi,[45] which is now called Tangqut, he was named Qashi. Being a heavy and confirmed drinker, he died in his youth of the deterioration brought on by excessive inebriety, his death occurring during his father's lifetime. The name Qashi was banned and thereafter the country was called Tangqut.[46] He had a son called Qaidu by Sebkine Khatun of the ————[47] people. [This son] lived to a great age and died only last year.[48] This Qaidu was brought up in the *ordo*[49] of Chingiz-Khan and after Ögetei's death was in attendance upon Möngke Qa'an, upon whose death he joined Arïq Böke and supported and worked for his elevation to the Khanate. When Arïq Böke went to Qubilai Qa'an and made his submission, Qaidu was filled with fear of Qubilai Qa'an; and since it was not the *yasa*[50] that anyone should disobey the command and order of the Qa'an, and whoever did so was a wrongdoer, he transgressed the *yasa*, committed acts of resistance, and became a rebel. From that time until

[43] (The country of) the Southern Chinese, from Chinese Nan-Chia, that is "people of the South."

[44] Blank in the MSS.

[45] From Ho-hsi, then the common Chinese name for the country. See *Polo I*, p. 125.

[46] On the Mongol taboo on the names of the dead, see Boyle 1956.

[47] Blank in the MSS. Elsewhere (Khetagurov, pp. 149–50) Rashīd al-Dīn says that Qaidu's mother belonged to the Bekrin, a tribe of mountaineers who were "neither Mongols nor Uighur."

[48] That is, in 1301. He was born, according to Jamāl Qarshi (*Four Studies*, I, p. 124) about 1235. The statement that he took part in the invasion of Hungary in 1241, often repeated, most recently by Dawson (p. xxxi, note 1), is due to a mistake of Wolff (*Geschichte der Mongolen*, Breslau, 1872, pp. 154 and 159). See *Polo I*, p. 125.

[49] See Glossary.   [50] See Glossary.

this present age, many Mongols and Tāzīks[51] have been destroyed and flourishing countries laid waste because of his rebellion. At first Qaidu had not many troops or followers, for when the seed of Ögetei Qa'an plotted against Möngke Qa'an, their troops were taken from them and distributed, except those of Köten's sons. However, he was an exceedingly intelligent, competent, and cunning man and accomplished all his affairs by means of craft and guile. He contrived to gather together, out of every corner, some two or three thousand men, and because Qubilai Qa'an had set up his headquarters in Khitai for the purpose of conquering Māchīn,[52] and because of the great distance [between them], Qaidu adopted a rebellious attitude. And when Qubilai summoned him and his family to a *quriltai*,[53] they made excuses in the first, second, and third years and did not go. Little by little he gathered troops around him from every side; and, making friends with Jochi's family, he captured a number of territories with their assistance. Qubilai Qa'an now saw fit to dispatch an army to deal with them, sending his son Nomoghan with a group of princes and emirs and a large body of troops. Upon the way, Nomoghan's uncles decided upon an act of treachery and, seizing him and Hantum Noyan, the commander of the army, they sent Nomoghan to Mengü-Temür, of the seed of Jochi, who was then ruler of that *ulus*, and Hantum Noyan to Qaidu, the details of which events will be given in the history of Qubilai Qa'an.[54] From that time until the present day when the world is adorned by the august splendor of the Lord of Islam[55] (*may his reign continue forever!*), [Qaidu] has been in rebellion against Qubilai Qa'an and Abaqa Khan and the seed of Abaqa Khan. He used to call Abaqa Khan and his seed *shīghaldash*, and they used to call him likewise. In former times they used to apply this term to one another: it means to feast with one another.[56] Qaidu repeatedly engaged in battle with Qubilai Qa'an and Abaqa Khan, as shall be mentioned in a [later] history. Qubilai Qa'an sent Baraq, the son of Yesün-To'a, the son of Mö'etüken, whom he had brought up, to

[51] *Tāzīk* or *Tājīk* (whence the modern Tajikistan) was the term applied by the Turks to the Iranians.
[52] The Persian name for South China.   [53] See Glossary.
[54] See below, pp. 266–67.
[55] That is, Rashīd al-Dīn's patron, the Il-Khan Ghazan (1295–1304).
[56] Rather, "feasting companion." See Doerfer, I, No. 245 (p. 368).

administer the *ulus*[57] of Chaghatai and make war on Qaidu. Baraq came, they fought, and Qaidu defeated him; and in the end they came to an agreement and both of them rebelled [together] against the Qa'an and Abaqa Khan, the account of which events shall be given in the relevant histories.[58] In the year 701/1301–1302, Qaidu and Du'a, the son of Baraq, jointly fought a battle against the army of Temür Qa'an. They were defeated, and both of them received a wound in the fighting: Qaidu died of his wound and Du'a is still suffering from his, which will not heal. Qaidu's eldest son, Chapar, has now been set in his place, but some of his brothers, Orus, and other princes do not agree to this, and their sister, Qutulun Chaghan, is at one with them, and it is said that there is a dispute between them. The number of Qaidu's [sons] is not known for certain. Some say that he has forty sons, but this is an exaggeration. Naurūz,[59] who was there for a time, states that there are twenty-four sons. However, those that are known in these parts are nine, as follows:

Chapar. He was born of —[60] of the —[61] tribe He has now succeeded Qaidu. Those who have seen him say that he is extremely lean and ill-favored and in face and beard like a Russian or Circassian.

Yangichar. He was born of —[62] of the —[63] tribe. He is handsome and talented, and his father was very fond of him. With a large army he is always guarding the frontier against Bayan, the son of Qonichi, of the seed of Orda, for they are at war with one another, because they[64] are allied with the Qa'an and the Lord of Islam (*may his kingdom endure forever!*) whereas their cousin Küilük inclines toward the sons of Qaidu and Du'a and they favor him lest Bayan should join the Qa'an and the Lord of Islam with an army and bring confusion to their affairs. And since Bayan belongs to the seed of Orda, Toqta, who occupies the throne of Jochi Khan, is assisting him, and they are thinking

---

[57] See Glossary.

[58] See below, p. 100, also Arends, pp. 70–87.

[59] The Emir Naurūz, the son of Arghun Aqa (on whom see above, pp. 230–31), had passed some time in Central Asia while in rebellion against the Il-Khan Arghun (1284–1291) and his successors. On this famous man, by whom the Il-Khan Ghazan was converted to Islam, see *CHI*, pp. 376–79, 380, and 382–84.

[60] Blank in the mss.   [61] Blank in the mss.

[62] Blank in the mss.   [63] Blank in the mss.

[64] That is, Bayan and the other princes of the White Horde, on which see Section 2, p. 100, note 13.

of making war on the sons of Qaidu and Du'a and have sent ambassadors here in this connection.

Orus. He was born of Qaidu's chief wife, Dörbejin[65] by name. Since his father's death he has disputed the kingdom, and in this dispute Tökme, the son of Tökme, the son of Hoqu, the son of Ögetei, is in agreement and alliance with him, as is his sister also. However, since Du'a favors Chapar, he exerted himself and set him up as Khan. Qaidu, the son of Qashi, had instructed Orus and given him a considerable army, and at the present time those troops are still with him and will not bow their necks, because strife and enmity have arisen between them and have resulted in war.

Örüg-Temür.

Töden.

Shāh Chungtai.

Il-Buyan.

'Umar Khwāja.

Nariqi (?)

Qahawur.

Quril.

Sorqa-Buqa.

Ekü-Buqa (?), born of ———.[66]

*Tai-Bakhshi(?) has many sons; they are not well known.

Sarban. This Sarban crossed the River Oxus with an army and is [encamped] in the region of Badakhshān and Panjāb.[67] He attacks Khurāsān on every occasion and the army of the Lord of Islam has repeatedly defeated him. In the autumn of the year 702/1302-1303 Prince Khar-Banda[68] went with an army toward Sarakhs and heard that Sarban's army was in the region of Maruchuq. He fell upon them, killed a great number, and plundered [their quarters]. It was Sarban's intention to enter Khurāsān that winter with a large army.

---

[65] DRNJYN.   [66] Blank in all the MSS.

[67] The name given in the 13th century to Mēla, a ford across the Oxus near the mouth of the Vakhsh. See *Turkestan*, p. 72.

[68] Ghazan's brother and successor, the Il-Khan Öljeitü (1304–1316). The name Khar-Banda, meaning, in Persian, "ass-herd" or "muleteer," was afterward changed to Khudā-Banda ("Servant of God"). He received the name, according to Ibn Baṭṭūṭa (Gibb II, p. 336), because a muleteer was the first person to enter the house after his birth.

Uighurtai, the son of Qutluq-Buqa, and Naurūz's brother, Oiradai, were with him inciting him to mischief. With that desire they advanced into the neighborhood of Ṭūs. Prince Khar-Banda withdrew from Sarakhs by way of Bāvard[69] and, putting his army in battle order at Eljigidei's Spring[70] suddenly fell upon them in the neighborhood of Ṭūs. When they drew up it was nighttime. They turned back and fled, and our army pursued them as far as the *ribāṭ*[71] of Sangbast.[72] They tried to make a stand but were unable and retreated in a rout. Snow and blizzards did their work upon them, and many men and animals perished. Such [was the cold] that the commander of Sarban's guard lost the use of his hands and feet: he embraced one of his *nökers*[73] and they both froze on the spot and so died. [Only] a few stragglers made their way back to their quarters. They had arranged with Qutluq-Khwāja, the son of Baraq, to join forces in the neighborhood of Herat, but since the mountains of Ghūr, Gharcha, and Ghazna were covered with snow they were unable to make their way thither, and the fortune of the Lord of Islam (*may God Almighty cause his kingdom to endure forever!*) scattered and destroyed them.

End of the list of his sons

Qaidu also had a daughter called Qutulun Chaghan. He loved her most of all his children. She used to behave like a young man, frequently taking part in campaigns and performing acts of heroism. She was held in high esteem by her father and was of great service to him. He would not marry her to a husband, and people suspected that there was some kind of relationship between him and his daughter. On several occasions when Qaidu's ambassadors came to the Lord of Islam (*may his kingdom endure forever!*) she sent greetings and *biligs* and said: "I will be thy wife and do not want another husband." In the last few years, Qaidu, out of excess of shame and the reproaches

---

[69] Bāvard or Abīvard lay near the present-day village of Abīvard, 5 miles west of Kahka, on the Transcaspian Railway. See *Ḥudūd*, p. 326.

[70] Presumably in Bādghīs, where Ögedei's general, Eljigidei, appears to have had his headquarters. See *HWC*, pp. 512 and 590.

[71] See Glossary.

[72] A day's march southeast of Meshed. See *Turkestan*, p. 448 and note 8.

[73] See Glossary.

of the people, gave her in marriage to a Khitayan.[74] When Qaidu died she had a desire to organize the army and administer the kingdom and wished her brother Orus to succeed her father. Du'a and Chapar shouted at her, saying: "Thou shouldst be working with scissors and needle. What concern hast thou with the kingdom and the *ulus*?" Offended on this account she has withdrawn from them and favors Orus, stirring up unrest.[75] The events and circumstances [which were in the life of] a single grandson of Ögetei called Qaidu, who by conquest, subjugation, and trickery has acquired a certain part of Ögetei's *ulus*, are in brief as has been stated. We shall return now, God willing, to describing the genealogy of the Qa'an's children.

Sixth son—Qadan Oghul

His mother was a concubine called Erkene, and he was brought up in the *ordo* of Chaghatai. At the time of Arïq Böke's rebellion, [Qadan Oghul] was in attendance on Qubilai Qa'an. When, for the second time,

[74] According to Verkhovsky's text, based on the Tashkent and Istanbul MSS., Qutulun's husband was "a certain Abtaqul of the Qorulas". There follows in his text a long passage absent from Blochet's text and MSS. It begins with an account of Qaidu's final battles with the Great Khan's troops: at a place called TKLKH near the Dzabkhan in western Mongolia, at another place called QRBH TAQ, in which the second element is apparently T. *taq*, "mountain," and finally in the mountains of QRALTW, apparently identical with the Ha-la-ha-t'ai of the *Yüan shih* (*Polo I*, p. 128). During the last named battle Qaidu had fallen ill and withdrawn his forces. He died a month later in a place called TAYKAN Na'ur, being between fifty and sixty years of age (actually about sixty-six, see above, note 48). It was said that his beard consisted only of nine grey hairs; he was of medium height and build and never took wine, kumyss, or salt. His remains and those of some of the princes who predeceased him were buried in high mountains called Shonqurlïq, between the Ili and the Chu. His daughter Qutulun still lived in that region; her husband, Abtaqul, was a vigorous man, tall and handsome. She herself had chosen him for her husband and she had had two sons by him. She lived there modestly, guarding her father's secret burial place. Qaidu had also another daughter, younger than she, called Qortichin (Hortochin?) Chaghan. He had given her in marriage to Tübshin, the son of Tarai Küregen of the Olqunut tribe. Tarai Küregen was married to the daughter of Hülegü's brother Sübedei. Tübshin had fallen in love with a slavegirl and had wished to elope with her to the Great Khan. He had confided his intention to a groom, who had denounced him, and Qaidu had put him (Tübshin) to death. Qaidu had other daughters also.

[75] Qutulun Chaghan is apparently the Aigiaruc (Ai-Yaruq, "Moonshine") of Marco Polo, on whom see *Polo I*, p. 15.

the Qa'an sent an army against Arïq Böke, he placed him in command of it [Qadan Oghul] killed 'Alam-Dār, the commander of Arïq Böke's army. Thereafter he was again in attendance on Qubilai Qa'an. He had six[76] sons, as follows:

Durchi. He had two sons: Söse and Eskebe.

Qïpchaq. It was he that was with Qaidu and brought about an agreement between him and Baraq. Qaidu sent him into Persia to reinforce Baraq. Because of some trick he turned back disappointed.[77] He had a son called Quril.

Qadan-Ebük. He had two sons: Lāhūrī and Mubārak-Shāh.

Yebe. He too was in attendance on Qaidu. He had two sons: Örüg-Temür and Esen-Temür.

Yesüder. His children are not known.

Qurumshi. His children are not known.

This Örug-Temür[78] was sent by Qaidu to the frontier of Khurāsān. When Naurūz fled and came to that region, he was together with Örüg-Temür and gave him his daughter in marriage. When he came back, Örüg-Temür was suspected of favoring the Lord of Islam (*may his kingdom endure forever!*). Qaidu sent for him and put him to death. He had eleven sons: Küresbe, Tuqluq-Buqa, Qutluq-Khwāja, Tuqluq-Temür, Abachi, Küch-Temür, Chïn-Temür, Chïn-Bolad, Arghun, Muḥammad, and 'Alī. Küresbe and some of his brothers are now on the frontier of Khurāsān in alliance with Sarban, the son of Qaidu. [Küresbe] too is now under suspicion for the same reason. It appears that Chapar sent for him and dispatched him thither.

Esen-Temür had a son called 'Alī Khwāja.

Seventh son—Melik

His mother too was a concubine, and he was brought up by Dānish-mand Ḥājib in the *ordo* of Ögetei Qa'an. [He had] ——— [sons:] Toqan-Buqa, Toqan, ———.[79]

---

[76] *Seven* according to Verkhovsky, p. 17.

[77] See below pp. 152–53; also Arends, pp. 74–75.

[78] Apparently the son of Yebe, who is perhaps out of order and should be the sixth son, as in Verkhovsky (p. 17), where, however, Örüg-Temür is shown as the son of a seventh son, Ajïqï.

[79] According to Verkhovsky's more complete text, Melik had six sons: Tuman, Toghan-Buqa, Toghanchar, Toghan, Turchan, and Qutlugh-Toqmïsh. The *Yüan shih* (*CVII*, p. 84) knows only of one son: Toqu.

PART

II

OF THE HISTORY OF ÖGETEI QA'AN

The [general] history of and [particular] anecdotes
regarding his reign;
a picture of his throne and wives and the princes and emirs
on the occasion of his ascending the throne of the Khanate;
an account of the battles he fought
and the victories he gained

ACCOUNT OF THE BEGINNING OF HIS REIGN AND
description of his ascension of the throne of the Khanate

In the *qaqa yïl*,[80] that is, the Year of the Pig, falling within the months of the year 624/1226–1227,[81] Chingiz-Khan, by reason of that condition which no mortal can escape, passed away in the region of Tangqut, having set out for the country of the Nangiyas and having reached the frontier [of that country]. As has been described in his history, his coffin was borne to Kelüren,[82] which is their original *yurt*, and the mourning ceremonies were performed. All the princes and emirs then consulted together regarding the kingdom and departed each to his own place of residence, where, as had been agreed, they took their rest. For nearly 2 years throne and kingdom were deprived of a king. [Then] they reflected that [if] something happened and no leader or king had been appointed, falsehood and confusion would

---

[80] Literally "Pig Year," from Mo. *qaqa*, "pig," and T. *yïl* (for Mo. *jil*, the Uighur script not distinguishing between *y* and *j*), "year." On the Twelve-Year Animal Cycle, see Minorsky 1942, pp. 80–82; also Poucha 1962.

[81] It actually began on the 5th February, 1227. According to Juvainī (*HWC*, p. 183), Genghis Khan died on the 18th August, 1227; according to the *Yüan shih* Krause, p. 40), he died on the 25th, having fallen ill on the 18th.

[82] More usually Onan-Kelüren, that is, the region between the Onan (Onon) and the Kelüren (Kerülen), Rubruck's Onankerule, "which is as it were their original home, and in which is the *ordu* of Chingis chan" (Rockhill, p. 165). On the site of Genghis Khan's tomb, see below p. 228, note 128; also *Polo I*, pp. 330–54.

29

find their way into the foundations of the kingdom. It was therefore advisable to make haste in the matter of the accession to the Khanate. And on this delicate business they dispatched ambassadors to one another from every side and busied themselves with preparing a *quriltai*. When the violence of the cold had abated and the first days of spring had come round, all the princes and emirs set out from every side and direction for the ancient *yurt* and great *ordo*. From Qïpchaq[83] [came] the sons of Jochi: Orda, Batu, Shiban, Tangqut, Berke, Berkecher, and Toqa-Temür; from Qayalïq[84] [came] Chaghatai Khan with all his sons and grandsons; from the Emil and the Qobaq, Ögetei Qa'an with his sons and descendants; from the East, their uncles Otchigin and Bilgütei Noyan and their cousin Elchidei Noyan, the son of Qachi'un; and from all sides [came] the emirs and great men of the army. All of these now presented themselves at Kelüren. Tolui Khan, whose title is Yeke-Noyan or Ulugh-Noyan,[85] the lord of his father's house and original *yurt*, was already there. The aforesaid company for 3 days and nights concerned themselves with pleasure, conviviality, and merrymaking, after which they spoke about the affairs of the empire and the kingship, and in accordance with the will of Chingiz-Khan they settled the Khanate upon Ögetei Qa'an. First all the sons and princes in one voice said to Ögetei Qa'an: "By the command of Chingiz-Khan it behoves thee with divine assistance to set thy [foot] upon the land of kingship in order that the haughty leaders may gird the loins of their lives with the girdle of servitude and that far and near, whether Turk or Tāzīk, [they] may be obedient and submissive to thy command." Ögetei Qa'an replied: "Although Chingiz-Khan's command was to this effect, yet there are my elder brother and uncles, and in particular my younger brother Tolui Khan is more worthy to undertake and accomplish this task, for in accordance with Mongol usage and custom the youngest son from the eldest house succeeds the father and administers his house and *yurt*,

---

[83] That is, the Qïpchaq Steppe, the territory of the Golden Horde, in what is now South Russia.

[84] The Cailac of Rubruck, a little to the west of the present-day Kopal, in the Taldy-Kurgan Region in southern Kazakhstan.

[85] Literally, "the great *noyan*," a title perhaps conferred posthumously on Tolui to avoid the mention of his real name. See Boyle 1956, pp. 146–48.

and Ulugh-Noyan is the youngest son of the eldest *ordu* and was ever in attendance on Chingiz-Khan day and night, morning and evening, and has seen and heard and learnt the *yosuns*[86] and *yasas*. Seeing that he is alive and they are here present, how may I succeed to the Khanate?" The princes said in one voice: "Chingiz-Khan has confided this task to thee of all his sons and brothers and has entrusted the tying and untying thereof to thee. How can we admit any change or alteration of his firm decree and inflexible command?" After much insistence and importunity, Ögetei Qa'an also deemed it necessary to obey the commandment of his father and comply with the suggestions of his uncles and brothers; and he gave his consent. They all doffed their hats and slung their belts across their backs; and in the *hüker*[87] *yïl*, that is, the Year of the Ox, falling in the months of the year 626/1228–1229,[88] Chaghatai taking his right hand, Tolui Khan his left, and his uncle Otchigin his belt, they set him upon the throne of the Khanate. Tolui Khan held a cup, and all present inside and outside the Court knelt in turn and said: "May the realm be blessed by his being Khan!" They gave him the name of Qa'an, and Qa'an commanded the goods in the treasuries to be produced, and he distributed them amongst kinsmen and strangers and all his limitless family to the extent of his own generosity. And when he had done with feasting and making presents he ordered that in accordance with the ancient *yasaq* and their usage and custom they should provide victuals for the soul of Chingiz-Khan, and should choose forty beautiful girls of the race and seed of the emirs that had been in attendance on him and having decked them out in precious garments embroidered with gold and jewels, dispatch them along with choice horses to join his spirit.[89]

The account of Qa'an's ascent to the throne of the kingdom being completed, we shall now begin and write his history as we wrote that of Chingiz-Khan, writing in separate sections of several years and mentioning at the end of each section the rulers of the surrounding countries and those persons of his family who reigned independently in the various kingdoms. We shall then return again to his history until it is completed. *It is God to Whom we turn for help and in Him that we trust.*

---

[86] See Glossary.   [87] An older form of Mo. *üker*, "ox."
[88] Actually 1229.
[89] On the elaborate tomb of the Mongol Khans, see Boyle 1965, pp. 14–15 and note 6.

◀ THE HISTORY OF ÖGETEI QA'AN FROM THE BEGIN-
ning of *hüker yïl*, that is, the Year of the Ox, falling in Rabī' I of the
year 626 of the Hegira [28th January–26th February, 1229], which
is the year of his accession, from the death of Chingiz-Khan[90] until
the end of the *morin*[91] *yïl*, that is, the Year of the Horse, falling in
Jumādā I of the year 631 [2nd February–3rd March, 1234], which
is a period of 6 years

During this period, after organizing and reducing to order the
affairs of the kingdom and the army, he proceeded against the countries of Khitai, where he subjugated the provinces which had not yet
been taken, and, having destroyed Altan-Khan,[92] he returned from
thence to his capital, victorious and triumphant, as shall be recorded
in detail in the accounts of these matters.

Account of Qa'an's beginning to issue ordinances, establish yasas, and organize the affairs of the kingdom

When Qa'an had been established on the throne of the kingdom, he
first of all made a *yasa* that all the ordinances that had previously been
issued by Chingiz-Khan should be upheld and preserved and protected
from change and alteration. [He also commanded:] "Any crime or
offence that has been committed by anyone up to the day of our accession, we have forgiven them all. If after today any person behaves with
impudence and proceeds to an act that contravenes the old and new
yasas, there shall befall him such chastisement and requital as are
fitting to his crime."

Before Qa'an ascended the throne, in the very year of Chingiz-
Khan's death, the princes and emirs who had remained in the *ordo*
of Chingiz-Khan, having consulted together, had sent Elchidei Noyan,
the nephew of Chingiz-Khan, and Güyük Khan, the son of Qa'an,
to the borders of the country of Qunqan[93] in order to capture it. They

[90] Verkhovsky has "and the third year following the death." One would expect
"second year," as Genghis Khan died in 1227.

[91] Mo. "horse."

[92] That is, the Chin Emperor, *altan* in Mongol, like *chin* in Chinese, meaning "gold."

[93] I have been unable to identify the name. This episode does not appear to be
mentioned in the other sources.

had plundered and subjugated it and sent an emir called Tangqut Bahadur with an army as *tama*[94] to protect that province. Everyone was disputing about this, and when Qa'an ascended the throne he silenced all of the claimants by means of the aforesaid *yasa*.

Thereafter he dispatched armies to all the borders and sides of the empire to protect the frontiers and the provinces. In the direction of Persia, unrest and insurrection had not yet abated, and Sultan Jalāl al-Dīn was still active there. He dispatched Chormaghun Noyan and a group of emirs with thirty thousand horsemen to deal with him.[95] He dispatched Kökctci[96] and Sübedei Bahadur with a like army against the Qïpchaq, Saqsïn,[97] and Bulghar;[98] toward Khitai, Tibet, Solanga,[99] Jürche,[100] and that general region he sent on in advance a party of great *noyans* with an army, whilst he himself with his younger brother, Möngke Qa'an, set out in the wake of that army toward Khitai, which had not yet submitted and where the Emperor of Khitai was still in possession.

Of the setting out of Qa'an with his brother Tolui Khan for the land of Khitai and the conquest of those parts which were still in rebellion

In the *bars*[101] *yïl*, that is, the Year of the Leopard, falling in Rabī' I, 627 [17th January–16th February, 1230], Qa'an set out with his brother Ulugh-Noyan for the land of Khitai, because in the reign of

94 "Auxiliary force consisting of various nationalities, only the commanders being Mongols." See Doerfer, I, No. 120 (pp. 255–56).

95 On Sultan Jalāl al-Dīn, see below, pp. 43–48.

96 Kökedei, "he of the swarthy countenance," the name borne by one of Ghazan Khan's ambassadors to Pope Boniface VIII. See Mostaert-Cleaves, pp. 469, 471, and 473–74.

97 The precise site of Saqsïn (identified by Minorsky with Ibn Khurdādbih's Sārighshin, one of the towns of the Khazar) is not known. It lay somewhere along the estuary of the Volga, according to one late authority, near New Sarai, that is, on the eastern bank of the Upper Akhtuba near the present-day Leninsk, about 30 miles east of Volgograd. See *Ḥudūd*, pp. 453–54, Minorsky 1955, p. 269, and *Horde d'Or*, pp. 165–74.

98 The ruins of Bulghar (Bolghar), the capital of the Volga Bulghars, are situated near the village of Bolgarskoe in the Spassk district, 115 kilometers south of Kazan and 7 kilometers from the left bank of the Volga. See *Ḥudūd*, p. 461.

99 North Korea.

100 Manchuria.

101 T. "leopard, cheetah," Mo. "tiger."

Chingiz-Khan, as has been described in the part of this history devoted to him, Altan-Khan, the king of Khitai, whose name was Shose,[102] had abandoned the town of Jungdu,[103] which was one of his capitals, together with many provinces dependent on it and gone to the town of Namging[104] and that region. He gathered many troops around him and was still reigning at that time, whilst the provinces which Chingiz-Khan and his army had taken remained in the possession of the Mongols. Qa'an[105] decided to overthrow him and conquer all those countries. He took with him Tolui Khan and Kölgen[106] of his brothers and certain of his nephews and sons, along with an extremely numerous army. Sending Tolui Khan with 2 *tümens*[107] of troops by way of Tibet, he himself proceeded on the right in the direction of a province of Khitai, the people of which are called Hulan-Degeleten,[108] that is, the people who wear red coats. And since the road to Qa'an was long, Tolui Khan traveled all that year, and in the next year, which was the Year of the Hare corresponding to the months of the year 628 [November 9, 1230–October 28, 1231],[109] the army was left without provisions or supplies and became very lean and hungry; and things came to such a pass that they ate the flesh of human beings and all [kinds of] animals and dry grass. They proceeded in *jerge*[110] over mountain and plain until first they came to a town, the name of which is *Hojanfu Balqa-sun,[111] on the banks of the Qara-Mören.[112] They laid siege to it and

---

[102] That is, Shou-hsü, the personal name of the last Chin Emperor (1224–1234), his posthumous Temple Title being Ai-tsung.

[103] That is, Chung-tu, "Middle Capital," the name given by the fourth Chin Emperor to Peking.

[104] That is, Nan-ching, "Southern Capital," now Kaifeng in Honan.

[105] That is, Ögedei. See Boyle 1956, pp. 152–53, where it is suggested that Qa'an, that is, the Qa'an *par excellence*, was his posthumous title.

[106] Genghis Khan's son by the Merkit princess Qulan. On his death in Russia, see below, p. 59 and note 237. [107] See Glossary.

[108] From Mo. *hulān* (*ulaghan*), "red," and *degelen* (*degelei*), "jacket." The Hulan-Degeleten are mentioned in §251 of *SH*.

[109] Beginning, in fact, on the 5th February, 1231.

[110] "Hunting circle; circular or semi-circular formation for the surrounding of the enemy." See Doerfer, I, No. 161 (pp. 291–94).

[111] This corrupt name apparently represents Ho-chung, the modern Puchow in Shansi. See *HWC*, p. 191, note 3.

[112] Literally Black River, from Mo. *qara*, "black" and *mören*, "river": the Mongol name for the Yellow River, Polo's Caramoran.

after 40 days the people of the town sued for quarter and surrendered the town; and about a *tümen* of troops embarked on a boat and fled. They carried off their women and children as prisoners, laid waste the province, and departed.

Account of Tolui's arrival at Tungqan Qahalqa,[113] where the army of Altan-Khan had built a stockade,[114] having seized that place, which is like a defile

When Tolui drew near to Tungqan Qahalqa, he reflected that since this place was a difficult pass in the middle of the mountains and a defile not easy to force, the enemy would certainly have seized and be guarding it so that it would be impossible to pass through. It was in fact so. When he arrived, 100,000 horsemen from Altan-Khan's army led by *Qada Sengüm, and *Höbegedür,[115] with several other emirs, had built a stockade on the plain and at the foot of the mountains on the far side of the army and, having made their dispositions, stood in ordered ranks waiting for battle, being exceedingly emboldened and encouraged by their own multitude and the smallness of the Mongol forces. When Tolui saw that they were many, he summoned one of the emirs, Shigi Qutuqu Noyan,[116] to him in private and consulted with him, [saying]: "Since the enemy have taken such a position and, having made their dispositions, are standing in battle-order it is difficult to fight them. The best course is for thee to ride up to them with three hundred horsemen to discover whether they will move from the spot." Qutuqu, in accordance with the command, rode forward.

[113] That is, Tungkuan, the celebrated pass at the bend of the Yellow River, the Tunggon of *SH* (§251). *Qahalqa* (Mo. *qaghalgh-a*) means literally "door" or "gate."

[114] *Chapar*, that is, a kind of wooden fence or paliside, such as the Mongols were accustomed to build around a town to which they were laying siege. See Boyle 1961, p. 156, note 3.

[115] On these two corrupt names, see *HWC*, p. 192, note 5. I have, at the suggestion of Professor F. W. Cleaves, identified them with the names of the two Chin generals mentioned in §§251 and 252 of *SH*.

[116] A Tatar foundling adopted by Genghis-Khan's wife or mother, Shigi Qutuqu was, at the great *quriltai* of 1206, appointed to the office of grand judge. In the campaign in the West he was defeated by Sultan Jalāl al-Dīn at the Battle of Parvān. He died at some time during the rebellion of Arīq Böke (1260–1264). See Boyle 1963, p. 241.

They did not move at all or budge from their position in order not to break the *jerge*[117] and to remain in proper order. And because of their own multitude and superiority and the fewness of the Mongols, pride and vanity had taken root in their brains and they looked with the glance of contempt upon the Mongol army and spoke big words, saying: "We shall encircle these Mongols and their king, and take them prisoner, and do this and that to their womenfolk." And they gave expression to shameful ideas and unworthy desires. God Almighty did not approve of their arrogance and pride, and in the end [He] caused them to be defeated. When they paid no attention to the galloping about of Qutuqu Noyan and his army and did not give way, Tolui Khan said: "As long as they do not budge it is impossible to fight them, and if I turn back, our army will be dispirited and they will be all the more insolent. The best course is for us to make in the direction of the provinces and towns that belong to their king and, if possible, join Ögetei Qa'an and the main army." And he appointed Toqolqu Cherbi, who was the younger brother of Borghuchin Noyan of the Arulat tribe,[118] with a thousand horsemen, to act as scouts and follow in the rear, whilst they themselves made off to the right. When the army of Khitai saw that they had turned their faces from battle and set off in another direction, they shouted out: "We are standing here. Come so that we may fight." But they, for their part, paid no attention and continued to withdraw, and the Khitayans of necessity moved out of their position and began to pursue them, and because the Khitayan army was large the Mongol army went in fear and apprehension.

All of a sudden the Khitayans struck at Toqolqu Cherbi, who was [in command of] the rearguard. They hurled forty Mongols into a muddy stream lying across their path and killed them. Toqolqu Cherbi joined his army and reported the situation. Tolui Khan gave order for the practice of rain magic.[119] This is a kind of sorcery carried

---

[117] See Glossary.

[118] According to the *SH*, Doqolqu—such is the correct form of the name—was the younger brother of Jedei Noyan of the Mangqut. See *Campagnes*, pp. 352–533, and Boyle 1956, p. 149. He was one of the six *cherbis*, or adjutants, appointed by Genghis Khan in 1206. See Boyle 1963, pp. 237–38 and 244.

[119] *Jadamīshī*, on which see Doerfer, I, pp. 286–89. On this practice in modern times, see Harva, pp. 221–23.

out with various stones, the property of which is that when they are taken out, placed in water, and washed, wind, cold, snow, rain, and blizzards at once appear even though it is in the middle of summer. There was amongst them a Qanqlï[120] who was well versed in that art. In accordance with the command he began to practice it, and Tolui Khan and the whole army put on raincoats and for 3 days and nights did not dismount from their horses. The Mongol army [then] arrived in villages in the middle of Khitai from which the peasants had fled, leaving their goods and animals, and so they ate their fill and were clothed. Meantime the Qanqlï continued to practice rain magic, so that it began to rain in the Mongols' rear and the last day the rain turned to snow, to which was added an icy wind. Under the effects of summer cold, such as they had not experienced in winter, the Khitayan army were disheartened and dismayed. Tolui Khan ordered [his] army to enter the villages, a unit of a thousand to each village, [and to] bring their horses into the houses and cover them up, since on account of the extreme severity of the wind and the icy blast it was impossible [to move about]. The Khitayan army, meantime, by force of necessity, remained out in the open country exposed to the snow and the wind. For 3 days it was altogether impossible to move. On the fourth it was still snowing, but Tolui observed that his own army was well fed and rested and no harm had come to them or their animals from the cold, whereas the Khitayans, because of the excessive cold, were like a flock of sheep with their heads tucked into one another's tails, their clothes being all shrunk and their weapons frozen. He ordered the kettledrum to be beaten and the whole army to don cloaks of beaten felt and to mount horse. Then Tolui said: "Now is the time for battle and good fame: you must be men." And the Mongols fell upon the Khitayans like lions attacking a herd of deer and slew the greater part of that army, whilst some were scattered and perished in the mountains. As for the two aforementioned generals, they fled with five thousand men, flinging themselves into the river, from which only a few were saved. And because they had jeered at the Mongols, speaking big words and expressing evil thoughts, it was

---

[120] The Qanglï Turks (the Cangitac of Carpini and the Cangle of Rubruck), were closely associated with the Qïpchaq (Comans).

commanded that they should commit the act of the people of Lot with all the Khitayans who had been taken prisoner.

So great a victory having been gained, Tolui Khan dispatched messengers to Qa'an with the good tidings thereof, and he too, victorious and triumphant, set out to join him. [In front of him was] the River Qara-Mören, which flows from the mountains of Kashmir and Tibet and separates Khitai from Nangiyas. It had never been possible to cross that river, and it was necessary for him to send Shin Chaghan-Buqa of the Uru'ut tribe[121] to search for a crossing. By chance that year there had been great floods which had brought down large quantities of stones and sand. These had collected in every part of the river and the water had in consequence spread out over the plain and was flowing in [a number of] branches, so that the river was a parasang broad and shallow. Chaghan-Buqa found that [place] and guided Tolui Khan so that they crossed safely over.

Because Tolui Khan had been separated from him for some time and he had heard that an enemy had overpowered him when far from the main army, Qa'an had been in great distress of mind. When the good news arrived of his victory and safe return, he was exceedingly pleased and happy. And when Tolui Khan himself arrived he showed him much honor and praised him greatly. And so unexpected a victory having been gained, he left Toqolqu Cherbi with some other emirs to deal with Altan-Khan and subjugate all the countries of Khitai, whilst they themselves auspiciously returned, in triumph. Tolui asked permission to go on in advance: he died suddenly on the way. It is related that several days before, Qa'an had been sick, and at his last breath. Tolui Khan went up to his pillow. The *qams*,[122] as is their custom, had pronounced their incantations and washed his sickness in water in a wooden cup. Because of his great love for his brother, Tolui snatched up that cup and cried out with great insistence: "O Eternal God, Thou art aware and knowest that if this is [because of] sins, I have committed more, for in all the lands I have rendered many people lifeless and enslaved their wives and children and made them weep. And if it is because of his handsomeness and accomplishments, I am handsomer and more accomplished. Forgive him and call

---

[121] On the Uru'ut, see Khetagurov, pp. 184–86, and *Campagnes*, pp. 32–33.
[122] See Glossary.

me to Thee in his stead." Having uttered these words with great insistence he drank down the water in which they had washed the sickness. Ögetei recovered and Tolui took his leave and departed. A few days later he was taken ill and died. This story is well known,[123] and Tolui Khan's wife, Sorqoqtani Beki, used always to say: "He who was my delight and desire went into the head of Ögetei Qa'an and sacrified himself for him."

Qa'an spent the summer in Khitai in the place [called] Altan-Kere[124] and then departed, arriving, triumphant and victorious, to his capital in [the *moghai yïl*, that is,] the Year [of the Snake].[125]

Account of the battle of Toqolqu Cherbi with the army of Khitai, his defeat, Qa'an's sending help to him, the arrival of the Nangiyas to his aid, the destruction of Altan-Khan and the complete conquest of Khitai

After a time, the army of Khitai gathered together and fought with Toqolqu Cherbi. He was defeated and put to flight and, withdrawing a long distance, [he] sent a messenger to Qa'an to ask for help. Qa'an said: "Since the reign of Chingiz-Khan we have fought many times with the army of Khitai and always defeated them; and we have taken the greater part of their lands. Now that they have beaten us it is a sign of their misfortune, a lamp which, at the time of going out, flares up and burns well and brightly and then goes out." And he commanded that an army should be sent to Toqolqu's aid. And since there was an ancient enmity between the kings of Māchīn which the Mongols call Nangiyas, and the kings of Khitai, who were of the race of the Jürche,[126] Qa'an issued a *yarligh*[127] that they should render assistance, approaching from their side whilst the Mongols approached from theirs, and lay siege jointly to Namging. In accordance with the command, they led a great army to the town of Namging, of which the circuit is said to be 40 parasangs; it has three walls and is

[123] It is told in *SH* (§272) also. According to Juvainī (*IIWC*, p. 549), Tolui's death was due to alcoholism.

[124] In Mo. "Golden Steppe," from *altan*, "gold," and *ke'ere (kegere)*, "steppe." Unidentified.

[125] That is, 1233. The date is supplied from Verkhovsky.

[126] That is, the Manchurians.   [127] See Glossary.

surrounded on two sides by the River Qara-Mören. The Mongol
and Nangiyas armies together laid siege to the town and set up mangonels and laid ladders against the walls and stationed sappers with
battering-rams at the foot of the walls. It became clear to the emirs and
army of Khitai that the town would be taken and they reflected:
"Our king is faint of heart. If we tell him, he will perish from excess of
fear and dread, and our cause will be completely lost." They concealed
[the truth from him] and, in accordance with their custom, he concerned himself with pleasure with his wives and concubines in his
mansions and palaces. When the wives and concubines realized that the
town would be taken, they began to weep. Altan-Khan asked why
this was and they told him of the plight of the town. He did not believe
them and, going up in the wall, saw with his own eyes. When he was
certain [of the town's fate] he decided to flee. Embarking with some of
his wives upon a boat, he set off along a canal which had been made
from the Qara-Mören into the town and continues into another
province, and so departed to another town. When the Mongols and
the Nangiyas people learnt [of his flight] they sent troops after him and
besieged him in that town. He fled from thence by boat and went to
another town.[128] Again they followed him and besieged him. Since
the way of escape was distant and blocked, the Mongol and Nangiyas
troops set fire to the town. Altan-Khan realized that they would
take the town. He said to his emirs and ladies: "After reigning so
long and enjoying all manner of honors I do not wish to become the
prisoner of the Mongols and die in ignominy." He dressed his *qorchi*[129]
in his clothes and, having set him in his place on the throne, went out
and hanged himself until he died. He was then buried. In some
histories it is stated that he donned rags after the manner of the *qalan-
dars* and went into hiding, and in the *History of Khitai*[130] it is stated
that when the town was set on fire he was burnt. Neither of these two
versions is correct. It is certain that he hanged himself and died; and
2 days later they captured the town and put to death the person whom
he had set in his place. The Nangiyas army entered the town, and the
Mongols learnt that the person they put to death was not Altan-Khan

[128] This was Ts'ai-chou (the present-day Junan). See Franke, IV, p. 290.
[129] See Glossary.
[130] Presumably the work on which Rashīd al-Dīn's own *History of China* was based.

and [they] began to look for him. They were told that he had been burnt. They did not believe this and asked for his head. And when the Nangiyas army learnt of this state of affairs, although they were enemies of Altan-Khan, they assisted in preventing his exhumation from the grave and the handing over of his head, and together with the Khitayans [they] pretended that he had been burnt. The Mongols, to make certain, asked for his head, and they knew that if they gave another head the Mongols would find out that it was not his head. In the end they gave them a man's hand. On this account the Mongols were offended with the Nangiyas, but at that time it was impossible to quarrel with them.[131] In short, Toqolqu Cherbi and the army, in the manner that has been mentioned, conquered all the countries of Khitai, and this victory was gained in the *morin yïl*, which is the Year of the Horse, falling in Jumada I, 631 [2nd February–3rd March, 1234].

In that same year they removed *turqaqs*[132] and *keziktens*[133] without number from the land of Solanqa and sent them to Qa'an; and their leader was Ong Sun.[134]

Six years of the history of Qa'an, from the beginning of the *hüker yïl*, that is, the Year of the Ox, falling in Rabī' I of the year 626 [28th January–6th February, 1229], to the end of the *morin yïl*, that is, the Year of the Horse, falling in Jumādā I of the year 631 [2nd February–3rd March, 1234], have been recorded in detail. We shall now begin recording, briefly and concisely, the history of the *khaqans*,[135] caliphs, *maliks*,[136] sultans, and *atabegs*[137] of the surrounding countries

---

[131] On the various Chinese accounts of Ai-tsung's death and the disposal of his body, see Franke, IV, p. 290, V, p. 157.

[132] The *turqaq* was the day-guard, as distinct from the *kebte'ül*, or night-guard. See Minorsky 1939, p. 163.

[133] Mo. *keshikten*, "body guard," Polo's *quesitan*, "a word that in our language signifies 'Faithful Knights of the Lord.'" See Doerfer, I, No. 333 (pp. 469–70), *Polo II*, p. 815, and Benedetto, p. 129.

[134] Identified by Ledyard (p. 14) with Wang Chun, a member of the Korean royal house who had gone to Qara-Qorum as a hostage in 1241. He regards this passage as a garbled version of Wang Chun's activities in Korea in the Year of the Horse corresponding to 1258, and sees in the *turqaqs* and *keshiktens* "a reference to those Koreans, probably defectors, who accompanied him." On Wang Chun or Wang Sun (1224–1283), the Duke of Yŏngnyŏng, see Henthorn, p. 118, note 13.

[135] See Glossary. [136] See Glossary.

[137] See Glossary.

to the East and West, as also of those persons who were governors of certain provinces with absolute authority as representatives of Qa'an. We shall then return to the history of Qa'an and relate what occurred hereafter, if God so wills.

✦ HISTORY OF THE *KHAQANS* OF KHITAI AND Māchīn, the caliphs, sultans, *maliks*, and *atabegs* of Persia, Syria, Egypt, etc., and the emirs, who were governors of certain provinces, [all] who were contemporary with Qa'an, from the beginning of the *hüker yïl*, that is, the Year of the Ox, falling in Rabī' I of the year 626 [28th January–26th February, 1229] to the end of the *morin yïl*, that is, the Year of the Horse, falling in Jumādā I, 631 [2nd February–3rd March, 1234] as also a further year of their history being the *qulquna*[138] *yïl*, that is, the Year of the Rat, corresponding to the months of the year 625/1227–1228,[139] the year of Chingiz-Khan's death and the accession of Qa'an, briefly and concisely

History of the emperors of Khitai who ruled during this period

Shousü ————.[140]

History of the emperors of Māchīn who ruled during this period

Lizun[141] ———— 41 years, ———— 7 years.[142]

History of the caliphs, sultans, maliks, and atabegs and the Mongol emirs who were governors of Certain provinces during this period

History of the caliphs

In Baghdad the Caliph of the 'Abbāsids, al-Nāṣir li-Dīn Allāh, ruled supreme. He died in the beginning of 627/1229–1230 and was

---

[138] Mo. *qulughana*, "mouse, rat."　　　[139] Actually 1228.

[140] See above, p. 34, note 102.

[141] The Sung Emperor Li-tsung (1224–1264).

[142] The blanks are in all the mss. The 41 years must refer to the total length of Li-tsung's reign and the 7 years to the length of his reign up to 1234; but in neither case are the figures exact.

succeeded by his son Ẓāhir. He in turn died in 628/1230–1231, and al-Mustanṣir bi'llāh was set upon [the throne of] the Caliphate.

History of the sultans

In 'Irāq[143] and Ādharbāijān, Sultan Jalāl-al-Dīn reigned supreme. In the beginning of 625/1227–1228, returning from Iṣfahān, he came to Tabrīz and set out for Georgia. And since the Sultan of Rūm and the *maliks* of Syria and Armenia and all that region were alarmed at his power and ascendancy, they all rose up to repel him and gathered together in one place with an army of Georgians, Armenians, Alans,[144] Sarir,[145] Lakz,[146] Qïpchaq, Svan,[147] Abkhaz,[148] and Chanet.[149] The Sultan encamped near them at Mindor.[150] He was embarrassed by the great numbers of the enemy's horsemen and consulted the vizier Yulduzchï and the other dignitaries. Yulduzchï said: "Since our men are not one hundredth of theirs in number, the best course is for us to pass through Mindor and remove and withhold the water and timber from them so that they may languish from hunger and thirst and their horses grow weak. We can then give battle when we see fit." The Sultan was annoyed at these words. He hurled a pencase at the vizier's head and said: "They are a flock of sheep. Does the lion complain of the size of the flock?" For that treachery Yulduzchï forfeited 50,000 dinars. The Sultan went on: "Though the case is hard, we must fight with our trust in God." The next day they drew up their lines, and the hostile army thought the Sultan in the midst of his troops to be a mountain in a plain. He ascended a hill in order to observe them and descried the standards of the Qïpchaq with twenty thousand men. He sent Qoshqar to them with a loaf and a little salt and reminded

---

[143] That is, 'Irāq-i 'Ajam, Persian 'Irāq or Central Persia.

[144] The Ossetes.

[145] The Avars of Daghestan. See *Ḥudūd*, p. 447.

[146] The present-day Lezghians in Daghestan. See *Ḥudūd*, pp. 411 and 455.

[147] This people still survives in modern Georgia along the Upper Ingur. See Allen, pp. 27–28.

[148] The Abkhaz on the Black Sea coast in the extreme northwest of Georgia are now citizens of the Abkhazian A. S. S. R.

[149] That is, the Chan or Laz, who still inhabit the southeastern shores of the Black Sea between Trebizond and Batum. See Allen, pp. 54–56.

[150] Mindori near Lori in what is now Soviet Armenia. According to the Georgian Chronicle, the battle was fought at Bolnisi.

them of their former obligations. The Qïpchaq at once turned rein and withdrew into a corner. The Georgian army now came forward and he sent [a messenger] to say: "Today you have just arrived and you are tired. Let the young men on either side lay hands upon one another in thrust and parry, and we shall watch from the side." The Georgians were pleased and all that day until nightfall both sides attacked and retreated. Finally one of the brave *aznaurs*[151] came forward, and the Sultan, like Munkar,[152]

Charged out from the army like a lion and came valiantly before Hujīr.[153]

And whilst men watched from every side the Sultan at full gallop

Thrust a lance at his girdle so that *khaftān* and clasps were split open.[154]

The man had three sons, who came forward separately one after the other, and the Sultan destroyed each of them in a single charge. Another *aznaur* of exceedingly fearful size rode on to the field, and because the Sultan's horse was tired he was about to vanquish him; but the Sultan in an instant sprang down from his horse and felled and killed the man with a single thrust of his lance. Seeing the Sultan thus, his troops in a single charge put the whole [of the enemy army] to flight.

The Sultan then proceeded to Akhlāṭ.[155] The inhabitants closed the gates and refused to accept advice. He laid siege to the town for 2 months and the townspeople were desperate with hunger. The Sultan ordered his men to attack at once from every side and make their way into the town. He took up his abode in the palace of Malik Ashraf,[156] while Mujīr al-Dīn, the latter's brother, and his slave 'Izz al-Dīn Ai-Beg entered the citadel without provisions. Mujīr al-Dīn came out first, and the Sultan treated him with great honor; and Ai-Beg also came out after him. The Sultan's treasury was replenished with the wealth of

---

[151] In Georgian *aznauri*. On this Georgian rank, see Allen, pp. 225–27.

[152] One of the two angels who question the dead in their graves.

[153] Vullers, p. 448, 1.252. See *HWC*, p. 441, note 12.

[154] Vullers, p. 236, 1.341. See *HWC*, p. 441, note 13. The *khaftān* (whence our *caftan*) was a kind of tunic worn under armor.

[155] The present-day Ahlât on the northwestern shores of Lake Van in eastern Turkey.

[156] On the Aiyūbid Malik Ashraf, afterward ruler of Damascus (1229–1237), see *Caucasian History*, pp. 149–56.

Malik Ashraf, and because he had defeated the Georgians and taken Akhlāt, the fame of his greatness and splendor was spread abroad. The *maliks* of Egypt and Syria, following the example of the caliphs of the City of Peace,[157] dispatched gifts and presents to his court; and his cause was again in the ascendant.

From thence he proceeded in the direction of Khartabirt,[158] being affected with some infirmity. It was at this time that the Sultan of Erzerum was distinguished with all manner of favors and kindnesses for having assisted the Sultan's army with provisions and fodder at the siege of Akhlāt. He reported that 'Alā al-Dīn of Rūm[159] had made peace with the *maliks* of Aleppo and Damascus; that they were allied together to attack the Sultan and were busy collecting their forces; and that they were constantly threatening him and saying that if the Sultan had not been helped by him with provisions at the gates of Akhlāt he could not have maintained himself. Hearing these words the Sultan, despite his infirmity, at once mounted horse. When he came to the plain of Mūsh,[160] six thousand men, who were going to the aid of that host, crossed the Sultan's path. In a single charge [the Sultan and his army] destroyed them all.

Some days after, the armies drew close to each other, and the Sultan of Rūm, Malik Ashraf, and the other *maliks* came together from the various provinces with such gear and equipment as will not enter into computation. They drew up their forces on a hilltop, the naphtha-throwers and crossbowmen standing with cowhide shields in front, and the horsemen and footmen behind. The Sultan decided to get out of his litter and mount his horse, but because of the strength of his illness he was unable to hold the reins, and the horse turned back. His attendants said that he should rest for awhile, and his personal standard was accordingly carried back. The right and left wings thought he was fleeing and themselves turned in flight. But the enemy imagined that the Sultan had had recourse to a trick in order to draw them down on to the plain, and a herald in the midst of their forces cried out that no one was to stir from his position. Such fear had overcome Sultan 'Alā al-Dīn that he had not even the faculty to remain

---

[157] That is, Baghdad. [158] Now Harput.
[159] The Seljuq ruler of Rūm, or Asia Minor, 'Alā al-Dīn Kai-Qubād I (1219–1236).
[160] The present-day town and district of Muş, to the west of Lake Van.

still, and Malik Ashraf ordered locks to be put on the fore and hind legs of his mule.[161]

His army having fled and scattered in every direction, the Sultan of necessity set out toward Akhlāṭ, and, summoning those whom he had detailed to defend it, he proceeded to Khoi. Mujīr al-Dīn, the brother of Malik Ashraf, he dismissed with full honors, while to Taqī al-Dīn[162] he gave leave to return and intercede for him with the Caliph al-Mustanṣir bi'llāh. As for Ḥusām al-Dīn Qaimarī,[163] he had fled. His wife, the daughter of Malik Ashraf, the Sultan sent back with every manner of kindness, her honor unsullied. As for 'Izz al-Dīn Ai-Beg, he had been imprisoned in the castle of Dizmār,[164] and there he died.

Meantime, news arrived that Chormaghun Noyan had crossed the Oxus with a great army to attack the Sultan. The Sultan deputed the vizier Shams al-Dīn Yulduzchï to defend the castle of Gīrān[165] and entrusted his womenfolk to him. He himself proceeded to Tabrīz, and although he had differences with the Caliph and the *maliks* and sultans of Rūm and Syria, he sent messengers to each of them and informed them of the Mongols' approach. The purport of his message was to the effect that the Tartars were exceedingly numerous and this time more so than ever and that the troops in that region were in terror of them. "If," he went on, "you will not assist with men and equipment, I, who am like a wall, shall be removed, and it will be impossible for you to resist them. Let each of you give aid to himself, his children, and the Muslims by [sending] a detachment and a standard, so that when the report of our concord reaches them they will be rebuffed and our own troops encouraged. But if you treat this matter lightly you shall see what you shall see.

Let each of you see to his life; exert your understanding in this matter."

---

[161] This detail is not in Juvainī (*HWC*, p. 451), whom Rashīd al-Dīn here follows very closely. For an account of the Battle of Arzinjān (Erzincan) according to the Arabic sources and Ibn Bībī, see Gottschalk, p. 191.

[162] Also a brother of Malik Ashraf.

[163] Afterward the Aiyūbid governor of Aleppo, from whence he fled upon the approach of Hülegü. See *HWC*, p. 451 and note 6.

[164] East of Marand in Azerbaijan.

[165] The present-day Kīlān, to the north of the Araxes.

The powerful fortune of Chingiz-Khan and his descendants threw their words into disagreement and changed the Sultan's hope into despair. Suddenly news arrived that the Mongol army had reached Sarāv.[166] The Sultan set out for Bīshkīn.[167] The roof of the palace in which he lodged at night caved in. He did not take this as an omen but bore it with patience and the next day set out for Mūghān.[168] After he had been there 5 days the Mongol army drew near, and the Sultan abandoned his encampment and entered the mountains of Qaban.[169] Finding the Sultan's encampment empty they turned back.

The Sultan passed the winter of 628/1230 in Urmīya[170] and Ush-nūya. The vizier Sharaf al-Dīn was falsely accused of having, at the time of the Sultan's absence when all news of him was cut off, cast covetous eyes at his harem and treasury. When the Sultan came to that district, [Sharaf al-Dīn] refused out of fear to come out of the castle and asked for a safe-conduct. At his request the Sultan sent Buqu Khan to bring him out. Then he said: "I raised Yulduzchï from the nadir of abasement to the zenith of exaltation; and this is how he shows his gratitude." He handed him over to the governor of the castle and distributed his belongings as plunder; and the vizier died in that prison.

The Sultan now set out for Diyār Bakr, and when the Mongol army came to Chormaghun, [the latter] chided them saying: "Why have you returned and not made the utmost exertion in seeking the Sultan? When such an enemy has grown weak how is it possible to give him grace?" And he dispatched in his pursuit the emir Naimas and a group of other emirs with a large force. Now the Sultan had sent back Buqu Khan to act as scout and reconnoiter the position of the Mongol army. When he came to Tabrīz, it was reported to him that from 'Irāq there had come news of the dispersal [of the Mongols] and that in that region also there was no trace of that people. Buqu Khan, acting without circumspection, turned back and bore the Sultan the

[166] Sarāb, on the road from Tabriz to Ardebil.

[167] Now Mīshkīn, the district around Ahar.

[168] That is, the Moghan Steppe, south of the Araxes on the western coast of the Caspian.

[169] The Armenian Kapan, now Kafan, a district in the extreme southeast of Soviet Armenia, noted as a copper-mining center.

[170] Now Rezaiyeh (Riżā'īya).

glad tidings that they had departed. In their joy and exultation, the Sultan and all the emirs and soldiers engaged in pleasure and merry-making and passed 2 or 3 days in folly and rejoicing. One day at midnight the Mongol army came upon them. The Sultan was deep in drunken sleep. Orkhan, learning of the Mongols' arrival, ran to [the Sultan's] bedside, but as much as he called him he did not awaken. They threw cold water on his face until he came to himself and realized the situation. He turned to flee, ordering Orkhan not to move his standard and to offer resistance until he had gained a little lead. Then he departed and Orkhan, after standing firm for awhile turned in flight; and the Mongols, thinking it was the Sultan, set out in his pursuit. When they realized [their mistake] they returned and slew all that they found. Meanwhile, the Sultan, having set out alone, was moving with great haste. Accounts differ as to how he met his end. Some say that he was sleeping at night under a tree in the Hakkār mountains when a party of Kurds came upon him and, coveting his clothes and horse, split open his stomach.[171] Then, putting on his garments and arms, they entered the town of Āmid.[172] Some of his retinue recognized the clothes and weapons and seized the men; and the ruler of Āmid, when he had ascertained the circumstances, put them to death. The Sultan's body was then brought to Āmid and buried there; and a dome was built over his tomb. Others say that he gave the men his arms and garments of his own free will, taking their coarse clothing in exchange, and began to wander through the lands in the garb of the Ṣūfīs. However that may be, his rule now came to an end.

As for Sultan Ghiyāth al-Dīn, in the year 624/1226–1227, when they were fighting the Mongols at the gates of Iṣfahān, he purposely abandoned the left wing, which his brother had entrusted to him, and made for Khūzistān by way of Luristān. The Caliph Nāṣir

---

[171] This differs considerably from Juvaini's version (*HWC*, p. 459): "Some say that upon arriving in the mountains of Amid he had encamped for the night in a certain place when a party of Kurds conceived a desire to despoil him of his clothes and stabbed him in the breast . . . ." By the Hakkār mountains is meant presumably the territory of the Hakkārī Kurds, the present-day province of Hakâri, to the south of Lake Van.

[172] The present-day Diyarbakir (Diyār Bakr), the chief town of the Turkish province of the same name.

sent his presents and letters-patent as Sultan. He then turned back, and when Sultan Jalāl al-Dīn was in Armenia and Georgia, he set out for Alamūt. 'Alā al-Dīn[173] received him with honor and respect and rendered suitable services. After some time he again set out for Khūzistān and sent a messenger to Baraq Ḥājib[174] in Kirmān to inform him of his arrival. Again a treaty was concluded between them, and it was agreed that Baraq should meet him in the desert near Abarqūh. The Sultan set out for Kirmān with his mother, and Baraq came to meet him in the aforesaid place with nearly four thousand horsemen and for 2 or 3 days behaved with proper respect. However, since the Sultan had no more than five hundred horsemen with him, Baraq conceived the desire to marry his mother. One day he came and, sitting on the same carpet with the Sultan, began to address him as his child. He allotted to each of his emirs the places of dignitaries and sent a message seeking his mother's hand. The Sultan, seeing no means of forestalling him, complied with his suggestions; and his mother, after objecting and refusing, agreed to the marriage. After much pressing, she entered [Baraq's house] with a number of her servants wearing mail under their tunics, and the marriage was consummated. When they reached the town of Guvāshīr,[175] which is the capital of Kirmān, and some days had passed, two of Baraq's kinsmen came to the Sultan and said: "Baraq is not to be trusted, for he is treacherous and deceitful. We have discovered an opportunity. If we make away with him, it is fitting that thou shouldst be the Sultan and we thy obedient slaves." The purity of his origin would not allow him to violate his covenant, but since the sun of that dynasty's fortune had reached its decline, one of his intimates told Baraq in private of these words. He at once examined his kinsmen and Sultan Ghiyāth al-Dīn and they admitted what had happened. He ordered their limbs to be cut to pieces in the Sultan's presence and the Sultan to be detained in a castle. Afterward he sent men to place a bowstring[176] round his neck

[173] Marco Polo's "Old Man of the Mountains, Alaodin by name," that is, Muḥammad III, the Grand Master of the Ismā'īlīs or Assassins (1221–1255), on whom see *HWC*, pp. 703–12, and Hodgson, pp. 256–58.

[174] On Baraq Ḥājib, the first of the Qutlugh-Khans of Kirmān, see *CHI*, pp. 323, 329, and 332.

[175] Now called Kirmān (Kerman) after the province of which it is the capital.

[176] A rope, according to Juvainī (*HWC*, p. 473).

49

and put him to death. The Sultan cried out: "After all, did we not make a covenant not to plot against each other? Why dost thou see fit to break it without cause?" His mother, hearing her son's voice, gave out a cry. They were both of them strangled and all his army put to death in the same manner. Baraq sent the head of Sultan Ghiyāth al-Dīn to Qa'an with the message: "You have two enemies, Jalāl al-Dīn and Ghiyāth al-Dīn. I have sent you the head of one of them."[177] Such was the fate of the Khwārazm-Shāhī Sultans.

In Rūm there reigned Sultan 'Alā al-Dīn. His history during this period has been told in the account of Jalāl al-Dīn.[178]

In Mosul there reigned Badr al-Dīn Lu'lu' ———.[179]

History of the maliks and atabegs

In Māzandarān ———.[180]

In Diyār-Bakr there reigned Malik Muẓaffar al-Dīn, the lord of Irbīl and all the towns except Mosul and that region.[181]

In Syria there reigned the sons of Malik 'Ādil ibn Ayyūb, Malik Mu'aẓẓam and Malik Ashraf. A little of the history of Malik Ashraf has been told in the account of Sultan Jalāl al-Dīn.[182]

In Egypt Malik Kāmil ibn Malik 'Ādil Saif al-Dīn Abū Bakr[183] reigned supreme.

In Maghrib ———.[184]

In Fārs there reigned the atabeg Muẓaffar al-Dīn Sa'd ibn Zangī.[185] He died in the year ———.[186] Khwāja Ghiyāth al-Dīn Yazdī, who was the vizier and the administrator of the kingdom, kept his death secret, and, sending his signet ring to the White Castle, he had his son, the atabeg Abū Bakr,[187] released from captivity and brought to his presence. Then flinging open the door of the pavilion, he said to the

[177] Juvainī does not mention this message to Ögedei.

[178] See above, pp. 45–46.   [179] Blank in all the MSS.

[180] Blank in all the MSS.

[181] Muẓaffar al-Dīn Kök-Böri (Blue Wolf), the last (1190–1232) of the Begteginids of Arbil.

[182] See above, pp. 44–46.   [183] 1218–1238.

[184] Blank in all the MSS.   [185] 1195–1226.

[186] Blank in all the MSS. The date should be 623/1226.

[187] 1226–1260.

emirs and the army: "The *atabeg* decrees that Abū Bakr is his successor."
The emirs cast their belts about their necks and he became *atabeg*.

In Kirmān Baraq Hājib reigned supreme. His history has been told
in the account of Sultan Ghiyāth al-Dīn.[188]

In Sīstān ———.[189]

History of the Mongol emirs who were governors of provinces

In Khurāsān, Chïn-Temür, [who belonged to one] of the tribes of
the Qara-Khitai,[190] was appointed to the governorship of that kingdom and the kingdom of Māzandarān. How this came about is as
follows. At the time of the conquest of Khwārazm, Toshi[191] Khan
left him there in the capacity of *shaḥna*.[192] During the reign of Qa'an,
when he was sending Chormaghun to Persia, he commanded the
leaders and *basqaqs*[193] of the provinces to accompany the levy in person
and render assistance to Chormaghun. In accordance with the command, Chïn-Temür set out from Khwārazm by way of Shahristāna,[194]
and from other directions came emirs representing each of the princes.
Chormaghun for his part left with Chïn-Temür, an emir to represent
each prince, Kül-Bolat representing Qa'an, Nosal Batu, Qïzïl-Buqa
Chaghatai, and Yeke Sorqoqtani Beki,[195] and the princes. And since
Chormaghun had neglected Khurāsān, rebels and [other] riffraff
were casting trouble and confusion into the provinces at every moment;
and Qaracha and Yaghan-Sonqur, two of Sultan Jalāl al-Dīn's emirs
used to make raids upon Nishapur and that region, killing the *shaḥnas*
whom Chormaghun had set over the provinces and seizing those who
breathed the breath of submission to the Mongols. Chormaghun
sent Kül-Bolat and Chïn-Temür into the region of Nishapur and

[188] See above pp. 49 50; also *HWC*, pp. 476–80.
[189] Blank in all the mss.
[190] Here Rashīd al-Dīn follows Juvainī (*HWC*, p. 482); elsewhere (Khetagurov,
p. 141), he says that Chïn-Temür belonged to the Öngüt.
[191] That is, Jochi, the eldest son of Chingiz-Khan. Here Rashīd al-Dīn reproduces
Juvainī's spelling of the name. On the etymology of Jochi, see below, p. 98, note 7.
[192] See Glossary.
[193] See Glossary.
[194] Shahristāna (Shahristān) lay 3 miles north of Nasā, near the present-day
Ashkhabad in Turkmenistan.
[195] On Princess Sorqoqtani, the widow of Tolui, see below, pp. 168–71.

Ṭūs[196] to drive off Qaracha, and Kül-Bolat returned after Qaracha had been put to flight. When news of the confusion in Khurāsān reached Qa'an, he gave orders for Tayir Bahadur[197] to lead an army from Bādghīs, drive off Qaracha, and flood their dwellings and habitations. He set out in accordance with these orders but heard on the way that Qaracha had been put to flight by Kül-Bolat and had taken refuge in the citadel of Sīstān. Tayir Bahadur proceeded thither to lay siege to it and toiled away for 2 years before he took it. From Sīstān he sent a messenger to Chïn-Temür to say: "The administration of Khurāsān has been entrusted to me: withdraw the hand of control from it." Chïn-Temür replied: "The report of a rebellion by the people of Khurāsān was false. How can so many lands and peoples be destroyed on account of Qaracha's crime. I will send a messenger to Qa'an to report on the situation and then proceed according to his command." Tayir Bahadur turned back in anger. Chormaghun also sent messengers to summon him and the emirs and make him hand over the affairs of Khurāsān and Māzandarān to Tayir Bahadur. Chïn-Temür now deputed Kül-Bolat, who was one of the confidential attendants of Qa'an, to proceed to his Court accompanied by the emirs of Khurāsān and Māzandarān. In the meantime, Malik Bahā al-Dīn of Ṣu'lūk[198] had come down from the castle on condition that he be sent to the Court of Qa'an. Chïn-Temür returned from Māzandarān, and the garrisons of most of the castles in Khurāsān surrendered because of the news of Bahā al-Dīn. When the latter came before Chïn-Temür he was distinguished with great honor. From Māzandarān there was designated the *ispahbad*[199] Nuṣrat al-Dīn of Kabūd-Jāma,[200] and the two of them set out for the Court of Qa'an in the company of Kül-Bolat in the year 630/1232–1233. Since none of the emirs of those countries had come thither before, Qa'an was pleased and delighted with their arrival. He ordered feasts to be held and treated them with great kindness. On that account Chïn-Temür and Kül-

[196] The ruins of Ṭūs are situated a few miles north of Meshed.
[197] Dayir—such is the correct form of the name—belonged to the Qonqotan tribe. In 639/1241–2, he invaded India and fell in battle before Lahore. See Boyle 1963, p. 240.
[198] This was a castle to the north of the town of Isfarāyin. See Mustaufī, p. 148.
[199] See Glossary.
[200] A district in the extreme east of Astarābād (Gurgān), the present-day Hajjilar.

Bolat were distinguished with all manner of favors, and Qa'an said: "During all this time since Chormaghun went and conquered so many countries he has sent no *malik* to us, whereas Chïn-Temür, despite the smallness of his equipment and resources, has served us thus. We approve thereof." And he settled the governorship of Khurāsān and Māzandarān upon him and commanded that Chormaghun and the other emirs were not to interfere. He made Kül-Bolat his partner in command and conferred upon the *ispahbad* the rank of *malik* [over the territory] from the frontier of Kabūd-Jāma to Astarābād, while he settled on the Malik Bahā al-Dīn the same rank over Khurāsān and Isfarāyin, Juvain, Baihaq, Jājarm, Jūrbad, and Arghiyān.²⁰¹ He gave them each a gold *paiza*²⁰² and two mandates with an *altamgha*.²⁰³

Chïn-Temür, being now confirmed in his office by the *yarlïgh*, appointed Sharaf al-Dīn, on account of his seniority, as vizier, and Bahā al-Dīn Muḥammad Juvainī as *ṣāhib-dīvān*:²⁰⁴ and each of the emirs sent a *bitikchi*²⁰⁵ to the Divan to represent the princes. The Divan being restored to a fairly flourishing condition, Chïn-Temür again sent Korguz upon an embassy to Qa'an. Kül-Bolat sought to prevent this, saying: "He is an Uighur and will do everything for himself. It is not advisable." But Chïn-Temür refused to listen. When Körgüz arrived and was questioned about the state of the provinces, he described it in accordance with [the Emperor's] taste. The latter was pleased with his manner of expression and sent him back with all his wishes gratified. Shortly afterward Chïn-Temür died. *And God knows what is best, and it is to Him that we return.*

The History has now been written of the *khaqans*, caliphs, sultans, *maliks*, *atabegs*, and Mongol emirs who were contemporary with Ögetei Qa'an during this period of 6 years. We therefore take up the history of Ögetei Qa'an after this period, which, God willing, we shall record in detail.

⁀ HISTORY OF ÖGETEI QA'AN FROM THE BEGINNING of the *qonin*²⁰⁶ *yïl*, that is, the Year of the Sheep, falling in Jumāda I of the year 632 [29th January–21st February, 1235], to the end of the

---

²⁰¹ On this area in Western Khurāsān, see Spooner 1965.
²⁰² See Glossary.   ²⁰³ See Glossary.   ²⁰⁴ See Glossary.
²⁰⁵ See Glossary.   ²⁰⁶ Mo. *qoni[n]*, "sheep."

hüker yïl, that is, the Year of the Ox, falling in Sha'bān of the year 638 [16th February–16th March, 1241], a period of 7 years, during which period he [held] two great *quriltais* of the princes, dispatched emirs to the lands of Qïpchaq, Māchīn, and elsewhere, and everywhere constructed fine buildings, both towns and palaces; in the last year of the period, which was the thirteenth since his accession and the fifteenth since the death of Chingiz-Khan, he died

History of the Qa'an's holding a quriltai *and dispatching*
princes and emirs to all the frontiers and borders of the lands

Having returned in the Year of the Horse[207] from his conquest of the lands of Khitai, Qa'an had called an assembly in Talan-Daba[208] and held a *quriltai*. In this Year of the Sheep he wished to reassemble all the sons, kinsfolk, and emirs and cause them to listen once again to the *yasas* and ordinances. They all presented themselves in accordance with his command, and he distinguished them everyone with every sort of kindness and favor. For one continuous month, in unison with his kinsmen, he joined the morning [draught] to the evening draught in feasting, and in his wonted manner and according to his practice, he bestowed upon that assembly all the valuables that had been gathered together in the treasuries. And when they had done with feasting and merrymaking he turned to the disposal of the affairs of the state and the army. And since some parts of the lands had not yet been conquered, and in certain countries some were practicing rebellion, he set about dealing with these matters, dispatching each one of his kinsmen in a different direction and intending to proceed in his own person to the Qïpchaq Steppe. However, Möngke Qa'an, who, although in the first flower of youth, had the perfect wisdom and counsel of an old man, remarked upon Qa'an's intention and said: "All of us brothers and sons stand awaiting thy ever-fulfilled command so that we may give our lives in whatever manner he may suggest whilst Qa'an busies himself with spectacles and pleasure and amusement and does not endure the toils and hardships of travel. Otherwise

[207] 1234.

[208] For Dalan-Daba, "Seventy Passes" (Mo. *dala(n)*, "seventy," and *dabagha(n)*, "mountain pass"). It was apparently the name of a mountain. See *Campagnes*, p. 244.

54

of what use are kinsmen and emirs, and a countless army?" All present approved these perfect words and made them their model and guide; and the august mind of Qa'an resolved that of the princes, Batu, Möngke Qa'an, and Güyük Khan, together with others of the princes and a great army, should set out for the countries of the Qïpchaq, Orus,[209] Bular,[210] Majar,[211] Bashghïrd,[212] Sudaq,[213] and [all] that region and subjugate them all.

In the same year in the plain of Asichang,[214] Ögetei Qa'an dispatched his own son, Köchü, and Prince Qutuqu, the son of Jochi-Qasar, into Māchīn, which they call Nangiyas. They set out and captured the towns of Sangyambu and Kerimbu,[215] laying waste the country of Tibet upon their way.

In the same year Hoqatur[216] was sent with an army toward Kashmīr and India. They captured and pillaged several provinces.

In the same year qubchur[217] on animals was fixed at the rate of one beast for every hundred. Also Qa'an commanded that a ṭaghār[218] of grain should be levied for every ten ṭaghārs to be distributed among the poor. And as there was [much] coming and going of ambassadors both from the princes [to the Court of Qa'an] and from the Court to the princes upon important and necessary business, yams were set up in all the lands which were called tayan yams,[219] and for the setting up of those yams ambassadors were designated and appointed on behalf of the princes as follows:

On behalf of Qa'an, Bitikchi Qoridai.

On behalf of Chaghatai, Emegelchin Tayichi'utai.

[209] The Mongol name for the Russians.
[210] The Bulgars, whether of the Volga or of the Danube. See Horde d'Or, pp. 124–39.
[211] The Magyars or Hungarians.
[212] The Uralian Bashkirs, now citizens of the Bashkir A. S. S. R.
[213] On the southeast coast of the Crimea, Polo's Soldaia.
[214] Unidentified.
[215] Hsiang-yang fu (Siangyang) and Chiang-ling fu (Kiangling) in Hupeh.
[216] The Oqotur of SH. He was in command of forces in the Baghlān-Qunduz-Badakhshan area. See Boyle 1963, pp. 242 and 247, note 68. On the invasion of Kashmīr see Jahn 1956, p. 177.
[217] On qubchur, originally as here a tax in kind (usually cattle), see Doerfer, I, No. 266 (pp. 387–91).
[218] A well-known dry-measure equivalent to 83.4 kilograms. See Hinz, p. 52.
[219] On yam (Mo. jam), "post station," and tayan yam, see below, p. 62 and note 270.

On behalf of Batu, Suqa Mulchitai.

On behalf of Tolui Khan, Alchïqa went at the command of Sorqoq-tani Beki.

The above-mentioned emirs went upon their way and established *tayan yams* in all the lands and countries throughout the length and breadth of the climes.

And Qa'an sent messengers to all the ends of the lands with the message that no mortal should molest another and the strong should not exercise their strength on the weak, nor seek more than their due of them, nor behave tyrannically toward them. And the people were at rest, and the fame of his justice was spread abroad.

Account of the battles fought by the princes and the Mongol army in the Qïpchaq Steppe, Bulghar, Orus, Magas, Alan, Majar, Bular, and Bashghïrd, and the conquest of those countries[220]

The princes deputed to conquer the Qïpchaq Steppe and the neighboring regions were: of the sons of Tolui, his eldest son Möngke Qa'an and his brother Böchek; of the family of Ögetei, his eldest son Güyük Khan and his brother Qadan; and the sons of Jochi, Batu, Orda, Shiban, and Tangqut. Of the principal emirs, there accompanied them Sübedei Bahadur and several other emirs. They all set out together in the spring of the *bichin yïl*, that is, the Year of the Monkey, falling in Jumādā II of the year 633 [12th February–12th March, 1236]. Having traveled throughout the summer, in the autumn, in the region of Bulghar, they joined the family [of Jochi], Batu, Orda, Shiban, and Tangqut, who had also been deputed to that region.

From thence,[221] Batu together with Shiban and Boroldai took the field with his army against the Bular and Bashghïrd[222] and in a short

---

[220] For an earlier translation of this chapter, see Minorsky 1952, pp. 224–26.

[221] This part of Rashīd al-Dīn's account has, as Minorsky (1952, p. 228) points out, been inserted in the wrong place. The operations in the Carpathians and Hungary took place later, in 1240. The present version is based on Juvainī (*HWC*, pp. 270–71); for Rashīd al-Dīn's own version, see below pp. 69–71.

[222] The phrase "Bular and Bashghïrd," like Juvainī's "Keler and Bashghïrd," seems to mean simply "the Hungarians." See *Horde d'Or*, p. 139. However, Minorsky (1952), follows Blochet in reading *Pūlū* for *Būlar* and thinks this may reflect "some memory of Poland, which was invaded before Hungary."

time and without great trouble captured that [country] and slaughtered and looted there. It happened as follows. The Bular were a numerous people of the Christian religion whose country bordered on [that of] the Franks. When they heard the report of the approach of Batu and the emirs, they made preparations and set out with 40 *tümens* of illustrious troops. Shiban, who was in the van with ten thousand men, sent word that they were double the size of the Mongol army, every one a *bahadur*.[223] When the two armies drew up opposite each other Batu, following the custom of Chingiz-Khan, went up on to a hilltop and for one day and night prayed and lamented to God Almighty; he also commanded the Muslims to offer up sincere prayers. A large river[224] lay between [the two armies]: Batu and Boroldai crossed it in the night and joined battle. Shiban, Batu's brother, attacked and fought in person; and the emir Boroldai and all the forces, attacking together, made for the pavilion of the *keler*[225] and cut the ropes with their swords. Their army lost heart and fled; and the Mongols, like a brave lion falling upon its prey, pursued them, smiting and slaying until they had destroyed the greater part of that army and that country had been conquered. This victory was one of their great deeds. Bular and Bashghïrd is a great region with [many] places difficult of access, and yet they conquered it. They have rebelled again and have not yet been completely subjugated. Their kings are called *keler*.

Thereafter,[226] in the winter, the princes and emirs gathered together on the River Jaman[227] and sent the emir Sübedei with an army into the country of the Ās and the region of Bulghar. They [themselves] went as far as the town of ———.[228] The emirs [of the town], Bayan and Chïqu, came and paid homage to the princes. They were received with honor, but upon their return [Bayan and Chïqu] again rose in revolt, and Sübedei Bahadur was sent [against them] for the second time in order to take them prisoner.

---

[223] See Glossary. [224] The Sayó.

[225] The Hungarian *király*, "king." See *Horde d'Or*, pp. 121–22.

[226] Here we seem to be back in an earlier period, ca. 1237. See Minorsky 1952, p. 228.

[227] Perhaps a corruption of Jayaq, the Mongol name of the Ural (T. Yayïq). See Minorsky 1952, p. 239.

[228] KRYK or KWYK.

Thereafter the princes held a council, and each with his army set out in an encircling movement and attacked and conquered the countries which lay across their path. Möngke Qa'an moved in such a circle upon the left along the bank of the river[229] and captured both Bachman, who was one of the chief emirs of those parts, of the *Ülirlik people in the *Qïpchaq federation,[230] and Qachir-Ukula of the Ās people.[231] This happened in the following manner. This Bachman, together with a number of other robbers, had escaped from the sword and a further group of fugitives had joined him. He would strike upon every side and carry something off, and day by day the mischief he caused grew greater. He had no fixed place of abode, and the Mongol army could not lay hands on him. In the daytime he used to lie hidden in the forests on the banks of the Etil.[232] Möngke Qa'an ordered two hundred boats to be constructed and one hundred fully armed Mongols to be set in each, while he and his brother formed a hunting ring and proceeded along the banks of the river. In one of the forests on the Etil they found some dung and other traces of an encampment that had been hurriedly abandoned. In the middle of this they found an old woman, from whom they learnt that Bachman had crossed on to an island and that all that he had acquired during that period by his wickedness and mischief was on that island. Because no boats were at hand, it was impossible to cross the Etil, but suddenly a strong wind arose, the water began to billow, and [it] receded from the passage leading from the island to the other side; and because of Möngke Qa'an's good fortune the bottom became visible. He ordered the troops to ride in. Bachman was seized and his army destroyed within an hour, some being flung into the river and some killed outright. The Mongols bore off their wives and children as prisoners, and they likewise carried off much valuable booty. Then they returned. The

---

[229] The Volga. This account of the operation against Bachman is reproduced from Juvainī (*HWC*, pp. 553–54).

[230] *Jamā'at*. So Minorsky 1952, p. 225. *Ülirlik* (AWLYRLYK) probably represents the "Ilberi" clan of the Qïpchaq, the conventional form of the name being "mal vocalisé," according to Pelliot (*Horde d'Or*, p. 212, note 3 to p. 210). Verkhovsky (p. 38) has *olburlik*. The name does not occur in Juvainī's version.

[231] That is, the Ossetes. The name of the Ossete leader has evidently undergone the influence of popular etymology, the first element being assimilated to Mo. *qachir* "mule." He is not mentioned in Juvainī's account.

[232] That is, the Volga. On the name Etil, see Boyle 1964, p. 178, note 18.

water began to move, and when the troops had crossed, it was back again without one soldier's having suffered harm. When Bachman was brought before Möngke Qa'an, he begged to be put to death by the latter's own hand. Instead Möngke ordered his younger brother Böchek to cut him in half. Qachir-Ukula, the Ās emir, was likewise put to death. That summer Möngke remained in that region.

Then, in the *taqiqu*[233] *yïl*, that is, the Year of the Hen, falling in the months of the year 634/1236–1237,[234] the sons of Jochi Khan, Batu, Orda, and Berke, the sons of Qa'an, Qadan and Güyük Khan, as also Möngke Qa'an, the grandson of Chaghatai Khan, Büri, and the son of Chingiz-Khan, Kölgen, went to war against the Boqshi and the Burtas[235] and conquered them in a short space of time.

In the autumn of the same year all the princes that were in those parts held a *quriltai*, and all together went to war against the Orus. Batu, Orda, Güyük Khan, Möngke Qa'an, Kölgen, Qadan, and Büri together laid siege to the town of Irezan,[236] which they took in 3 days. They then also captured the town on the Ika,[237] where Kölgen was wounded and died. One of the Orus emirs, Orman[238] by name, advanced at the head of an army; he was defeated and slain. They likewise jointly captured the town of Makar[239] in a space of 5 days and killed the emir of the town, Ulai-Temür[240] by name. Laying siege to the town of Great Yurgi,[241] they took it in 8 days.[242] The people fought hard, but Möngke Qa'an in person performed deeds of valor until he had defeated them. They captured the town of ———,[243]

---

[233] T. taqaghn/taqïghu, "fowl."

[234] Actually 1237.

[235] The Boqshi are apparently the Moksha, a division of the Mordvins. Burtas (Burṭās) seems to have been a general Islamic name for the Mordvins, who survive to this day as citizens of the Mordvinian A. S. S. R.

[236] Ryazan, which fell on the 21st December, 1237.

[237] That is, the Oka. The town was Kolomna.

[238] Prince Roman, the defender of Kolomna.

[239] MKR or MAKARD. Apparently Moscow, then only a secondary town in the Suzdal principality.

[240] Vladimir, son of the Grand Duke Yuri.

[241] That is, Vladimir, the capital of the Grand Duke Yuri.

[242] According to the Russian sources, the siege lasted from 2nd to the 8th February, 1238.

[243] QYRQLA or QYRNQLA. According to Berezin Pereyaslavl', according to Pelliot Torzhok. See *Horde d'Or*, p. 115, note 1 to p. 114.

which is the original country of ————,[244] jointly in 5 days. The emir of that province, Yeke-Yurgu,[245] fled into a forest; he too was captured and put to death. Then they turned back, and [after] holding a council [they] decided to proceed in a hunting ring, *tümen* by *tümen*, capturing and destroying any town, province, or castle that lay in their path. In passing, Batu came to the town of Kosel-Iske.[246] He laid siege to it for 2 months but was unable to capture it. Then Qadan and Büri arrived and they took it in 3 days. Then they entered the houses and rested.

Thereafter in the *noqa*[247] *yïl*, that is, the Year of the Dog, corresponding to the months of the year 635/1237–1238,[248] in the autumn, Möngke Qa'an and Qadan proceeded against the Cherkes[249] and, in the winter their king, Tuqar[250] by name, was killed. Shiban, Böchek, and Büri proceeded against the region of Qïrïm[251] and conquered Tatqara[252] of the Qïpchaq people. Berke proceeded against the Qïpchaq and captured Arjumaq, Quranmas, and Qïran,[253] the leaders of the Mekrüti.[254]

Thereafter, in the *qaqa*[255] *yïl*, that is, the Year of the Pig, corresponding to the months of the year 636/1238–1239,[256] Güyük Khan, Möngke Qa'an, Büri, and Qadan proceeded against the town of Magas[257] and took it in the winter, after a siege of 1 month and 15 days. They

---

[244] WZYRLAW. Minorsky (1952, p. 229) thinks this is Vsevolod III (1176–1212), the father of the Grand Duke Yuri.

[245] The Grand Duke Yuri. He actually fell in battle on the Sit' on the 4th March, 1238.

[246] Kozel'sk. The siege lasted 7 weeks according to the Russian chroniclers.

[247] Mo. *noqai*, "dog."   [248] Actually 1238.

[249] That is, the Circassians.

[250] TWQAR. So with Verkhovsky (p. 39), according to the Tashkent MS. Blochet has BWQAN.

[251] That is, the Crimea.

[252] So in Verkhovsky (p. 39). Blochet has *tā be-qarār*, "up to the agreement," which does not seem to make sense.

[253] Verkhovsky (p. 39) reads these names as follows: Arjumak, Kuran-bas, and Kaparan. Blochet has the phrase *az jamāl-i vufūr-i ū* (translated by Minorsky, with a query, as "thanks to his good luck") in place of the first name and the first two syllables of the second.

[254] Verkhovsky (p. 39) has Berkuti. Unidentified.

[255] Mo. *ghaqai*, "pig."   [256] Actually 1239.

[257] Reading MKS for the MNKS of the text. On Magas, the capital of the Alan or Ossetes, see Minorsky 1952, pp. 232–37.

were still upon that campaign when the Year of the Rat[258] came around. In the spring, they appointed troops and gave them to Buqadai,[259] whom they sent to Temür-Qahalqa[260] to capture the town and the region. As for Güyük Khan and Möngke Qa'an, by the *yarligh* of Qa'an they turned back in the autumn of the Year of the Rat, and in the Year of the Ox, corresponding to the months of the year 638/1240–1241,[261] [they] alighted in their own *ordos*.

Account of the buildings which he constructed in the period between the princes' departure to Qïpchaq and their return; also a description of his houses and dwelling places and summer and winter residences

From the beginning of the *qonin yïl*,[262] corresponding to the months of the year 632/1234–1235,[263] when he sent the princes to the Qïpchaq Steppe, until the *hüker yïl*,[264] corresponding to the months of the year 638/1240–1241,[265] when Güyük Khan and Möngke Qa'an returned, a period of 7 years, [Ögetei Qa'an] concerned himself with pleasure and merrymaking, moving happily and joyously from summer to winter residences and from winter to summer residences, constantly employed in the gratification of all manner of pleasures in the company of beauteous ladies and moon-faced mistresses and on all occasions turning his august mind to the diffusion of justice and beneficence, the removal of tyranny and oppression, the restoration of the lands and provinces, and the creation and construction of all manner of buildings. And in no way did he neglect the finest points in whatever related to laying the foundations of world sovereignty and raising the edifices of prosperity. Having brought with him from Khitai masters of every craft and trade, he commanded them to build in the *yurt* of Qara-Qorum, where he for the most part had his auspicious residence, a palace exceedingly tall in structure and with lofty pillars, such as was in keeping with the high resolve of such a king. The length of every wing of it was the distance of a bowshot,

---

[258] 1240.

[259] Verkhovsky's Bukdai: Blochet's text has QWQDAY.

[260] "Iron Gate," that is, Darband.　　　[261] Actually 1241.

[262] The Year of the Sheep (Mo. *qoni(n)*).

[263] Actually 1235.　　　[264] The Year of the Ox (Mo. *üker*).

[265] Actually 1241.

and in the middle they raised up an exceedingly tall pavilion. These buildings were finished off in the best possible fashion and painted with all kinds of designs and pictures. They called it Qarshi:[266] he made it his residence and orders were given that each of his brothers and sons and the rest of the princes that were in attendance should build tall houses in that neighborhood. They all obeyed the command, and when those buildings were completed and joined one to another they covered a great area. He then ordered distinguished goldsmiths to fashion, for the wine cellar, utensils[267] of gold and silver in the shape of animals such as elephants, lions, horses, etc. These were laid down in place of vats and filled with wine and kumys. In front of each of them was a silver basin, and wine and kumys came out of the mouths of those animals and poured into those basins.[268]

He asked: "Which is the fairest city in the whole world?" They answered: "Baghdad." He ordered a great city to be built on the banks of the Orkhon and given the name of Qara-Qorum.[269]

Between the countries of Khitai and that town other *yams*[270] were established in addition to the *tayan yams*. At every stage a *tümen* was posted for the protection of the *yams*. And he had issued a *yasa* to the effect that every day five hundred wagons fully loaded with food and drink should arrive thither from the provinces to be placed in stores

[266] Mo. *qarshi*, "palace." It was built in 1235, its Chinese name being Wan-an kung ("Myriad Tranquillities Palace"). See Cleaves 1952, p. 25. This must be the "great palace" described by Rubruck (Rockhill, p. 207) as "situated next to the city walls, enclosed within a high wall like those which enclose monks' priories amongst us."

[267] These utensils cannot have been seen by Juvainī during his stay in Qara-Qorum, for he speaks of them (*HWC*, p. 237) as real animals ("elephants, camels, horses, and their attendants") used in lifting up the various beverages, that is, presumably in raising the great vats "which could not be moved because of their weight."

[268] This contrivance is surely identical with the "magic fountain" constructed by the Parisian goldsmith, William Buchier, for the Great Khan Möngke. See Rockhill, p. 208; also Olschki, pp. 45 ff.

[269] In fact, though Qara-Qorum was not walled till 1235, the capital seems to have been fixed there as early as 1220. See *Polo* I, p. 167.

[270] T. *yam*, Mo. *jam*, "post station." For the fullest account of this postal relay system, see Benedetto, pp. 152–57. There were, according to the Chinese sources, three kinds of stations with the Mongol names: *morin jam*, "horse station," *tergen jam*, "wagon station," and *narin jam*, "secret station," the last-named used for urgent military matters. See Olbricht, p. 45, note 101. The *tayan yam* of Rashīd al-Dīn—the spelling of the first element (*TAYAN*) is quite uncertain—seems to stand in opposition to the *narin jam* and so to mean something like "ordinary post station."

and then dispensed therefrom. For [corn] and [wine]²⁷¹ there were provided great wagons drawn by six²⁷² oxen each.

He ordered the Muslim *uzan*²⁷³ to build a pavilion a day's journey from Qara-Qorum, in a place where were in ancient days the falconers of Afrāsiyāb²⁷⁴ and which is called *Gegen-Chaghan.²⁷⁵ He would be in this place in the spring because he used to fly hawks there.²⁷⁶ In the summer he would be in Örmügetü.²⁷⁷ There he had pitched a great tent which held a thousand persons and which was never struck. The outside was adorned with gold studs and the inside covered with *nasīj*.²⁷⁸ It is called Sira-Ordo.²⁷⁹ In the autumn he was in Köke-Na'ur,²⁸⁰ 4 days' journey from Qara-Qorum, where he would

²⁷¹ The words in brackets are supplied from Verkhovsky (p. 41). Blochet's text has the unintelligible NKTY and SRMH.

²⁷² Eight, according to Verkhovsky (p. 41).

²⁷³ *Ūzān*: Persian plural of T. *uz*, "skillful, craftsman."

²⁷⁴ Probably Bügü Khan, the legendary ruler of the Uighur, is meant. See *HWC*, p. 54 and note 5. Already in the 11th century Kāshghari had identified Alp-Er Tonga, a mythical Turkish hero, with Afrāsiyāb, the hereditary enemy of Iran in the Persian National Epic. So too the Qara-Khanids claimed to be of the "house of Afrāsiyāb" (*āl-i Afrāsiyāb*). See *Turcs de l'Asie Centrale*, p. 70.

²⁷⁵ In Blochet's text the first element of the name appears as KR, a reading which Verkhovsky adopts in his translation (Karchagan), though his own text has KHZ, which is much nearer to an original *KKN. Gegen-Chagan ("Bright and White") was apparently the name given to a series of lakes about 25 miles north of Qara-Qorum, probably on the Orkhon near the old Uighur capital at Qara-Balghasun. See Boyle 1970. The pavilion was built in 1237 at the same time as a "city" called Sa'uri(n). See Cleaves 1952, pp. 25–27.

²⁷⁶ Juvaini (*HWC*, p. 237) speaks of his watching the hunting of waterfowl in front of the pavilion, which he calls Qarshi-yi Sūrī, that is, apparently, "the Qarshi of Sa'uri."

²⁷⁷ AWRMKTW. The name occurs otherwise only in the *Altan Tobchi* (p. 147 of the translation), where it is mentioned as the place in which Güyük ascended the throne of the Khanate. Örmügetü was apparently the name given to a mountainous area to the south-east of Qara-Qorum between the Orkhon and the Khögshin Gol. See Boyle 1970.

²⁷⁸ See Glossary. There were in fact, according to Carpini, two other pavilions in this area: the "Golden Orda," where Güyük's enthronement took place and where he afterward received the Pope's envoys, and "a wonderful tent, all of red purple, a present of the Kitayans [that is, the Chinese]." See Boyle 1970.

²⁷⁹ The Sira-Orda of Carpini. See Becquet-Hambis, pp. 28 and 119.

²⁸⁰ For the first element of the name, Blochet's text has KWSH and Verkhovsky's KWSH. Köke-Na'ur ("Blue Lake")—not to be confused with the Köke-Na'ur of *SH* (§89), which lay on the Sengkür within the great bend of the Kerülen, and still less with the Koko Nor in Chinghai, where there were no Mongols in the 13th century

remain for 40 days. His winter quarters were at Ongqïn,[281] where he would pass his time hunting in the Bülengü and Jelingü[282] mountains and so complete the winter. In short, his spring quarters were in the neighborhood of Qara-Qorum, his summer quarters in the meadows of Örmügetü, his autumn quarters between Köke-Na'ur and Usun-Qol,[283] a day's journey from Qara-Qorum, and his winter quarters at Ongqïn. And when he was on his way to Qara-Qorum, there was a tall pavilion which he had built 2 parasangs from the town named Tuzghu-Balïq;[284] here he would eat *tuzghu* from the town and make merry for one day. Then on the next day the people would don garments of one color, and he would proceed from thence to Qarshi, where tender youths would stand before him and for the space of a month he would devote himself to pleasure. He would open the doors of the treasuries and cause noble and base to share his general bounty; and every night he would pit archers, crossbowmen, and wrestlers against one another and would show favor and make presents to the winners.

In his winter quarters at Ongqïn he had ordered a wall of wood and clay, 2 days' journey in length, to be erected and gates set in it.[285] This they called *jihik*.[286] When hunting, the soldiers on every side were all instructed to form themselves gradually into a hunting ring and make for the wall, driving the game toward it. From a distance of a month's journey, proceeding with the utmost caution, they would

---

—is mentioned further on (p. 180) as the place where the princes assembled to elect Güyük to the Khanate. It was situated, perhaps, in the extreme south of Örmügetü.

[281] AWNK QYN, that is, the River Ongin. Here is meant some point along the course of the river, perhaps the region around the present-day Arbai Kheere.

[282] BWLNKW (Blochet) or TWLWNKW (Verkhovsky) and J̌ALYNKW. Unidentified. These mountains must be somewhere in the Gurban-Bogdo or Gurban-Saikhan chains in the Gobi Altai.

[283] For the second element of the name Blochet's text has QWL, but two of the MSS. (as Verkhovsky's) have BWL. Unidentified. It was probably in the extreme north of Örmügetü. See Boyle 1970.

[284] A derivative of T. *tuzghu*, "food offered to a passing traveler," and *balïq*, "town." According to Juvainï (*HWC*, p. 213), it lay to the east of Qara-Qorum. According to the *Yüan shih*, it was 30-odd *li* from the town, that is, 10-odd miles. It was built in 1238. See Cleaves 1952, pp. 25 and 27–28.

[285] According to Juvainï (*HWC*, p. 29), this wall was built between Ögedei's winter quarters and the "land of Khitai," that is, North China.

[286] J̌YHK. The word does not seem to be recorded.

slowly form themselves into a ring and drive the animals into the *jihik*, [at which point] the soldiers would stand shoulder to shoulder in a circle. Then, first of all, Ögetei Qa'an would enter the circle with his personal retinue and amuse himself for awhile killing game. When he grew tired he would ride up on to high ground in the middle of the ring, and the princes would enter in due order; then the common people and soldiers would do their killing; then some [of the animals] would be released for breeding and the rest of the game would be distributed by the *büke'üls*[287] to all the various princes and emirs of the army, so that no one went without his share. All that company would perform the ceremony of *tikishmishi*,[288] and then after 9 days of feasting each tribe would return to its own *yurt* and home.[289]

Account of Qa'an's illness and death

Qa'an was extremely fond of wine, and [he] drank continuously and to excess. Day by day he grew weaker, and though his intimates and well-wishers sought to prevent him, it was not possible, and he drank more in spite of them. Chaghatai appointed an emir as *shaḥna*[290] to watch over him and not allow him to drink more than a specified number of cups. As he could not disobey his brother's command, he used to drink from a large cup instead of a small one, so that the number remained the same. And that emir-supervisor also used to give him wine and act as a drinking companion in order to make himself one of his confidants; and so his attendance brought no benefit to Qa'an.

Ibaqa Beki, the sister of Sorqoqtani Beki, whom Chingiz-Khan had given to Kehetei Noyan,[291] had a son who was a *ba'urchi*.[292] This

---

[287] See Glossary.

[288] See Glossary.

[289] On the Mongol *bultues*, see *HWC*, pp. 27–29; also Doerfer, I, No. 286 (pp. 411–14).

[290] Used here in the sense of "supervisor," the word was normally at this period a synonym of *basqaq*, that is, the representative of the conqueror in conquered territory, responsible in particular for the collection of tribute.

[291] Genghis Khan had first taken Ibaqa Beki as his own wife and had then bestowed her on Jürchedei of the Urut (not his son Kehetei). See *Campagnes*, p. 236, and *Conquérant*, p. 181.

[292] See Glossary.

Ibaqa Beki used every year, on the advice of Sorqoqtani Beki, to come from Khitai, where her *yurt* was, to attend [on Qa'an], and arrange a banquet in which she would hold his cup. In the thirteenth year from his accession she came as usual and, together with her son, who was the *ba'urchi*, she acted as his cupbearer. In the night Qa'an died in his sleep from excess of drink, and in the morning the princesses and the emirs raised an accusation against Ibaqa and her son saying that they had been the cupbearers and so must have poisoned Qa'an. But Elchidei Noyan, who was a foster brother [of Qa'an] and an important emir of the Jalayir tribe, said: "What foolish words are these? Ibaqa Beki's son was the *ba'urchi* who always held the cup, and Qa'an was constantly drinking to excess. Why should we slander Qa'an by saying that he died at the hands of others? His appointed time had come. No one must repeat these words." Being a sensible man he realized that the cause of his death was excessive and habitual drinking; he realized also that excessive drinking has such injurious consequences.[293]

According to the Mongols, Qa'an ascended the throne in a *hüker yïl*[294] and died in the next *hüker yïl*, corresponding to the months of the year 638/1240–1241, being the thirteenth year [of his reign].[295] But in the history of Master 'Alā ad-Dīn Ṣāḥib,[296] it is stated that he died in the Year of the Leopard, corresponding to the 5th Jumādā I, 639/11th December, 1241.[297] Ögetei Qa'an had a physician called

[293] Some garbled version of this story must be the basis of Carpini's statement (Rockhill, p. 25, and Becquet-Hambis, p. 122) that Ögedei was poisoned by his "paternal aunt."

[294] Year of the Ox.

[295] The two years correspond in effect to 1229 and 1241, respectively.

[296] That is, Juvainī.

[297] There is some confusion here. Juvainī never makes use of the Animal Cycle, and the year 639 A.H., which began on the 12th July, 1241, and ended on the 30th June, 1242, fell half in the Year of the Ox (1241) and half in the Year of the Leopard (1242). There follows, in Verkhovsky's version, an account of Ögedei's place of burial that is absent from the MSS. used by Blochet. According to this passage, the Great Khan was buried at a distance of 2 days' journey from the Irtysh, on a high mountain, covered with eternal snow, from which two of the tributaries of that river take their source. See Boyle 1968, where it is suggested that the tombs of Ögedei and his son Güyük are situated somewhere on the southern slopes of the Saur mountains, which separate northern Sinkiang from the basin of the Upper Irtysh.

————,[298] who composed a chronogram on the date of his death and sent it to a friend in Transoxiana. It runs as follows . . ..[299]

The history of Ögetei Qa'an has been completed from the beginning of the *qonin yïl*, that is, the Year of the Sheep, corresponding to the months of the year 632/1234–1235,[300] until the end of the *hüker yïl*, that is, the Year of the Ox, corresponding to the months of the year 639/1241–1242,[301] a period of 7 years, in the last of which he died. We shall now, concisely, with God's aid, record the history of the *khaqans* of Māchīn, the caliphs, certain sultans who still remained, the *maliks* and *atabegs* of Persia, and certain Mongol princes and emirs who ruled the surrounding countries.

History of the khaqans *of Māchīn, the caliphs, the remaining sultans,* maliks, *and* atabegs *of Persia, Rūm, Syria, Egypt, etc., certain princes who were in the Qïpchaq Steppe, the Mongol emirs in Khurāsān and other provinces, who were contemporary with Qa'an during this period of 7 years, beginning with the* qonin yïl, *corresponding to the months of the year 632/1234–1235;*[302] *also of the strange and unusual occurrences recorded as happening during this period of 7 years, briefly and concisely related, if God so wills*

History of the emperors of Khitai and Māchīn
who ruled during this period

Lizun ———— 41 years, ————, the 7 preceding years, [and] ———— 7 years.[303]

---

[298] Blank in all the MSS.

[299] The chronogram, omitted from Blochet's MSS., runs as follows in Verkhovsky's version:

"In the year *khalaṭ* his phlegm (*khilṭ*) increased more than in [any] other year.
Day and night it made [even] the ignorant aware of heavy drinking.
[This] contributed in full measure to the destruction of his health.
Let [people] be informed of this and of the help of wine [in bringing] this [about]."

As Verkhovsky points out (p. 43, note 2), there is a play on words in the chronogram between *khilṭ*, "phlegm," and *khalaṭ*, that is, the year 639 in the *abjad* or alphabetical notation.

[300] Actually 1235. [301] Actually 1241.
[302] Actually 1235. [303] The blanks are in all the MSS.

History of the caliphs, sultans, maliks, *and* atabegs
who ruled during this period

History of the caliphs. In Baghdad al-Mustanṣir bi'llāh[304] was the 'Abbāsid caliph. During this period he founded and completed the Mustanṣirīya College.

History of the sultans. In Mosul there reigned Badr al-Dīn Lu'lu'
―――――.[305]

In Rūm there reigned Sultan 'Alā al-Dīn ―――――.[306]

In Kirmān there reigned Rukn al-Dīn Qutlugh-Sulṭān, the son of Baraq.[307] His history is as follows. During this period, in the year 63[2]/1234–1235, his father Baraq Ḥājib sent him to the Court of Qa'an. Whilst still *en route*, he received the news of his father's death. When he reached his destination Qa'an, as was his royal wont, conferred all manner of favors upon him and, because he had hastened to pay him homage, gave him the title of *qutlugh-sulṭān*[308] and issued a *yarlīgh*[309] to the effect that he should be ruler of the countries of Kirmān and that his brother, Quṭb al-Dīn, who had been in charge of the affairs of the kingdom since his father's death, should make haste to Court and wait in attendance. Upon Rukn al-Dīn's arrival in Kirmān, Quṭb al-Dīn set out for Court by way of Khabīṣ.[310] When he arrived there, he was for a time in attendance on Maḥmūd Yalavach, whilst Rukn al-Dīn was busy as Sultan.

History of the maliks *and* atabegs

In Mazandarān ―――――.[311]
In Diyār Bakr ―――――.[312]
In Syria ―――――.[313]
In Egypt ―――――.[314]

――――――――――――――
[304] 1226–1242. Blank in the MSS.
[305] 1233–1259. Blank in the MSS.
[306] That is, 'Alā al-Dīn Kai-Qubād I (1219–1236).
[307] On Rukn al-Dīn, the second of the Qutlugh-Khans of Kirmān, see *HWC*, pp. pp. 479–82.
[308] That is, *fortunate sultan*, a variant of *qutlugh-khan*, the hereditary title of the dynasty.
[309] See Glossary.
[310] Now Shāh-Dād, to the east of Kerman, on the edge of the Dasht-i Lūt.
[311] Blank in the MSS.
[312] Blank in the MSS.
[313] Blank in all the MSS.
[314] Blank in the MSS.

In the Maghrib ———.[315]

In Fārs there reigned Abū Bakr ibn Sa'd, and during this period ———.[316]

In Sīstān ———.[317]

History of certain princes in the Qïpchaq Steppe and the emirs of Khurāsān and other provinces

History of the princes in the Qïpchaq Steppe[318] In the autumn of the qulquna[319] yïl, that is, the Year of the Rat, corresponding to the months of the year 637/1239 1240,[320] when Güyük Khan and Möngke Qa'an had, in accordance with the yarlïgh of Qa'an, returned from the Qïpchaq Steppe, the princes Batu and his brothers [together] with Qadan, Büri, and Böchek took the field against the land of the Orus and the people of the Blackcaps,[321] and in 9 days [they] captured the great town of the Orus called Men-Kermen.[322] Then they proceeded in a hunting ring, tümen by tümen, against all the towns of Üledemür,[323] seizing the castles and lands that lay across their path. Together they laid siege to the town of Üch-Oghul-Üledemür[324] and took it in 3 days

In the hüker yïl[325] Qa'an died, and in the middle of the spring month they crossed the *Qazaq-Taq[326] mountains in the direction of the Bular and the Bashghïrd.[327]

---

[315] Blank in the MSS.

[316] The second part of the phrase is not in Verkhovsky.

[317] Not in Verkhovsky.

[318] For an earlier translation of this chapter, see Minorsky 1952, pp. 227–28.

[319] Mo. qulughan-a, "rat."　　　　　[320] Actually 1240.

[321] The name given by the Russians to the Turks whom they established as frontier guards on the Middle Dnieper. See Minorsky 1952, p. 230.

[322] The Turkish name of Kiev. See Minorsky 1952, p. 230.

[323] That is, Vladimir, apparently as the name of a person. See above, p. 59, note 240.

[324] Vladimir Volynsky. In Turkish, üch oghul means "three sons (children)," and Minorsky (1952, p. 230), sees in this epithet a reference to the two sons (Daniel and Vasilko) and daughter (Salome) of Roman of Galicia.

[325] 1241.

[326] Following Pelliot's suggestion (Horde d'Or, p. 130, note 3), the Carpathians. See also Minorsky 1952, p. 231.

[327] See above, p. 56, note 222.

Orda, setting out on the right, passed through the land of the Ïla'ut.[328] ————[329] came against them with an army, but they defeated him.[330]

Qadan and Büri took the field against the Sasan[331] people and defeated that people after three battles.

Böchek proceeded by way of the Qara-Ulagh,[332] crossing the mountains of those parts and defeating the Ulagh peoples.[333] From thence, through the forests and mountains of *Qazaq-Taq,[334] they reached the territory of Mishlav[335] and attacked the rebels who were standing in readiness there.

The princes, proceeding by these five[336] routes, seized all the territories of the Bashghïrd, Majar,[337] and Sas,[338] and put their king, Keler,[339] to flight. They spent the summer on the Tisa[340] and Tanha rivers.[341]

Qadan now took the field with an army, captured the territories of the Taqut,[342] Arbaraq,[343] and Asraf[344] and pursued Keler, the king

[328] The Poles. See *Horde d'Or*, p. 159.

[329] BZRNDAM, perhaps a corruption of BWLZLAW, that is, Boleslaw. Prince Boleslaw of Sandomir attempted to halt the Mongols near Opole. See Minorsky 1952, p. 231.

[330] There occurs here in Verkhovsky's text the following sentence: "Then Batu [made his way] toward ASTARYLAW and fought with the king of the Bashghïrds, and the Mongol army defeated them."

[331] The text has *Sāsān*, the Persian, as the *Sasut* of *SH* (§§262 and 274) is the Mongol, plural of *Sās*, that is, the Hungarian *szász* "Saxon." It is, of course, the Saxons of Transylvania that are meant.

[332] That is, Moldavia. See *Horde d'Or*, p. 153.

[333] That is, the Vlachs. See *Horde d'Or*, p. 153.

[334] That is, the Carpathians. See above, p. 69, note 326.

[335] MYŠLAW. Minorsky (1952, p. 231) follows Strakosch-Grassmann in assuming that Böchek's route lay through Transylvania and sees in this name a possible corruption of Szászvár (Szászváros, Rumanian Orăştie, German Broos), on the southern bend of the Maros. Macartney, on the other hand, basing his premise on Bretschneider's version of this passage (i, 329–30), identifies Mishlav with Mieczyslaw, Duke of Opole, who was present at the Battle of Liegnitz.

[336] The *Yüan shih* too speaks of five routes followed by the invaders. See Bretschneider, i, 331.

[337] Both Bashghïrd and Majar, of course, refer here to the Hungarians.

[338] See above, note 331.

[339] See above, p. 57, note 225.

[340] TYSH: the Tisza.

[341] TNHA: the Danube.

[342] TAQWT (Verkhovsky's text). Blochet has MAQWT. Apparently a Mongol plural in *-ut*. Perhaps the Croatians are meant.

[343] ARBRQ (Verkhovsky). Blochet has AWYRQ.

[344] ASRAF (Verkhovsky). Blochet has SRAN. Perhaps the Serbs.

of those countries, to the seacoast. When [Keler] embarked on a ship in the town of ———,[345] which lies on the coast, and put to sea, Qadan turned back and after much fighting captured Qïrqïn[346] and Qïla[347] in the town of the Ulaqut.[348]

The news of Qa'an's death had not yet reached them. Then in the Year of the Leopard,[349] a number of Qïpchaq had come to fight with Köten and Shingqur,[350] the son of Jochi.[351] They gave battle and the Qïpchaq were defeated. In the autumn they returned again and passed into the region of Temür-Qahalqa[352] and the mountains of those parts. They gave an army to Ïla'udur[353] and dispatched him against them. He proceeded thither and defeated the Qïpchaq, who had fled to that region. They subjugated the Urungqut and Badach[354] and brought [back] their envoys.

The whole of that year was passed in that region. In the beginning of the taulai yïl, that is, the Year of the Hare, corresponding to the months of the year 640/1242–1243,[355] having completed the task of conquering that country, they turned back. Traveling throughout the summer and winter, they reached their ulus[356] in the mogha yïl, that is, the Year of the Snake, corresponding to the months of the year

---

[345] Verkhovsky's text has TLNKYN, Blochet's MLYKYN. Minorsky (1952, p. 231) sees in the latter form a probable corruption of an original SPLYT, that is, Split. On the other hand, TLNKYN could be a corruption of TRWKYR, that is, Trogir, the Serbian name of Trav, where Béla did in fact embark his family in March, 1242. See Strakosch-Grassmann, p. 168.

[346] QRQYN.

[347] *QYYLH* (Blochet), QYLH (Verkhovsky). Minorsky (1952, p. 231) regards these as the names of Turks captured in the town (chief town?) of the Vlachs.

[348] That is, the Vlachs. See above, p. 70, note 333.

[349] 1242.

[350] Minorsky (1952, p. 231) suggests that the text is out of order here and should be emended to read: ". . . a number of Köten's Qïpchaq had come to fight with Shinqur . . . ." Köten, if this is the same person, was a Qïpchaq prince who had taken refuge in Hungary, where he had been lynched by the mob at the time of the Mongol invasion. His followers had then crossed the Danube into Bulgaria and may well have made their way into the Caucasus area. See Strakosch-Grassmann, pp. 72–75.

[351] Shingqur was Jochi's ninth son. See below, p. 114.

[352] Darband. See above, p. 61, note 260.

[353] AYLAWDWR.

[354] Neither name can be identified. These were presumably Qïpchaq tribes.

[355] Actually 1243.   [356] See Glossary.

641/1243–1244,[357] and alighted in their own *ordos*. *And God best knows the truth.*

History of the emirs of Khurāsān

When Chïn-Temür died, a messenger was sent to the Court of Qa'an to report his death. A decree was issued that the Emir Nosal should succeed him in Khurāsān and 'Irāq. He was an aged Mongol[358] more than one hundred years old. In accordance with that decree the emirs and the *bitikchis*[359] in the Divan transferred themselves from Chïn-Temür's house to his, where they busied themselves with the affairs of the Divan. Sharaf al-Dīn Khwārazmī departed to wait on Batu, and Körgüz, as usual, traveled to and fro.

All at once, Bahā al-Dīn had a dispute with Maḥmūd Shāh of Sabzavār and set out for the Court of Qa'an, where he presented the case. A decree was issued that no decision could be reached in the absence of his adversaries; they must attend together so that an inquiry might be made. When the *malik* Bahā al-Dīn returned and communicated the decree, Nosal and Kül-Bolat were not pleased that Körgüz had been sent for. Nevertheless, he set out and returned having obtained the governorship for himself, and Nosal had to content himself with the command of the army until 637/1239–1240 [when] he died.[360]

Körgüz now brought the *bitikchis* and agents [under his own roof] and busied himself with the work [of government]. He restored the affairs of Khurāsān and Māzandārān to order, carried out a census, fixed the assessment of taxes, founded workshops in an excellent fashion, and created [conditions of] the most perfect justice and equity. However, Sharaf al-Dīn returned from Batu, and he and certain others, being deprived of authority by the presence of Körgüz, prevailed upon Edgü-Temür, the eldest son of Chïn-Temür, to seek his father's office. He sent Tonquz to Qa'an to report how affairs were proceeding in Khurāsān. Certain opponents of Chinqai, Qa'an's vizier, found an opportunity to report Edgü-Temür's words. The order

---

357 There is some mistake here. 1245 was the Year of the Snake.
358 Actually a Kereit. See *Horde d'Or*, pp. 54–55.
359 See Glossary.
360 See *HWC*, pp. 488–89.

was given that the Emir Arghun Aqa, Qurbagha, and Shams al-Dīn Kamargar should proceed thither and investigate these matters. When Körgüz received news of this he set out for the Court of Qa'an. He came upon the messengers at Fanākat[361] and refused to turn back at their suggestion. Tonquz grappled with him and broke his teeth. In the night Körgüz sent his bloodstained clothes to Qa'an by the hand of Temür and, of necessity, turned back. When he arrived in Khurāsān, Kül-Bolat, Edgü-Temür, and Nosal gathered together and with clubs drove the *bitikchis* out of Körgüz's house and brought them to their own quarters, where they began the investigation. Körgüz kept procrastinating until after 45 days [when] Temür returned bringing a decree to the effect that all the emirs and *maliks* should present themselves [at Court] and that no inquiry should be conducted on the spot. Qa'an had been angry when he had been shown the bloodstained clothes, and he sent a message to Körgüz saying that he was to present himself in accordance with the decree. [Körgüz] at once mounted horse with a group of trustworthy persons, the most capable of the age. Kül-Bolat and Edgü-Temür also set out with a party of *aiqaqs*.[362] In Bukhārā, Sain-Malik-Shāh entertained them in his house. Kül-Bolat went outside to pass water, and some *fidā'īs*,[363] who were following him, stabbed and killed him. When they reached the Court they first pitched the tent which Chïn-Temür had provided. Qa'an began to feast in it, and when he went outside to pass water a wind sprang up and blew down the tent injuring a concubine. Qa'an ordered the tent to be taken to pieces and distributed as plunder; and on this account Edgü-Temür's cause was ruined. A week later they pitched the tent that Körgüz had brought, and Qa'an made merry in it. Among the presents was a belt studded with jaundice stones.[364] Out of curiosity he fastened it round his waist. A little discomfort which he had felt in that region from indigestion was dispelled. He took this as a good omen, and Körgüz's cause prospered.

For a period of 3 months they continued to be examined and no decision was reached. In the end, Qa'an examined them himself

---

[361] Fanākat (or Banākat) lay on the right bank of the Sïr Daryā, near the mouth of the Angren (Āhangarān).

[362] See Glossary.   [363] See Glossary.

[364] The *icterias* of Pliny. See *HWC*, p. 496, note 15.

and Edgü-Temür and his followers were found guilty. He said: "Thou belongest to Batu. I will send thy case to him: he knows about thee." But Chinqai, Qa'an's vizier, said: "Qa'an is Batu's superior. Who is this fellow that his case should require the consultation of princes? Qa'an knows what to do with him." Qa'an pardoned him and having made peace between them sent them all back in the company of Körgüz, ordering them to be told: "It is the Great Yasa of Chingiz-Khan that a lying *aiqaq* be put to death. You ought all of you to be put to death, but since you have come a long way and your wives and children are awaiting you, I have spared your lives. Henceforth do not engage in such action." And he ordered Körgüz to be told: "If thou continue [to bear a grudge against them] for their former crime, thou too wilt be at fault."

A decree was issued that Körgüz should administer all the countries that Chormaghun had subjugated beyond the Oxus. He sent on bearers of these good tidings in advance into Khurāsān, whilst he himself went to visit Tangqut, the brother of Batu. From thence he set out for Khurāsān by way of Khwārazm and alighted at his own house in Jumādā II, 637 [November–December, 1239]. Then, summoning the emirs and chief men, he had the edicts read out to them. He also dispatched his son to 'Irāq, Arrān, and Ādharbāijān, where, after much disputation with the emirs of Chormaghun, he took control of those countries in accordance with the decree and fixed the taxes.

Körgüz chose Ṭūs[365] as his place of residence and began to construct buildings there. He arrested and imprisoned Sharaf al-Dīn and conferred the office of vizier upon Aṣīl al-Dīn Rūghadī. Sending Temür to Qa'an to report his action against Sharaf al-Dīn, he himself followed in person. On his way back he had an argument over money with one of Chaghatai's emirs, called Küje'ür,[366] somewhere in Transoxiana. The emir said: "What if I report thee?" And Körgüz replied: "To whom wilt thou report me?" Chaghatai had recently died. The emir wept before Chaghatai's wife and said: "Körgüz said this." The princess sent to Qa'an saying: "Because Chaghatai is

[365] The ruins of Ṭūs lie a few miles to the north of Meshed.
[366] Elsewhere (Khetagurov, p. 142) Rashīd al-Dīn calls him Sartaq-Küje'ür and says that he was a page (*ev-oghlan*) of Oghul-Ghaimish.

dead a *qarachu*[367] like Körgüz has spoken such big words." Qa'an gave orders that he was to be arrested and his mouth filled with earth until he died. [Körgüz] had in the meantime returned to Khurāsān. The messengers of that princess brought to the son of Kül-Bolat a *yarligh* commanding him to seize Körgüz and hand him over to them. Körgüz fled and entered the castle of Ṭūs. After 3 days' fighting he was taken out, dragged off in chains and delivered up to them. They took him away and put him to death by thrusting earth into his mouth.[368] *Praise be to God, Lord of the worlds!*

History of the strange and unusual occurrences
that happened during this period ——————[369]

[367] That is, "man of the people," "commoner."

[368] The whole section on Körgüz, with the exception of the detailed account of his quarrel with Küjc'ür, is abridged from Juvainī (*HWC*, pp. 493–505).

[369] Blank in all the MSS.

PART

III
OF THE HISTORY OF ÖGETEI QA'AN

His praiseworthy character and morals;
the excellent biligs, *parables, and pronouncements*
which he uttered and promulgated;
and such events and happenings as occurred during his reign
but have not been included in the two previous parts,
the information having been acquired
on separate occasions and at irregular intervals
from various books and persons

Qa'an was imbued with the fairest of dispositions and the noblest of qualities and customs. He was always exercising the utmost generosity and liberality toward all classes of men. The love of justice and bounty had gained such mastery over his nature that not for the twinkling of an eye would he neglect the spreading of equity and the diffusion of beneficence. Sometimes the pillars of state and the great men of the Court would object to his excessive generosity and he would say: "It is known of a certainty to all mankind that the world is faithful to none and that wisdom requires a man to keep himself alive by the perpetuation of a good name.

Lasting fame has been called a second life: this treasure is enough for thee *like good works that abide.*"[370]

And whenever the customs and usages of the sultans and kings of olden times were mentioned and reference was made to their treasures, he would say: "Those who strove after these things were devoid of their share of intellect, for no difference can be imagined between buried treasure and dust, both being of equal advantage. Since it will be impossible to return from that other world, we shall lay down our treasure in the corners of men's hearts, and whatever is ready and

[370] Cf. Koran, xix, 79: "*And good works which abide are in the Lord's sight better in respect of guerdon, and better in the issue* than all worldly good."

76

present or may come to hand we shall give it all to our subjects and to petitioners so that we may store up a good name."

To confirm these statements that have been made in brief regarding his deeds and words, a few anecdotes will be recounted in detail, being one out of a thousand and little out of much.[371]

[i] It is the *yasa* and *yosun*[372] of the Mongols that in spring and summer no one may sit in water by day, nor wash his hands in a stream, nor draw water in gold and silver vessels, nor lay out washed garments upon the plain; it being their belief that such actions increase the thunder and lightning, which they greatly dread and shun. One day Qa'an had been hunting with Chaghatai, and as they were returning they beheld a Muslim sitting in midstream washing himself. Chaghatai, who was extremely precise in the enforcement of the *yasa*, wished to put the man to death. But Qa'an said: "Today it is late and we are tired. Let him be held in custody tonight, and tomorrow he can be tried and punished." He handed the man over to Dānishmand Ḥājib, telling him in secret to have a silver *bālish* thrown in the water where the man had been washing and to have him instructed to say, at the time of the trial, that he was a poor man, that all the capital he possessed had fallen into the water, and that he had plunged in in order to pull it out. On the next day, at the time of the examination, the man had recourse to this excuse, and some persons were sent to the place and found the *bālish* in the water. Then Qa'an said: "Who would dare to contravene the Great Yasa? But this poor man, because of his great distress and helplessness, has sacrificed himself for this wretched amount." He pardoned him and commanded that he should be given 10 more *bālish* from the treasure; and a written statement was taken from him that he would not commit a similar action again. On this account the freemen of the world became the slaves of his nature, which is better than much treasure. *Praise be to God, Lord of the worlds!*

[ii] When they first rose to power they made a *yasa* that no one should cut the throats of sheep and other animals slaughtered for food

---

[371] The above is abridged from Juvainī (*HWC*, pp. 201–204). The anecdotes that follow are also reproduced from Juvainī, for the most part in a somewhat abridged form. Four however (nos. [xxiv], [xxvi], [xxxiv], and [xliv] in *HWC*) are omitted.

[372] See Glossary.

but should slit open their breasts or shoulders after their own fashion. A Muslim bought a sheep in the market, took it home, closed the doors securely, and slaughtered it inside after the Muslim fashion. A Qïpchaq had seen him in the market and had followed watching him. He climbed on to the roof, and when the Muslim drew the knife across the sheep's throat he leapt down, bound him, and dragged him off to the Court of Qa'an. Qa'an sent out officials to investigate the matter. When they reported the circumstances of the case, he said: "This poor man has observed the *yasa* and this Turk has infringed it, for he climbed on to the roof of his house." The Muslim was saved and the Qïpchaq was put to death.

[iii] From Khitai there had come some players, and they displayed from behind a curtain wonderful Khitayan plays.[373] One of these consisted of a kind of picture of every people, among which they showed an old man with a white beard and a turban wound round his head being dragged along bound to the tail of a horse. Qa'an asked who this was meant to portray. They replied that it represented a rebellious Muslim because the soldiers dragged them out of the towns in this manner. Qa'an ordered the show to be stopped and [commanded his attendants] to fetch from the treasury precious clothes and jewel-studded objects such as are brought from Baghdad and Bukhārā, Arab horses, and other valuable things such as jewels, gold, silver, etc., which are found in these parts. They produced Khitayan wares also and laid them side by side. The difference was enormous. Qa'an said: "The poorest Tāzīk Muslim has several Khitayan slaves standing before him, while not one of the great emirs of Khitai has a single Muslim captive. And the reason for this can only be the wisdom of God, Who knows the rank and station of all the peoples of the world; it is also in conformity with the auspicious *yasa* of Chingiz-Khan, for he made the blood money for a Muslim 40 *bālish* and that for a Khitayan a donkey. In view of such clear proofs and testimonies how can you make a laughing stock of the people of Islam? You ought to be punished for your action, but this time I will spare your lives. Depart from my presence and do not commit such actions again."

[373] Otto Spies, *Türkisches Puppentheater* (Emsdetten, 1959), p. 29, takes this as a reference to puppet plays. See also his review of HWC in *Die Welt des Islams*, N.S., Vol. VI, 1–2, pp. 152–53.

[iv] One of the rulers of Persia [374] sent a messenger to Qa'an and accepted allegiance, sending among other gifts a polished ruby which he had inherited from his forefathers. The blessed name of the Prophet had been engraved at the top and the names of the sender's ancestors beneath. He ordered the jewelers to leave the name of the Prophet for luck's sake but to erase the other names and engrave his own name beneath that of the Prophet. And then he sent it back.

[v] An Arabic-speaking apostate from Islam came to Qa'an and, kneeling, said: "I saw Chingiz-Khan in a dream and he said: 'Tell my son to kill many of the Muslims, for they are exceedingly evil people.'" After reflecting for a moment Qa'an asked whether he had spoken to him through an interpreter or personally with his own tongue. "With his own tongue" said the man. "Dost thou know the Mongol language" asked Qa'an. "No", said the man. "There is no doubt," said Qa'an, "that thou art lying. I know for certain that Chingiz-Khan knew no language but Mongol." And he ordered the man to be put to death. [375]

[vi] There was a poor man who was unable to earn a living and had learnt no trade. He sharpened pieces of iron into the shape of awls and mounted them on pieces of wood. He then sat waiting where Qa'an would pass. His auspicious glance fell upon him from afar and he sent someone to inquire into his circumstances. The poor man told him that he was of feeble condition and small property and had a large family; and he had brought these awls for Qa'an. He gave the awls to that emir, who told Qa'an about him but did not show him the awls because they were so ill-made. Qa'an said; "Bring me what he has brought." And taking those awls into his auspicious hand he said: "Even this kind will serve for herdsmen to mend the seams in their kumys skins with." And for each awl, which was not worth a barley-corn, he bestowed a *bālish*.

[vii] A very old and feeble man came to Qa'an and asked for 200 gold *bālish* to form a company with him. He ordered them to give that amount to him. His courtiers said: "The day of this man's life has reached its evening, and he has no dwelling, children, or kin, and no

---

[374] "A certain ruler from . . ." (*HWC*, p. 207). One MS. of Juvainī has: "Someone sent a messenger to him who was son of the king [*pādshāh*] of Badakhshān . . . ."

[375] This story occurs further on in Juvainī (No. [xl] in *HWC*).

one is acquainted with his circumstances." He replied: "All his life he has cherished this wish and sought such an opportunity. To send him from our Court disappointed would be remote from magnanimity and unworthy of the royalty which God Almighty has bestowed upon us. Give him what he has asked for quickly. He must not meet his destiny without having achieved his wish." In accordance with his command they delivered the *bālish* to him. He had not received them all when he yielded up his soul to God.

[viii] A person asked to be given 500 gold *bālish* from the treasury by way of capital so that he might engage in trade. Qa'an ordered the amount to be given. His attendants pointed out that this was a man of no standing, with no money and owing debts to that amount. He ordered them to give him 1,000 *bālish*, so that he might pay half to his creditors and use the other half as capital.

[ix] A document was found which told that in such-and-such a place near those parts, where their *yurts* were, was a treasure that had been laid up by Afrāsiyāb.[376] And it was written in the document that all the beasts of burden in that region could not raise up that treasure. But Qa'an said: "What need have we of the treasure of others? Whatever we have we dispense it all to the servants of God and our subjects."

[x] An *ortaq*[377] came to him and took 100 gold *bālish* from the treasury by way of capital. He returned after awhile and offered some unacceptable excuse for the loss of those *bālish*. Qa'an ordered him to be given another 500 *bālish*. He took them and returned a year later still poorer and offering some other excuse. Qa'an ordered him to be given the same amount again. He returned and offered some excuse. The *bitikchis* were afraid to communicate his words. In the end they said: "Such-and-such a person wastes and devours the money in the towns." "How," asked Qa'an, "can one devour *bālish*?" They replied that he gave them to worthless persons and spent them on food and drink. "Since the *bālish* themselves are still there," said Qa'an, "and since those who take them are also our subjects, the money remains in our hands. Give the same as you gave him the other times and tell him not to be extravagant."

[376] See above, p. 63, note 274.   [377] See Glossary.

[xi] The people of *Tayanfu,[378] one of the towns of Khitai, presented a petition saying, "We owe a debt of 8,000 *bālish*, which will be the cause of our undoing, for our creditors are demanding payment. If an order is given for our creditors to be easy with us, we shall gradually pay them off and shall not be utterly ruined." Qa'an said: "To force the creditors to be easy with them will cause them to suffer loss and to do nothing will cause these people distress. It will be better to pay the amount out of the treasury." He commanded a herald to proclaim that the creditors should produce documentary proof so that they might present themselves and receive cash from the treasury. And there were many who pretended to be debtor and creditor and obtained *bālish* by fraud; and so they received the double of what they had mentioned.

[xii] On his hunting-ground, someone brought him three melons. Having neither gold nor garments available he told Möge Khatun[379] to give the man two pearls which she had in her ears. They said: "This poor man does not know the value of these pearls. Let him present himself tomorrow and receive whatever is commanded in the way of gold and clothing." "The poor fellow cannot bear to wait," said Qa'an "and the pearls will come back to us." At his command she gave the pearls to him, and the poor man went away rejoicing and sold them for a small sum. The buyer said to himself: "Such fine jewels are fit for kings," and the next day he brought them as a present to Qa'an. Qa'an declared: "I said that they would come back to us and that the poor man would not be disappointed." He gave them back to Möge Khatun and distinguished the bearer with all kinds of favors.

[xiii] A stranger brought a pair of arrows and knelt down. They inquired into his circumstances and he said: "My trade is that of an arrowsmith and I have a debt of 70 *bālish*. If it is commanded that I be paid this amount from the treasury I will deliver ten thousand arrows every year." Said Qa'an: "The poor fellow's affairs must be entirely distraught for him to accept these *bālish* for so many arrows. Give him 100 *bālish* in cash so that he can mend his affairs." The *bālish* were delivered immediately, but he was unable to carry them.

---

[378] See *HWC*, p. 210, note 20; also below, Section 3, p. 146, note 30.
[379] Ögedei's favorite wife. See *HWC*, p. 211, note 21.

Qa'an laughed and commanded him to be given a yoke of oxen and a wagon also. He loaded the *bālish* on the wagon and went his way.

[xiv] At the time when he had laid the foundations of Qara-Qorum, he one day entered the treasury, where he saw nearly 2 *tümens* of *bālish*. "What profit," he said, "do we derive from storing all this, for it has to be constantly guarded? Proclaim that whoever wants some *bālish* should come and take them." The people of the town, noble and base, rich and poor, set out for the treasury, and everyone received his full share.

[xv] There had been no agriculture in the neighborhood of Qara-Qorum on account of the excessive cold, but a beginning was made during Qa'an's reign. A certain person planted radishes and a few of them grew. He brought them to Qa'an, who ordered them to be counted with their leaves. The number came to a hundred, and he ordered the man to be given 100 *bālish*.

If heart and hand are sea and mine, it is the heart and hand of the king.[380]

[xvi] A certain person planted a number of willow and almond trees near the pavilion, which he had built 2 parasangs from Qara-Qorum, and to which he had given the name of Tuzghu-Balïq.[381] No trees will grow in that region because of the violent cold, but it so happened that these ones put out leaves. He ordered the man to be given a gold *bālish* for every tree.

[xvii] When the fame of his bounty and beneficence had been spread throughout the world, merchants made their way to his court from every side. He would command their wares to be bought, whether they were good or bad, and the full price paid. And it usually happened that he would give them away without having looked at them. They for their part would make their calculations [by] fixing the price of one item at that of ten. All the merchants, when they realized what happened, would leave their goods unopened and withdraw for 2 or 3 days, until he had disposed of them all. Then they would return and state whatever price they liked; and it was his command that whatever it amounted to an additional 10 percent should be

---

[380] The opening line of a famous *qaṣīda* by Anvarī, in praise of Sultan Sanjar.
[381] See above, p. 64 and note 284.

paid. One day the officers of the Court represented to him that it was unnecessary to add this 10 percent seeing that the price of the goods was already in excess of their real value. "The dealings of the merchants with the treasure," said Qa'an, "are for the sake of increasing their profit. And indeed they have expenses to pay to you *bitikchis*. It is their debt to you that I am discharging, lest they depart from our presence having suffered a loss."

[xviii] Some people from India brought him two tusks of ivory. He asked what they wanted and was told "500 *bālish*." Without the slightest hesitation he ordered them to be given this amount. The officers of the Court made a great outcry, asking how he could give so large a sum for so contemptible a matter, when these people had come from an enemy country. "No one," he replied, "is an enemy of mine. Give them the money and let them go."

[xix] Someone, at a time when he was drunk, brought him a cap of the kind worn in Persia. He ordered a draft to be written for 200 *bālish*. [The secretaries] delayed [affixing] the *al-tamgha*,[382] thinking he had made such an order on account of his drunken state. The next day his glance fell upon that person. The secretaries laid [the draft] before him, and he ordered the man to be paid 300 *bālish*. They held up the matter again for the same reason; and every day he increased the amount until it came to 600 *bālish*. Then, summoning the emirs and *bitikchis*, he asked them whether there was anything in the world that would endure forever. They replied with one voice that there was not. Then, addressing himself to the Minister Yalavach he said: "That is wrong, for good repute and fair fame will endure forever." To the *bitikchis* he said: "You are my real enemies, for you do not wish fair fame and a good name to remain as a memorial to me. You think that I give presents because I am drunk, and so you delay payment and hold up what is due. Until one or two of you have been punished for [these] deeds as a warning to the rest, no good will come of you."

[xx] At the time when Shiraz had not yet submitted, a person came from that place and kneeling said: "I am a man with a family and have a debt of 500 *bālish*. I have come from Shiraz because of the fame of thy generosity, O Emperor." Qa'an ordered him to be given 1,000 *bālish*. The officials hesitated, saying: "To add to what he asked for is

[382] See Glossary.

nought but extravagance." He answered: "Because of our fame he has traversed many mountains and plains and experienced heat and cold. What he has asked for will not cover his debt and his expenses. Unless it is added to, it will be as though he returned disappointed. That cannot be considered right. Pay him the amount I told you in full so that he may return home rejoicing."

[xxi] A poor man came to the Court of Qa'an with ten thongs tied to a stick. Opening his mouth in prayer [for Qa'an] he said: "I had a kid. I made its flesh the sustenance of my family, and out of its hide I fashioned thongs for men-at-arms, which I have brought with me." Qa'an took the thongs and holding them in his august hand he said: "The poor fellow has brought us what is the best part of the goat."[383] And he ordered him to be given 100 *bālish* and one thousand head of sheep, and he added that when this was consumed he should come again and he would give him more.

[xxii] It was Qa'an's custom to pass the three winter months in hunting, and during the remaining nine months of the year he would sit every day, after he had finished his meal, on a chair outside his Court, where every kind of merchandise that is to be found in the world was heaped up in piles. These wares he used to give away to all classes of Mongols and Muslims, and it would often happen that he would command persons of great size to take as many of the wares they wanted as they could lift up. One day a person of this description picked up a whole pile of garments. As he went away one of them fell down. He came back to pick it up. "How," said Qa'an, "can a man have the trouble of a journey for a single garment?" And he commanded him once again to take as much as he could carry.

[xxiii] A man brought him two hundred whip handles made of the wood of the red willow, which they burn in those parts as firewood. He ordered him to be given 200 *bālish*.

[xxiv] A man brought him two hundred arrow-heads. He gave him the like number of *bālish*.[384]

[xxv] He was passing through the market of Qara-Qorum, when he caught sight of a shop full of jujubes. He felt a craving for this fruit

---

[383] Not "what is better than goats" (*HWC*, p. 216).

[384] This anecdote seems to correspond with No. [xxi] in *HWC*, p. 216, in which a hundred bone arrowheads are paid for with the same amount of *bālish*.

and upon alighting ordered Dānishmand Ḥājib to buy jujubes from that shop with a *bālish*. [Ḥājib] went and brought a dish of jujubes, having paid a quarter of the *bālish*, which was double the price. When he brought them, Qa'an said: "One *bālish* is a very small price for so many jujubes." Dānishmand Ḥājib produced the rest of the *bālish* and said: "What I paid was more than ten times the price." Qa'an upbraided him and said: "When in all his life has he had a customer like us?" And he commanded the man to be given the whole of the *bālish* and ten *bālish* more.

[xxvi] He gave a poor man 100 *bālish*. The officials said: "Surely Qa'an must think that 100 *bālish* are 100 dirhems." They scattered this quantity where he would pass by. He asked: "What is this?" They replied that it was the *bālish* that were to be given to the poor man. "It is a miserably small amount," he said. "Give him twice as much."

[xxvii] A certain person had made a deal for 100 *bālish* with his emirs and treasurers. He gave orders for the *bālish* to be paid him in cash. The next day a poor man was standing at the door of Qarshi.[385] Thinking that this person was the merchant he asked: "Why have you not yet paid him his due?" At once 100 *bālish* were brought to the poor man and he was told: "This is the price of your goods." "I have sold no goods," said the poor man. The attendants returned and reported that this was not the man. "Since you have taken the *bālish* out of the treasury," said Qa'an, "you cannot take them back again. It is this man's good fortune. Give it all to him."

[xxviii] One day he saw an Indian woman with a child on her back. He ordered her to be given 5 *bālish*. The official kept back one *bālish* and gave her only four. She pleaded with him and Qa'an asked, "What was the woman saying?" He was told that she was a woman with a family and was uttering a prayer. "She has a family?" asked Qa'an. "Yes," they said. He went into the treasury, called the woman and told her to take as many garments of every kind as she could lift. She took as many *nasīj*[386] garments as might be the capital of a wealthy man.

[xxix] One day a falconer brought a falcon, of which he said that it was sick and that its medicine was the flesh of fowls. Qa'an ordered him to be given a *bālish* to buy some fowls with. The treasurer gave

the *bālish* to a banker and had the man credited with the price of several fowls. Qa'an asked the treasurer about the falconer and he told him about his own efficiency. Qa'an was angry and said: "I have placed in thy hands all the wealth of the world, such as cannot be calculated, and it is not enough for thee. That falconer did not want a fowl, he used that as an excuse to seek something for himself. Everyone that comes to us—the *ortaqs* who say that they will take *bālish* in order to give interest, those who bring merchandise, and those people of every kind that make their way to this Court—I know that they have each of them fashioned a net in order to get something. But I wish everyone to have comfort from us and receive his share of our fortune." And he commanded that several *bālish* should be given to the falconer.

[xxx] There was a bowmaker who made exceedingly bad bows. He was so well known in Qara-Qorum that no one would buy his wares. One day he bound twenty bows at the end of a stick, brought them to the gate and took his stand there. When Qa'an came out he caught sight of him and sent someone to inquire into his circumstances. "I am," he said, "that bowmaker whose bows no one will buy, and I have become exceedingly poor. I have brought these twenty bows to present to Qa'an." He ordered his attendants to take the bows from him and give him 20 gold *bālish*.

[xxxi] A valuable jeweled belt of elegant design was brought to Qa'an as a present. He bound it round his waist, and a stud became loose at one end. It was given to a goldsmith to have the stud fastened. The goldsmith sold the belt and whenever they came to claim it offered some different excuse. In the end he was arrested and confessed that he had got rid of it. He was bound and taken to Court, where the case was explained to Qa'an. "Although he has committed a great crime," said Qa'an, "yet his resorting to such an action is proof of the utmost impotence and constraint. Give him 150 *bālish* so that he may mend his affairs and not presume to do the like again."

[xxxii] Someone brought him an Aleppo goblet. His attendants took it and showed it to him without admitting the bearer. "He that brought this," said Qa'an, "has endured hardships in order to bring so fine a jewel hither. Give him 200 *bālish*." The bearer of the goblet

was seated at the gate wondering whether his message had been delivered. Suddenly the glad tidings were brought to him, and at once the *bālish* were handed over to him also. The same day there was talk about Abyssinian eunuchs and Qa'an said, "Ask this person whether he can obtain eunuchs." "That is my profession," said the man. He ordered him to be given another 200 *bālish* and a *yarlīgh* for the journey. The man never returned.

[xxxiii] There was a person in Qara-Qorum who was in extremely distressed circumstances. He made a cup out of the horn of a mountain goat and sat down upon the highway. When Qa'an arrived, he stood up and held out the cup. Qa'an took it and ordered him to be given 50 *bālish*. One of his secretaries repeated the number of the *bālish*, and Qa'an said: "How long must I tell you not to deny my bounty and begrudge petitioners my property? Though it goes against your will, give him 100 *bālish*."

[xxxiv] A Muslim had borrowed 4 silver *bālish* from an Uighur emir and was unable to pay the money back. They seized him and took him to task, insisting that either he should abandon the pure faith of Muhammad and, girding the *zunnār*, embrace idolatry or else be paraded naked through the market and receive a hundred blows of the bastinado. He asked for 3 days' grace, went to the audience-hall of Qa'an and told of his plight. Qa'an ordered his creditors to be sent for and found them guilty of coercing the Muslim. He gave the Muslim the Uighur's house and wife[387] and ordered the Uighur to receive a hundred blows of the bastinado naked in the market-place, while he presented the Muslim with 100 *bālish*.

[xxxv] An 'Alid from Chargh near Bukhārā, who was called the 'Alid of Chargh, had received some *bālish* from the treasury for a commercial enterprise. When the time came to make a payment he said that he had already handed over the interest. They asked for the receipt. He said that he had given the money to Qa'an in person. He was brought into the audience hall, and Qa'an said: "I do not know thee. Where, in whose presence, and when didst thou hand it over?" "Thou wert alone," he said. Qa'an reflected for awhile and then said: "It is clear and certain [that he is lying], but if he is called to

[387] Not "an Uighur wife and house" as in *HWC*, p. 223.

account, people will say that Qa'an has gone back on his word and called the man to account." He went on: "Let him be, but do not purchase any of the wares which he has brought to the treasury to dispose of." A number of merchants had come that day: their wares were purchased and Qa'an gave each of them a greater sum than the actual price. Suddenly he said: "Where is that *saiyid*?" They brought him in and he said: "Is thy heart sore because they will not buy thy goods?" The 'Alid began to weep and lament. "What is the price of thy goods?" asked Qa'an. "30 *bālish*," he replied. Qa'an ordered him to be given 100 *bālish*.

[xxxvi] One day a kinswoman of Qa'an came in and gazed at the clothes, pearls, and jewel-studded ornaments of his ladies. He ordered Yalavach to bring in the pearls that were held in readiness. He produced twelve trays of pearls which had been purchased for 80,000 dinars. Qa'an ordered them to be poured into her sleeves and lap and said: "Now that thou art sated with pearls, how many glances wilt thou cast at others?"

[xxxvii] Someone brought him a pomegranate as a present. He commanded the seeds to be counted and distributed among those present. And for each seed he gave the man a *bālish*.

[xxxviii] A Muslim from the Tangqut region, from a place called Qara-Tash,[388] brought a wagon-load of victuals and sought permission to return to his own country. Qa'an granted permission and gave him a gold *bālish*.

[xxxix] On the day of a feast, when all the *turqaqs*[389] were buying drink, someone stole a gold cup from the *ordo*. Though an inquiry was made it could not be found, and Qa'an caused a proclamation to be made that whoever picked it up and brought it in would have his life spared and would be granted whatever he asked for. The next day the thief brought back the cup. He was asked why he had committed this impudent act, and he replied: "In order that it might be a warning to the World-Emperor Qa'an not to trust the *turqaqs*." "I have spared his life," said Qa'an "and in any case cannot put a fellow like this to death. Otherwise I should have ordered his breast to be cut open to see what sort of heart and liver he had." He gave him 500 *bālish* and

---

[388] According to Mustaufī (p. 250), Eriqaya and Qara-Tash were "the best-known towns" in the Tangut country.   [389] See Glossary.

many horses and garments, made him the commander of several thousand soldiers, and sent him to Khitai.

[xl] One year when the crops were growing, hail fell and destroyed them. Because of the fear of a dearth, a maund could not be obtained for a dinar in Qara-Qorum. He ordered a proclamation to be made that whoever had sown corn should not give way to anxiety, because whatever might be lost would be made good from the treasury. They should water their fields again, and if there was no harvest, they would receive the full equivalent from the granaries. They acted accordingly, and that year such a harvest was reaped as had no ending.

[xli] He was very fond of watching wrestling and at first [his wrestlers] were Mongols, Qïpchaq and Khitayans. Afterward he was told of the wrestlers of Khurāsān and 'Irāq, and he sent a messenger to Chormaghun and ordered him to send him such wrestlers. From Hamadān he dispatched, with relay horses and forage, the *pahlavāns* Fīla and Muḥammad Shāh with thirty [other] wrestlers. When they came to Qa'an he was extremely pleased with Fīla's appearance and size and the symmetry of his limbs. The Emir Elchidei of the Jalayir tribe was present and said: "A pity that relay horses, forage, and other expenses were wasted on these." "Bring thy own wrestlers," said Qa'an "to wrestle with them. If they win I will give thee 500 *bālish*. If they are beaten give me five hundred horses." So it was agreed.[390] Qa'an sent by night for Fīla, gave him a cup and spoke to him kindly. Fīla laid his head on the ground and said: "My hope, based on the fortune of the World-Bestowing Emperor, is that fate in this matter will be in accordance with his desire." Elchidei for his part brought from his *tümen* a man called Orghana Böke. They presented themselves in the morning. Elchidei said: "It is a condition that they lay hold of each other by the leg." The fight began. Orghana threw Fīla on all fours. Fīla said: "Hold me with all the strength and force that thou hast and do not let go." Then he made a play, turned Orghana Böke round and round like a wheel, and struck him on the ground with [so] much force that the sound of his bones could be heard far and near. Qa'an leapt up like a lion and said to Fīla: "Hold thy opponent well." And to Elchidei he said: "What now? Was he

---

[390] The account of the bout with Elchidei's champion is absent from Juvainī's version ([xli], pp. 227–28, in *HWC*).

worth the relay horses and forage?" And he forced him to produce the five hundred horses. To Fīla he gave, apart from presents and gratuities, 500 *bālish*, and to Muḥammad Shāh also he gave 500 *bālish*, while to each of their *nökers* he gave 100 *bālish*. Then he said to Muḥammad Shāh: "Wilt thou wrestle with Fīla?" "I will," said Muḥammad Shāh. "You are fellow-townsmen and kinfolk," said Qa'an.

After some time he gave Fīla a moon-faced maiden. In accordance with his custom and in order to conserve his strength he did not lay hands on her but avoided her company. One day the girl came to the *ordo*, and Qa'an asked her in jest: "How hast thou found the Tāzīk? Hast thou received thy full share of pleasure from him?" For it is a standing joke with the Mongols to credit the Tāzīks with great sexual powers. "I have had no taste of it so far," said the girl, "for we live apart." Qa'an sent to Fīla and questioned him about this state of affairs. "I have become famous as a wrestler in the Emperor's service," said Fīla, "and no one has vanquished me. If I do this my strength will wane, and I must not lose my rank in Qa'an's service." "My intention is," said Qa'an, "that thou shouldst have children. From now on I exempt thee from the competition of wrestling."

[xlii] In the country of Rūm there was a person in embarrassed circumstances who earned his bread by buffoonery. At that time, the fame of Qa'an's bounty and beneficence had spread to all parts, and that person conceived the desire to visit his Court, but he had neither traveling provisions nor a mount. His friends contributed together and bought him a donkey on which he set forth. Three years later he returned. Seeing one of his friends in the market place, he dismounted, greeted him, and carried him off to his house, where he brought him all kinds of elaborate food and drink in gold and silver vessels and dishes, whilst Khitayan slaves stood before him and many horses and camels were tethered in his stable. All the time he was busy questioning his friend, who did not recognize him. After 3 days had passed the friend asked him [who he was], and he replied: "I am that buffoon that went on his travels with a single donkey." His friends asked what had happened and he recounted as follows: "I went a-begging on that same donkey to the Court of Qa'an. I had a little dried fruit with me, and I sat down on a hilltop in a place that he would pass by. His august glance fell upon me from afar and he sent someone to inquire

into my circumstances. I told how I had come from Rūm because of the fame of Qa'an's bounty and liberality and had set my foot on the road with a hundred thousand privations in order that his fortune-bestowing glance might fall upon me and my horoscope might become auspicious. They held the tray up to him and told him what I had said. He dropped some of the fruit into a *suluq*.[391] Then, perceiving that his ministers inwardly objected to his action, he said to them: 'This man has come a long way. In traveling hither he has passed through many sacred shrines and holy places and has waited upon many great men. To seek a blessing from the breathings of such a person is a profitable action. I took the fruit in order to give some to my children. Share some among yourselves also.' With that he urged his horse on. When he dismounted in the *ordo*, he asked Dānishmand Ḥājib where the poor man was lodging. He replied that he did not know. 'What sort of a Muslim art thou?' said Qa'an. 'A poor man comes to us from a great distance and thou art negligent of his weal and woe, his lodging, eating, and drinking. Seek him out in person, place him in good lodgings, and attend to him in every way.' I had halted in the great market. He sent people running right and left inquiring about me until one of them came upon me and carried me off to his house. The next day, when Qa'an had mounted horse, he saw several wagon-loads of *bālish* being taken into the treasury, the number of *bālish* being 700. He said to Dānishmand Ḥājib: 'Call that person.' When I appeared he gave me all those *bālish* and encouraged me with other promises. And so my affairs of poverty entered the broad plain of prosperity."[392]

[xliii] A man came from Baghdad and sat down in the roadway. When Qa'an came along he inquired into his circumstances. "I am old and feeble and poor," said the man, "and I have ten daughters, and because of my extreme poverty I cannot find husbands for them." "Why does not the Caliph give thee something," asked Qa'an, "and help thee to find husbands for thy daughters?" "Whenever I ask the Caliph for alms," said the man, "he gives me 10 gold dinars, and that is not sufficient for a week." He ordered him to be given 1,000 silver *bālish*. "How shall I carry all these *bālish*?" asked the man. Qa'an

[391] A Turkish word meaning "vessel for holding water."

[392] Juvainī tells this story (No. [xlvi], pp. 228–31 in *HWC*) on the authority of a friend and sets it in the reign of 'Alā al-Dīn Kai-Qubād I (1219–1236).

ordered him to be supplied with relay horses and other facilities for transport. The old man said: "Many friendly and unfriendly territories lie across my path. How shall I get these *bālish* to my own country?" Qa'an gave him ten Mongols as an escort to bring him and the money safely through to friendly territory. The man died upon the way and they informed Qa'an. He ordered them to take the *bālish* to Baghdad, deliver them at his house and say that the Emperor had sent alms so that husbands might be found for those daughters.

[xliv] The daughter of one of his courtiers was being married. He had given her for her dowry a casket of pearls that had to be carried by eight persons. When it was brought before him he was carousing and making merry. He ordered the lid to be taken off. All the pearls were unique, varying in weight between a *mithqāl*[393] and two-sixths of a *mithqāl*. He distributed them all amongst those present. It was represented to him that this was the casket which they had brought, at his command, for the dowry of such-and-such a maiden. "Give her" he said, "the casket that is the fellow of this one."

[xlv] The *atabeg* of Shiraz[394] sent his brother Tahamtan to Qa'an with gifts and presents, amongst which were two carboys of extremely fine pearls. When they were shown to Qa'an and he learnt that the pearls were of value in the eyes of him that sent them, he ordered his attendants to bring in a long casket filled with royal pearls. The envoy and all present were dumbstruck at the sight. Qa'an ordered these pearls to be tossed into the wine cup during the feast so that they were all shared out amongst those present.

[xlvi] There was a Mongol called Minquli who had a flock of sheep. One night a wolf fell upon that flock and destroyed the greater part of it. The next day the Mongol came to Court and told about his flock. Qa'an asked where the wolf had gone. It so happened that at this juncture some Muslim wrestlers arrived bringing a live wolf with its jaws bound which they had caught in those parts. Qa'an bought the wolf from them for 1,000 *bālish*, and said to the Mongol: "No good will come to thee from killing this animal." He ordered him to be given a thousand sheep and said: "We will release this wolf so that it

---

[393] Equivalent in Persia, until the late Middle Ages, to 4.3 grams. See Hinz, pp. 5–7.

[394] Abū Bakr (1226–1260).

can inform its friends of what happened and they may leave this region." When the wolf was released the dogs fell upon it and tore it to pieces. Qa'an was angry and ordered the dogs to be put to death for killing the wolf. He entered the *ordo* in a sad and thoughtful mood and, turning to his ministers and courtiers, he said: "I set that wolf free because I felt a weakness in my constitution and I thought that if I saved a living creature from destruction the Eternal God would grant that I too should be spared. The wolf did not escape from the dogs, neither surely shall I come forth from this danger."[395] Now it is not concealed that kings are raised up by divine aid and receive inspirations and so are aware of [future] events.

We have given some description of Qa'an's generosity, liberality, clemency, and forgiveness, the qualities with which the Necessarily Existent had distinguished him, in order that it may be known and confirmed to all that in this world there is no virtue above the acquisition of a good name, for after the lapse of many years the mention of the bounty, generosity, beneficence, and justice of Ḥātim[396] and Nūshīnravān[397] is still upon the tongues of all mankind.

O Sa'di, the breath of a good name never dies; he [only] is dead of whom men do not speak well.

We shall now tell one story also of his severity, awesomeness, and fury in order to illustrate his perfection in both of the categories upon which the foundations of world sovereignty are laid.

❧ STORY

A rumor once sprang up amongst the Mongol tribe of the Oirat[398] that in accordance with a decree the daughters of that tribe were to be affianced to a certain group of people. In fear they affianced most of their daughters to husbands within the tribe, and some they actually delivered up to them. News of this reached Qa'an's ear, and he

---

[395] See below, Section 6, p. 206, note 39.

[396] A pre-Islamic Arab famous for his generosity and hospitality.

[397] Nūshīrvān (Khusrau I), the Sassanian ruler (531–578), always represented in Persian literature as the personification of justice.

[398] The name of the tribe is omitted in Juvainī's version (*HWC*, p. 235).

investigated the matter. It being just as had been reported, orders were given to gather all the girls of that tribe over seven years of age and to take back all who had been given that year to their husbands. Four thousand girls were thus assembled. He ordered those who were daughters of emirs to be separated from the rest and made a *yasa* that all who were present should have intercourse with them. Two of the girls expired. As for the rest, he drew them up in two rows. Those who were worthy of the *ordo* he dispatched to the harem, some he gave to the cheetah-keepers and falconers, and some to the various attendants at Court; others again he sent to the brothel and the hostel for ambassadors. As for those that still remained, he ordered all present, whether Mongols or Muslims, to carry them off whilst their brothers, husbands, and kinsmen looked on not daring to breathe.

◀ STORY

Qa'an had placed all the countries of Khitai under Maḥmūd Yalavach; [the region] from Besh-Balïq[399] and Qara-Khocho,[400] which is the land of Uighuristān, Khutan, Kāshghar, Almalïq,[401] Qayalïq,[402] Samarqand, and Bukhārā, to the banks of the Oxus under Mas'ūd Beg, the son of Yalavach; and (the region) from Khurāsān to the frontiers of Rūm and Diyār Bakr under the Emir Arghun. They used to gather together all the taxes of all these countries and deliver them to Qa'an's treasury.[403]

End of the history of Ögetei Qa'an, the son of Chingiz-Khan.

[399] "Pentapolis." The ruins of Besh-Balïq are situated some 47 kilometers west of Guchen, near Jimsa. See *Ḥudūd*, p. 272.
[400] Or Qocho, of which the ruins are situated about 45 kilometers east of Turfan.
[401] "Apple Orchard." It lay somewhere near the later Kulja.
[402] See above, p. 30, note 84.
[403] This story is not in Juvainī. It appears to be incomplete.

History of Jochi Khan,

Son of Chingiz-Khan,

which is in Three Parts

HISTORY OF JOCHI KHAN,
SON OF CHINGIZ-KHAN,
WHICH IS IN THREE PARTS

❧ PART I. An account of the lineage of Jochi Khan; also of his wives, sons, and grandsons in the branches into which they have divided down to the present day; his portrait; and a genealogical table of his descendants.

❧ PART II. The [general] history of and [particular] episodes in his reign; a picture of his throne and wives and the princes and emirs on the occasion of his accession; an account of his summer and winter residences, the battles he fought and the victories he gained and the length of his reign.

❧ PART III. His praiseworthy character and morals; miscellaneous anecdotes and also the excellent parables, *biligs*, and pronouncements which he uttered, such as have not been included in the two previous parts, the information having been acquired on separate occasions and at irregular intervals from various books and persons.

PART I

OF THE HISTORY OF JOCHI KHAN

An account of the lineage of Jochi Khan and also
his wives, sons, and grandsons
in the branches into which they have divided down to the present day;
his portrait;
and a genealogical table of his descendants

Jochi Khan was the eldest of the children of Chingiz-Khan, except [for] a sister, called Fujin Beki, who was older than he. He was born of the eldest wife, called Börte Fujin, the daughter of Dei Noyan of the Qonqïrat[1] people, who was the mother of four sons and five daughters. In the early days of Chingiz-Khan, when the indications of world sovereignty were not yet apparent on the pages of his life, his wife, the aforesaid Börte Fujin, became pregnant with Jochi Khan. About that time the Merkit[2] people found an opportunity to raid the encampment of Chingiz-Khan and carry off his wife, who was pregnant. Now although that people hitherto had been for the most part unfriendly and hostile toward Ong-Khan,[3] the ruler of the Kereit, there was at that time peace between them. They therefore sent Börte Fujin to Ong-Khan, and since he had been the friend of Chingiz-Khan's father and also called Chingiz-Khan his child, he treated her with honor and respect and bestowed upon her the rank and status of

---

[1] On the Qonqïrat (Qonggirat or Onggirat), a tribe in the extreme east of Mongolia, see Khetagurov, pp. 160–66, *Campagnes*, pp. 402 ff, *Polo I*, No. 375 (pp. 869–70).

[2] A forest people in the region of the Lower Selenga, along the southern shores of Lake Baikal.

[3] The Unc of Rubruck and the Unc Kan of Marco Polo, who identified him with Prester John. His real name was Toghrïl (To'oril), Ong being the Mongol pronunciation of the Chinese title *wang*, "prince," conferred on him by the Chin in recognition of the part he had played in one of their campaigns against the Tatar. See *Conquérant*, pp. 116–20. His people, the Kereit, were Nestorian Christians; they lived along the Orkhon and Tula, between the Khangai and Kentei mountains.

a daughter-in-law, protecting her from the gaze of strangers. And because she was exceedingly beautiful and capable the emirs of Ong-Khan said to one another: "Why does not Ong-Khan take Börte Fujin for himself," But Ong-Khan said: "She is in the position of a daughter-in-law to me and has been placed with us for safe keeping. To look at her with perfidious eyes is not the way of chivalry." When Chingiz-Khan learnt of her whereabouts, he sent an emir of the Jalayir[4] called Sebe (the grandfather of Sartaq, who during the infancy of Arghun[5] was by virtue of the *yarlïgh* of Abaqa[6] Khan emir of the *ordo* in Khurāsān and Māzandarān) to Ong-Khan to seek and fetch Börte Fujin. Having treated her with respect and consideration, Ong Khan dispatched her along with Sebe. Upon the way a son was suddenly born to her, and for that reason he was called Jochi.[7] Since the road was dangerous and there was no opportunity for halting, it was impossible to make a cradle, and [so] Sebe kneaded a little flour and, wrapping it round the child, took him in his lap so that he might not be harmed. And carrying him carefully, he brought him to Chingiz-Khan.[8]

When he grew up he always accompanied and was in attendance upon his father, assisting him in weal and woe, but there was constant strife, quarreling, and disagreement between him and his brothers Chaghatai and Ögetei. And because of ———,[9] the path of unity was trodden upon both sides between him and Tolui and his family and none of them ever uttered that taunt but regarded his ———[10] as genuine.

[4] On the Jalayir, see Khetagurov, pp. 92–98.

[5] The Il-Khan of Persia (1284–1291).

[6] The father of Arghun, Il-Khan of Persia from 1265 to 1281.

[7] Later authorities have explained Jochi's name as meaning "unexpected guest," from Mo. *jochin*, "guest," but it would seem that Rashīd al-Dīn had some other word in mind. See *Horde d'Or*, pp. 10–28, and Doerfer I, No. 167 (pp. 299–300).

[8] The *SH* gives an altogether different version (§§ 104–11) of the events, according to which Börte was rescued from the Merkit by an expedition led jointly by Genghis Khan, Ong Khan, and Genghis Khan's *anda*, or "oath brother," Jamuqa, and it is implied in a later passage (§254) that the Merkit Chilger Bökö was Jochi's real father. See also below, note 10.

[9] There is a blank in the MSS.

[10] There is a blank in one of Blochet's MSS and in his text, but not in Verkhovsky's. Presumably some such word as *nasab*, "genealogy, parentage," is missing. The "taunt" must in any case be a reference to the circumstances of Jochi's birth.

In his childhood and youth, Jochi Khan had sought in marriage a daughter of Jagambo[11] called Bek-Tutmïsh Fujin, the sister of Ibaqa Beki, the wife of Chingiz-Khan, and of Sorqoqtani Beki, the wife of Tolui Khan. She was Jochi Khan's eldest wife; apart from her he had many wives and concubines and many children by them. According to reliable informants he had nearly forty sons, and grandchildren without number descended from them. However, on account of the great distance and because no authority could be found, it has not been possible to ascertain their genealogies with exactitude, but such of his sons and grandsons as are well known shall be described in detail. *And God Almighty knows best what is right.*

✎ ACCOUNT OF THE SONS OF JOCHI KHAN AND HIS grandsons that have been born up to the present time

The sons of Jochi Khan, those that are famous and well known, are fourteen. Their names and those of their descendants, insofar as these are known, are as follows: first son, Orda; second son, Batu; third son, Berke; fourth son, Berkecher; fifth son, Shiban Khan; sixth son, Tangqut; seventh son, Bo'al; eighth son, Chila'uqun; ninth son, Shingqur; tenth son, Chimtai; eleventh son, Muḥammad; twelfth son, Udur; thirteenth son, Toqa-Temür; [and] fourteenth son, Shinggüm.

We shall now begin and give an account of each of these sons one by one in the order given above; we shall also give a detailed account of their descendants.

First Son of Jochi Khan—Orda

He was born of [Jochi Khan's] chief wife, Sorghan by name, of the Qonqïrat people. He was held in very great honor and respect both during his father's lifetime and after his death. And although Jochi Khan was succeeded by his second son, Batu, yet in the *yarlïghs* which he wrote with respect to decrees and *yasas* Möngke Qa'an placed the

---

[11] The brother of Ong-Khan.

name of Orda first. Orda was content with Batu's being the ruler and caused him to be enthroned in his father's place. Of Jochi Khan's armies, half was held by Orda and half by Batu. He with his four brothers Udur, Toqa-Temür, Shingqur, and Shinggüm were the army on the left, and to this day they are called the princes of the left hand.[12] Their posterity is still today together with the posterity of Orda, and his *yurt* and that of his brothers and their armies are on the left in the region of ———.[13] His descendants and their *ulus* are still there, and from the very beginning it has never happened that any of the members of Orda's family that have succeeded him have gone to the khans of Batu's family, for they are far distant from each other and independent rulers of their own *ulus*. Nevertheless, it has been their custom to recognize those who have succeeded Batu as their lords and rulers and to write their names at the head of their *yarlighs*. Bayan, the son of Qonichi, who is the ruler of the *ulus* of Orda in the present age, has come to the border of the territory of Toqta, who is the ruler of the *ulus* of Batu, because his cousin Küilük had rebelled against him and he was afraid of him, and he has gone to Toqta on the pretext of holding a *quriltai*, as shall be related in detail hereafter.

Orda had three chief wives, one of them being Jüke Khatun of the Qonqïrat people, another Tobaqana, also of the Qonqïrat, and another ———,[14] likewise of the Qonqïrat, whose father's name was Öge Khan; [Orda] married her after her father's death. He had concubines also. By these wives he had seven sons, as follows: Sartaqtai, Quli, Qurumshi, Qongqïran, Chormaqai, Qutuqu, and Hülegü. The circumstances of these seven sons and their sons and grandsons are such as shall now be recounted in detail separately for each one.

First Son of Orda—Sartaqtai

This son was born of Jöge Khatun, who belonged to the Qonqïrat people. He had four chief wives and several concubines. By the wife called Hujan, who was the sister of Qutui Khatun, the wife of Hülegü

---

[12] That is, the East.

[13] Blank in the MSS. Orda's *ulus*, known later as the White Horde, occupied the region stretching northward from the right bank of the Sïr Daryā to the Ulu-Tau mountains, in what is now Central Kazakhstan.

[14] Blank in all the MSS.

Khan, he had a son Qonichi,[15] who was for a long time ruler of the *ulus* of Orda: he was on friendly terms with Arghun[16] Khan and afterward with the Lord of Islam (*may God cause him to reign forever!*), to whom he was constantly sending ambassadors to express his affection and devotion. He was excessively fat and corpulent and was growing fatter every day, until it reached a point where the *kezikten*[17] used to watch over him night and day to prevent his sleeping, lest some fat should come out of his throat and he should perish. Because of his extreme bulk no horse would carry him, and he used to travel in a wagon. In the end he accidentally fell asleep, some fat came out of his throat, and he died.

Qonichi had four chief wives, the first, Toquluqan of the Qonqïrat people, the second, Buqulun of the Merkit people, the third, Chingtüm of the Qonqïrat people, and the fourth, Barquchin of the Jajirat[18] people, of the family of a great emir, who was the chief of the *qorchis*. He had four sons; Bayan, Bachqïrtai,[19] Chaghan-Buqa, and Maqudai.[20] The circumstances of these four sons of Qonichi and the genealogy of their sons and grandsons are such as shall now be described in detail separately for each one.

First Son of Qonichi—Bayan. He was born of Buqulun Khatun of the Qonqïrat people. After his father's death, he married three of his wives: the first, Barquchin, the second, Chingtüm, and the third, Altaju. He had also three other wives: the first, Ilgen of the Qonqïrat people, the daughter of Temüge of the family of Keles Elchi, who came here; the second, Qutulun of the Arghun[21] people, the daughter

---

[15] Marco Polo's Conchi. See *Polo I*, p. 404.

[16] The Il-Khan of Persia (1284–1291).

[17] A variant form of *keshikten*, on which see above, Section 1, p. 41, note 133.

[18] The Jadaran or Jajirat were the tribe of Genghis Khan's old rival, Jamuqa. On the name, see *Campagnes*, pp. 28–29.

[19] "Ile of the Bachqïrd (Bashqïrd)." On the Bashghïrd, the modern Bashkirs, see above, Section 1, p. 55, note 212. The Mongols, as Pelliot remarks, "were often called by ethnical names, without any regard to their own tribal origin . . . ." See *Polo II*, p. 782.

[20] "He of the Maqud (Maqut)." On the Maqut or Taqut, see above, Section 1, p. 70, note 342.

[21] Reading ARΓWNAN for the AWʿWNAN of two of Blochet's MSS, whence apparently Verkhovsky's *ugnan*. Blochet himself reads AWΓWZYAN, that is, apparently Oghuz, which is, of course, impossible. On the Arghun, the Argons of Marco Polo, see *Polo I*, pp. 48–51.

of ———;[22] and the third, Altaju of the Qonqïrat people, the daughter of Tödei Bahadur, who was a kinsman of the Great Lady Bulaghan Khatun.[23] Bayan has four sons, as follows: Shādī, born of Ilgen, the daughter of Temüge; Sati-Buqa, born of Qutulun Khatun; Tekne, born of Altaju Khatun; and Salji'utai, whose mother's name is not known.

Bayan has now succeeded his father Qonichi and administers his *ulus*. He is on friendly terms with the Lord of Islam (*may God cause him to reign forever!*) and is constantly sending ambassadors. Some time ago Küilük, the son of Temür-Buqa, made the claim that previously his father had administered the *ulus* and [that] therefore it came to him by inheritance. He held an assembly, obtained troops from Qaidu and Du'a, and made a sudden attack upon Bayan. Bayan fled and went to a region where Toqta, the successor of Batu, is settled. He passed the winter there and in the spring came to Toqta for a *qurutai* and asked him for help. Toqta, being at war with Noqai and at the same time apprehensive regarding the Lord of Islam (*may God cause him to reign forever!*), made some excuse and did not give him any troops. Instead, he sent ambassadors to Qaidu and Du'a calling on them to send Küilük to him; he also issued a *yarligh* that the *ulus* was still be be administered by Bayan. Up to the present Bayan has fought fifteen battles with Küilük and the troops of Qaidu and Du'a, and on six occasions he was present in person in the battle. And although Toqta sends ambassadors to Chapar, the son of Qaidu, and Du'a, calling on them to send Küilük, they do not agree and made excuses, it being their intention to help Küilük so that he may become ruler of the *ulus* and be their ally in their dispute with Ghazan Khan. Last year, which was 702/1302–1303, Bayan sent ambassadors to the Lord of Islam (*may God cause him to reign forever!*) headed by Keles of the Qonqïrat, who was an emir during the reign of Qonichi, and Toq-Temür of the Besüt,[24] along with other *nökers*. They reached the Lord of Islam (*may God cause him to reign forever!*) in the neighborhood of Baghdad at the beginning of Jumādā II of the same year [end of

[22] Most of the diacritical points are missing in Blochet's MSS and text. Verkhovsky reads the name Tukuyana-Tukutai.

[23] Bulaghan was the wife of the Il-Khan Abaqa and afterward became the wife of his son Arghun.

[24] On the Besüt (misspelled Yisut), see Khetagurov, pp. 193–96.

January, 1303], bringing falcons and other presents. They bore this message: "It is requested that you constantly send ambassadors with good tidings and wait until the emirs go to war in whatsoever direction is commanded and render service. For this year we have gone to war against Chapar, and Toqta is allied with us and has been sending troops."

Toqta had sent 2 *tümens* to link up with the troops of the Qa'an at Deresü,[25] for the frontier of their territory is close to that of the Qa'an and they had joined forces before. Some years ago Qaidu, fearing they might link up with the troops of the Qa'an, sent his second son, called Bayanchar, another son called Shāh, Töde-Temür, the son of Shiregi, the son of Möngke Qa'an, and Malik Temür, the son of Arïq Böke, with an army to the frontier of Bayan's country and handed over that region to them so that they might form a screen between the troops of the Qa'an and those of Bayan and not allow them to link up. And Küilük, with the troops that have gone over from Bayan and those which have come to assist him from Qaidu and Du'a, has seized part of the territories and *ulus* of Bayan, though Bayan still administers the greater part of the *ulus* of Orda, but on account of these constant battles his troops have become empoverished, some mounted and some on foot; nevertheless he continues to struggle against his powerful enemy and seeks help in money from here. The Lord of Islam (*may God cause him to reign forever!*) sent back from Tabriz his ambassadors that had reached him in Baghdad; with them he sent gold, clothing, and other presents for Bayan and his wives.

Second Son of Qonichi—Bachqïrtai. He was born of Buqulun Khatun of the Merkit and had a wife called Kökelün of the Kereit, by whom he had a son called Yeke.

[25] DRSW. In a letter dated the 20th February, 1968, Professor Francis W. Cleaves suggests that this name is "almost certainly the Mongolian *deresü*(n), a kind of high grass, which occurs very frequently in proper names." Cf. the Tersüt of the *SH*, the T'a-la-su of the *Shêng-wu ch'in-chêng lu*, in which Pelliot (*Campagnes*, pp. 224–26) sees a plural of this same *deresü*(n). Deresü is perhaps to be identified with this place, in which, in 1201, Ja-gambo, the brother of Ong-Khan, made his submission to Genghis Khan, or else with Yeke-Deresün, where, according to the *Yüan shih* (quoted by Pelliot, *Campagnes*, p. 226), the Great Khan Möngke gave an audience to his brother Qubilai at the beginning of 1258. Unfortunately, we know nothing about the location of either of these places. For a description of *deresü*(n) "broom grass, *lasiagrostis splendens*" and the effect it produces on the steppe landscape, see Thiel, p. 136.

Third Son of Qonichi—Chaghan-Buqa. He was born of Chingtüm Khatun, who has already been mentioned, and had a wife called Sürmish, the daughter of Qush-Temür, of the Kereit people, by whom he had a son called Jiretei.

Fourth Son of Qonichi—Maqudai. He was born of Barquchin Khatun of the Jajirat people: he had no children.

End of the branch of Sartaqtai, the father of Qonichi, the first son of Orda.

The Second Son of Orda—Quli

When Hülegü Khan was coming to Persia the decree was issued that from each of the princely houses a prince should join him with an army to assist him, and it was this Quli who was sent from the *ulus* of Orda.[26] By way of Khwārazm he arrived in Dihistān[27] and Māzandarān. He had several senior wives; one called Nendiken of the Qonqïrat people, another called Qadaqan of the ———[28] people and one called Kökteni, who came here and died in this country.[29] He had five sons, as follows: Tümeken, Tümen, Mingqan, Ayachi, and Musalmān. The account of the descent of these five sons and of their circumstances is such as shall now be given of each of them individually.

First Son of Quli—Tümeken. This Tümeken had three senior wives: one called Bulaghan, the daughter of Soghal Noyan, of the Tatar people, the second, Boralun Khatun of the ———[30] people; the third, called Öljei, was a concubine. He had three sons in the order in which they are enumerated below.

Charuq. He had a wife called Yaqur ———,[31] by whom he had two sons: Noqai and Satïlmïsh.

Mubārak. He was born of the aforesaid Boralun Khatun and had two sons: El-Buqa and Töre-Temür.

Küchük. He was born of the aforesaid concubine called Öljei.

[26] According to Grigor (pp. 327–31), Quli (whom he calls Khul) had previously been governor of Armenia. He implies that he met a violent end, though this is not confirmed by Rashīd al-Dīn (Arends, p. 54), who says only that his death occurred after those of Balaghai and Tutar. See below, p. 123.

[27] Dihistān, "the land of the Dahae," was a district north of the Atrek on the eastern shores of the Caspian, in what is now Turkmenistan. See *Ḥudūd*, p. 386.

[28] Blank in the MSS.   [29] That is, Persia.

[30] Blank in the MSS.   [31] Rest of the name is corrupt.

Second Son of Quli—Tümen. He was born of Nendiken Khatun and had several wives and concubines. The name of one of his senior wives was Boralun of the ——[32] people. He had six sons, as enumerated: Aq-Köpek: he had a son called Boralqï; Dashman; Qurtaqachi; Qutlugh-Buqa; Qutlugh-Temür; and El-Temür. These [latter] five sons had no children, and the names of Aq-Köpek's mother and those of Dashman, Qurtaqachi, and Qutlugh-Temür are not known: Qutlugh-Buqa was born of Boralun.

Third Son of Quli—Mingqan. He was born of ——[33] Khatun and had wives and concubines, but their names have not been ascertained. he had three sons, in the order enumerated: Khalīl, Bashmaq, and Olqutu. This Mingqan, when his father Quli came to this country, came also accompanied by all the three above-mentioned sons.[34]

Fourth Son of Quli—Ayachi. The names of his wives have not been ascertained. He had one son, called Qazan, by the daughter of Qutluq-Buqa, the son of Körgüz. This Ayachi came here as a child and during the reign of Abaqa Khan was with Arghun Khan in Khurāsān. Having treated him with kindness and favor, they dismissed him together with his son as an act of friendship and expediency, sending them back to their own *ulus.*

Fifth Son of Quli—Musalmān. He was born of Qadaqan Khatun. He had many wives, one of them called Orda-Tegin of the Naiman people. He had four sons in the order enumerated: Yaqutu, Khwāja, Yailaq, and Ilyās, all born of Orda-Tegin.

End of the branch of Quli, the second son of Orda.

Third Son of Orda—Qurumshi[35]

This Qurumshi has no sons, and his wives are not known.

Fourth Son of Orda—Qongqïran

He administered the *ulus* of Orda after his death. He had no sons.

---

[32] Blank in the MSS.

[33] Blank in Blochet; Verkhovsky has Bilan.

[34] According to Grigor (pp. 339–41), Mingqan (whom he calls Mighan) was imprisoned by Hülegü on an island in Lake Urmīya. He speaks elsewhere (p. 331) of his succeeding his father as governor of Armenia.

[35] Identified by Pelliot (*Horde d'Or*, p. 9) with the Mongol chieftain Corenza, encountered by John de Plano Carpini on the Dnieper.

Fifth Son of Orda—Chormaqai

He also had no children, and his wives are unknown.

Sixth Son of Orda—Qutuqu

It is not known whether or not he had any children.

Seventh Son of Orda—Hülegü

He had two senior wives, one of these called Soluqu[36] Khatun of the ———[37] people and the other ———[38] of the Qïpchaq people: by them he had two sons, Temür-Buqa and Olqutu.

His name was Hüle'ü, and he had no children. The children attributed to him are those of Qutuqu. This was ascertained from the books of genealogies which are most trustworthy. *And God knows best.*[39]

First Son of Hülegü—Temür-Buqa. He had four senior wives: the first, Kökejin, the daughter of Yisün Noyan, of the Qonqïrat people; the second, Arghun-Tegin of the Arghun[40] people, the daughter of Quri-Qochghar; the third, Qutujin of the ———[41] people; and the fourth, Bayalun of the Qonqïrat, the sister of Qutui Khatun, the wife of Hülegü Khan. Apart from these, he also had concubines. The aforesaid wives had six sons: (1) Küilük, born of Kökejin; (2) Buqa-Temür, born of Arghun-Tegin; (3) Jangqut, by Qutujin; (4) Toqa-Temür, whose mother was Bayalun; (5) Saisi, also by Qutujin; and (6) Ushanan, also born of Kökejin.

Second Son of Hülegü—Olqutu. He was born of the aforesaid ———[42] Khatun and had four sons in the order in which they are enumerated: Üch-Qurtuqa, Besh-Qurtuqa,[43] Buqa-Temür, and Derek.

---

[36] Verkhovsky has Sulukan (Soluqan).

[37] Blank in all the MSS.

[38] Verkhovsky has Turbarchin.

[39] All of this paragraph, according to Blochet, is a marginal note occurring in only one of his MSS: the information it contains agrees with the data of the *Mu'izz al-Ansāb*. In Verkhovsky it is placed before the preceding paragraph.

[40] See above, p. 101, note 21.   [41] Blank in all the MSS.

[42] See above, note 38.

[43] The names are Turkish and mean, respectively, "Three Old Women" and "Five Old Women." For the former, Verkhovsky has Üch-Buqa, that is, "Three Oxen." Presumably the old women had been present at the birth. It was the Mongol custom to name a child after the first person or thing that caught the mother's eye after her confinement. Cf. above, p. 25, note 68.

This Hülegü was born of a concubine of the Tangqut people called Ernük Egechi. He had extremely long hair such that it reached the ground. He had no children.[44]

With the aid of God Almighty the branch of Orda, the first son of Jochi Khan, has been completed.

The Second Son of Jochi Khan—Batu

Batu was born of Öki[45] Fujin Khatun, the daughter of Alchi Noyan, of the Qonqirat people. He was called Sayin-Khan[46] and stood in high honor and enjoyed great power, administering the *ulus* and army in place of Jochi Khan and living a long life. When the four sons of Chingiz-Khan died, he became the senior of all [of the Khan's] grandsons and occupied a position of great honor and magnificence amongst them. In the *quriltai*, no one dared to contravene his word, nay, all the princes were obedient and submissive to him. It had been previously ordained by a *yarlïgh* of Chingiz-Khan that Jochi should proceed with an army and seize and take possession of all the northern countries, such as Ibir-Sibir,[47] Bular, the Qïpchaq Steppe, and the lands of the Bashghïrd, Rus,[48] and Cherkes[49] as far as Darband on the Caspian, which the Mongols call Temür-Qahalqa.[50] Jochi neglected this command, and when Ögetei Khan acceded to the Khanate, he charged Batu with that same undertaking, deputing his nephew Möngke Qa'an, the latter's brother Böchek, and his own son Güyük Khan, along with such great emirs as Sübetei Bahadur, the army

---

[44] This paragraph is not in Verkhovsky. It apparently belongs together with the paragraph referred to above, p. 106, note 39, and is therefore an interpolation from some other source.

[45] On the name, see *Horde d'Or*, pp. 28–29.

[46] Literally, "Good Khan," "good" not in the sense of "kind, benevolent" (Barthold), or of "wise, sensible" (Pelliot), but of "late, deceased," the name being a posthumous title bestowed on Batu to avoid the mention of his real name. See Boyle 1967.

[47] That is, Siberia. See Bretschneider, II, p. 37, note 811.

[48] Russians.

[49] Circassians.

[50] See above, Section 1, p. 61, note 260.

commander of the Uriyangqat[51] people who came to this country[52] with Jebe, at the head of an army, to gather all together with the other princes under Batu and set about the conquest of the northern countries. In the *bichin yïl*, that is, the Year of the Monkey, falling in Jumādā 11 of the year 633 [February–March, 1236], they set out and conquered the greater part of those countries, and in the spring of the *qulquna yïl*, that is, the Year of the Rat, corresponding to the months of the year 637/1239–1240,[53] Güyük Khan and Möngke Qa'an, in obedience to the *yarlïgh* of Qa'an, turned back and proceeded to the Court of Qa'an. After a lapse of time, Batu, with his brothers and the emirs and army, continued the conquest of those countries, as his posterity are still doing.

Batu had many senior wives and concubines. He had four sons, in the following order: Sartaq, Toqoqan, Ebügen, and Shinggüm. The descendants of these four sons and their circumstances are such as are recorded separately for each of them.

First Son of Batu—Sartaq[54]

He was born of ———[55] Khatun and had no son.[56]

Second Son of Batu—Toqoqan

He had five sons, in the following order: Tartu, Möngke-Temür, Töde-Möngke, Toqïqonqa, and Ügechi. The details regarding the descendants of these five sons are as follows.

[51] Rashīd al-Dīn distinguishes between the Uriyangqat proper and the forest Uriyanqat, the latter (the Orengai of Rubruck) inhabiting the Barghujin-Tögüm or "Barghu Depression," that is, the region to the east of Lake Baikal, Marco Polo's "plain of Bargu." The Uriyangqat proper, so Pelliot thinks, "may have been the ancestors of the present Uryangqai tribes of the Republic of Tuva." See Khetagurov, pp. 123–25, and 156–60, and *Polo* I, pp. 77 and 337.

[52] That is, Persia. The reference is to the two generals' pursuit of Sultan Muḥammad across Persia in 1220, on which see *HWC*, pp. 142–49.

[53] Actually 1240.

[54] On Sartaq, apparently a Nestorian Christian, who succeeded his father as ruler of the Golden Horde (1255–1256), see *Horde d'Or*, p. 34, *Steppes*, 473–74, Spuler 1943, p. 33, and Vernadsky, pp. 148–50.

[55] Blank in all the MSS.

[56] Actually, Sartaq had at least two sons, one of whom, Ulaghchï, succeeded him as ruler of the Golden Horde. See *Horde d'Or*, pp. 34–44. Rashīd al-Dīn also fails to mention Sartaq's "six wives" and his eldest son's "two or three" (Rockhill, p. 101).

First Son of Toqoqan—Tartu. He had wives and concubines, but their names are not known. He had two sons: Töle-Buqa,[57] whose children are not known, and Könchek, who had a son called Boz-Buqa.

Second Son of Toqoqan—Möngke-Temür.[58] This Möngke-Temür had wives and concubines, and the names of all three senior wives are known: Öljei of the Qonqïrat people, Sultan Khatun of the Üshin[59] people, and Qutuqui[60] Khatun of the ———[61] people. He had ten sons, in the following order: Alqui, born of Öljei; Abachi; Tödeken, born of Sultan Khatun; Börlük, born of Qutuqui Khatun; Toqta,[62] born of Öljeitü Khatun, the sister of Kelmish-Aqa, the sister of Möngke Qa'an, who was the wife of Saljidai Küregen (Toqta is now the ruler of the *ulus* of Jochi and has two wives, one called Bulaghan and the other Tükünche, of the Qonqïrat people, and one son called ———);[63] Sarai-Buqa; Molaqai;[64] Qadan; Qoduqai;[65] and Toghrïl-cha.[66]

Ended with the aid of God and His excellent guidance.

*Third Son of Toqoqan—*Töde-Mongke.[67] His mother and Möngke-Temür's was Köchü Khatun, the sister of Öljei Khatun and the

---

Pelliot (*Horde d'Or*, p. 44, note 1) suggests that this curious lack of information may be due to a conspiracy of silence imposed upon the Muslim world by Sartaq's uncle and successor, Berke (1258–1266), a bigoted convert to Islam.

[57] Marco Polo's Tolobuga. He ruled the Golden Horde from 1287 to 1291. See Spuler 1943, pp. 70–72, Vernadsky, pp. 178–85; also below, pp. 124–26.

[58] The successor of Berke, he ruled the Horde from 1266 or the beginning of 1267 until 1280. See Spuler 1943, pp. 52–62, and Vernadsky, pp. 163–74; also below, pp. 123–24.

[59] On the Üshin or Hüshin, see Khetagurov, pp. 171–72, and *Campagnes*, pp. 72–73.

[60] Qutui in Verkhovsky's text.　　　　　　　　[61] Blank in all the mss.

[62] Toqta or Toqto—on the name see *Horde d'Or*, pp. 67–71—was the ruler of the Golden Horde from 1291 to 1312. See Spuler 1943, pp. 72–85, and Vernadsky, pp. 185–95; also below, pp. 126–30.

[63] Blank in all Blochet's mss. He had three sons according to Verkhovsky's text: Yavarïsh (Yabush?), Iksar (?), and Tugel-Buka, the latter two being the El-Basar and Tükel-Buqa of the Egyptian sources. See *Horde d'Or*, pp. 71–72 and note 4.

[64] Holaqai according to Verkhovsky's text, which gives him a son called Ulus-Buqa.

[65] Qoduqan according to Verkhovsky's text, which also mentions a son—Künges.

[66] Verkhovsky's text also names his son Öz-Beg, the future ruler of the Golden Horde (1313–1341), on whom see *Horde d'Or*, pp. 92–94, Spuler 1943, pp. 85–99, and Vernadsky, pp. 195–204.

[67] Successor of Möngke-Temür (1280–1287). See Spuler 1943, pp. 63–70, and Vernadsky, pp. 174–82; also below, p. 124.

daughter of Buqa-Temür of the Oirat people. This Töde-Möngke had two wives: Arïqachi of the Qonqïrat people and Töre-Qutlugh of the Alchi-Tatar people. He had three sons, in the following order: Or-Menggü, born of Ariqachi; Chechektü, by Töre-Qutlugh; and Töbetei, whose wives are unknown and who had two sons, as follows: ——[68] has no children.

Fourth Son of Toqoqan—Toqïqonqa. He had wives and two sons, in the order that follows: Babuch, Tükel-Buqa ——.[69]

Fifth Son of Toqoqan—Ügechi. He had no children.

Third Son of Batu—Ebügen

He had wives and concubines and seven sons, in the order that follows: Baraq, Bular, Tutuch, Daquqa, Aḥmad, Sabir, and Döngür. The last-named had no children, and the names of his wives are not known.[70]

The branch of Batu, the second son of Jochi Khan, has been completed, with God's assistance.

Third Son of Jochi Khan—Berke

He had no children. His history will be included in the sections on Hülegü Khan and Abaqa Khan, if God so wills.[71]

Fourth Son of Jochi Khan—Berkecher

He had a wife and concubines and two sons, in the order that follows:

The first son of this Berkecher, Kökechü, had four sons: Ejil-Temür, Bïlïqchï, Doqdai, and Toq-Temür.

---

[68] Blochet's MSS omit the sons' names, and Verkhovsky's text omits all these details, stating instead that Töbetü's mother was not known.

[69] So in Verkhovsky. Blochet's text has "seven," although it gives the two names.

[70] Here follows in Verkhovsky's text: "Fourth Son of Batu, Ulakchi. He had no children, and the names of his wives are not known." See above, p. 108, note 56.

[71] See Arends, pp. 59–61 and 68–69; also below, pp. 122–23. Cf. Spuler 1943, pp. 33–52, and Vernadsky, pp. 151–63.

The second son of this Berkecher, Yesü-Buqa, had one son, called Sarai-Buqa.

The branch of Berkecher, the son of Jochi Khan, has been completed with the help of God and His excellent guidance.

Fifth Son of Jochi Khan—Shiban[72]

He had many wives and concubines and twelve sons, as follows: Bainal, Bahadur, Qadaq, Balaqan, Cherik, Mergen, Qurtuqa, Ayachi, Sailqan, Bayanchar, Majar, and Qonichi. The details of the branches of these twelve sons and their grandsons are given below.

First Son of Shiban—Bainal

He had three sons in this order: Ilaq-Temür, Beg-Temür, and Yesü-Temür.

Second Son of Shiban—Bahadur

He had two sons. It is not known whether the first son of Bahadur, Qutlugh-Buqa, had any issue. The second son of Bahadur, Jochi-Buqa, had four sons, as follows: Badaqul, Beg-Temür, Nangkichar, and Yesü-Buqa.

Third Son of Shiban—Qadaq

He had one son, called Töle-Buqa, and this Töle-Buqa had two sons: the elder, Mingqutai, and the younger, Tümen-Temur. Tümen-Temür had a son called Üchüken.

Fourth Son of Shiban—Balaqan[73]

He had three sons in the following order: Türi, Tügen, and Toqdai. This Toqdai is called Murīd-Toqdai and Tama-Toqdai. His winter quarters are near the River Terek, toward Darband, and for some time past he has been at the head of the patrol of scouts. He has three sons: Baqïrcha, Küchük, and Ja'uqan.

---

[72] On the name, see *Horde d'Or*, pp. 44–47. From Shiban's line there sprang, besides occasional rulers of the Golden Horde, the Tsars of Tiumen and the Uzbeg Khans of Bokhara and Khiva. See *Steppes*, pp. 556–68.

[73] Balaghai is the more usual form of the name: he came to the West in the train of Hülegü. See *HWC*, p. 608 and note 1; also below, pp. 122–23.

Fifth Son of Shiban—Cherik

This Cherik had one son called Toq-Temür.

Sixth Son of Shiban—Mergen

He had two sons, as follows: Buqa-Temür and El-Buqa.

Seventh Son of Shiban—Qurtuqa

This Qurtuqa had one son, called Kines.

Eighth Son of Shiban—Ayachi

This Ayachi had one son, called Üch-Qurtuqa.[74]

Ninth Son of Shiban—Sailqan

He had one son, called Qutlugh-Temür. This Qutlugh-Temür had seven sons: Boraltai, Beg-Temür, Boralghï, Otman, Sainaq, Yesü-Buqa, and Temürtei.

Tenth Son of Shiban—Bayanchar

He had one son, called Ebügen Küregen, and this Ebügen Küregen had one son, called Toghanchar.

Eleventh Son of Shiban—Majar[75]

He had one son, called Dorchi.

Twelfth Son of Shiban—Qonichi

He had no issue.
The branch of Shiban is completed with His excellent guidance.

Sixth Son of Jochi Khan—Tangqut

He had two sons: Sübügetei and Toquz. The descendants of these two sons are as follows.

---

[74] On the name, see above, p. 106, note 43.
[75] That is, "Hungarian." See above, Section 1, p. 55, note 211.

First Son of Tangqut—Sübügetei

He had two sons: Majar, who had a son called Kürk, and Kichik-Qonichi, who had four sons: Borachar, Küch-Temür, Ishten,[76] and Duratu.

Second Son of Tangqut—Toquz

He had three sons, as follows: Qalumtai, Arslan, and Boralghï.
The branch of Tangqut, the sixth son of Jochi Khan, is completed.

Seventh Son of Jochi Khan—Bo'al

He had two sons: Tatar and Mingqadur. The descendants of these two sons are as follows.

First Son of Bo'al—Tatar

He had a son, Noqai,[77] and this Noqai had three sons, as follows: Jöge, Tüge, and Torai.

Second Son of Bo'al—Mingqadur

He had nine sons, as follows: Tutar,[78] who has a son called Kirdi-Buqa; Begdüz; Orus, who has two sons, Tödüken and Qutlu-Bai; Ebügen, who has two sons, Toquch and Aḥmad; Öz-Beg, who has no issue; Sasïq, who has one son, Basar; Öz-Beg-Qurtuqa; Toqlucha; and El-Basmïsh.

The Branch of Bo'al, the seventh son of Jochi Khan, has been completed with the assistance of God Almighty.

Eighth Son of Jochi Khan—Chilaqa'un

He had no issue.

---

[76] AYSTAN. Apparently the Hungarian *Isten*, "God."

[77] Marco Polo's Nogai, on whom see Spuler 1943, pp. 59–78, and Vernadsky, pp. 174–189; also below, pp. 125–29.

[78] He too accompanied Hülegü to the West (*HWC*, p. 608 and note 2). He was accused and convicted of sorcery and put to death on the 2nd February, 1260 (Arends, p. 54), the mode of execution according to Grigor (p. 339), being strangulation with the bowstring. See also below, p. 123.

Ninth Son of Jochi Khan—Shingqur

He had three sons. Their names and those of their descendants are as follows.

First Son—Yesü-Buqa

He had five sons, as follows: Boralqï, Küilük, Tödeken, Tödechü, and Akhtachi.

Second Son—Shiremün

He had three sons: Khwārazmī,[79] whose mother was Bora'ujin of the Tatar; Jaqutu, whose mother was Qutluqan of the Süldüs; and Bairam, whose mother was Qoldaq, a concubine.

Third Son—Majar[80]

He had three sons: Urusaq, Bayan, and Baiqu.

The branch of Shingqur, the ninth son of Jochi Khan, has been completed, thanks be to God.

The Tenth Son of Jochi Khan—Chimtai

He had wives and concubines and two sons, Hindu and Töde'ür, whose descendants are as follows.

First Son of Chimtai—Hindu

He had one son, called Yekü. This Yekü had three sons, in this order: Jalayirtai, Köndelen-Mangqutai, and Taqachu. He reigned for 2 full years after Chimtai's death, after which Toqta put him to death.

Second Son of Chimtai—Töde'ür

He had two sons: Majar, who had three sons: Melik, Khwāja Temür, and Qurtuqachuq; and Tariyaji, who had no issue.

The branch of Chimtai, the tenth son of Jochi Khan, has been completed by His grace and favor.

[79] "Khwārazmian." The same name as Qurumshi (p. 105). See *Horde d'Or*, p. 9 and note 3.
[80] See above, p. 112, note 75.

Eleventh Son of Jochi Khan—Muḥammad

He was also called Bora.[81] He had no issue.

Twelfth Son of Jochi Khan—Udur

He had one son called Qarachar. This Qarachar had five sons, as follows.

First Son of Qarachar—Qurtuqa

His mother was called El-Tutmïsh of the Tögeles, that is, Töles.[82] This Qurtuqa had a son called Sasi.

Second Son of Qarachar—Dorji

This Dorji had one son, called Ananda.

Third Son of Qarachar—Abishqa

He had no issue.

Fourth Son of Qarachar—Emegen

He too had no issue.

Fifth Son of Qarachar—Tükel

He too had no issue.

The branch of Udur, the twelfth son of Jochi Khan, has been completed.

Thirteenth Son of Jochi Khan—Toqa-Temür[83]

This Toqa-Temür had four sons. Their names and those of their descendants are as follows.

---

[81] Bora ("Grey") was presumably the name he bore before his conversion (like that of his brothers Berke and Berkecher) to Islam. See *Horde d'Or*, pp. 49–50.

[82] Tögeles represents the Uighur spelling, in which the intervocalic *g* is purely graphic. The Tö'eles are mentioned in *SH* (§239) as one of the forest peoples subjugated by Jochi in 1207. They lived in close proximity to the Barghut and Qori, in the Barghujin-Tögüm, to the east of Lake Baikal.

[83] The ancestor of the Khans of Kazan and the Crimea.

First Son—Bai-Temür

He had three sons: Toqanchar, Yïlqïchï, and Kökechü. None of them had issue.

Second Son—Bayan

He had two sons: Qazan and Dashman. They had no issue.

Third Son—Ürüng-Temür

He had four sons: Achïq, who had a son called Bakhtiyār; Arïqlï, who had three sons, 'Ādil, Saqrïchï, and Anbarchi; Qaraqïr, who had three sons, Negübei, Kereiche, and Shibaghuchi; and Saricha, who had one son called Könchek.

Fourth Son—Ked-Temür

He had two sons; Qara-Khwāja and Abai.

The branch of Toqa-Temür, the thirteenth son of Jochi Khan, has been completed by His grace and favor.

Fourteenth Son of Jochi Khan—Shinggüm

This Shinggüm had no issue.

The sons of Jochi Khan, according to the reports of trustworthy persons, are these fourteen, whose names, and those of their sons and grandsons, have been recorded in detail, and whose genealogical table is as here shown.

PART
II
OF THE HISTORY OF JOCHI KHAN

The [general] history of and [particular] episodes in his reign;
a picture of his throne and wives
and the princes and emirs on the occasion of his enthronement;
an account of his summer and winter residences[84]
and some of the battles he fought and the victories he gained;
the length of his reign

Chingiz-Khan had entrusted to Jochi Khan all the countries and *ulus* which lie in the region of the Erdish [the Irtysh] and the Altai mountains, and the summer and winter ranges in that area. He had also issued a *yarligh* that he should take possession of the Qïpchaq Steppe and the countries that had been conquered in that direction. His *yurt* was in the region of the Erdish, and his residence was there, as shown upon this picture.

◆ BRIEF ACCOUNT OF THE CAREER OF JOCHI KHAN

Since Jochi Khan died before his father, it is impossible to record separately those events which refer to him personally. Accordingly, a brief summary is given here of his career, as it is recounted in detail in the history of Chingiz-Khan;[85] an account will also be given of his illness and death.

By Chingiz-Khan's command he always took part in his campaigns and had conquered and subdued many countries and provinces. When Chingiz-Khan set out against the Tāzīk countries and came to the region of Otrar, he charged him with the conquest of the town and

---

[84] This account was apparently never written. There is only a passing reference (p. 118) to his various *yurts*.
[85] See Smirnova, pp. 198–201 and 214–17.

left him there. As is recorded in the history of Chingiz-Khan, he took Otrar and captured and destroyed the fortress. He then returned [to the main army], subjugating the regions which lay across his path until he joined his father in the neighborhood of Samarqand. From thence he was dispatched by Chingiz-Khan together with his brothers Chaghatai and Ögetei to capture Khwārazm. When they laid siege to the town it was impossible to capture it because of a disagreement between him and Chaghatai. Chingiz-Khan ordered Ögetei to take command of that operation; by his competence he brought about agreement between the brothers, and they took Khwārazm. Chaghatai and Ögetei then set off to join their father, and they reached Chingiz-Khan before the fortress of Ṭālaqān. As for Jochi, he set out from Khwārazm for the Erdish, where his heavy baggage was, and reached his *ordos*. Previously, Chingiz-Khan had ordered Jochi to set out upon the conquest of the northern countries, such as those of the Bular, Bashghïrd, Orus, Cherkes, and the Qïpchaq Steppe, and to subjugate them. As [Jochi] had held back from this operation and returned to his own tents, Chingiz-Khan was extremely annoyed and said: "I will put him to death without seeing his face." Jochi was taken suddenly ill, and on that account, when Chingiz-Khan returned from the Tāzīk countries and alighted at his *ordos*, he was unable to present himself but sent several *kharvārs*[86] of game and offered his excuses. Thereafter on several occasions Chingiz-Khan summoned him to his presence, but on account of his illness he did not come but sent excuses. Then a man of the Mangqut[87] people was passing through the *yurts* of Jochi. Jochi had set out and was proceeding from *yurt* to *yurt*, still ill, when he came to a mountain, which was his hunting ground. Being too weak himself, he sent the emirs of the hunt to hunt [for him]. That man, seeing them hunting, thought that it was Jochi. When he came to Chingiz-Khan the latter asked him about Jochi's illness. He replied: "I know nothing about any illness, but he is hunting in such-and-such a mountain." At these words, the flame of Chingiz-Khan's anger flared up and he thought: "He has surely become a rebel not to pay attention to his father's words." And he said: "Jochi is mad to commit such actions." He ordered the armies to set out against him with

[86] See Glossary.
[87] On the Mongol tribe of the Mangqut, see *Campagnes*, pp. 167–69.

Chaghatai and Ögetei in the van, while he himself brought up the rear. In the meantime, news came of Jochi's death in the year ———.[88] Chingiz-Khan was extremely grieved. He made an inquiry, and the words of that person were shown to be false and it was established that Jochi had been ill at that time and not in the hunting ground. He sought for that person to put him to death, but he could not be found.

Trustworthy ambassadors coming on various occasions from the *ulus* of Jochi stated that at the time of his death he was between thirty and forty, and this approximates to the truth. Some say that he died at twenty, but this is altogether wrong.[89] After his death and that of Chingiz-Khan, when Qa'an ascended the throne he entrusted the conquest of the northern countries to Jochi's family because [of] the *yarlïgh* which Chingiz-Khan had previously issued with respect to Jochi; and they with the help of one another set about the task.

Completed by the power of God Almighty.

⁂ HISTORY OF THE FAMILY OF JOCHI KHAN AFTER his death; the succession of each of them to the throne; the various wars which they waged and the victories which they gained; and other events which occurred.

History of the succession of Batu to his father and an account of his reign

When Jochi died, his second son, Batu, mounted the throne as his father's successor in the *ulus*, and his brothers tendered their allegiance to him. During the reign of Ögetei Qa'an, as has been told in detail in his history, he was in accordance with a previous edict entrusted along with his brothers and other princes with the conquest of the northern countries. They all assembled in his *ordo* and set out together; and, as has already been described, they subjugated the greater part of those countries. After the return of the princes Möngke Qa'an and

---

[88] Blank in the MSS. He died several months before his father, that is, presumably early in 1227.

[89] As Jochi was at least 2 years older than Ögedei, who was born in 1184, he must have been approximately forty-three years of age at the time of his death.

Güyük Khan, he and his brothers, as has been mentioned in the appendix to the account of his branch of the family, set about the subjugation of the remainder of those countries.[90]

In the beginning of the year 639/1241–1242,[91] when Ögetei Qa'an died, he was seized, because of his great age, with a sudden attack of paralysis.[92] And when he was summoned to the *quriltai*, he held back on that excuse, and because of his absence, he being the senior of them all, the question of the Khanate was not determined for nearly 3 years. The eldest of Ögetei Qa'an's wives, Töregene Khatun, governed [the realm], and during this period confusion found its way into the borders and center of the Empire. Qa'an had made his grandson Shiremün his heir-apparent, but Töregene Khatun and some of the emirs objected, saying that Güyük Khan was older, and they again summoned Batu to take part in the enthronement. Though he was offended with them and apprehensive because of the alarming nature of the past events, he set out, proceeding at a slow pace. Before his arrival and without the attendance of *aqa* and *ini*,[93] they arbitrarily settled the Khanate upon Güyük Khan. Güyük Khan was afflicted with a chronic disease, and on the pretext that the climate of his old *yurt*, which his father had given him, was beneficial to his condition, he set out with a large army for the region of Emil-Qochin.[94] When he approached this area, Batu became a little apprehensive. Sorqoqtani Beki, the eldest wife of Tolui Khan, because of the foundation of friendship that had been laid and consolidated between Jochi Khan and Tolui Khan and the families of either side since the time of Chingiz-Khan, sent the message that Güyük Khan's coming to that region was not devoid of some treachery. On that account, his apprehension was increased and he awaited the arrival of Güyük Khan with vigilance and caution.

---

[90] See above, pp. 56–57 and 69–71.   [91] Actually November, 1241.

[92] *Istirkhā*. Elsewhere (see below, pp. 170 and 200) his infirmity is described as *dard-i pā*, "pain in the foot," that is, apparently gout.

[93] See Glossary.

[94] The phrase seems to occur in the *Yüan shih*. It is stated in the biography of Sübedei that after conquering the countries north of the Caucasus he returned home, according to the translation of Bretschneider (II, p. 43), by way of "Ye-mi-li and Ho-dji," that is, presumably Yeh-mi-li Ho-chi. Emil-Qojin, like Onan-Kelüren (see above, Section 2, p. 29 note 82), would appear to be the name of a region between two rivers, one of the rivers in this case being the Emil, while Qojin is perhaps another name for the Qobaq. See above, Section 1, p. 19 and note 23.

When the latter reached Samarqand,[95] from whence it is a week's journey to Besh-Balïq, he died of the disease from which he was suffering, in the year 640/1242–1243.[96]

Again for a time the throne was without a king, and once again Töregene Khatun acted as regent. When the report of his illness was spread abroad, Sorqoqtani Beki sent her son Möngke Qa'an to Batu. Batu was pleased at his arrival, and perceiving the signs of power and greatness upon him and being offended with the sons of Ögetei Qa'an, he said: "Möngke Qa'an is the eldest son of Tolui Khan, who was the youngest son of Chingiz-Khan, and administered his ancient *yurt* and original home. This prince is extremely competent, talented, and fit for kingship. When he is present how can another be Qa'an, especially when the sons of Ögetei Qa'an have gone against their father's word and not given authority to the aforesaid Shiremün? Moreover, infringing the ancient *yasa* and *yosun*, and without consulting *aqa* and *ini*, they put to death the youngest daughter of Chingiz-Khan, whom he loved more than all his other children and whose husband's title was Cha'ur Sechen, although she had committed no crime.[97] On this account the Khanate should not go to them." And he himself raised Möngke Qa'an to the Khanate, making all his brothers, kinsmen, and emirs tender their allegiance to him and sending his brother Berke and his son Sartaq, who was his heir-apparent, to accompany him with an army of 3 *tümens*. In Onan-Kelüren,[98] which is the original *yurt* of Chingiz-Khan, they set him upon the throne of the Khanate and the seat of world-empire and frustrated the wiles of the sons of Ögetei Qa'an, who had meditated treachery. In short, the bringing of the Khanate to the house of Tolui Khan and the placing of the right in its due place were due to the competence and shrewdness of Sorqoqtani Beki and the help and assistance of Batu, because of their friendship for one another. Thereafter, until the end

[95] An old mistake for Qum-Sengir (T. "Sand Promontory"), which lay somewhere along the upper course of the Urungu, probably at the point where it ceases to flow from North to South and makes a sharp turn to the West. See *Papauté*, pp. 196–97, *Campagnes*, pp. 315–16, and *HWC*, p. 261, note 42.

[96] In fact, Güyük died in April, 1248.

[97] This was Altalun, on whom see Smirnova, p. 70. Her execution does not appear to be mentioned elswhere.

[98] See above, p. 29 and note 82.

of his life, and, after his death, during the reigns of Sartaq and Ulagh-chi and the greater part of the reign of Berke, the path of friendship and unity was trodden between the family of Tolui Khan and that of Batu.

It was still during Batu's lifetime that Möngke Qa'an dispatched his third brother, Hülegü Khan, at the head of large forces against the countries of Persia. Of the armies of the princes, he appointed two out of every ten men to accompany Hülegü Khan and render assistance to him. Orda dispatched his eldest son, Quli, with an army of 1 *tümen* by way of Khwārazm and Dihistān. Batu sent Balaqan, the son of Shiban, and Tutar, the son of Mingqadur, the son of Bo'al, the seventh son of Jochi Khan, by way of Darband. They came and rendered service as a reinforcement to the army of Hülegü Khan.

Batu died at Sarai[99] on the banks of the Etil in the year 650/1252–1253, being forty-eight years of age.[100] Möngke Qa'an received his son Sartaq with honor, settled the throne and the kingdom upon him, and gave him permission to return. He died upon the way, and Möngke Qa'an sent ambassadors and, having won over his wives, sons, and brothers, set Ulaghchi, the grandson of Batu, upon the throne and distinguished them all with every kind of favor. Ulaghchi too died after a short time and left the throne and the kingdom to others.[101]

History of the accession of Berke as ruler of the ulus of Jochi and the events of that period

When Batu passed away and his son Sartaq, and Sartaq's son Ulaghchi, who succeeded him, died one after the other, his younger brother Berke sat in his place, in the year 652/1254–1255. His rule was absolute within his *ulus*, and he continued to tread the path of friendship and affection with the family of Tolui Khan.

In 654/1256–1257 Balaqan, who was in this country, plotted treason and treachery against Hülegü Khan and had recourse to witchcraft. An informer came forward, and he was questioned and confessed. In

---

[99] That is, Old Sarai (so called to distinguish it from the "New Sarai" founded by Berke) on the eastern bank of the Akhtuba, about 65 miles north of Astrakhan.

[100] In fact, Batu's death probably occurred about the middle of 1255. See *Horde d'Or*, p. 29.

[101] See above, p. 108, note 56.

order not to cause ill-will, Hülegü Khan sent him to Berke accompanied
by the Emir Sunjaq. When they arrived and Berke had been convinced of his guilt, he sent him back to Hülegü Khan with the message:
"He is guilty and is under thy authority." Hülegü Khan put him to
death. Shortly afterward, Tutar and Quli died also, and it was alleged
that they had been poisoned. On this account an estrangement arose,
and Berke became hostile to Hülegü Khan, as shall be related in the
history of Hülegü Khan.[102] In Shauwāl of the year 660 [July–August,
1262], a battle was fought, and the greater part of the troops which
had come to this country with Quli and Tutar took to flight, some of
them by way of Khurāsān; and they seized the territory from the
mountains of Ghazna and Bīnī-yi Gāv[103] to Multan and Lahore, which
are on the frontier of India. The chief of the emirs that were in command of them was Negüder.[104] Ötegü-China[105] and ———,[106] two
of the emirs of Hülegü Khan, went in pursuit of them. Others rejoined
their homes by way of Darband. This dispute between Berke and
Hülegü Khan lasted the length of their lifetimes. Berke's commander-
in-chief was Noqai, the son of Tatar and grandson of Bo'al, a great
warrior and fighter. When Hülegü Khan died in his winter quarters
at Jaghatu[107] in the year 663/1264–1265,[108] and his son Abaqa Khan
succeeded him on the throne, the enmity between Berke and him
continued. In the year 663/1264–1265, Berke turned back from battle
with Abaqa Khan in the region of Shīrvān; he passed through Darband
and died near the River Terek in the year 664/1265–1266.

History of the accession of Möngke-Temür, the son of Toqoqan, the second son of Batu, as ruler of his ulus

When Berke died, the aforesaid Möngke-Temür was set upon the
throne in his stead. For a time he too was in conflict with Abaqa

[102] Arends, pp. 59–61.

[103] "Ox's Nose," apparently in the vicinity of Ghazna. See Boyle 1963, p. 247, note
74.

[104] The Negodar of Marco Polo, from whom the bands of marauders known as
Nigūdārīs received their name. See Boyle 1963, pp. 242–43 and 247, note 74.

[105] See Boyle 1963, p. 239.   [106] Blank in the mss.

[107] That is, the valley of the Jaghatu (the present-day Zarrīna Rūd), one of the
four rivers that discharge into Lake Urmiya from the south.

[108] Actually on the 8th February, 1265.

Khan; they fought several battles and Abaqa Khan gained victories over them. In the end, in the year 66—,[109] they[110] were obliged to make peace, as shall be related in the history of Abaqa Khan,[111] and forsook hostilities from that time onward until the reign of Arghun Khan, when in Ramaḍān of the year 687 [October–November, 1288] there came a great army of theirs led by Tama-Toqta. Arghun Khan had set out from his winter quarters in Arrān for his summer quarters. When he heard the news of their approach, he turned back, sending the emirs on in advance with an army. They gave battle and killed a great number of their advance forces, while the remainder withdrew in a rout.[112] From that time until the auspicious reign of the Lord of Islam (*may God cause him to reign forever!*) they have committed no further hostile action and out of weakness have chosen concord in preference to discord. They outwardly profess friendship and unity and upon every occasion send ambassadors to the Lord of Islam to report on events and bring gifts and presents.

History of the accession of Töde-Möngke, the brother of Möngke-Temür; his dethronement by Töle-Buqa and Könchek-Buqa; their joint rule; Toqta's fleeing from them; and his killing them by guile with the help of Noqai

When Möngke-Temür died in the year 681/1282–1283, after a reign of 16 years, Töde-Möngke, the third son of Toqoqan, ascended the throne in the same year. He was ruler for awhile, and then the sons of Möngke-Temür, Alghu and Toghrïl, and the sons of Tartu (who was the eldest son of Toqoqan), namely Töle-Buqa and Könchek, deposed him from the Khanate on the pretext that he was insane, and [they] themselves ruled jointly for 5 years. As for Toqta, the son of Möngke-Temür, whose mother, Öljei Khatun, was the grandmother of Kelmish-Aqa Khatun, they were plotting against him because they saw in his face the marks of valor and manliness. Becoming aware of their intention he fled from them and took refuge with Bïlïqchï, the

---

[109] Presumably 664/1265–1266.　　　[110] That is, the Golden Horde.

[111] See Arends, pp. 68–69, where, however, there is mention only of their defeat, not of peace negotiations.

[112] See Arends, p. 127.

son of Berkecher. He then sent the following message to Noqai, who had been the commander-in-chief of Batu and Berke: "My cousins are trying to kill me, and thou art the *aqa*. I will take refuge with thee so that thou mayst preserve me and prevent the hand of their oppression from reaching me. As long as I live I shall be commanded by my *aqa* and shall not contravene thy will." When Noqai learnt of his plight he was filled with indignation. Setting out from the country of the Orus, Ulakh,[113] and ———,[114] which he had conquered and made his *yurt* and place of abode, on the pretense of being ill he crossed the River Uzï,[115] and whenever he came upon a *hazāra* or an emir he would ingratiate himself with them, saying: "The time of old age is at hand, and I have renounced rebellion, strife, and contention. I have no mind to dispute and no intention of fighting with anyone. We have a *yarlïgh* from Chingiz-Khan, which says that if anyone in his *ulus* and family goes astray and disturbs the *ulus* we are to investigate the matter and incline their hearts to agreement with one another." When the *hazāras* and soldiers heard this advice and experienced his kindness toward them, they all of them yielded obedience to him. And when he drew near to the *ordo* of the aforesaid princes, he pretended to be ill, drinking a little blood and then bringing it up from his throat in a vomit, and treading the pathway of dissimulation and cajolery. He had secretly sent a message to Toqta bidding him hold himself in readiness and when he received word [to] come with such forces as were at hand. The mother of Töle-Buqa heard the report of Noqai's weakness and ill health, and how he was vomiting blood. She upbraided her sons, saying: "Speak at once with the feeble old man, who has bidden farewell to this world and is preparing for the journey into the next. If you see fit to neglect and slight him, may your mother's milk be forbidden to you!" The princes, listening carelessly and incautiously to their mother's words, came on a visit to Noqai. He said to them by way of advice: "Children, I have served your fathers old and young and have acquired all manner of rights. Therefore

[113] Reading AWLAX for the ARTAH of Blochet's text. Apparently a variant of Ulaq or Ulagh, that is, the Vlachs. See *Horde d'Or*, p. 153.

[114] KHRT or KHRB. Perhaps a corruption of a form LHWT, *Lahut, that is, the Poles. Noqai's territory extended westward from the Dnieper to the Lower Danube area. See Vernadsky, p. 180.

[115] The Dnieper.

you should listen to my disinterested words so that your discord may be changed into true accord. Your interest is in peace. Hold a *quriltai* so that I may give you peace." And with every breath he brought up clotted blood from his throat. He had sent word to Toqta, while keeping the princes off their guard with his smooth words. All at once Toqta arrived with several *hazāras*, seized the princes, and immediately put them to death. Noqai straightway turned back and, crossing the River Etil, made for his accustomed *yurt*. *And God knows best what is right.*

History of Toqta's accession as ruler of his ulus; *the outbreak of hostilities between him and Noqai; their warring with one another; Toqta's battle against Noqai; Noqai's death*

When, with the aid and assistance of Noqai, Toqta had killed the aforesaid princes and was firmly established as absolute ruler upon the throne of Jochi, he repeatedly sent ambassadors to Noqai and, encouraging him with fair promises, summoned him to his presence, but Noqai refused to come.

Now Toqta's father-in-law, Saljidai Küregen of the Qonqïrat people, who was the husband of Kelmish-Aqa Khatun, had sought the hand of Noqai's daughter Qïyaq for his son Yailaq; and Noqai had agreed. Some time after the consummation of the marriage, Qïyaq Khatun became a Muslim. Yailaq, being an Uighur, could not accommodate himself to this and there were constant disputes and quarrels because of their religion and beliefs. They treated Qïyan with contempt, and she told her father, mother, and brothers. Noqai was greatly offended and sent an ambassador to Toqta with the following message: "It is known to all the world what toil and hardship I have endured and how I have exposed myself to the charge of perfidy and bad faith in order to win for thee the throne of Sayin-Khan.[116] And now Saljidai Küregen has authority over that throne. If my son Toqta wishes the basis of our relationship to be strengthened between us, let him send Saljidai Küregen back to his *yurt*, which is near Khwārazm." Toqta did not agree. Again Noqai sent an ambassador to ask for Saljidai. Toqta said:

---

[116] That is, Batu. See above, p. 107, note 46.

"He is to me like a father, tutor, and emir. How can I hand him over to an enemy?" And he refused to do so.

Noqai had a clever and competent wife called Chübei, who was constantly going to Toqta upon missions for him. And he had three sons: the eldest Jöge, the middle one Tüge, and the youngest Torai. They suborned several of Toqta's *hazāras* and made them subject to themselves; and crossing the Etil they stretched out the hand of insolence and violence against the territory of Toqta and ruled it as absolute rulers. Toqta was annoyed and asked for the return of the *hazāras*. Noqai refused, saying: "I will send them when Saljidai, his son Yailaq, and Tama-Toqta are sent to me." On this account the flame of discord and enmity flared up between them, and Toqta gathered his forces and in the year 698/1298–1299 reviewed nearly 30 tümens on the banks of the River Uzï. But since the Uzï had not frozen over that winter, he was unable to cross, and Noqai did not stir from his position. Toqta turned back in the spring and spent the summer on the banks of the River Tan.[117]

The next year Noqai crossed the Tan with his sons and wives and began to practise his wiles, saying: "I am coming for a *quriltai* so that I may take my pleasure with you." And knowing that Toqta's armies were scattered and that he had but few men with him, he hurried forward in order to fall upon him unawares. Toqta learnt of his approach and collected an army; and they met and fought at ———,[118] on the banks of the River Tan. Toqta was defeated and fled back to Sarai. Three emirs, Maji, Sutan, and Sanqui, deserted Noqai and made their way to Toqta. Toqta sent for Tama-Toqta, the son of Balagha, who for some time past had been the guardian and defender of Darband, and again mobilized a great army and went to war against Noqai. Noqai had not the power to resist. He turned face and, crossing the Uzï, pillaged the town of Qïrïm[119] and carried off many slaves. The inhabitants came to the court of Noqai and asked for the release of the slaves and prisoners. Noqai ordered the prisoners to be returned. His army became disaffected and sent the following message

---

[117] The Don.
[118] Verkhovsky (p. 85) reads this corrupt name as Bakhtiyar.
[119] The Crimean port of Soldaia, or Sudaq. See above, p. 55, note 213.

to Toqta: "We are the servants and subjects of the Il-Khan.[120] If the king will pardon us we will seize Noqai and deliver him up to him." The sons of Noqai learnt of the message and prepared to attack the *hazāras*.[121] Meanwhile the commanders of the *hazāras* sent someone to Tüge, the second son of Noqai, to say: "We have all agreed together about thee." Tüge went to them, and they at once imprisoned him. Jöge, who was the elder brother, collected his army and gave battle to the great *hazāras*. The *hazāras* were defeated, and one commander fell into [Jöge's] hands. He sent his head to the other *hazāra* which had captured Tüge, and the three hundred men who formed his guard made one with him, made off in the night, and went to Noqai and his sons.

When Toqta heard of the conflict between the *hazāras* and the army, he crossed the Uzï with an army of 60 *tümens* and encamped on the bank of the River ———,[122] where Noqai's *yurt* was. Again feigning illness, [Noqai] lay down in a wagon and sent ambassadors to Toqta with this message: "I did not know that the king was coming in person. My kingdom and army are the Il-Khan's, and I am a feeble old man who has spent his whole life in the service of your fathers. If there has been some trifling error, it is the fault of my sons. It is to be expected of the king's magnanimity that he will forgive that fault." But in secret he had sent Jöge with a large army to cross the ———[123] higher up and attack Toqta and his army. However, Toqta's guards caught a scout, who told them the state of affairs, and Toqta, on being informed of Noqai's guile, ordered his troops to make ready and mount horse. Battle was joined between the two sides, and Noqai and his

[120] In the sense of subordinate to the Great Khan, this title was applied to the rulers of the Golden Horde as well as to those of Persia.

[121] See Glossary.

[122] Verkhovsky (p. 86) reads the name as Tarku; Spuler (1943) takes the river to be the Terek in the Caucasus but Noqai's *yurt* lay in quite a different region, between the Dnieper and the Lower Danube. Taking an alternative reading of the name (*N*RKH), we can perhaps see in it the Mongol *nerge*, "hunting circle," and connect it with the "plain of Nerghi" in which, according to Marco Polo, the earlier battle between Noqai and Toqta was fought. Vernadsky (pp. 187–88) believes "that the name refers to the ancient fortified line between the Dniester and the Pruth rivers in Bessarabia and Moldavia, called Emperor Trajan's Wall, remnants of which still exist." The river, whatever its Mongol or Turkish name, would appear to be the Dniester, or perhaps the Bug.

[123] See above, note 122.

sons were defeated, large numbers being killed in that battle.[124] Noqai's
sons with a thousand horsemen set off for the Keler and Bashghïrd.
Noqai was fleeing with seventeen horsemen when he was wounded by
an Orus horse soldier in Toqta's army. He said: "I am Noqai. Take
me to Toqta, who is the Khan." The man seized his bridle and was
leading him to Toqta, when he gave up the ghost.[125]

Toqta returned to Batu's Sarai, which is their capital, while Noqai's
sons wandered here and there. Seeing no profit in such a life, Tüge,
his mother Chübei, and Yailaq, the mother of Torai, said to Jöge:
"It is to our advantage that we abandon strife and contention and go
to Toqta." But Jöge was frightened of this idea. He killed his brother
and his father's wife and wandered about with a group of followers and
finally took refuge in a castle, the path to which was as narrow as
Ṣirāṭ,[126] or as the hearts of misers. Let us see what will happen to him
in the end.

Noqai had previously begun to establish friendly relations with
Abaqa Khan and Arghun Khan. In the year ———[127] he sent his
wife Chubei with his son Torai and an emir called ———[128] to
Abaqa Khan and asked for his daughter[129] in marriage. Abaqa
Khan gave his daughter to Torai, and they remained there for awhile,
after which he dismissed them kindly. And when war and strife arose
between Noqai and Toqta, he was always sending trustworthy ambassadors to the Lord of Islam[130] (*may God cause him to reign forever!*)
to ask for help and request that he might be a dependent of this Court.
In truth, it was an extremely excellent opportunity, but the Lord of
Islam (*may God cause him to reign forever!*), in his magnanimity, would

---

[124] It was fought, according to the Egyptian authorities, at a place called Kūlkānlïk,
which Vernadsky (p. 188 and note 197) identifies with the Kagamlïk, a small river
flowing into the Dnieper near Kremenchug.

[125] According to the Egyptian authorities, the Russian soldier killed Noqai and
brought his head to Toqta expecting a reward. The Khan ordered him to be put to
death. "Obviously," comments Vernadsky (p. 189), "Tokhta was indignant that
Nogay was not given the privilege of dying without his blood being shed."

[126] The bridge, according to Muslim traditions, across the infernal fire, described
as being finer than a hair and sharper than a sword.

[127] Blank in all the MSS.

[128] Blank in Blochet's text. Verkhovsky (p. 86) has simply "an emir."

[129] "Two daughters" in Verkhovsky (p. 86).

[130] That is, Ghazan.

not agree and refused to abuse his advantage, saying: "In the present time treason and ill faith are remote from chivalry, and guile and deceit are condemned and forbidden by reason, religious law, and the *yasa*. And although we have a great friendship for Noqai yet we shall not intervene in the quarrel, for the abuse of opportunities is a reprehensible quality, especially among great kings."

Toqta, being in fear and apprehension, used to send ambassadors with professions of friendship in order to prevent this from happening. And the Lord of Islam (*may God cause him to reign forever!*) used to send for the ambassadors of both sides and would say to them to their faces: "I shall not intervene between you and abuse my advantage, but if you make peace with one another, it will be good and praiseworthy." And in order to allay their suspicions he used not to go in his august person to Arrān to pass the winter but made his winter quarters in Baghdad and Diyār Bakr in order that their minds might be set at rest. And up to the present time he is on terms of sincere friendship both with Toqta and with the sons of Noqai and has said on many occasions: "None of the *aqa* or *ini* is to stir up strife between them or engage in hostile actions against them. We for our part shall never start a quarrel or take any step that might lead to strife, lest the blame for some harm that might come to the *ulus* might rest on us."

It is as though God Almighty had created his pure being and radiant person out of sheer goodness and absolute beneficence. He is a ruler distinguished by his noble character and known for his equity and kindness throughout the world, a monarch who protects religion, spreads justice, musters armies, cherishes the people, is of happy omen, and possesses the best of virtues. May God Almighty grant him abundant years and endless ages over the people of the world and give him enjoyment of life and fortune and kingdom and sovereignty through the honor of the Chosen Prophet Muḥammad and his pious family!

PART

III

OF THE HISTORY OF JOCHI KHAN

On his praiseworthy character and morals;
the excellent biligs, parables, and pronouncements
which he uttered and promulgated,
such as have not been included in the two previous parts
but have been ascertained
on separate occasions and at irregular intervals
from various books and persons

———————131

131 The text of this section is absent in all the MSS, presumably because it was never written.

History of Chaghatai Khan,

the Son of Chingiz-Khan,

which is in Three Parts

HISTORY OF CHAGHATAI KHAN,
THE SON OF CIIINGIZ-KHAN,
WHICH IS IN THREE PARTS

◈ PART I. An account of his lineage; an account of his wives, sons, and grandsons in the branches into which they have divided down to the present day; his portrait; and a genealogical table of his sons and grandsons.

◈ PART II. The [general] history and [particular] episodes of his reign; a picture of his throne and wives and the princes; an account of his *ulus* and certain battles which he fought and victories which he gained; the length of his reign.

◈ PART III. His praiseworthy character and morals; miscellaneous events and happenings; the excellent parables and *biligs* which he uttered and promulgated; and whatever has not been included in the two previous parts, having been ascertained at irregular intervals from various books and persons.

PART

I
OF THE HISTORY OF CHAGHATAI[1] KHAN

An account of his wives, sons, and grandsons
in the branches into which they have divided down to the present day;
his portrait;
and a genealogical table of his sons and grandsons

Chaghatai was the second son of Chingiz-Khan, his mother, the latter's chief wife and the mother of his four sons, [was] Börte Fujin of the Qonqïrat people, the daughter of Dei Noyan, the ruler of that people. Chaghatai had many wives, but the most important of them were two. The first, Yesülün Khatun, who was the mother of all his chief sons, was the daughter of Qata Noyan, the son of Daritai, the brother of the ruler of the Qonqïrat. Börte Fujin, the chief wife of Chingiz-Khan, and Yesülün Khatun, were cousins. The second was Tögen Khatun, the sister of the aforesaid Yesülün Khatun, whom he married after Yesülün's death.

✎ ACCOUNT OF HIS SONS AND GRANDSONS IN THE branches into which they have divided down to the present day

Chaghatai had eight sons, in the following order: first, Mochi-Yebe; second, Mö'etüken; third, Belgeshi; fourth, Sarban; fifth, Yesü-Möngke; sixth, Baidar; seventh, Qadaqai; [and] eighth, Baiju.

The detailed description of these eight sons is such as shall now be given with respect to each of them separately, with the help of God Almighty.

---

[1] On the name, see Cleaves 1949, pp. 417–18. The original form was perhaps Cha'adai, as the name is always spelt in *SH*. Cf. the Chiaaday of Carpini and the Russian family name Chaadayev directly derived from Chaghatai.

First Son of Chaghatai Khan—Mochi-Yebe

The mother of this Mochi-Yebe was a slave-girl in the *ordo* of Yesülün Khatun. One night she was laying the bedclothes and the *khatun* had gone out. Chaghatai pulled her to him and made her with child. For this reason he did not hold Mochi-Yebe of much account and gave him fewer troops and less territory. He had eleven sons as follows.

First Son—Tegüder

It was this Tegüder who was sent from the *ulus* of Chaghatai to accompany Hülegü Khan to Persia. He remained here, and in the reign of Abaqa Khan [he] rose in rebellion and made for the mountains of Georgia, where he wandered in the forests with the emirs of Abaqa Khan at his heels. He was captured by Shiremün Noyan, the son of Chormaghun, and brought to Abaqa Khan, who pardoned him. For a time he wandered about here alone and then died.[2]

Second Son—Aḥmad

This Aḥmad was in attendance on Baraq. When Baraq fled across the river his army was scattered, and every detachment withdrew into a different corner. Aḥmad set out for Besh-Balïq. Baraq, who was ill, followed him upon a litter, sending Te'ülder, who was the commander of a thousand, in advance. When he came up with Aḥmad he tried to coax him to turn back, but Aḥmad was violent, and in the end they came to blows, and Aḥmad was killed. He had three sons: 'Umar, Mubārak-Shāh, and Mö'etü.

Third Son—Tekshi

He had a son called Tabudughar, who had four sons: Toghan, Hoqolqu, Qorïqtai, and Qutluq-Temür.

Fourth Son—Nom-Quli

Fifth Son—Bük-Buqa

Sixth Son—Temüder

[2] On Tegüder's revolt against the Il-Khan Abaqa (1265–1284), see *CHI*, p. 356.

Seventh Son—Qotan

Eighth Son—Cheche

Ninth Son—Chichektü

He had two sons: Shādbān and Qushman.

Tenth Son—Ishal

He had two sons: Qan-Buqa and Uladai.

Eleventh Son—Toghan

He had three sons: Qorïqtai, Bük-Buqa, and Nom-Quli.

Second Son of Chaghatai Khan—Mö'etüken

This Mö'etüken was born of Yesülun Khatun, and his father loved him more than his other children. Since Chingiz-Khan also loved him greatly, he was mostly in attendance on him. When he sent his father Chaghatai along with Jochi and Ögetei to lay siege to Khwārazm and was himself investing the castle of Bāmiyān, this Mö'etüken was hit by an arrow from the castle and died. Chingiz-Khan was greatly distressed on this account, and when he captured the castle he destroyed it utterly, put all the inhabitants to death, and called it Ma'u-Qurghan.[3] When Chaghatai arrived, while the castle was still being destroyed, Chingiz-Khan gave orders that no one was to tell him of his son's death, and for several days he would say that Mö'etüken had gone to such-and-such a place. Then, one day, he purposely picked a quarrel with his sons and said: "You do not listen to my words and have ignored what I told you." Chaghatai knelt down and said: "We shall act as the Khan commands and if we fall short may we die!" Chingiz several times repeated this question: "Is it true what thou sayest and wilt thou keep thy word?" He answered: "If I disobey and do not keep my word, may I die!" Chingiz-Khan then said: "Mö'etüken is dead, and thou must not weep and lament." Fire fell into Chaghatai's bowels, but obeying his father's command he

[3] In Mongol, "Bad Fortress." Cf. Smirnova, p. 219. Juvainī (*HWC*, p. 133) has the hybrid form Ma'u-Balïgh, in which the second element is T. *balïq*, "town." See *Horde d'Or*, p. 110.

exercised forbearance and did not weep. After awhile he went out on the pretext of some necessity and wept in secret in a corner for a moment or two. Then, wiping his eyes, he returned to his father.

Mö'etüken had four sons, in this order: Baiju, Büri, Yesün-To'a, and Qara-Hülegü. His sons and the grandsons of these sons are divided into branches as set out below.

First Son of Mö'etüken—Baiju

He had a son called Töden, and this Töden had a son called Böjei, and Böjei a son 'Abdallāh.

Second Son of Mö'etüken—Büri

The circumstances of his birth have been described as follows: Formerly it was the custom for the wives of the *ev-oghlans* to gather together in the *ordos* in order to work. One day Mö'etüken entered the *ordo* and saw a crowd of women, one of them very beautiful. He took her into a corner and had intercourse with her. It occurred to him that she might become pregnant, and he ordered her to be kept apart from her husband. It so happened that she did become pregnant and gave birth to Büri. She was then given back to her husband.

This Büri was very headstrong and brave and would utter harsh words when he drank wine. Things reached such a pitch that during the reign of Möngke Qa'an, when he was drinking wine, he abused Batu on account of the enmity which he nourished against him. When Batu heard of his words, he asked for [Büri] to be handed over to him. At Möngke Qa'an's command, Mengeser Noyan took him to Batu, who put him to death.[4]

Büri had five sons.

First Son—Abishqa. This Abishqa had no issue. At the time of Arïq Böke's revolt[5] against Qubilai Qa'an, he was in the service of the Qa'an. He was sent to take the place of Qara-Hülegü as ruler of the *ulus* of Chaghatai and to marry Orqïna Khatun. On the way he was taken prisoner by Arïq Böke's troops and remained with them until Asutai,

[4] Büri had taken part in the campaign in eastern Europe and had brought back a number of German slaves, who appear to have been the subject of a pontifical letter to their master. See *HWC*, p. 588, note 124.

[5] See below, pp. 252 ff.

the son of Möngke Qa'an, who was allied with Arïq Böke, put him to death.

Second Son—Ajïqï. This Ajïqï was in attendance on Qubilai Qa'an and is now with Temür Qa'an. He is extremely old and the most respected of all the princes there, possessing great power and authority. He has three sons, Örüg, Örüg-Temür, and Ershil Küregen, who also have issue and are in attendance on the Qa'an.

Third Son—Qadaqchi Sechen. He has five sons: Nalïghu, who has three sons, Temür, Oradai, and Tümen; Bughu, who has two sons, Dhu'l-Qarnain and 'Alï; Buqa-Temür, who has two sons, Örüg-Temür and Öljei; and Buqa.

Fourth Son—Aḥmad. He has two sons: Baba, who has three sons, Hābïl-Temür, Qābïl-Temür, and Yulduz-Temür; and Sati.

Fifth Son—Ebügen.

Ended, praise be to God, the Lord of the Worlds, and blessing and peace upon our Master Muḥammad and all his good and pure family.

Third Son of Mo'etuken—Yesun-To'a

He had three sons, in the following order.

First Son—Mu'min. He had two sons, the first called Yebe, whose son is called Bilge-Temür, and the second Örüg.

Second Son—Baraq. He had five sons: Beg-Temür, Du'a, Toqta, Uladai and Bozma.

Third Son—Yasa'ur. He came here to tender submission in the year in which Abaqa Khan had gone to Herat to drive off the Qaraunas.[6] And when Aḥmad fled from Khurāsān the emirs put him to death.

Mu'min was a great drinker. As for Baraq, since he had been in attendance on Qubilai Qa'an and had rendered praiseworthy services Qubilai Qa'an commanded that he should administer the *ulus* jointly with Mubārak-Shāh. When he arrived there he affected friendship for awhile, and then one of Mubārak-Shāh's emirs, called Bitikchi, and certain other army leaders made one with Baraq and deposed Mubārak-Shāh, and Baraq became the absolute ruler. And since the frontier of the *ulus* of Chaghatai adjoined Qaidu's territory, certain areas were

[6] On the Qaraunas, Polo's Caraunas, also called Nïgūdarïs, bands of Mongol freebooters with their main base in southern Afghanistan, see *Polo I*, pp. 183–96, and Boyle 1963, pp. 212 and 217. See also below, p. 154, note 40.

occupied by Qaidu, [and] Baraq fought several battles with Qaidu. In the first, Qaidu was victorious, and when they resumed hostilities Qïpchaq, the son of Qadaqan, of the family of Ögetei Qa'an, made peace between them, and they swore an oath and became *anda*[7] to each other—and to this day their descendants are also *anda* to one another. They then rose in rebellion against the Qa'an and also against Abaqa Khan. Baraq seized their dependents within his territory, confiscated their property, opened the hand of tyranny and domination against the people, and consulted with Qaidu about crossing the Oxus and making war on Abaqa Khan. Qaidu, being concerned about Baraq's disaffection, and being himself in rebellion against the Qa'an and Abaqa Khan, agreed to this in order that Baraq might be far away from his own kingdom. And he sent Qïpchaq, the son of Qadaqan, and Chabat, the son of Naqu, the son of Güyük Khan, both of them nephews of Qaidu, to accompany Baraq, each of them at the head of an army. When they crossed the river, Qïpchaq lost heart and turned back, and Chabat also. Baraq sent his brothers Mu'min, Yasa'ur, and Negübei Oghul after him with instructions to bring him back if he came willingly and otherwise to hold him up with words until Jalayirtai should arrive and seize him. When they came up to Qïpchaq he would not turn back. They sought to give him drink and so keep him occupied, but he perceived their intention and said: "This is what you intend. If you will go back of your own accord, well and good. Otherwise I will seize you and take you with me." For fear of this they turned back, and when they saw Jalayirtai they said: "He has gone a long way and thou wilt not come up with him." And he too returned with them.

When Baraq crossed the Oxus defeated, and most of his kinsmen and military leaders had deserted him, he sent Yasa'ur to Qaidu with the following message: "The *aqa* and *ini* and those whom thou hadst sent did not keep faith and stand firm, but each of them turned back on some pretext; and the first to do so was Qïpchaq. And this conduct was the cause of the army's defeat." When he had heard the message to the end, Qaidu asked Yasa'ur: "When he sent thee, Mu'min, and Negübei after Qïpchaq, did he send an army to follow you?" "No,"

[7] In Mongol, "sworn brother." On the term and the practice, see Doerfer, I, No, 33 (pp. 149–52).

replied Yasa'ur. Qaidu, who knew what had happened, said: "The reason for your defeat is that your tongues are not true to your hearts. In that affair did not Jalayirtai follow you with an army in order to capture Qïpchaq?" Yasa'ur was frightened, and Qaidu seized and imprisoned him. Then, after consulting his emirs, he set out as though to aid Baraq, hoping by some means to get rid of him. When he drew near there came a report that those who had gone in pursuit of Negübei Oghul and Aḥmad, had killed them. Baraq sent a messenger to say: "Why has my *anda* Qaidu taken the trouble to come back, since there is no need for help?" Qaidu ignored the message, and arriving in the evening [he] encamped for the night all round Baraq's *ordo*. That very night Baraq died. In the morning, since no one came forward, Qaidu sent someone to investigate. Baraq was indeed dead. Qaidu entered his *ordo*, performed the mourning ceremonies, and sent his body on to a mountain to be buried there.

After Baraq's death his nephew, Buqa-Temür, the son of Qadaqchi, became the ruler of the *ulus* of Chaghatai. After his death it was given to Du'a, the son of Baraq, who is in alliance with Qaidu and his sons. Previously, when he was gradually gathering together the armies of Chaghatai, Naurūz,[8] who had risen in rebellion, went to him and Qaidu and, being familiar with the roads and general conditions in Khurāsān, prevailed upon them to invade that province and lay waste Isfarāyin. And because of Naurūz, much damage was done to these territories and many Muslims were killed, as shall be described in the history of the Lord of Islam.[9] Afterward, Uighurtai, the son of Qutluq-Buqa, fled and went to Du'a. He had a good knowledge of the roads of Māzandarān, and when Baidu betrayed Geikhatu and the emirs turned against him and put him to death and the Lord of Islam (*may God cause him to reign forever!*) came with an army and captured the throne of the Khanate, Du'a, guided by Uighurtai, availed himself of the opportunity when the army had left Khurāsān in this direction, entered Māzandarān by way of the desert, carried off some of the heavy baggage belonging to the military leaders of the Lord of Islam (*may God cause him to reign forever!*) that had been left in that region, and returned home. These events will be described

[8] On Naurūz, see above, Section 1, p. 24, note 59.
[9] See Arends, pp. 150 and 153.

in the history of the Lord of Islam (*may God cause him to reign forever!*).[10]

On several occasions Du'a, in alliance with Qaidu, fought the army of the Qa'an. On the most recent occasion both of them were wounded, Qaidu dying of his wound and Du'a becoming paralyzed.[11]

Du'a has sons, one of whom is Qutluq-Khwāja, to whom they have entrusted the province of Ghaznīn and the Qarauna army, which has long had connections with them. In the summer they sit in the region of Ghūr[12] and Gharchistān[13] and in the winter in the province of Ghaznīn and that area. They have constantly to do battle with the Sultan of Delhi, and the army of Delhi has frequently defeated them. On every occasion they enter the borderlands of this country, robbing and plundering. Bozma wished to go to the Qa'an, but Qaidu learnt of this and put him to death.

Fourth Son of Mö'etüken—Qara-Hülegü

He had a son called Mubārak-Shāh, and this Mubārak-Shāh had five sons: Öljei-Buqa, who had a son called Qutluq-Shāh; Boralqï, who had a son called Tutluq; Horqadai; Esen-Fulad; and Qadaq. Chaghatai had made this Qara-Hülegü his heir in place of his father. His wife was Orqïna Khatun, who gave birth to Mubārak-Shāh. When Qara-Hülegü died, Alghu, the son of Baidar, who was [Qara-Hülegü's] cousin, became ruler of the *ulus* of Chaghatai by command of Arïq Böke and married Orqïna Khatun. After awhile he died, and this Mubārak-Shāh succeeded his father. Baraq now arrived, at the command of Qubilai Qa'an. Finding Mubārak-Shāh established as ruler, he said not a word; he gradually gathered a scattered army about him and seized the rulership of the *ulus*. Convicting Mubārak-Shāh of some crime, he ended by making him the supervisor of his cheetah-keepers. When Baraq entered Khurāsān to make war on Abaqa Khan, Mubārak-Shāh accompanied him, [at which time] he fled

---

[10] In the passage apparently referred to (Arends, p. 153), Rashīd al-Dīn makes no mention of Du'a but speaks only of a raid on Gurgān (not Māzandarān) by Uighurtai.

[11] See below, p. 329.

[12] The region of Afghanistan east and southeast of Herat.

[13] The modern Firuzkuh in northwest Afghanistan.

to Abaqa Khan. This event shall be described in detail hereafter in the proper place, if God Almighty so wills.[14]

Third Son of Chaghatai—Belgeshi [15]

When Mö'etüken, who was Chaghatai's heir-apparent, died, [Chaghatai] wished to make this son his heir, but he died at the age of thirteen and left no issue. He then made Qara-Hülegü, the son of Mö'etüken, his heir. *Peace unto those that follow Divine Guidance.*

Fourth Son of Chaghatai—Sarban

He had two sons: Qushïqï and Negübei.

Fifth Son of Chaghatai—Yesü-Möngke

This Yesü-Möngke was a great drinker. It is said that he was not sober long enough to give a falcon to the falconers. He had a wife called Naishi, who enjoyed great authority and power. Her husband being always drunk, she used to perform his duties. [Yesü-Möngke's] career was as follows. He was on friendly terms with Güyük Khan, and although Qara-Hülegü was Chaghatai's heir-apparent, Güyük made [this Yesü-Möngke] ruler of the *ulus* of Chaghatai because of his opposition to Möngke Qa'an. Afterward, when Möngke Qa'an became Qa'an, he ordered Qara-Hülegü to administer the *ulus* and put Yesü-Möngke to death. Qara-Hülegü died *en route* and his wife, Orqïna Khatun, put Yesü-Möngke to death and herself reigned for 10 years. Then Arïq Böke gave that *ulus* to Alghu, the son of Baidar, and when Alghu rebelled against Arïq Böke, Orqïna Khatun became his wife, as has already been related. Yesü-Möngke had no son.

Sixth Son of Chaghatai—Baidar

He was a short man and an extremely good archer. It is said that ———[16] joked with him once and said: "Thou art short of height.

---

[14] See below, pp. 152–53; also Arends, pp. 70–83. In neither passage, however, is there any mention of Mubārak-Shāh.

[15] The remainder of the chapter is absent from Verkhovsky's text.

[16] Blank in Blochet's text and one MS.

Come, let us shoot together." He had a son called Alghu, who had three sons:

First Son—Qaban

Second Son—Chübei[17]

He lived and died in the service of the Qa'an. He had fifteen sons, whose histories will be given later: Toqta, Yasa'ur, Düküles, Ejil-Buqa, Nom-Quli, Nom-Dash, Aq-Buqa, Sati, Dā'ūd, Gambo Dorji, Chigin-Temür, Jirghudai, Mingtash, and Könchek Dorji.

Third Son—Toq-Temür

He had two sons: Esen-Böke and Oqruqchï.

Seventh Son of Chaghatai—Qadaqai

His mother was Tögen Khatun. This Qadaqai had five sons: Naya, Buqu, Naliqo'a, Buqa-Temür, and Buqa.

Eighth Son of Chaghatai—Baiju

He had a son called Mochi. It was this Mochi who was the commander of the *cherig* of Qarauna in the Ghaznïn area. [Mochi] has a son called 'Abdallāh, who is a Muslim. ['Abdallāh's] father was in that area and summoned him to him, and [he] sent his own son, Qutluq-Khwāja, there in his stead.

[17] These are the Cibai and Caban of Marco Polo, on whom see below, pp. 265 and 300; also *Polo I*, pp. 262–63.

PART II

OF THE HISTORY OF CHAGHATAI KHAN

The [general] history and [particular] episodes of his reign,
a picture of his throne and wives and the princes;
an account of his ulus and
certain battles which he fought and victories which he gained;
the length of his reign;
the history of his descendants down to the present day

Chaghatai was a just, competent, and awe-inspiring ruler. His father, Chingiz-Khan, said to the emirs: "Whoever wishes to learn the *yasa* and *yosun* of kingship should follow Chaghatai. Whoever loves property, wealth, chivalrous manners, and comfort should walk in the footsteps of Ögetei. And whoever wishes to acquire politeness, good breeding, courage, and skill in the handling of weapons should wait in attendance on Tolui."[18] And when he was sharing out the armies he gave him four thousand men, as is set forth in detail in his history in the section on the division of the armies. Of the emirs he gave him Qarachar of the Barulas people and Möge, the father of Yesün Noyan, of the Jalayir people; and of the lands and *yurts* from the Altai, which is the *yurt* of the Naiman peoples [to the banks of the Oxus].[19] And, in accordance with the command of Chingiz-Khan, he went forth with the armies, and carried out the operations with the utmost zeal and endeavor, and conquered the various countries in the manner already described. In the *qonin yïl*, that is, the Year of the Sheep, corresponding to Sha'bān of 607 of the Hegira [January–February, 1211], when Chingiz-Khan set out against the land of Khitai, Chaghatai together with Ögetei and Tolui captured five towns: Un-Ui,[20] Tung-Cheng,[21]

[18] Cf. above, p. 18.
[19] Only in Verkhovsky.
[20] Yün-nei, northwest of Urot Banner in Suiyuan.
[21] Tung shêng, the modern Tokoto, in Suiyuan.

145

Fu-Jiu,[22] Suq-Jiu,[23] and Fung-Jiu.[24] Then, when they had besieged and taken the town of Jo-Jiu,[25] he sent all three to the edge of a mountain[26] and its environs, and they captured all the towns, provinces, and castles between the towns of Fu-Jiu[27] and Khuming.[28] From thence they went to the River Qara-Mören, and then, turning back, [they] captured and plundered the towns of Pung-Yang-Fu[29] and Tai-Wang-Fu[30] and their dependencies; and the plunder of Tai-Wang-Fu went to Chaghatai.

Thereafter, in the *lu yïl*, that is, the Year of the Dragon, of which the beginning corresponds to the Dhu'l-Ḥijja of the year 616 [February –March, 1220], when Chingiz-Khan set out for the Tāzīk country and came to the town of Otrar, he left him with his brothers Ögetei and Tolui to lay siege to it. They took the town and thereafter captured Banākat and most of the towns of Turkistān and then joined their father in Samarqand after its fall. Then he sent him with Jochi and Ögetei to lay siege to Khwārazm, and since he and Jochi did not

[22] Wu-chou, the modern Wuchai, in Shansi.

[23] Shuo-chou, the modern Shohsien in Shansi. These three towns are mentioned in the *Yüan shih* (Krause, p. 30), in the same order, as having been captured by the three princes in 1211.

[24] Fêng-chou, 20 *li* south of Kweisiu (Huhehot), in Suiyuan, mentioned in the *Shêng-wu ch'in-chêng lu*, 62a, as captured by the three princes in 1211. I am indebted to Dr. Igor de Rachewiltz for this reference which was made available to me in a letter dated the 13th April, 1966.

[25] Cho-chou, the modern Chohsien, in Hopeh. See *Polo II*, p. 736, where Pelliot points out that Cho-chou "occurs in the parallel text of *Shêng-wu ch'in-cheng lu*." It was captured by Genghis Khan himself in the seventh month of 1213. See Krause, p. 31.

[26] The Taihang Shan, from which, in the autumn of 1213, the princes descended into the North China Plain, sweeping southward through Hopeh and Honan to the Hwang Ho and then returning northward through Shansi to the Great Wall. See Krause, p. 32.

[27] Fu-chou, near Changpeh in Hopeh, captured by Genghis Khan in the spring or summer of 1212. See Krause, p. 31.

[28] Reading XWMYNK with the Leningrad, British Museum, and Tehran MSS. Apparently the Huai and Mêng of the *Yüan shih* (Krause, p. 32) regarded as a single name. These two places—Tsingyang and Menghsien in northern Honan—form the southernmost point in the princes' thrust.

[29] Polo's Pianfu, that is, P'ing-yang fu, the present-day Linfen, in Shansi. I adopt the reading proposed by Pelliot (*Polo I*, p. 803). Blochet takes this to be T'ung-p'ing fu (Tungping) in Shantung, which, as Pelliot says, "is irreconcilable with the trend of the narrative."

[30] Polo's Taianfu, that is, T'ai-yüan fu (now Yangku) in Shansi. See *Polo I*, p. 842.

agree, their father commanded Ögetei, though he was the youngest, to take command, and he, by his competence, brought about agreement between the brothers and together they took Khwārazm. Then Jochi went to his heavy baggage, and the others, in the summer of the *morin*[31] *yïl*, that is, the Year of the Horse, corresponding to the year 619/1222–1223,[32] joined their father and were received in audience at Ṭālaqān. Having passed the summer in that area Chaghatai, Ögetei, and Tolui all three together accompanied their father in pursuit of Sultan Jalāl al-Dīn. They went to the banks of the Indus and defeated the Sultan's army, while [the Sultan] himself escaped across the river. That summer they were engaged in conquering the countries of those parts and then accompanied their father back to their original *yurt* and abode.

In the *daqïqu*[33] *yïl*, that is, the Year of the Hen, corresponding to the year 622/1225–1226,[34] when Chingiz-Khan set out against the land of the Tangqut, who had risen in rebellion, he commanded Chaghatai to remain with the wing of the army behind the *ordos*. In accordance with this command, Chaghatai continued so occupied until his brothers Ögetei and Tolui, who had accompanied their father, returned: they then brought Chingiz-Khan's coffin to the *ordos*, and, having jointly performed the mourning ceremonies, each departed to his own *yurt* and tents.

And since Chaghatai had a particular friendship for his brothers Ögetei and Tolui, he spared no efforts to seat Ögetei upon the throne of the Khanate and went to great pains to have him so enthroned in accordance with his father's command. Together with Tolui and the other kinsmen, he knelt nine times and made obeisance. And although he was the elder brother he used to treat Ögetei with the utmost respect and rigidly observe the niceties of etiquette, one example of which is the following. One day they were riding on easy-paced horses and Chaghatai, being drunk, said to Ögetei: "Let us race our horses for a bet." And having made a bet, they ran a race, and Chaghatai's horse, being a little faster, won by a head. At night in his tent, Chaghatai was reminded of this incident and he reflected: "How was it possible for me to make a bet with Qa'an and let my horse beat his?

---

[31] Mo. *mori*(*n*), "horse."
[33] T. *taqaghu/taqïghu*, "fowl."

[32] Actually 1222.
[34] Actually 1225.

Such conduct was a great breach of etiquette. Judging by this we and the others are becoming insolent, and this will lead to harm." And before morning he summoned the emirs and said: "Yesterday I was guilty of a crime of committing such an action. Let us go to Ögetei so that he may convict me of my crime and carry whatever is a fitting punishment." And setting out with the emirs in a great throng he came to the audience-hall earlier than usual. The guards reported to Ögetei that Chaghatai had come with a great multitude, and Ögedei, although he had complete confidence in him, was apprehensive of the situation, wondering what his motive could be. He sent some persons to his brother to ask him. [Chaghatai] said: "We, all of us, *aqa* and *ini*, spoke great words in the *quriltai* and gave written undertakings that Ögetei was the Qa'an and that we should tread the path of loyalty and obedience and in no way oppose him. Yesterday I made a bet and raced my horse against his. What right have we to make a bet with the Qa'an. Therefore I am guilty and have come to confess my guilt and submit to punishment. Whether he puts me to death or beats me is for him to decide." Ögetei Qa'an was filled with shame at these words. He became more loving and tender and humbled himself before his brother, but though he sent someone to say, "What words are these ? He is my *aqa*. Why pay attention to such trifles?" [Chaghatai] would not listen. However, in the end he agreed that the Qa'an should spare his life and made an offering of nine horses. The *bitikchis*[35] proclaimed that the Qa'an had spared Chaghatai's life, so that everyone heard and knew that he was making the offering because he had been pardoned. He then entered the *ordo* and explained this to all present with the eloquence that he possessed.

On this account the concord between them increased, and the other kinsmen laid their heads upon the letters of the Qa'an's command and took the road of obedience to him. And those countries which had not been conquered in the age of Chingiz-Khan were all subjugated during the reign of Ögetei Qa'an. And the sovereignty of his family and the state of his army were strengthened. And since Chaghatai lived after this manner with Ögetei Qa'an, the Qa'an made his son Güyük his attendant and placed him in his guard, where he used to serve him. And Chaghatai's greatness became such as cannot be

[35] See Glossary.

described, and he ruled over his *ulus* and the army that Chingiz-Khan had given to him; he was firmly established on the throne of his kingdom in the region of Besh-Balïq.[36] And in all important affairs Ögetei Qa'an used to send messengers and consult Chaghatai and would undertake nothing without his advice and approval. He himself in all matters trod the path of agreement and co-operation and in every decision used to say whatever occurred to him. Whenever there was an important undertaking he would attend the *qurïltai*, and all the princes and emirs would come to welcome him; he would then enter the Court of the Qa'an, make obeisance and go into the inner chamber. During the 13 years that Ögetei was established on the throne, Chaghatai agreed and co-operated with him in this fashion: he died 7 months before Ögetei Qa'an, in the year 638/1240–1241.[37]

◈ HISTORY OF THE *ULUS* OF CHAGHATAI AFTER HIS death and the accession

Of his descendants one after another till the present day

After the death of Qa'an and Chaghatai, although Qara-Hülegü was the most senior of Chaghatai's descendants and the eldest son of Mö'etüken (who during his father's lifetime, in the reign of Chingiz-Khan, had been killed by an arrow before the castle of Bāmiyān, having been the heir-apparent), nevertheless Güyük Khan, because Yesü-Möngke, the fifth son of Chaghatai, was opposed to Möngke Qa'an, sent him instead to rule over the *ulus* of Chaghatai. However, when Möngke Qa'an became Qa'an, he gave Qara-Hülegü a *yarlïgh* commanding him to put Yesü-Möngke to death and, as heir-apparent, become the ruler of that *ulus*. Qara-Hülegü died *en route* before reaching the *ulus*, and his wife, Orqïna Khatun, the daughter of Törelchi Küregen of the Oirat, put Yesü-Möngke to death in accordance with

---

[36] That is, from Besh-Balïq westward. His main residences were in the valley of the Ili. See *HWC*, pp. 271–72; also *Four Studies*, pp. 114–15.

[37] Ögedei died on the 11th December, 1241: according to Juvainī (*HWC*, p. 272), Chaghatai survived his brother for a brief period.

the *yarlïgh* and ruled herself in her husband's stead. When Möngke Qa'an passed away, Qubilai Qa'an sent Abishqa, who was the eldest son of Büri, the second son of Mö'etüken, to marry Orqïna Khatun and rule the *ulus* of Chaghatai in place of Qara-Hülegü. At that time there were hostilities between Qubilai Qa'an and Arïq Böke. He ordered Asutai, the son of Möngke Qa'an, to put [Abishqa] to death. Alghu, the son of Baidar, the sixth son of Chaghatai, was with Arïq Böke. He gave him a *yarlïgh* appointing him ruler of the *ulus* of Chaghatai and commanding him to guard those frontiers against the army of Qubilai Qa'an and that of Chaghatai's descendants and to collect money, provisions, and equipment for the army from the province of Turkistān and to send it all to him so that he might proceed with an easy mind to make war on the army of Qubilai Qa'an. Alghu arrived and communicated the *yarlïgh*, and established himself as ruler. Orqïna Khatun went to Arïq Böke and made complaints about Alghu. She remained there for awhile, and after some time Arïq Böke sent envoys to those parts to levy two out of every ten cattle and to arrange [the supply of] great quantities of money and arms for the army. The names of those envoys were: Erkegün, Büritei Bitikchi, and Shādī. They set off and, having delivered the *yarlïgh* to Alghu, began to collect the cattle, money, and arms in that province. When a certain amount had been assembled, they sent it off. In 661/1262–1263 Alghu detained them, saying: "When the other *nökers* have completed their task and arrived, go all together." Some time afterward, when [the envoys] arrived, they rebuked the *nökers*, saying: "Why did you delay?" They replied that Alghu had held them up. Thereupon they went to the gate of Alghu's *ordo* and sent the following message: "We came in accordance with Arïq Böke's *yarlïgh* and collected imposts. What authority has thou over us to hold up our *nökers*?" Being covetous of all those goods, Alghu was angered with the ambassadors' sharp words and seized and imprisoned them. He then consulted his emirs, saying, "What is the best course of action?" They answered: "Thou shouldst have consulted us before seizing them. Now that we have risen against Arïq Böke the only course is to break with him entirely and render assistance to Qubilai Qa'an." Accordingly, he put the ambassadors to death and retained all those goods and arms. His position was greatly strengthened thereby, and, Orqïna Khatun having returned, he married her and secured absolute possession of the throne of the *ulus* of Chaghatai. When the news of this reached Arïq Böke, he led an army against Alghu and they joined battle. In the first two encounters Arïq Böke was defeated: in the third Alghu was put to flight and came to Bukhārā and Samarqand, where he seized money, arms, and animals from the rich. Arïq Böke plundered his heavy baggage and after the lapse of a year returned from that region to repel the army of the Qa'an.

The next year, which was the year 662/1263–1264, Alghu died, and Orqïna Khatun, having all the emirs and army under her command, installed her son Mubārak-Shāh, the eldest son of Qara-Hülegü, as ruler. The army continued as before to pillage and commit irregularities; but Mubārak-Shāh, being a Muslim, would not allow any violence against the peasants. When Arïq Böke was forced to surrender to the Qa'an and rebellion subsided in that region, Baraq, who was the son of Yesün-To'a, the third son of Mö'etüken, and had for a time been in attendance at the court of the Qa'an, was sent by him to the *ulus* of Chaghatai and given a *yarlïgh* to the effect that Mubārak-Shāh and he were to rule the *ulus* [jointly]. When Baraq arrived and found Mubārak-Shāh and Orqïna firmly established and in a strong position, he did not show the *yarlïgh*. Mubārak-Shāh asked him why he had come. He replied: "For some time I have been far away from my *ulus* and home, and my people are scattered and distressed. I have sought permission and have come to gather my followers together and wander about with you." Mubārak-Shāh was pleased with these words, and Baraq lived with him practising craft and dissimulation whilst gathering military men around him out of every corner. All of a sudden an emir, called Bitikchi, and certain army leaders joined him. They deposed Mubārak-Shāh, and Baraq became absolute ruler, while Mubārak-Shāh was reduced to the position of being his head cheetah-keeper.

Now Qaidu had been in league and alliance with Arïq Böke and had refused to present himself before the Qa'an, and the latter had sent Baraq in order to ward off Qaidu. In obedience to that command, as soon as he had gathered strength, [Baraq] led an army against [Qaidu] and they joined battle. In the first encounter Baraq was defeated. When they began a second battle, Qïpchaq Oghul, the son of Qadan Oghul, the son of Ögetei Qa'an, who was a friend of Baraq, made

151

peace between them and drew up a treaty; and they became *anda*[38] to each other. Being now reassured and encouraged with respect to Qaidu, Baraq himself became firmly established on the throne of the *ulus* of Chaghatai, after which he held a *quriltai*, and said to Qaidu: "My army has increased in size and this land cannot support it. I will cross the river in order to seize the lands of Khurāsān, and my *anda* Qaidu ought to help me." Qaidu, wishing him to be absent from the region [of the *ulus* of Chaghatai] and being hostile to Abaqa Khan, gave his agreement and dispatched Qïpchaq Oghul together with Chabat, the son of Naqu, the son of Güyük Khan, each with an army, to Baraq's assistance. Baraq led forth his army, crossed the river, and encamped near Merv. And when Tübshin, the brother of Abaqa Khan, gave battle, a *tümen* commander called Shechektü, hearing that Qïpchaq had come with Baraq, deserted to Baraq's army and said: "I am Qïpchaq's subject and [have come] to my lord." And he brought fine horses as a present for him. Thereafter Qïpchaq ordered him to bring some horses and present them to Baraq, and Shechektü did so. The next day, in Baraq's *ordo*, Jalayirtai said to Qïpchaq: "Baraq has come with all these thousands of soldiers to wield his sword for thee." "What does that mean," asked Qïpchaq. "What should it mean?" said Jalayirtai. "If Shechektü is thy subject and belongs to thee, why did he not come to thee for so long a time? When, thanks to Baraq, he came here, thou tookest him to thy self and laidst thy hands on the fine horses that were fit for Baraq, whilst ordering him to present to Baraq the horses that were only fit for thee." "Who art thou," said Qïpchaq, "to come between *aqa* and *ini*?" "I am Baraq's servant," replied Jalayirtai, "and not thine for thee to ask me who I am." "When," said Qïpchaq, "has a *qarachu* ever argued with the seed of Chingiz-Khan, for a dog like thee to give me an unmannerly answer?" "If I am a dog," said Jalayirtai, "I am Baraq's, not thine. See to thy own honor and keep to thy place." Qïpchaq was filled with rage. "Dost thou answer me thus?" he said. "I will cut thee in half. Will not my *aqa* Baraq say something to me on thy behalf?" Jalayirtai laid his hand on his knife and said: "If thou attack me I will rip open thy belly." When matters had come to this pass, Baraq said not a word, and Qïpchaq realized that he was on Jalayir-

38 See Glossary and p. 140, note 7.

tai's side. Filled with rage, he came out of Baraq's *ordo* and, having consulted his army, left his own *ordo* below Maruchuq and fled with the army across the river. When Baraq learnt of this, he sent his brothers Yasa'ur and Negübei after him and dispatched Jalayirtai to follow them with three thousand horses, as has been recorded in detail in the appendix to the account of Baraq's branch.[39] Then Chabat too fled and went to Qaidu. In short, Baraq was defeated, and the greater part of his troops were destroyed by the army of Abaqa Khan, while the few that remained were scattered far and wide. Baraq came fleeing to Bukhārā and became ill from chagrin and grief. He set out in a litter to attack Aḥmad Oghul, the son of Mochi Yebe, the son of Chaghatai, who had refused to come to his aid. And he gave the following message to Yasa'ur and sent him to Qaidu: "The princes have failed to render assistance and on that account the armies have been defeated. Weak as I am I am pursuing them. If my *anda* too will help we shall seize and punish them." As has already been related, Qaidu arrested and imprisoned Yasa'ur. Then he advanced with his army, ostensibly to help Baraq [but in reality] to get rid of him entirely now that he was weak. Baraq, having captured and executed Aḥmad's men, repented of having sent for Qaidu. He sent someone to say: "There is no need for my *anda* Qaidu to trouble himself; let him turn back." Qaidu ignored the message and, advancing, encamped in a circle near Baraq's *ordo*. As has been related in the account of Baraq's branch, he died that very night, and Qaidu performed the mourning ceremonies and buried him. The emirs and princes who were in his *ordo* came to Qaidu and kneeling said: "Hitherto Baraq was our ruler, but now Qaidu is our *aqa* and king. We shall serve him in whatever way he commands." Qaidu treated them kindly. He distributed Baraq's goods amongst his troops and carried them off; and [then he] turned back and betook himself to his own *yurt*.

Thereafter Beg-Temür, the eldest son of Baraq, and Chübei and Qaban, the sons of Alghu, rose in rebellion and went to the Qa'an. And Chabat, the grandson of Ögetei, with a group of emirs likewise went to join the Qa'an. Thereafter Mubārak-Shāh, the son of Qara-Hülegü, came to Abaqa Khan and was distinguished with honor and

[39] See above, p. 140.

attention. He was appointed a commander in the army of Negüder[40] in the Ghaznīn region.

After Baraq's death, the rulership of the *ulus* was given to Negübei, the son of Sarban, his cousin.[41] He reigned for 3 years, and then Qaidu gave it to Buqa-Temür, the son of Qadaqai, the seventh son of Chaghatai, who ruled for awhile and then fell sick of alopecia; all his hair and beard fell out, and he died of that disease. Qaidu then gave the rulership of the *ulus* to Du'a, the son of Baraq. He is still reigning today but is sick and weakly, because last year[42] he and Qaidu were wounded in a battle with the army of the Qa'an: Qaidu died of his wound and Du'a was crippled by his, which is incurable.

❧ ACCOUNT OF CHAGHATAI'S MINISTERS, VAZIR[43] and Ḥabash 'Amīd

Chaghatai had two viziers, one called Vazir and the other Ḥabash 'Amīd. The history of Vazir is as follows: He was by origin from Khitai and had been the servant of a Khitayan physician in attendance on Chaghatai. After the death of that physician he became the herdsman of Qushuq Noyan, one of Chaghatai's emirs. It so happened that one day Qushuq Noyan of the Jalayir people, who was an old and experienced man and an authority on past events, was asked by Chaghatai about the history of Chingiz-Khan and which countries he had conquered each year. Not being well informed, he went home and questioned each of his dependants and they were telling him what they knew.

[40] See above, p. 123. Here follows in Verkhovsky a sentence absent from Blochet's text: "And in the year when Abaqa Khan went to the town of Herat to repel the Qaraunas, there came to him the sons of Mubārak-Shāh with all their *ordus*, and they were here [in Persia] until the end." On the whole problem of the Qaraunas, see now Jean Aubin, "L'Ethnogénèse des Qaraunas," *Turcica* I (1970), pp. 65–94.

[41] The relationship is rather more complicated than this, Sarban being the brother of Baraq's grandfather. See Table IV in Appendix.

[42] 1301. See above, p. 142, and *Four Studies*, p. 138.

[43] The resemblance to the Arabo-Persian *vazīr*, "vizier," is coincidental. The word is a Turkish borrowing from the Sanskrit *vajra*, "thunderbolt." The weapon of Indra, it "was early used metaphorically to suggest immutability, permanence, and the like. In late Buddhism, it became the symbol of the absolute." See Lessing, p. 1188, *s.v.* VACIR. Cf. the modern Mongolian *ochir* with the form of the name in Juvainī— HJYR (Hujir in *HWC*, p. 272).

That Khitayan, who was his herdsman, was listening outside the house and demonstrating the truth or falsehood of the various statements in such a manner that it was clear to them all, and they all agreed with what he said. Qushuq called him in and asked him from whence he had acquired this knowledge. He produced a book in which he had recorded day by day all the past events and histories that were now required. Qushuq was pleased and took him to Chaghatai together with the book. Being extremely fond of *biligs* and aphorisms, Chaghatai approved of those words. He asked Qushuq for that Khitayan and made him one of his attendants. Within a short time [the Khitayan] acquired absolute freedom of speech in Chaghatai's service and became honored and famous. Qa'an recognized and approved of his intelligence and, seeing him to be Chaghatai's favorite, gave him the name of Vazir.[44] He was short of stature and of mean appearance, but extremely brave, quick-witted, intelligent, and eloquent, and also a great eater and drinker. His status became such that he sat above most of the emirs and enjoyed greater freedom of speech than anyone in Chaghatai's service, to such an extent that one day, when Chaghatai's wife interrupted him Vazir shouted out: "Thou art a woman and hast no say in this matter." Again, one of Chaghatai's daughters-in-law was accused [of adultery] with a certain person. [Vazir] put her to death without consulting Chaghatai. When [Chaghatai] learnt of this Vazir said: "How is it fitting that a daughter-in-law of thine should commit a blameworthy act and blacken the names of thy other womenfolk?" Chaghatai approved of his action. Now it was the custom in those days to write down day be day every word that the ruler uttered; and for the most part they would make use of rhythmical and obscure language. Everone had appointed one of his courtiers to write down his words. The aforesaid Vazir did this for Chaghatai. Now Qa'an had an Uighur minister called Chingqai, and one day he asked Chaghatai: "Which is better, thy vizier or mine?" "Certainly, Chingqai is better," said Chaghatai. One day, at a feast, they were both reciting *biligs*. Having memorized these, Vazir went outside to write them down. Chaghatai and Qa'an had themselves memorized the *biligs* and had recited them as a test to see whether or not Vazir could write them down exactly [as he had heard them]. Vazir was

44 See above, p. 154, note 43.

busy writing when Möngke Qa'an passed by and spoke to him. "Do not disturb me," said Vazir, "until I have written down what I heard." When he brought it back and they looked at it it was written down exactly [as they had recited it], and he had remembered it all except that some of the words were in the wrong order. Qa'an admitted that Chaghatai was in the right because his vizier was better than his own. As long as Chaghatai lived, Vazir enjoyed such authority in his service.

It is said that during the reign of Ögetei Qa'an Chaghatai wrote a *yarligh* and gave some of the provinces of Transoxiana (which by the command of Qa'an were under the control of Yalavach) to someone else. Yalavach reported the matter to Qa'an and he sent a *yarligh* to Chaghatai rebuking him and ordering him to write an answer. Chaghatai wrote in his reply: "I acted from ignorance and without guidance. I have no answer that I can write, but since Qa'an has ordered me to write I am emboldened to write this much." Qa'an was pleased and accepted this excuse; and he gave that province to Chaghatai as *injü*.[45] Thereafter Yalavach came to visit Chaghatai, who rebuked and abused him. Yalavach said to Vazir: "I should like a word with thee in private." And when they were closeted together he said to Vazir: "I am Qa'an's minister, and Chaghatai cannot put me to death without consulting him. If I complain of thee to Qa'an, he will put thee to death. If thou wilt set matters to rights for me, well and good; otherwise I shall denounce thee to Qa'an. And if thou repeatest these words to Chaghatai I will deny them however much I am questioned, and thou hast no witness." On this account Vazir was forced to put matters to rights. There are many stories about this Vazir of which only a few have been recounted. He had often said to Chaghatai: "For thy sake I have left no man my friend, and when thou art dead none will have pity on me." When Chaghatai died, [Vazir] was put to death on the charge of having poisoned him.

As for the history of Ḥabash 'Amīd it is as follows: He was a Muslim, Chaghatai's *bitikchi*, and by origin from Otrar.[46]

———————[47]

45 See Glossary.

46 Part II seems to break off abruptly at this point. On Ḥabash Amīd, see *HWC*, pp. 272–75.

47 Verkhovsky has here the heading of Part III (cf. above, p. 131, note 131), of which the text would seem never to have been written.

Beginning of the History of Tolui Khan,

the Son of Chingiz-Khan:

History of Tolui Khan,

which is in Three Parts

BEGINNING OF THE HISTORY OF
TOLUI KHAN,
THE SON OF CHINGIZ-KHAN

History of Tolui Khan, which is in three parts

❧ PART I. Account of his lineage; an account of his wives, sons, and grandsons in the branches into which they have divided down to the present day; his portrait; and a genealogical table of his sons, and grandsons except those born of his sons who were rulers, the history of each of whom will be given separately.

❧ PART II. The [general] history of and [particular] episodes in his life, except such as it was necessary to include in the histories of his father and mother of which only a summary is given; a picture of his throne and wives and the princes and emirs on the occasion of his enthronement; an account of the battles he fought, the countries he conquered, and the victories he gained; the length of his reign.

❧ PART III. His praiseworthy character and morals; miscellaneous events and happenings; the excellent parables and *biligs* which he uttered and promulgated and whatever has not been included in the two previous parts, having been ascertained at irregular intervals, from various books and persons.

PART I

OF THE HISTORY OF TOLUI KHAN

Account of his lineage;
an account of his wives, sons, and grandsons
in the branches into which they have divided down to the present day;
his portrait; and a genealogical table of his sons,
and grandsons except those born of his sons who were rulers,
the history of each of whom will be given separately

Tolui Khan was the fourth son of Chingiz-Khan, the youngest of his four chief sons, who were called the four *külüks*,[1] that is, they were like four pillars. His mother was Chingiz-Khan's chief wife, Börte Fujin, who was also the mother of his three older brothers. His title was Yeke-Noyan, or Ulugh-Noyan, that is, the Great Noyan,[2] by which he was best known: Chingiz-Khan used to call him *nöker*. He had no equal in bravery, valor, counsel, and policy. In his childhood his father had asked for the daughter of Jagambo, the brother of Ong-Khan, the ruler of the Kereit peoples, for him in marriage. Her name was Sorqoqtani Beki, and she was Tolui Khan's senior and favorite wife and the mother of his four chief sons, who, just as the four sons of Chingiz-Khan, were like the four pillars of the kingdom. He had other wives and concubines besides her and ten sons in the order enumerated as follows: (1) Möngke Qa'an, (2) Jörike, (3) Qutuqtu, (4) Qubilai Qa'an, (5) Hülegü Khan, (6) Arïq Böke, (7) Böchek, (8) Möge, (9) Sögetei, [and] (10) Sübügetei.

❧ FIRST SON OF TOLUI KHAN—MÖNGKE QA'AN

He was born of Sorqoqtani Beki. As he was a ruler, there will be a separate history devoted to him, and an account of his branch will be given there.

[1] On *külük*, "hero," see *Campagnes*, p. 340, and Doerfer, III, No. 1686 (pp. 653–54).
[2] See Boyle 1956, pp. 146–48, where it is suggested that this title was conferred upon Tolui posthumously to avoid the mention of his real name.

159

SECOND SON OF TOLUI KHAN—JÖRIKE

He was born of a wife called Saruq Khatun. He died young and left no issue.

THIRD SON OF TOLUI KHAN—QUTUQTU

He was born of [Linqum Khatun].[3] He had no son, only one daughter called Kelmish-Aqa, who was married to Saljidai Küregen of the Qonqïrat people. That emir was with the ruler of the *ulus* of Jochi: he died in the year 701/1301–1302. Kelmish-Aqa is still alive there and held in high esteem by Toqta and the other princes. And because she is of the family of Tolui Khan, she is always on friendly terms with the Lord of Islam and constantly sends ambassadors to inform him of the events that occur in that country. And through her efforts, the foundations of friendship have been strengthened between Toqta and the other descendants of Jochi Khan and the descendants of Tolui Khan, and she has put a stop to strife and enmity between them. When Nomoghan, the son of Qubilai Qa'an, was captured by his cousins, united for evil, and dispatched by them to Möngke-Temür, the ruler of the *ulus* of Jochi, Kelmish-Aqa exerted her efforts to secure his restoration to his father with every mark of respect along with certain princes and great emirs, as has been related in detail in the history of Jochi. As for the estrangement between Toqta, the ruler of the *ulus* of Jochi, and Noqai, the son of Tatar, who commanded the army of the right hand of that *ulus* and by whose help Toqta became the ruler, and the battles they fought against each other, it was all due to [Kelmish-Aqa's] husband, Saljidai Küregen, as has been mentioned in the history of Jochi;[4] it ended in Noqai's being killed and his sons' dwindling away.

FOURTH SON OF TOLUI KHAN—QUBILAI QA'AN

He was born of the chief wife, Sorqoqtani Beki. As he was Qa'an, there will be a separate history devoted to him, and the branches of his children will be given there.

[3] The name has been supplied by Blochet from Berezin's text (Khetagurov, p. 138). See also below, Section 7, p. 312 and note 294.

[4] See above, pp. 126–27.

FIFTH SON OF TOLUI KHAN—HÜLEGÜ KHAN

He too was born of the aforesaid chief wife. He was a great king
and the Lord of the Ascendant; and his circumstances were very like
those of his grandfather Chingiz-Khan. And down to the present day
there have been and are great kings of his race in the country of
Persia and other lands. And the cream of that house and the choice
and pick of the pillars thereof is the faith-defending king, Nāṣir
Dīn Allāh Ghazan (*may God cause him to reign forever!*), the monarch
of august glance and auspicious influence, selected from his sons in
particular and all the princes in general.

May the sun of fortune shine forth; may his shadow endure and
he himself live forever!

An account of him and his branch will be given separately in the
history devoted to his reign.

SIXTH SON OF TOLUI KHAN—ARĪQ BŪKE

He too was born of the aforesaid chief wife. Since for some time he
disputed the throne and the Khanate with Qubilai Qa'an, and they
were several times at war and fought battles against each other, his
history has been included in that of Qubilai Qa'an, but the branch of
his sons is given here. He had five sons in the following order: first son,
Yobuqur; second son, Melik-Temür; third son, Qutuqa; Fourth
son, Tamachi; [and] fifth son, Naira'u-Buqa.

SEVENTH SON OF TOLUI KHAN—BÖCHEK

He was born of———[5] Khatun and had many wives and concubines,
by whom he had sons. The one who succeeded him was called Sebilger,
because he had a hundred sons.[6] At the present day they are at the
court of Temür Qa'an, and their names are not properly known:
such as have been ascertained so far are recorded below.

[5] Blank in all the MSS.
[6] Rashīd al-Dīn has evidently confused Sebilger with his son, Ja'utu (see note 7
below), whose name, as read by the historian's informants, means literally "He
who has a hundred."

Sayin-Bugha. He has two sons: Dashman and Ïla'udar.

Ja'utu.[7] He has one son: Töre-Temür.

Tekshi. Nothing is known of his children.

Tübshin. He has four sons: Bültecher, Süt, Bektei, and Boralghï.

༄ EIGHTH SON OF TOLUI KHAN—MÖGE

He had two sons: first son, Chingtüm [and] second son, Ebügen.

༄ NINTH SON OF TOLUI KHAN—SÖGETEI

He was born of ———[8] and had one son called Toq-Temür, who was extremely brave and a very good archer. In battle he rode a grey horse and used to say: "People choose bays and horses of other colors so that blood may not show on them and the enemy not be encouraged. As for me, I choose a grey horse, because just as red is the adornment of women, so the blood of a wound on a rider and his horse, which drips on to the man's clothes and the horse's limbs and can be seen from afar, is the adornment and decoration of men." Because of his great bravery his brain was full of rebellion. When Qubilai Qa'an sent Nomoghan against Qaidu along with [other] princes at the head of the army of Deresü,[9] this Toq-Temür was with them, and it was he who incited the other princes to seize Nomoghan, as shall be related in the history of Qubilai Qa'an.

༄ TENTH SON OF TOLUI KHAN—SÜBÜGETEI

Here is the portrait of Tolui Khan, also the genealogical table of his descendants.[10]

---

[7] His name, in fact, as appears from the *Yüan shih*, was Yaqudu, Ja'utu and Yaqudu being identical in the Uighur script. See *Chapitre CVII*, p. 101.

[8] Blank in the mss.

[9] See above, Section 2, p. 103, note 25.

[10] In the original ms the table is given directly following this sentence.

PART
II
OF THE HISTORY OF TOLUI KHAN

The [general] history of and [particular] episodes in his life
except such as it was necessary to include
in the histories of his father and mother, of which only a summary is given;
a picture of his throne and wives
and the princes and emirs on the occasion of his enthronement;
an account of the battles he fought and the victories he gained;
the length of his reign

HISTORY OF TOLUI KHAN DURING HIS FATHER'S lifetime; his attendance upon the latter, his fighting of battles and conquering of towns

Tolui Khan was for the most part in attendance on his father, and Chingiz-Khan used to consult him on all occasions on matters of general and particular importance, calling him his *nöker*. The *yurt*, *ordos*, property, treasury, *irakhta*,[11] emirs, and private army of Chingiz-Khan all belonged to him, for it has been the custom of the Turks and Mongols from ancient times for [the ruler] during his lifetime to send out his elder sons [into the world] after dividing amongst them his property, herds, flocks, and followers, and what then remains goes to the youngest son, whom they call *otchigin*, that is, the son who is attached to the fire and hearth of the house, referring to the fact that the house is founded thereon. In the original Turkish, the term is composed of *ot*, "fire," and *tegin*, "emir," meaning "emir or lord of the fire."[12] Since *tegin* is difficult to pronounce in the Mongol dialect, they say *otchigin* and some of them *otchi*, but the original and correct form of the expression is as has been stated.

[11] That is, cavalry. See Doerfer, II, No. 638 (pp. 178–81).
[12] This etymology is rejected by Doerfer (I, pp. 156–58).

Chingiz-Khan had thought of setting him upon the path to the Khanate and the throne of kingship and making him his heir-apparent, but he said: "Thou wilt be better off and easier of mind with the administration of my *yurt*, *ordo*, army, and treasury, and in the end, when thou shalt have a large army, thy children will be stronger and more powerful than all the other princes." And, indeed, since he perceived the signs and marks of fortune upon them, it occurred to his mind that in the end the Khanate would be settled upon them, as all have seen [come to pass]. All the armies and commanders of *tümens* and *hazāras*, of the right and left hand, have been enumerated at the end of the history of Chingiz-Khan. From thence it may be ascertained what he gave to the other sons and brothers and which these were; and whatever he did not so distribute all belonged to Tolui Khan. And that army and those emirs still belong, by way of inheritance, to the descendants of Tolui Khan, as one may see with one's own eyes, except such as have, on account of rebellions, been dispersed against their will upon every side under the control of various princes; the remainder are some of them in attendance on the Qa'an and some in the service of the Lord of Islam (*may God cause him to reign forever!*).

Tolui Khan was a great winner of battles, and no prince conquered as many countries as he. A summary will be given of all that occurred during his father's lifetime, and something will be told of what happened afterward. When Chingiz-Khan went to war against the country of Khitai, he came to the town of Tayanfu,[13] which is extremely large. There was a great throng of people within it, strong and powerful, such that none dared approach it. Chingiz-Khan dispatched Tolui Khan along with Chigü Küregen, the son of Alchu Noyan, of the Qonqïrat people, at the head of an army. Giving battle, they mounted the walls and took the town. Afterward he besieged and took the town of Joju[14] and then sent armies to the right and left under his elder sons and the emirs, while he himself with Tolui Khan advanced in the

---

[13] That is, T'ai-yüan (the modern Yangku). See above, Section 3, p. 146 and note 30. Here, however, it is a mistake for Tê-hsing fu, that is, the modern Paonan, south of Suanhwa in northern Shansi, a town captured in the seventh month of 1213, a month earlier than T'ai-yüan; Tolui and Chigü were the first to scale the walls. See Krause, pp. 31 and 32.

[14] Cho-chou, the modern Chohsien, in Hopeh. See above, p. 146 and note 25.

middle, which they call *qol*, up to the town of Bi-Jiu.[15] Every town and country which lay across their path they conquered and laid waste. The plunder of the town of Jing-Din-Fu, which is one of the large towns of Khitai and is called Chaghan-Balghasun[16] by the Mongols, went to Tolui Khan. And the plunder which Tolui Khan obtained from that country and which has been inherited by his descendants in Khitai, the Qïpchaq Steppe and the other lands, is all exactly specified. Such goods and treasures as are still in Khitai and belong to the share of Hülegü Khan and his descendants, the Qa'an has ordered to be registered and kept until they have the means and opportunity to send them.

After they returned from the countries of Khitai, Chingiz-Khan set out for the Tāzīk country. When he came to Otrar, he left Jochi, Chaghatai, and Ögetei to besiege and capture it, while Tolui Khan accompanied him to Bukhārā. They took it and proceeded from thence to Samarqand, which they conquered with all the [neighboring] country. From thence they came to Nakhshab and Tirmidh, and from Temur-Qahalqa,[17] which is in the region of Badakhshān, he sent Tolui Khan to conquer the province of Khurāsān. [Tolui] set out and in the winter captured Merv, Maruchuq, Sarakhs, Nishapur, and all that region within the space of 3 months. In the spring, at the command of Chingiz-Khan, he returned from Nishapur and on the way captured Quhistān and all that region as well as Herat. He joined Chingiz-Khan at Ṭālaqān when he had just taken the castle and was engaged in destroying it. That same summer, together with his brothers Chaghatai and Ögetei, he accompanied his father in pursuit of Sultan Jalāl al-Dīn to the banks of the Indus. They defeated the Sultan's army, and [the Sultan] himself fled across the river. Returning thence they came to their ancient *yurt* and their *ordos*.

---

[15] Probably to be read Pei-Jiu and identified with P'ci, the modern Peichow, in northern Kiangsu, mentioned in the *Yüan shih* (Krause, p. 32) amongst the eleven towns north of the Hwang Ho still uncaptured at the end of 1213.

[16] Polo's Achbaluch, that is, T. Aq-Balïq, which, like the Mongol name, means "White Town." Jing-Din-Fu is Chêng-ting fu (Chengting in Hopeh). See *Polo I*, pp. 8-9.

[17] "Iron Gate." On the name, see above, Section 1, p. 61, note 260. It is here applied, not of course to Darband, but to the pass, some 55 miles south of Shahr-i Sabz in Uzbekistan, known today as the Buzghala Defile.

Afterward, when Chingiz-Khan went to war against the Tangqut country, he left Chaghatai with an army at the rear of the *ordos* to defend them, and Ögetei and Tolui both accompanied him until he was overcome by an illness. As is related in detail in his history,[18] he spoke in private with both sons and, having made his will, sent them back. They returned to their country and dwelling places, and he died on that campaign.

۞ HISTORY OF THE CAREER OF TOLUI KHAN AFTER his father's death; how he became settled in his father's original *yurt* and residence; his concord with his brothers; the battles he fought and the victories he gained; his latter end

Tolui Khan, in obedience to his father's command, returned from the Tangqut country in the company of his brother Ögetei, who by virtue of Chingiz-Khan's testament was the heir-apparent, and came to his dwelling-place and *ordos*. Chingiz-Khan died shortly afterward, and when they had brought his coffin to the *ordos* and performed the mourning ceremonies, the other brothers and princes and everybody else departed to their accustomed *yurts* and Tolui Khan sat firmly upon the throne of kingship in the original *yurt*, where Chingiz-Khan's residence and his great *ordos* were situated.

His concord with his brothers and his battles and victories after
his father's death

After his father's death Tolui Khan rendered such services and showed such attentions to his brothers and the *aqa* and *ini* that they were all of them grateful to him. Most of the time he was in attendance on Ögetei Qa'an and made great efforts to ensure his elevation to the Khanate. When Ögetei Qa'an went to war against Altan-Khan, he made for Namging in the land of Khitai on the banks of the Qara-Mören and sent Tolui Khan by another route. He proceeded by way of Tibet and passed through a province of Khitai, the people of which are called Hulan-Degeleten, that is, the people who wear red

[18] Smirnova, p. 232.

coats. And since the road taken by Qa'an was long, Tolui Khan twisted and turned and traveled slowly until the next year. His men were left without provisions, and things came to such a pass that they ate the flesh of human beings and dead animals, and dry grass. Forming a *jerge*, he came down on to the plain, and at a place which they call Tungqan Qahalqa they came face to face with the main army of Altan-Khan. Tolui Khan, as has been recounted in detail in the history of Qa'an,[19] exerted great efforts so that by excellent strategy he defeated all that great army, which was twice the size of his own; then, finding a ford over the Qara-Mören, which had never been forded before, [he] crossed it and, triumphant and victorious, joined his brother. Qa'an was greatly pleased and delighted at his arrival. He praised his brother, and they feasted and celebrated because of their rejoicing.

His latter end and the cause of his illness and death

After Tolui Khan had returned from the aforesaid war he came to his brother Ögetei. Having been engaged in that campaign for some considerable time, Qa'an had left Toqolqu Cherbi with a great army to finish with Altan-Khan and had returned home. Tolui Khan accompanied his brother. It so happened that Qa'an was overtaken with an illness and, as is their custom, the *qams* had gathered together and exercising their craft had made a spell for his illness and were washing it in water. It was at this juncture that Tolui Khan arrived. In earnest supplication he turned his face toward the heavens and said: "O great and eternal God, if Thou art angry because of sins, my sins are greater than his, and I have killed more men in battle, and carried off their wives and children, and enslaved their mothers and fathers. And if Thou wishest to take Thy servant to Thee because of his fairness of face, elegance of stature, and many accomplishments, then I am more fitting and suitable. Take me instead of Ögetei, and cure him of this sickness, and lay his sickness upon me." He uttered these words with all possible earnestness and, taking the cup of water in which the *qams* had washed the spell for Qa'an's sickness, he drank it down. By divine providence Qa'an recovered, and Tolui Khan, having taken

---

[19] See above, pp. 33–38.

leave, set out earlier [than he had intended] to join his heavy baggage. On the way thither he fell ill and died in the *moghai yïl*, that is, the Year of the Snake, corresponding to the months of the year 630/1232–1233. As for the best of his descendants, the Lord of Islam, Ghazan Khan (*may God cause him to reign forever!*), who is the cream of all the sultans of the world, may God Almighty make him the heir to eternal life and cause him to enjoy for ever and ever a broad kingdom and an ample sultanate, by the grace of the Prophet and his good and pure descendants!

⚜ HISTORY OF TOLUI KHAN'S WIFE, SORQOQTANI Beki, and his sons after his death until the time when they became *qa'ans* and rulers through the efforts and endeavors of their mother and as the result of her ability and intelligence

After the death of Tolui Khan his sons together with their mother were in attendance on Ögetei. He greatly honored and respected them and used to grant their petitions immediately. One day Sorqoqtani Beki asked Qa'an for one of the *ortaqs*. He made difficulties about it, and Sorqoqtani Beki wept and said: "He that was my longing and desire, for whom did he sacrifice himself? For whose sake did he die?" When these words reached Qa'an's ear he said "Sorqoqtani Beki is right." And he begged her pardon and granted her request. She was extremely intelligent and able and towered above all the women in the world, possessing in the fullest measure the qualities of steadfastness, virtue, modesty, and chastity. Thanks to her ability, when her sons were left by their father, some of them still children, she went to great pains in their education, teaching them various accomplishments and good manners and never allowing the slightest sign of strife to appear amongst them. She caused their wives also to have love in their hearts for one another, and by her prudence and counsel [she] cherished and protected her sons, their children and grandchildren, and the great emirs and troops that had been left by Chingiz-Khan and Tolui Khan and were now attached to them. And perceiving her to be extremely intelligent and able, they never swerved a hair's breadth from her command. And just as, when Chingiz-Khan was left an orphan by his father, his mother, Hö'elün Eke, trained him and all the army, sometimes even going into battle herself and equipping and maintaining them until Chingiz-Khan became independent and absolute, and attained to the degree of world-sovereignty, and accomplished great things thanks to his mother's endeavors, so too Sorqoqtani Beki followed the same path in the training of her children. It is said, however, that in one respect she was more long-suffering than the mother of Chingiz-Khan and won the palm from her for constancy. After a time Chingiz-Khan gathered from a cryptic remark of his mother that she wanted a husband and he gave her in marriage to Menglik Echige. [In the same way] Ögetei Qa'an sent for Sorqoqtani Beki to give her in marriage to his son Güyük and sent ———[20] as his ambassador in this affair. When he had delivered Qa'an's *yarligh*, she answered: "How is it possible to alter the terms of the *yarligh*? and yet my thought is only to bring up these children until they reach the stage of manhood and independence, and to try to make them well mannered and not liable to go apart and hate each other so that, perhaps, some great thing may come of their unity." Since she had no mind for Güyük Khan and had rejected that proposal by this excuse, no doubt was left that she did not wish to marry. On this account she was considered superior to Hö'elün Eke, the mother of Chingiz-Khan.

During the reign of Ögetei Qa'an, after Tolui Khan's death, two *hazāras* of Süldüs, part of the army belonging to Tolui Khan and his sons, were given by [Ögetei] to his son Köten on his own authority without consulting the *aqa* and *ini*. The *tümen* and *hazāra* commanders who had been connected with Yeke-Noyan, such as ———,[21] when they learnt of this action, made a joint statement before Sorqoqtani Beki, Möngke Qa'an, and their *aqa* and *ini*, to this effect: "These two *hazāras* of Süldüs troops belong to us by virtue of the *yarligh* of Chingiz-Khan, and now he is giving them to Köten. How can we allow this and in so doing contravene the edict of Chingiz-Khan? We shall make representations to the Qa'an." Sorqoqtani Beki replied: "What you say is true, but we have no shortage of possessions, whether inherited or acquired, and are in no kind of need. The army and we ourselves all belong to the Qa'an: he knows what he is doing, and it is for him to command and for us to submit and obey." And when

---

[20] Blank in all the MSS.   [21] Blank in all the MSS.

Sorqoqtani Beki spoke thus, the commanders were silenced, and all who heard approved.

There is no doubt that it was through her intelligence and ability that she raised the station of her sons above that of their cousins and caused them to attain to the rank of *qa'ans* and emperors. The main reason that her sons became *qa'ans* was as follows. When Ögetei Qa'an died, Töregene Khatun did not allow Shiremün, who by virtue of his will was heir-apparent, to become *qa'an*, but ruled for awhile herself. When she set up her eldest son Güyük Khan as Emperor, Batu, who was the senior of them all, did not attend on the excuse that he was suffering from gout. Güyük Khan was offended at this and in his heart was meditating an act of treachery against Batu. On the pretext that the climate of Emil was good for his sickness, he set out in that direction. Sorqoqtani Beki, learning of his intention, secretly sent a message and warned Batu. Shortly afterward Güyük died, and the sons and kinsmen of Ögetei Qa'an wished to set up Shiremün as Qa'an, but first they sent to summon Batu. He said: "I am suffering from gout. It would be better for them to come to me." Töregene Khatun and the family of Ögetei Qa'an objected to this suggestion saying: "Chingiz-Khan's capital is here: why should we go thither?" Now Batu was old and honored and the eldest of all the princes; and his was the right to nominate a new ruler. Sorqoqtani Beki said to her eldest son Möngke Qa'an: "The others will not go to Batu, and yet he is the senior of them all and is ill. It is for thee to hasten to him as though upon a visit to a sick bed." In obedience to his mother's command he proceeded thither and Batu, in gratitude for this gesture and in consideration of previous obligations, swore allegiance to him and set him up as Qa'an. Now, as has already been mentioned, Sorqoqtani Beki, because of her ability, had not begrudged Köten the Süldüs troops, and he was in consequence on terms of friendship with them. When, therefore, the descendants of Ögetei Qa'an disputed the Khanate with Möngke Qa'an and meditated guile and treachery against him, Köten was in alliance with him and rendered him assistance. And when Köten died, Möngke Qa'an settled the troops that he had with him in the Tangqut country upon his sons, whom he always treated with respect and honor. The same arrangement continues till the present day, and these troops now belong to

Öljeitü Qa'an.[22] These matters will be recounted in detail in the history of Möngke Qa'an, if God Almighty so wills. *Praise be to God, the Lord of the Worlds, and blessings and peace upon our Master Muḥammad and all his holy family!* [23]

[22] That is, Temür Öljeitü (1294–1307), the grandson and successor of Qubilai.

[23] Here, in Verkhovsky, follows the heading of Part III (cf. above, pp. 131 and 156) with a note to the effect that the text is absent from all the MSS.

History of Güyük Khan,

the Son of Ögetei Qa'an, the Son of Chingiz-Khan

HISTORY OF GÜYÜK[1] KHAN,
THE SON OF ÖGETEI QA'AN,
THE SON OF CHINGIZ-KHAN

❧ PART I. An account of Güyük himself and a detailed account of his wives and the branches into which his descendants have divided down to the present time. (Since his genealogical table was included in this history of his father it is omitted here.)

❧ PART II. The [general] history of and [particular] episodes in his reign; a picture of his throne and wives and the princes and emirs on the occasion of his ascending the throne of the Khanate; an account of the battles he fought and the victories he gained; the events leading up to his accession.

❧ PART III. His praiseworthy character and morals; the excellent *biligs*, parables, and pronouncements which he uttered and promulgated; such events and happenings as occurred during his reign and have not been included in Part II, the information having been acquired on separate occasions and at irregular intervals from various books and persons.

[1] Or Küyük. On the name, see *Polo I*, 570.

PART I

OF THE HISTORY OF GÜYÜK KHAN

An account of his lineage;
a detailed account of his wives and the branches into which
his sons and grandsons have divided down to the present day
(As for his genealogical table,
it has been included in that of his father)[2]

Güyük Khan was the eldest son of Ögetei Qa'an, being born of his senior wife Töregene Khatun. He had many wives and concubines, the most senior being Oghul-Qaimish, and three sons, the name of the eldest being Khwāja Oghul and that of the second Naqu, both born of Oghul-Qaimish. Naqu had a son called Chabat. When Baraq crossed the river to make war on Abaqa Khan, Qaidu had sent this Chabat with a thousand horsemen, that were part of his private army, to accompany Baraq as an auxiliary force. He fell out with Baraq and turned back. When he reached Bukhārā he was attacked by Beg-Temür and fled with nine horsemen and went to Qaidu by way of the desert. He became ill with fear and died. Güyük Khan's third son was called Hoqu. He was born of a concubine and had a son called Tökme, who had a son also called Tökme, who is now disputing the kingdom with Chapar, the son of Qaidu, and refuses to obey him. Khwāja Oghul had no known son. The genealogical table of these sons was included in the history of Ögetei Qa'an.[3]

---

[2] See above, pp. 19–20.   [3] See above, p. 20.

PART

II

OF THE HISTORY OF GÜYÜK KHAN

The [general] history of and [particular] episodes in his reign;
a picture of his throne and wives and the princes and emirs
on the occasion of his ascending the throne of the Khanate; an account of
the battles he fought
and the victories he gained

❧ PRELIMINARY HISTORY

When Ögetei Qa'an passed away, his eldest son, Güyük Khan, had not yet returned from the Qïpchaq campaign. Möge Khatun too died shortly afterward, and Töregene Khatun, who was the mother of the eldest sons, making use of all the arts of diplomacy, seized possession of the kingdom by herself without consulting *aqa* and *ini* and wooed the hearts of kinsfolk and emirs with all manner of gifts and presents until they all inclined toward her and came under her control. Meanwhile, Chinqai and the other ministers and viziers of Qa'an continued in office, and the governors on every side remained at their posts. Having been offended by certain persons during Qa'an's reign, and these feelings of resentment [having been] rooted in her heart, she resolved, now that she was absolute ruler, to wreak vengeance upon each of those persons. She had an attendant called Fāṭima, who had been carried off from Meshed at the time of the conquest of Khurāsān. She was extremely shrewd and competent and the confidant of the *khatun* and the repository of her secrets. Great men upon every side used to make her their intermediary in the conduct of important affairs. In consultation with that attendant, Töregene Khatun dismissed emirs and pillars of state who had been appointed to high office during the reign of Qa'an and appointed a crowd of fools in their place. They tried to arrest Chinqai, who was Qa'an's chief vizier, but he learnt of their intention and, fleeing to Köten,

176

took refuge in his protection. Fāṭima had an old grudge against Maḥmūd Yalavach, whom Qa'an had appointed *ṣāḥib-dīvān*. Biding her time, she nominated a man called 'Abd al-Raḥmān in his stead and sent Oqal Qorchi along with him as ambassador to arrest Yalavach and bring him back with his *nökers*. When the ambassadors arrived, Yalavach came in with a cheerful face and performed the ceremonies of honor and respect. For 2 days he detained them with acts of kindness saying, "Today, let us drink a draught and tomorrow we will hear the terms of the *yarlīgh*." But in secret he was preparing for flight. Oqal Qorchi ordered his *nökers* to be arrested and imprisoned. Yalavach instructed them to make an outcry against him and exclaim: "We are informers against Yalavach. For what crime have you arrested and imprisoned us? We have prayed to God for such a day as this." On the third night, Yalavach plied the ambassadors with drink until he had made them completely intoxicated and put them to sleep. Then he fled with a few horsemen to Köten and was secure from their evil. Both he and Chinqai made Köten their asylum and were enveloped in his favor. The next day, when Oqal Qorchi learnt of Yalavach's flight, he released the *nökers* from their bonds and set off in pursuit of Yalavach. When he came to Köten he delivered his mother's edict that Yalavach was to be arrested and brought back. At his heels there came another messenger on the same errand. Köten said: "Tell thy mother: 'The kite that takes refuge in a thicket from the talons of the falcon is safe from its enemy's fury. Since these men have sought refuge with us, to send them back is remote from the rules of chivalry. A *qurïltai* is shortly to be held. I shall bring them thither myself, and their crime can be investigated in the presence of kinsmen and emirs and they can be punished and chastised accordingly.'" She sent messengers several times again, and Köten excused himself in the same manner. And when the Emir Mas'ūd Beg, who was governor of the countries of Turkistān and Transoxiana, observed this state of affairs he too thought it inadvisable to remain in his own territory and saw fit to hasten to the Court of Batu. And Qara Oghul and Orqïna Khatun and some others of Chaghatai's wives had sent Qurbagha Elchi along with the Emir Arghun Aqa into Khurāsān to arrest Körgüz. When the Emir Arghun brought Körgüz and he was put to death, he was sent to Khurāsān as Körgüz's successor.

In that time of interregnum and confusion, everyone sent ambassadors in every direction and broadcast drafts and assignments; and on every side they attached themselves to parties and clung to such protection, each with a different pretext—except only Sorqoqtani Beki and her sons, who kept to the path of the *yasa* and did not swerve a hair's breadth from the great *yosun*. As for Töregene Khatun, she had sent ambassadors to the East and West of the world to summon the princes, the sons of Chaghatai, the emirs of the right and left hand, the sultans, *maliks*, great men, and *ṣadrs* and invite them to the *quriltai*.

Meanwhile, the field was still clear, Güyük Khan not having returned, and Otchigin Noyan, the brother of Chingiz-Khan, thought to seize the throne by force and violence. With this intention he set out for the *ordo* of Qa'an at the head of a large army and with much gear and equipment. On that account the whole army and *ulus* were filled with alarm. Töregene Khatun sent a messenger to say: "We are thy *kelins*[4] and have set our hopes on thee. What is the meaning of thy coming with an army and so much gear and equipment? The whole *ulus* and army have been disturbed." And she sent Otchigin's son *Orutai,[5] who had been in attendance on Qa'an, along with Mengli Oghul, the grandson of ———,[6] at the head of his people and followers to approach him the second time. Otchigin repented of his design and excused himself with the pretense that some disaster had befallen him and he was in mourning. In the meantime, there came tidings of Güyük Khan's arrival at his *ordo* on the bank of the Emil, whereupon his repentance increased and he returned to his own home and *yurt*.

In short, for nearly 3 years the throne of the Khanate was under the control of Töregene Khatun; her writ ran throughout the Empire and she displaced all the great officers because no *quriltai* was held as the princes did not appear and meet together. And when Güyük Khan

---

[4] T. *kelin*, "daughter-in-law."

[5] AWTAY in the Tashkent and Istanbul MSS, the Wo-lu-t'ai (Orutai) of the *Yüan shih* (*Chapitre CVII*, p. 35), according to which he was Temüge-Otchigin's seventh son. He is not mentioned in Juvainī's briefer account of Temüge's rebellion (*HWC*, p. 244).

[6] There is a blank in all the MSS (though not in those of Juvainī). Melik or Mengli was the son of Ögedei and therefore the grandson of Chingiz-Khan. See above, p. 28; also *HWC*, p. 244, note 15.

came to his mother he took no part in affairs of state, and Töregene continued to execute decrees until the Khanate was settled upon her son. Two or three months later Töregene Khatun died.

An 'Alid from Samarqand called Shīra, the cupbearer of Qadaq,[7] hinted that Fāṭima Khatun had bewitched Köten and caused him to be indisposed. When Köten's illness grew worse, he sent a messenger to his brother Güyük Khan to say that he had been attacked by that illness because of Fāṭima's sorcery and that if anything happened to him Güyük should seek retribution from her. Following [on this message] came news of Köten's death. Chinqai, who was again a person of authority, reminded [his master] of that message, and when Güyük Khan ascended the throne, his first act was to hold a trial at which Fāṭima was questioned. She confessed after being beaten and tortured, her lower and upper orifices were sewn up, and she was thrown into the river. Her dependants perished also.

After Güyük Khan's death, 'Alī Khwāja of Emil accused the aforesaid Shīra the 'Alid of the same crime, saying that he was bewitching Khwāja Oghul. He was cased into bonds and because of torture and all manner of unendurable questioning despaired of his life. He confessed to a crime which he had not committed, and he too was flung into the river and his wives and children put to the sword.

After the throne of the Khanate had, in a happy and auspicious hour, been honored with the accession of Möngke Qa'an, he set *Bürilgitei[8] over the region of Besh-Baliq. When Khwāja was brought to him, he sent a messenger to fetch 'Ali Khwāja, who was one of his courtiers. Someone else accused him of the same crime, and Möngke Qa'an ordered him to be beaten from the left and the right until all his limbs were crushed. He died of the pain, and his wives and children were cast into the abasement of slavery.

When thou has done evil, think not thyself secure from calamities for punishment is necessary for [the whole of] Nature.

This was the brief account of Töregene Khatun and her attendant that has been given. We shall now begin and recount in detail the particulars of Güyük Khan's accession, if God Almighty so wills.

---

[7] On Qadaq, see below, p. 188.

[8] On the spelling of the name—Pu-lin-chi-tai (Bürilgidei) in the *Yüan shih*—see *HWC*, p. 246, note 9.

❧ HISTORY OF GÜYÜK KHAN'S ACCESSION TO THE throne of the Khanate

During his lifetime Ögetei Qa'an had chosen his third son, Köchü, who was born of Töregene Khatun, as his heir and successor. He died however, while Qa'an was still living, and since Qa'an loved him more than all his other sons, he brought up [Köchü's] eldest son, Shiremün, who was exceedingly fortunate and intelligent, in his own *ordo* and decreed that he was to be his heir and successor.

In the year in which Qa'an was to bid farewell to this life he had sent messengers to summon Güyük. In compliance with this command Güyük turned back, but before his arrival Fate's inevitable decree was carried out and no opportunity was given for father and son to brighten their eyes with each other's beauty. When Güyük was informed of his father's death, he hurried forward until he reached the Emil. From thence he made for his father's *ordo*; and the hopes of the ambitious were dashed by his arrival.

And when messengers had gone to the ends and corners of the lands near and far, to summon and invite the princes, emirs, sultans, *maliks*, and scribes, each of them set out from his home and country in obedience to the command. And when the spring of the Year of the Horse, falling in Rabī' II[9] of the year 643 [26th September–23rd October, 1245] came round, the princes and emirs of the right and left hand arrived, each with his followers and retainers, and they gathered together in Köke-Na'ur[10]—all except Batu, who was offended with them for some reason and held aloof, excusing himself on the grounds of his feeble condition and an attack of gout. The first to arrive were Sorqoqtani Beki and her sons with all manner of gear and full equipage. From the East came Otchigin with eighty[11] sons, Elchitei, and the other uncles and cousins, and from the *ordo* of Chaghatai Qara-Hülegü, Yesü-Toqa and the other sons, grandsons, and nephews

---

[9] This must be a mistake for Ramaḍān, that is, 20th January–18th February, 1246, the Year of the Horse in question beginning on or about the 27th January of that year.

[10] See above, Section 1, p. 63, note 280.

[11] Perhaps a mistake for *eight*, the number of Temüge-Otchigin's sons according to the *Yüan shih* (*Chapitre CVII*, p. 34).

of Chaghatai. From the *ordo* of Jochi, Batu had sent his brothers
Orda, Shiban, Berke, Berkecher, Tangqut, and Toqa-Temür. And
important *noyans* and great emirs, who had connections with one or
another party, came in attendance on the princes. From Khitai there
came emirs and officials; from Turkistān and Transoxiana the Emir
Mas'ūd accompanied by the grandees of that region; from Khurāsān,
the Emir Arghun with the emirs and notables of that province and
those of 'Irāq, Lūr, Ādharbāijān, and Shīrvān; from Rūm, Sultan
Rukn al-Dīn;[12] from Georgia, the two Davids;[13] from Aleppo, the
brother of the ruler;[14] from Mosul, the envoy of Sultan Badr al-Dīn
Lu'lu';[15] and from the Caliphate of Baghdad, the chief cadi Fakhr
al-Dīn. There came also envoys from the Franks,[16] and from Fārs and
Kirmān; and from 'Alā al-Dīn,[17] the ruler of Alamūt, the governors
of Quhistān Shihāb al-Dīn and Shams al-Dīn. And this assembly
came all of them with such baggage and presents as befitted such a
court. Nearly two thousand tents had been made ready for them, and
in the neighborhood of the *ordo*, because of the multitude of people,
no place was left to alight in, and food and drink fetched a high price
and were unobtainable.

The princes and emirs spoke as follows about the Khanate: "Since
Köten, whom Chingiz-Khan had appointed to be successor to Qa'an,
is somewhat sickly, and Töregene Khatun favors Güyük, and Shiremün,
Qa'an's heir, has not yet reached maturity, it is advisable that we
set up Güyük Khan, who is the eldest son of Qa'an." Now Güyük
Khan was known for his power and authority, and Töregene Khatun
favored him and most of the emirs were in agreement with her. After a
discussion they agreed to set him on the throne. He for his part,
as is the custom, rejected [the honor], recommending each and every
prince [in his stead] and having recourse to the excuse that he was
sickly and indisposed. After the emirs had insisted he said: "I accept

---

[12] Qïlïj-Arslan IV (1257–1265).

[13] David IV, the son of Queen Rusudani, and David V, the illegitimate son of her
brother King Giorgi.

[14] This was the Aiyubid Nāsir Salāḥ al-Dīn Yūsuf, the ruler of Aleppo (1236–
1260) and Damascus (1250–1260).

[15] The Zangid *atabeg* of Mosul (1233–1259).

[16] Apparently a reference to the mission of John de Plano Carpini.

[17] See above, Section 1, p. 49, note 173.

on condition that henceforth the Khanate shall be settled in my family." They all of them made the following written undertaking: "As long as there remains of thy race a piece of flesh such as an ox or dog would not accept wrapped in fat or grass, we shall give the Khanate to no other."[18] Then, the science of the *qams* having been practiced, all the princes took off their hats, loosened their belts, and set him upon the throne of the Khanate, in the *morin yïl*, that is, the Year of the Horse, corresponding to Rabī' II of the year 643 [16th September–13th October, 1245].[19] In accordance with their custom, they took their cups and feasted for a whole week. When they had finished, he presented great quantities of goods to the *khatuns*, princes, and commanders of *tümens*, thousands, hundreds, and tens. Then they began to deal with important affairs of state. First they held a court of inquiry to try Fāṭima Khatun, and then they took up the case of Otchigin, which they examined minutely. And since this examination was a matter of great delicacy and not everyone could be taken into their confidence, Möngke Qa'an and Orda were the examiners and they would admit no one else. When they had completed the enquiry, he was put to death by a group of emirs.

Qara Oghul was the successor of Chaghatai, and Yesü-Mongke, who was his direct son, was not allowed to intervene. And because Güyük Khan had a friendship for the latter he said: "How can a grandson be heir when there is a son?" And he settled Chaghatai's position upon Yesü-Möngke and strengthened his hand in all matters.

After Qa'an's death, every one of the princes had set their hand to actions without number; they had written drafts on the Empire and issued *paizas* to all sorts of persons. Güyük Khan ordered these to be called in, and since they were outside the *yosun* and *yasaq* they were ashamed and hung their heads in confusion. And the *paizas* and

[18] Juvainī mentions neither Güyük's condition of acceptance nor the emirs' undertaking. The latter seems to be a garbled version of the formula which, in *SH* (§255), is placed in the mouth of Genghis Khan: "Und wenn als Ogodais Nachkommen solche Minderwertigen geboren werden, dass das Gras, in das sie gewickelt sind, vom Rinde nicht gefressen und das Fett, in das sie gewickelt sind, vom Hunde nicht gefressen wird, warum dann sollte aus meiner sonstigen Nachkommenschaft nicht ein tüchtiger Knabe geboren werden?" (Haenisch, p. 128).

[19] See above, p. 180, note 9. According to Carpini, who was present in person, the ceremony took place on the feast of St. Bartholomew (24th August) 1246. See Rockhill, p. 22, and Becquet-Hambis, p. 119.

yarlīghs of each of them were taken from them and laid before the author with the words: "*Read thy Book: there needeth none but thyself to make out an account against thee this day.*"[20] [Only] Sorqoqtani Beki and her sons preserved their honor and held their heads high, for they had been guilty of no breach of the *yasa*. In his speeches Güyük used to hold them up as an example to the rest; and he praised them while he held the others lightly.

He confirmed all the *yasas* of his father and gave orders that every *yarlīgh* that had been adorned with the *al-tamgha*[21] of Qa'an should be signed again without reference [to himself].

Thereafter he assigned and dispatched armies in every direction, sending Sübedei Bahadur and Jaghan Noyan[22] with a large army into Khitai and parts of Manzi and assigning Eljigitei[23] with another army to the West. And he commanded that of the Tāzīk armies in Persia two out of every ten men should set out and reduce the rebellious territories, beginning with the Heretics.[24] He himself intended to follow after. And though he had placed all those armies and conquered peoples under the command of Eljigitei, he especially entrusted to him the affairs of Rūm, Georgia and Aleppo, in order that no one else might interfere with them and the rulers of those parts might be answerable to him for their tribute. He put to death 'Abd al-Rahmān, whom Töregene Khatun had sent as governor to Khitai, and gave the countries of Khitai to the Ṣāḥib Yalavach. Turkistān and Transoxiana he transferred to the Emir Mas'ūd, and Khurāsān, 'Irāq, Ādharbāijān, Shīrvān, Lūr, Kirmān, Georgia, and [the region] bordering on India he entrusted to the Emir Arghun Aqa. And to all the emirs and *maliks* that were dependent on each of them he gave *yarlīghs* and *paizas*, and important business was confided to them. He gave the Sultanate of Rūm to Sultan Rukn al-Dīn and deposed his brother.[25] David, the son of Qïz-Malik, he made subject to the other David.

---

[20] Koran, xvii, 15.   [21] See Glossary.

[22] On Jaghan, the commander of Genghis Khan's "chief *hazāra*" and afterward Ögedei's commander-in-chief on the borders of China, see *HWC*, p. 256, note 26.

[23] This was the Elcheltay, "king of the Tartars," who sent an embassy to Louis IX. See *Papauté*, pp. [154]–[155].

[24] That is, the Ismā'īlīs, or Assassins.

[25] For the somewhat complicated details of the rival Sultans' reigns, see *Steppes*, p. 423.

And by the ambassador from Baghdad be sent threats and menaces to the Caliph because of a complaint which Shiremün, the son of Chormaghun, had made about them. So also he ordered a reply to be written in the harshest language to the memorandum brought by the ambassadors from Alamūt. As for Chinqai, he showed favor to him and conferred on him the rank of vizier. And all the great men from every side returned home. *Praise be to God, the Lord of the Worlds!*

HISTORY OF THE END OF GÜYÜK KHAN'S REIGN; his generosity and liberality; his setting out for the Emil; and his passing away in the region of Samarqand[26]

Now Qadaq, who was of the Christian religion, had been, since his childhood, in attendance on Güyük Khan in the capacity of *atabeg*, and his nature was impressed with that picture. To this was afterward added the influence of Chinqai. He therefore always went to great lengths in honoring priests and Christians, and when this was noised abroad, priests set their faces toward his Court from the lands of Syria and Rūm and the Ās and the Orus. And because of the attendance of Qadaq and Chinqai he was prone to denounce the faith of Islam, and the cause of Christians flourished during his reign, and no Muslim dared to raise his voice to them.

Now because Güyük Khan wished the fame of his own generosity to surpass that of his father's, he used to exceed all bounds in his munificence. He commanded that the goods of merchants who had come from all sides should be valued in the same way as had been done in his father's day and their dues paid to them. On one occasion these dues amounted to 70,000 *bālish*, for which drafts had been written upon every land. The wares of every clime were piled up in heaps such that it was difficult to transport them. The pillars of state represented this to him. "It will be a trouble to guard it," he said, "and it will be of no profit to us. Distribute it amongst the soldiers and all present." For days they distributed it and sent it to all the subject peoples; and still much was left. He ordered it to be scrambled for.

[26] See above, Section 2, p. 121, note 95.

That year he wintered in that place, and when the new year came around he said: "The air of the Emil is agreeable to my constitution and the water of that region is beneficial to my ailment." And setting out from thence he proceeded, with the greatest possible awesomeness and majesty, toward the countries of the West. And whenever he came to cultivated land or saw people in the roadway, he would command them to be given enough *bālish* and clothes to free them from the humiliation of poverty. Now Sorqoqtani Beki, being an intelligent woman and extremely shrewd, realized that his haste in that journey was not devoid of guile. She secretly dispatched a courier to Batu to say: "Be prepared, for Güyük Khan has set out for those regions at the head of a large army." Batu was grateful and made ready for battle with him. However, when [Güyük Khan] reached the confines of Samarqand,[27] a week's journey from Besh-Balïq, the predestined hour arrived and did not grant him respite to advance one step beyond that place, and he passed away ————.[28] The length of his reign had been one year. May the Lord of Islam enjoy many years of life, youth, and fortune!

After the death of Güyük Khan, the roads were closed and a *yasaq* was issued to the effect that everyone should halt in whatever place he had reached, whether it was inhabited or desert.[29] And at Oghul-Qaimish's command, Güyük Khan's tomb was transferred to the Emil, where his *ordo* was. Sorqoqtani Beki, as is the custom, offered her words of advice and consolation and sent her clothing and a *boqtaq*.[30] And Batu consoled and comforted her in the like manner and said: "Let Oghul-Qaimish continue, as heretofore, to administer affairs in consultation with Chinqai and the [other] ministers, and let her neglect nothing, for on account of old age, weakness, and gout I am

[27] See above, Section 2, p. 121, note 95.

[28] Blank in Blochet's ms. Güyük died, according to the *Yüan shih*, in the third month (27th March–24th April) of 1248. See *Papauté*, pp. [195]–[196].

[29] Juvainī (*HWC*, p. 262) adds "as is their custom and wont whenever a king dies." Rashīd al-Dīn (Arends, p. 66) records the observance of this practice upon the death of the Il-Khan Hülegü.

[30] The *boghtaq* was the headdress of ladies of rank. It was "extremely tall" and "usually of dark silk, extended on a frame, sewn with pearls and precious stones, with a square top bearing a stone and/or small feathers." The *hennin* worn by noblewomen in medieval Europe is thought to have been derived from travelers' accounts of it. See Cammann, pp. 161–62.

unable to move, and you, the *inis*, are all there; therefore concern yourselves with whatever is necessary." Little was done, however, except for dealings with merchants. Most of the time Oghul-Qaimish was closeted with the *qams*, carrying out their fantasies and absurdities. As for Khwāja and Naqu, they set up two courts in opposition to their mother, so that in one place there were three audience chambers of different rulers. Elsewhere also the princes made dealings and issued orders in accordance with their own wishes. And because of the differences between mother, sons, and the rest, and their divergent counsels and policies, affairs passed out of their control. As for Chinqai, he was perplexed in the conduct of affairs, and no one listened to his words and advice. And of their kinsfolk, Sorqoqtani Beki used to send words of admonishment and counsel, but the sons in their childishness behaved in an arbitrary manner, and with the encouragement of Yesü-Möngke [they] continued to misrule until the Khanate was settled upon Möngke Qa'an and public affairs were strung upon the string of order.

This is the history of Güyük Khan that has been written.

PART
III

OF THE HISTORY OF GÜYÜK KHAN

His praiseworthy character and morals;
the excellent biligs, parables, and pronouncements
which he uttered and promulgated;
such events and happenings as occurred during his reign
and have not been included in the two previous parts,
the information having been acquired
on separate occasions and at irregular intervals
from various books and persons

Güyük Khan was a ruler who was a very heaven of magnificence and regality and a whole ocean of grandeur, being filled with the arrogance of greatness and the haughtiness of pride. When the report of his auspicious accession was published throughout the world, the severity and terror of his justice became so well known that before the armies reached his opponents fear and dread of him had already produced their effect upon the hearts of the froward. Every lord of the marches who heard that report, for fear of Güyük's fury and dread of his ferocity, found rest and repose neither night nor day. And his ministers, favorites, and courtiers were unable to raise one foot in front of the other, nor could they bring any matter to his attention, before he had taken the initiative in speaking of it. And visitors from near and far did not step a span higher than the place where the horses were tethered except such as he sent for. In the days of his reign, emirs, governors, agents, and deputies made their way to his *ordo* from north, south, east, and west, so that at the time of the *quriltai* two thousand tents were made ready for the guests. In the neighborhood of the *ordo* no room was left to alight in, and still great men and nobles were arriving from every side. No one had ever witnessed such an assembly nor has the like been read of in any history.

"Because of the many tents, and men, and pavilions there remained no level place on the plain."[31]

When the Khanate was settled upon him, just as his father Qa'an had upheld the *yasa* of his grandfather and [had] not admitted any change or alteration of his statutes, [so] he too kept the *yasas* and statutes of his own father immune from the contingencies of redundance and deficiency and secure from the corruption of change. And he commanded that every *yarligh* that had been adorned with the august *al-tamgha* of Ögetei Qa'an should be signed again without reference to his own august counsel.

Güyük had by nature a weak constitution, and most of the time he was not free from some kind of illness. Nevertheless, he was, on most days, engaged from morning till evening and from dawn to dusk with the quaffing of cups of wine and the contemplation of peri-faced, sweet-limbed maidens. These habits had the effect of aggravating his malady, but he would not abandon them.

A number of Christians, such as Qadaq, who was his *atabeg*, and Chinqai, who was his minister, had been in attendance on him since the days of his childhood; and physicians also of that religion were in attendance on him. His nature had therefore been impressed therewith, and that picture was left on the page of his bosom "*like a picture carved on stone.*" He went to great lengths in honoring Christians and priests, and when this was noised abroad, priests and monks set their faces toward his Court from all the ends of the world. He was naturally prone to denounce the faith of Muḥammad (*God bless him and give him peace!*). At the time of his reign he was in a melancholic frame of mind and had no inclination for conversation. He had therefore entrusted all the tying and untying and binding and loosing of affairs to Qadaq and Chingqai and made them entirely responsible for good and ill, weal and woe. The cause of the Christians flourished therefore during his reign, and no Muslim dared to raise his voice to them.

In munificence he exceeded all bounds, wishing his fame to surpass his father's, but he was not granted the time.

❧ A BRIEF AND CONCISE HISTORY OF THE EMPERORS of Khitai and Māchīn and the emirs, caliphs, sultans, *maliks*, and

[31] Vullers, p. 474, 1. 652.

atabegs of Persia, Egypt, Syria, and the Maghrib that were contemporary with Töregene Khatun and Güyük Khan from the beginning of the *bars yïl*, that is, the Year of the Panther, falling in Sha'bān of the year 639 [5th February–14th March, 1242], to the end of the *morin yïl*, that is, the Year of the Horse, corresponding to Ramaḍān of the year 643 [21st January–19th February, 1246], a period of 5 years

History of the emperors of Khitai and Māchīn that reigned
during this period of 5 years

The kingdom of Khitai was by this time completely under the control of the family of Chingiz-Khan. The last of their emperors, Shousü by name, was vanquished at the beginning of the reign of Ögetei Qa'an, and the dynasty came to an end. As for the emperor of Māchīn during this period, his name was Lizun, and the length of his reign was as follows:

Lizun. 41 years less 7 years past and 29 years to come, 5 years.[32]

History of the emirs, caliphs, sultans, maliks, and atabegs that
reigned during this period

History of the emirs

The Emir Körgüz, who was the governor of Khurāsān, had quarreled with a member of Chaghatai's family over a sum of money and had uttered harsh words. By virtue of a *yarlïgh* of Ögetei Qa'an, as has been recorded in his history, he was seized, bound, and carried off. When his escort arrived there, Ögetei Qa'an had passed away. They took him to the *ordo* of Ulugh-Ef,[33] where the emirs began to examine him. He said: "If you can decide my case, let me speak. Otherwise it is better to remain silent." On that account his case was held up and he was taken to the *ordo* of Töregene Khatun. Chinqai had fled from here, and Körguz had not paid much attention to the other emirs that were involved, nor had he any money with him to mend his affairs. He was taken to the *ordo* of Chaghatai and, after his guilt had

---

[32] See above, Section 1, p. 42, note 142.
[33] The *ordo* of Chaghatai's successors; in Turkish, "Great House."

been established, was put to death. At the end of his life he had become a Muslim. The Emir Arghun Aqa was sent in his place as governor of Khurāsān, and Sharaf al-Dīn Khwārazmī was made his deputy.[34]

History of the caliphs

At the beginning of this period the 'Abbāsid caliph was al-Mustanṣir bi'llāh.[35] The Mongol army, on Baiju Noyan's[36] orders, was raiding the Baghdad area in small detachments. They laid siege to Irbīl and took it by storm, whereupon the people of the town took refuge in the citadel. They continued to fight fiercely, but when no water was left in the citadel many people perished and, it being impossible to bury them, they were burnt with fire. Having laid waste the town, the Mongols set up their mangonels on the [walls of the] inner town. When the caliph received tidings of this he sent Shams al-Dīn Arslan-Tegin[37] with three thousand horsemen to reinforce them. The Mongols, learning of their approach, left abruptly and fled. The caliph now inquired of the jurisconsults whether the pilgrimage was more excellent than holy war. They issued a joint *fatwā* that holy war was more excellent. He commanded that no one should go on the pilgrimage that year and the jurisconsults and ulema, nobles and commoners, strangers and townsmen, all busied themselves with archery and the handling of weapons. He also ordered the moat and walls of Baghdad to be repaired and mangonels to be set on the walls. The Mongols now returned to attach Irbīl a second time, and the population was filled with alarm. The Emir Arslan-Tegin, with an army in full array, took his stand outside the town, awaiting their arrival. Learning of this the Mongols turned back and made for Daqūq and the dependencies of Baghdad, massacring and pillaging and carrying off prisoners. Sharaf al-Dīn Iqbāl Shārābī,[38] the preacher, urged the people to holy war, and they issued forth [from the town]. Jamāl al-Dīn Qush-

---

[34] For a fuller account of Körgüz, see above, pp. 72–75.

[35] 1226–1242.

[36] On Baiju, who replaced Chormaghun as commander-in-chief of the Mongol forces in western Asia, see *Steppes*, pp. 328 and 420 ff.

[37] One of Mustanṣir's emirs.

[38] Sharaf al-Dīn Iqbāl Shārābī (not Shīrāzī as in Blochet and Verkhovsky), one of Mustanṣir's *mamlūks*, was first his *shārābī* ("butler") and then rose to be his commander-in-chief.

Temür[39] was the commander of the army, and the armies met at Jabal Ḥamrīn. The Caliph Mustanṣir came out of the town of Baghdad and, summoning the nobles and commoners, he addressed the people as follows: "Assailants and enemies of the Faith have attacked our country from every side, and I have nothing to repel them with but this sword. I intend to go into battle against them in person." The *maliks* and emirs exclaimed: "The Caliph must not take the trouble. We, his slaves, will go." And they all went forth and fought with a stout heart, and the Mongols retired in a rout from Jabal Ḥamrīn. The Caliph's Turks and *ghulāms* pursued them, killing many of the Mongols and recovering the prisoners they had taken at Irbīl and Daqūq. And on Friday the 10th Jumādā II, 640 [6th November, 1242], the Commander of the Faithful, al-Mustanṣir bi'llāh, passed away and his son al-Musta'ṣim bi'llāh[40] succeeded him in the Caliphate.

History of the sultans

In Rūm, Sultan 'Izz al-Dīn was in charge of the Sultanate, while his brother Rukn al-Dīn went to the Court of Qa'an. After the accession of Möngke Qa'an, the Sultanate was given to him and his brother was deposed.[41]

In Mosul there reigned Sultan Badr al-Dīn Lu'lu', who was at the zenith of greatness. He sent an ambassador to the Court of the Qa'an, and when Möngke Qa'an ascended the throne he dismissed him with the greatest honor, showing favor to Badr al-Dīn Lu'lu' and sending him a *yarligh* and a *paiza*. During these years Sultan Badr al-Dīn Lu'lu' took Nisibīn.

In Egypt Malik Ṣāliḥ Najm al-Dīn Aiyūb ibn al-Kāmil ibn al 'Ādil[42] was Sultan. He was afflicted with a chronic disease and was always at war with the Franks.

In Kirmān there reigned Sultan Rukn al-Dīn,[43] busy with justice and equity. And no strange happening occurred.

---

[39] It was he who opposed Sultan Jalāl al-Dīn when he approached Baghdad in 1225. See *HWC*, p. 422.

[40] The last of the line, put to death by the Mongols after the sack of Baghdad (February, 1258).

[41] See above, p. 183, note 25.   [42] 1240–1249.

[43] See above, Section 1, p. 68, note 307.

In Sīstān there reigned Malik Shams al-Dīn Kart.[44]

History of the maliks *and* atabcgs

In Māzandarān ———.[45]

In Diyār Bakr and Syria in the year 639/1241–1242, Saiyid Tāj al-Dīn Muḥammad Salāya was appointed governor of Irbīl. In the same year, Baraka Khan,[46] the son of Daulat-Shāh, one of the emirs of Sultan Jalāl al-Din, who commanded what was left of the defeated army of Khwārazm, sought the hand of the daughter of Malik 'Ādil,[47] who was the mother of the ruler of Aleppo.[48] He[49] ordered the messenger to be humiliated, and Baraka Khan gathered his army together and invaded their territory. The army of Aleppo came out and they fought at Manbij. The Khwārazmīs beat the men of Aleppo, massacring, looting, and carrying off prisoners. Then the rulers of Aleppo and Ḥims[50] attacked the Khwārazmīs jointly, and neither side was defeated. In the same year certain Khwārazmīs who had been in Kirmān joined the rest in 'Āna. And Muḥammad, the son of Baraka Khan, came to Baghdad and was enrolled amongst the companions of Mujāhid al-Dīn Ai-Beg the Davāt-Dār.[51] In the year 640/1242–1243 there was again a battle between the Khwārazmīs and the people of Aleppo. The Khwārazmīs were defeated, abandoning their wives, children, horses, and cattle, and the men of Aleppo obtained much booty.[52] In the year 642/1244–1245 a Mongol army again entered

[44] The founder (1245–1278) of the Kart dynasty of Herat.

[45] Blank in the MSS.

[46] According to Nasawī (Houdas, p. 128), Baraka's father (whom he calls Daulat Malik), a maternal uncle of Sultan Ghiyāth al-Dīn, was killed in a battle with the Mongols near Zanjān some time in 1222; and Baraka, then only a young child, made his way to Azerbaijan, where in due course he entered the service of Sultan Jalāi al-Dīn.

[47] The Aiyūbid Sultan of Egypt, al-Malik al-'Ādil II (1238–1240).

[48] Al-Malik al-Nāṣir Ṣalāḥ al-Dīn Yūsuf (1236–1260).

[49] Presumably al-Malik al-Nāṣir. It cannot, as supposed by Verkhovsky (p. 125) be al-Malik al-'Ādil, who had died in the previous year.

[50] The Aiyūbid Sultan of Ḥims was then al-Manṣūr Ibrāhīm (1239–1245).

[51] Actually, the Lesser Davāt-Dār or Vice-Chancellor. He was afterward to play a considerable part in the defense of Baghdad against Hülegü. See below, p. 232; also Boyle 1961, pp. 154 ff.

[52] Rashīd al-Dīn does not mention their sacking of Jerusalem and subsequent defeat of the Crusaders in a battle near Gaza (17th October, 1244).

Diyār Bakr, where they captured Ḥarrān and Ruhā[53] and took Mārdīn by peaceful means. Shihāb al-Dīn Ghāzī[54] fled to Egypt, where he settled and obtained support.

In Fārs there reigned the Atabeg Abū Bakr, who was busy organizing his army.

[53] Edessa, the modern Urfa.

[54] Al-Muẓaffar Shihab al-Dīn Ghāzī, the Aiyūbid ruler of Maiyāfāriqīn (1230–1245).

Beginning of the History of Möngke Qa'an,

the Son of Tolui Khan, the Son of Chingiz-Khan:

History of Möngke Qa'an,

which is in Three Parts

BEGINNING OF THE HISTORY OF MÖNGKE[1] QA'AN,

THE SON OF TOLUI KHAN,
THE SON OF CHINGIZ-KHAN

History of Möngke Qa'an, which is in Three Parts

◆ PART I. An account of his lineage; a detailed account of his wives and of the branches into which his descendants have divided down to the present day; his portrait; and a genealogical table of his descendants.

◆ PART II. The history of his accession; a picture of his wives, the princes, and emirs on the occasion of his ascending the throne of the Khanate; a history of the events of his reign; an account of the battles he fought and the victories he gained.

◆ PART III. His praiseworthy character and morals; the excellent *biligs*, parables, and pronouncements which he uttered and promulgated; such events and happenings as occurred during his reign but have not been included in the two previous parts, the information having been acquired on separate occasions and at irregular intervals from various books and persons.

[1] The native Mongol form of his name. The Turkish form, Mengü, is represented by the Mengu of Carpini and the Mangu of Rubruck.

PART I

OF THE HISTORY OF MÖNGKE QA'AN

An account of his lineage;
a detailed account of his wives and the branches
into which his descendants have divided down to the present day;
his portrait;
and a genealogical table of his descendants

Möngke Qa'an was the eldest son of Tolui Khan, being born of his
senior wife Sorqoqtani Beki, the daughter of Jagambo, the brother of
Ong-Khan, the ruler of the Kereit. He had many wives and concubines,
his senior wife being Qutuqtai Khatun,[2] the daughter of Uladai, the
son of Buqu Küregen, of the Ikires bone,[3] who was the son-in-law
of Chingiz-Khan. By this wife he had two sons, the elder Baltu[4]
and the younger Ürüng-Tash. Ürüng-Tash had two sons, the elder
Sarban and the younger ———.[5] Both died young and had no issue.
Sarban had accompanied Nomoghan on the Deresü campaign.[6] Acting
in concert with Shiregi, he seized Nomoghan and carried him off
to Möngke-Temür, who was the ruler of the *ulus* of Jochi. Shiregi
was taken to Qubilai Qa'an, who sent him to the coast and the hot
region, where he died. By the same wife, Möngke had a daughter called
Bayalun, whom he gave in marriage to Prince Jaqurchin ———,[7]

---

[2] The Cotata Caten of Rubruck.

[3] The Persian *ustukhwān*, a literal translation of the Mongol *yasun*, "bone," in the
sense of "tribal sub-division, clan," and often simply "tribe." On the Ikires, a branch
of the Qonqïrat, see *Campagnes*, pp. 31–32.

[4] From Rubruck's account (Rockhill, p. 189–90), Baltu appears to have been a
Nestorian Christian.

[5] Blank in all the MSS. According to the *Yüan shih*, the second son's name was Öljei.
See *Chapitre CVII*, pp. 109–10.

[6] See below, pp. 267–69.

[7] MRYK in Blochet's text. According to the *Yüan shih* (quoted by Verkhovsky,
p. 127, note 8), his name was Hu-lin, that is, apparently Qurin.

who was the brother of Huludai, Huludai being the maternal grandfather of this daughter. He had another senior wife, called Oghul-
Qoimïsh,[8] of the Oirat bone[9] and of the family of Qutuqa Beki;[10]
she was the sister of Öljei Khatun.[11] This wife was extremely masterful.
She had first of all been betrothed to Tolui Khan and on this account
used to call her husband's brothers Qubilai Qa'an and Hülegü
Khan her children, and they used to be afraid of her. He had no sons
by this wife but two daughters, the elder called Shirin[12] and the
younger Bichqa, who was also called Kö'ünen. He had given Shirin
in marriage to ————,[13] the son of Taiju Küregen. Taiju had married
[Altalun], the youngest daughter [of Chingiz-Khan];[14] he belonged
to the Olqunut bone.[15] When Shirin died, Bichqa too was given in
marriage to the son of Taiju Küregen. He had two chief concubines,
one called Baya'ujin of the Baya'ut[16] people, by whom he had a son
called Shiregi, who had a son called Ulus-Buqa. The reason for his
taking this Baya'ujin was as follows. Her father stole a bowstring from
the armory, and it was found in the leg of his boot. He was to be
put to death for that crime and was brought before [the Qa'an]
along with his daughter. Möngke Qa'an was pleased with her and took
her to him. The other concubine was called Küiteni, of the Eljigin
bone.[17] By her he had one son, Asutai, who joined Arïq Böke and
rebelled against Qubilai Qa'an. Asutai had four sons: the eldest,
Öljei, the second, Hulachu, the third, Hantum, and the fourth,
Öljei-Buqa. These were at the Court of the Qa'an. There is no detailed

---

[8] Rubruck (Rockhill, pp. 172 and 190) describes her as a "Christian lady:" she
was already dead at the time of his visit to the Mongol court.

[9] See above, p. 197, note 3.

[10] The ruler of the Oirat at the time of Genghis Khan. Oghul-Qoimïsh was his
daughter. See Khetagurov, p. 119.

[11] Öljei Khatun, one of the wives of Hülegü, was actually Oghul-Qoimïsh's grand-
niece. See Khetagurov, p. 119.

[12] The Cirina or Cherina of Rubruck, who describes her (Rockhill, p. 172) as "a
very ugly, full-grown girl."

[13] His name was Chochimtai. See Khetagurov, p. 164.

[14] The words in brackets are added in accordance with Khetagurov, p. 164: there
is a blank in all the MSS.

[15] See above, p. 197, note 3.

[16] On the Baya'ut, see Khetagurov, pp. 175–77, and Campagnes, pp. 82 ff.

[17] Apparently a branch of the Qonqïrat.

information about their circumstances. The genealogical table of these sons is as shown.

∿ ACCOUNT OF THE REASON FOR THE TRANSFER OF the Khanate to Möngke Qa'an and the events that led up to his accession to the throne of the Khanate and the Empire

The reason for the transfer of the Khanate to him and the exertions and measures of his mother, Sorqoqtani Beki, by virtue of her ability

When Güyük Khan passed away confusion again found its way into the affairs of the Empire, and matters of state were administered by Oghul-Qaimïsh and the ministers. Previously, when Ögetei Qa'an had gone to war against Khitai and the inevitable disaster had overtaken Tolui Khan, Qa'an was always bemoaning the pain of separation from him, and when he was drunk he used to weep a great deal and say: "I am exceedingly sad because of separation from my brother and for that reason I choose to be drunk, in the hope of quenching the flame a little for awhile." And because of the great concern that he had for his children he commanded that the affairs of the *ulus* and the control of the army should be entrusted to the counsel of his chief wife, Sorqoqtani Beki, who was the most intelligent woman in the world, and that the princes and the army should be under her command. And Sorqoqtani Beki, in the care and supervision of her sons and in the management of their affairs and those of the army and the *ulus*, laid the foundation of such control as no turban-wearer was or could be capable of. Qa'an used to consult her on all affairs of state and would never disregard her advice or suffer any change or alteration of her words. Her dependants were distinguished by her protection, solicitude, and respect, and in no period of unrest did they do anything contrary to the old and new *yasas*. At the time of each Emperor's accession all the princes were put to shame because of their actions, all except Sorqoqtani Beki and her noble sons, and this was because of her great ability, perfect wisdom, and shrewdness and consideration of the latter end of things. And from the time of Tolui Khan's death she had always conciliated her kinsfolk and relations by the bestowing of gifts and presents and by her bounty and favors had rendered troops and strangers her obedient adherents, so that after the death of Güyük Khan most men were of one mind as to the entrusting of the Khanate to her eldest son, Möngke Qa'an. And so she continued to conciliate every side until the time when God Almighty, through the mediation of her experience, laid the bride of kingship in the bosom of Möngke Qa'an. And though she was a follower and devotee of the religion of Jesus she made great efforts to declare the rites of the law of Muṣṭafā and would bestow alms and presents upon imams and shaikhs. And the proof of this statement is that she gave 1,000 silver *bālish* that a *madrasa* might be built in Bukhārā, of which the *shaikh al-Islām* Saif al-Dīn of Bākharz (*may God sanctify his noble spirit!*) was to be administrator and superintendent; and she commanded that villages should be bought, an endowment made, and teachers and students accommodated [in the *madrasa*]. And always she would send alms to all parts and dispense goods to the poor and needy of the Muslims. And she continued to tread this path until Dhu'l-Ḥijja of the year 649 [February–March, 1252], when she passed away. *And God knows best and is most able to decide.*

The events preceding his accession

At the time of Güyük Khan's death Batu was suffering from gout. In his capacity as *aqa* he sent a relay of messengers in every direction to summon his relations and kinsmen, saying: "Let all princes come here, and we shall hold a *quriltai* and set upon the throne someone who is fitting and of whom we approve." But the sons of Ögetei Qa'an, Güyük Khan, and Chaghatai refused, saying: "The original *yurt* and residence of Chingiz-Khan is [the region of] the Onan and Kelüren. We are under no obligation to go to the Qïpchaq Steppe."[18] And Khwāja and Naqu send Qonqurtaqai and Temür Noyan, who was the emir of Qara-Qorum, as their representatives, instructing them to give written undertakings according as the princes agreed, "for Batu," they said, "is the *aqa* of all the princes, and all are subject to his command. We shall in no way deviate from his decision."

[18] According to Juvainī's version, Batu summoned the princes not to his own territory but to a place a week's distance from Qayalïq, the present-day Kopal in southern Kazakhstan. See *HWC*, p. 263 and note 3.

After this Sorqoqtani Beki said to Möngke Qa'an: "As the princes have disobeyed the *aqa* and not gone to him thou must go with thy brothers and pay him a visit." In accordance with his mother's suggestion, Möngke Qa'an set out for the Court of Batu. When he arrived there and Batu perceived upon his brow the signs of maturity and ability, he said: "Of all the princes Möngke Qa'an alone is fitted and qualified for the Khanate, for he has experienced the good and ill of life and tasted the bitter and the sweet of every affair, and on several occasions led armies in various directions, and is distinguished from all by his wisdom and ability; his dignity and honor were and are as great as they can be in the eyes of Ögetei Qa'an and the other princes, the emirs, and the army. Qa'an sent him, his brother Kölgen, and Güyük with me, that is, Batu, Orda, and the family of Jochi against the land of the Qïpchaq and the countries in that region in order to conquer them. And it was Möngke Qa'an who subdued the *Ülirlik[19] and Qïpchaq peoples and the Uruqsaq[20] and Cherkes peoples and captured Bachman, the leader of the Qïpchaqs, Tuqar,[21] the leader of the Cherkes peoples, and Ajis,[22] the leader of the As peoples. He also took the town of *Men-Kermen[23] massacring and pillaging, and reduced it to subjection. Then in the *ut*[24] *yïl*, corresponding to the year 638/1240–1241[25] Qa'an sent a *yarlïgh* that the princes should return, but before they arrived he had already died, having issued a *yarlïgh* that Shiremün, his grandson, was to be heir. Töregene Khatun disobeyed and ignored his ordinance and set up Güyük Khan as Khan. Today it is Möngke Qa'an who is best fitted and most suitable to be ruler. He is of the family of Chingiz-Khan, and what other prince is there who by his penetrating thought and straight-hitting

---

[19] See above, Section 1, p. 58, note 230.

[20] Unidentified.

[21] Not in Verkhovsky. Spelt here *TWQQAS*, but cf. above, p. 60.

[22] Not in Verkhovsky. Above, p. 58, his name is given as Qachir-Ukula.

[23] Reading MN KRMAN for the MR KRMAN of Verkhovsky's text. On Men-Kermen, the Turkish name for Kiev, see above, Section 1, p. 69, note 322. According to the Russian sources, Möngke had at least reconnoitred Kiev. See Vernadsky, p. 52. That he was present at the capture of the town, which fell on the 6th December, 1240, is inconsistent with the statement above (p. 61) that he and Güyük had already set out on the return journey to Mongolia in the autumn of that year.

[24] T. *ud*, "ox."

[25] Actually 1241.

counsel can administer the Empire and the army, except Möngke Qa'an, who is the son of my good uncle, Tolui Khan, who was the youngest son of Chingiz-Khan and held his chief *yurt*? (It is well known that according to the *yasa* and custom the position of the father passes to his youngest son.) Therefore Möngke Qa'an has all the qualifications for kingship."

When Batu had finished this speech he sent messengers to the wives of Chingiz-Khan, the wives and sons of Ögetei Qa'an, the wife of Tolui Khan, Sorqoqtani Beki, and the other princes and emirs of the right and left hand, saying: "Of the princes the only one who has seen with his eyes and heard with his ears the *yasaq* and *yarligh* of Chingiz-Khan is Möngke Qa'an. It is in the interest of the *ulus*, the army, the people, and us princes that we set him up as Qa'an." And he commanded his brothers Orda, Shiban, and Berke and all the descendants of Jochi and, of the princes of the right hand,[26] Qara-Hülegü, a descendant of Chaghatai, to hold an assembly. They feasted for a number of days and then agreed upon raising Möngke Qa'an to the Khanate. Möngke Qa'an refused and would not consent to accept that great office nor to take upon himself that immense charge. And when they pressed him he persisted in his refusal. Thereupon his brother, Möge Oghul, rose to his feet and said: "In this assembly we have all promised and given written undertakings that we shall abide by the command of Sayin-Khan[27] Batu. How can Möngke Qa'an seek to deviate from his advice?" Batu approved his words and praised them; and Möngke Qa'an was convinced. Thereupon Batu rose up, as is the Mongols' custom, and all the princes and *noyans* together loosened their belts and knelt down, while Batu seized a cup and placed the Khanate in its proper place. All present swore allegiance, and it was agreed to hold a great *quriltai* in the new year. With this intention each turned back and departed to his own *yurt* and encampment; and the report of these good tidings was spread abroad.

Then Batu ordered his brothers Berke and Toqa-Temür to accompany Möngke Qa'an with a large army to the Kelüren, which is the residence of Chingiz-Khan, to hold a *quriltai*, at which all of the princes

[26] That is, the West.
[27] See above, Section 2, p. 107, note 46.

should be present, and set him upon the throne of kingship.[28] They set out from Batu—

Glory and fortune on the right and victory and triumph on the left

—and encamped in *jerge*[29] formation.

Sorqoqtani Beki began to win over kinsmen and relations with acts of courtesy and attention and to invite them to the *quriltai*. Certain princes of the family of Qa'an and Güyük Khan as well as Yesü-Möngke and Büri, the descendants of Chaghatai, spoke evasively and postponed [a decision] on this matter on the pretext that the Khanate ought to remain in the family of Qa'an and Güyük Khan. And again and again they sent messengers to Batu to say: "We dissent from this agreement and do not acquiesce in this covenant. The kingship belongs to us. How canst thou give it to another?" Batu replied: "We have planned this with the agreement of *aqa* and *ini*, and this matter is now completed in such a manner that it is impossible to abrogate it. And if the matter were not feasible in this way and if another than Möngke Qa'an were to be nominated, the affairs of the Empire would suffer harm to such an extent that it would be impossible to set things to rights. If the princes ponder over this business and look at it with the glance of farsightedness it will be clear to them that the interests of the sons and grandsons of Qa'an have been respected, for the administration of so vast an empire, which stretches from the East to the West, is beyond the strength of children's arms." Amid such exchanges, the appointed year came to an end and the next year was half over. With each year, affairs of the world and the Empire became more desperate, and because of the great distance between them there was no possibility of mutual consultation. Möngke Qa'an and Sorqoqtani Beki continued to send messages to each of [those princes] and to tread the pathway of consideration and friendliness. But since their admonishments and exhortations produced no effect upon them, they sent message after message to them, now cajoling and now threatening them. They continued to make excuses, [and they] repeated their arguments on every occasion hoping that they might be restrained by kindness and conciliation and aroused from the slumber of pride and negligence.

[28] Juvainī (*HWC*, p. 563) speaks of Berke and Toqa-Temür only as representing Batu at the *quriltai*, not as accompanying Möngke on his return journey.
[29] See above, Section I, p. 36 and note 117.

When that year drew to an end, they had sent messengers in every direction calling upon the princes and their kinsmen to gather together on the Kelüren. They sent Shilemün Bitikchi to Oghul-Qaimish and her sons Khwāja and Naqu, and 'Alam-Dār Bitikchi to Yesü Möngke, with the following message: "Most of the family of Chingiz-Khan have gathered together and the business of the *quriltai* has been delayed until now because of you. There is no more time for excuses and procrastination. If you have a mind to concord and unity you must come to the *quriltai* in order that the affairs of the realm may be dealt with in unanimity." When they realized that they had no alternative, Naqu Oghul set out, as did also Qadaq Noyan and some of the emirs of Güyük Khan's Court. Yesün-To'a, too, the grandson of Chaghatai, set out from his place of residence and went with them to Shiremün; and all three gathered together in one place. Then Khwāja also started out, all of them still imagining that the business of the *quriltai* could not proceed without them. Berke now sent the following message to Batu: "For 2 years we have been waiting to set Möngke Qa'an on the throne, and the sons of Ögetei Qa'an and Güyük Khan and Yesü-Möngke, the son of Chaghatai, have not come." Batu sent this reply: "Set him on the throne. Whoever turns against the *yasa*, let him lose his head."[30]

All the princes and emirs that were with Möngke Qa'an—such as Berke; Harqasun, one of the great emirs; Yekü and Yesüngge, the sons of Jochi-Qasar;[31] Elchitei, the son of Qachi'un; Taghachar, the son of Otchi Noyan;[32] and the sons of Bilgütei,[33] all of them nephews of Chingiz-Khan, representing the princes of the left hand;[34] and Qara-Hülegü,[35] the son of Chaghatai; Qadan, the son, and Möngedü, the grandson of Ögetei Qa'an;[36] and Hülegü Khan, Qubilai Qa'an, Möge and Arïq Böke, the brothers of Möngke Qa'an, representing

[30] This exchange of messages between Berke and Batu is not mentioned by Juvainī.
[31] They are not mentioned by Juvainī as being present.
[32] Juvainī (*HWC*, p. 568) speaks only of the "sons of Otegin." According to the *Yüan shih* (*Chapitre CVII*, pp. 35 and 38, note 11), Taghachar was Temüge-Otchigin's grandson.
[33] Not mentioned by Juvainī.   [34] That is, the East.
[35] Rashīd al-Dīn repeats below, p. 207, Juvainī's statement (*HWC*, p. 573) that Qara-Hülegü and Qadan arrived *after* the enthronement ceremony.
[36] Juvainī speaks of the sons of Köten (of whom Möngedü was one); also the sons of Kölgen, who, according to the *Yüan shih* (*Chapitre CVII*, p. 64), had only one.

the princes of the right hand—now gathered together, and the astrologers selected an auspicious horoscope. It was one of the indications of his increasing fortune that in those few days the atmosphere of those regions had been covered with a veil of clouds, and there was constant rain, and no one could see the face of the sun. It so happened that at the hour selected by the astrologers when they wished to observe the heavens, the world-illuminating sun suddenly appeared from behind the clouds and the sky was sufficiently cleared to reveal its disc, so that the astrologers were able to take the altitude with ease. All those present—the aforementioned princes, the great and important emirs, the leaders of every people, and troops beyond measure—took off their hats, slung their belts over their shoulders and, it being the *qaqa yil*, that is, the Year of the Pig, falling in Dhu'l-Ḥijja of the year 648 [February–March, 1251],[37] set Möngke Qa'an upon the throne of command and the seat of kingship in the neighborhood of Qara-Qorum, which is the residence of Chingiz-Khan. And the emirs and troops outside the *ordo* knelt nine times together with the princes

At the time of his auspicious accession they had given thought to how they should make a *yasaq* to define the order of precedence. It was decided that Berke, on account of his gout, should sit where he was, that Qubilai should sit beneath him, and that all should attend to Qubilai's words. He ordered Möngke to stand at the door so that he could prevent the princes and emirs [from entering], and Hülegü to stand in front of the *ba'urchis* and *qorchis*, so that none should speak or listen to unconsidered words. It was arranged in this fashion, and both of them walked to and fro until the business of the *quriltai* had been settled.[38]

And when he was auspiciously seated on the throne of the Empire, he desired in his great and perfect magnanimity that on that occasion some ease should be enjoyed by every species and variety [of creature]. He therefore made a *yasa* that on that fortunate day no man should tread the path of strife and contention but should enjoy himself and make merry. And just as the human species was receiving its due of life in all manner of enjoyment and self-indulgence, so too every kind

[37] According to Juvainī (*HWC*, p. 567), the ceremony took place on the 1st July, 1251.

[38] These details are not given by Juvainī.

205

of living creature and every variety of inorganic matter should not go without their share, and therefore those domesticated animals used for riding or as beasts of burden should not be subjected to the discomfort of loads, chains, and hobbles, while as for those that may be eaten as food in accordance with the just Sharī'at, their blood should not be shed. And as for the wild creatures that fly or graze, on land and in the water, they should be secure from the arrows and snares of hunters and beat their wings to their heart's content in the gardens of safety. So too the surface of the earth should not be made to suffer the pain caused by tent-pegs and the headache induced by horses' hoofs; and running water should not be polluted by the discharge of impurities. Praise God for a being whom the Almighty makes the source of compassion and the meeting place of all kinds of equity to such an extent that he desires the comfort of all living creatures and inorganic matter! What limit can there be to the concern of his august mind for improving the lot of the weak and spreading justice and mercy among nobles and commoners? May God Almighty grant his illustrious family the enjoyment and pleasure of empire and fortune for long years and into distant ages, by His grace and favor![39]

In this manner they passed that day till nightfall. The next day they feasted in the tent which Ṣāḥib Yalavach had provided, made of nasīj[40] and gold-embroidered cloths in various colors such that no one before had pitched such a tent or constructed such a pavilion. And as the picture shows, the World Emperor was seated upon a throne, the princes, like the necklace of the Pleiades, gathered on his right, his seven illustrious brothers[41] standing on the feet of courtesy at his service, and his wives, like black-eyed houris, seated upon his left. And silver-limbed cupbearers circulated cups of koumiss and wine in ewers and goblets. Among the noyans there stood, slave-like, in the

[39] The account of this curious truce with Nature is taken from Juvainī (*HWC*, pp. 569–70). Cf. the story of Ögedei's releasing a captured wolf (above, pp. 92–93, *HWC*, p. 231). Cf. too the T. *ïdhuq*, "holy, sacred," of which the basic meaning is "released." "This name," says Kāshgharī(I, p. 65), "is given to an animal that has been set free. No load may be placed on such an animal and it may not be milked or shorn; it is spared because of a vow that its master has made."

[40] See Glossary.

[41] Qubilai, Hülegü, Arïq Böke, Möge, Böchek, Sögetei, and Sübügetei (Sübetei). See *HWC*, p. 571 and note 60.

station of the *qorchis*,[42] their leader Mengeser,[43] and the *bitikchis*, viziers, chamberlains, and ministers, with their leader Bulgha Aqa,[44] were drawn up in rows in their proper station, while the other emirs and retinue stood on the feet of courtesy outside the pavilion.

For a whole week they feasted and revelled in this fashion, and the daily ration of drink and food was two thousand wagon-loads of wine and koumiss, three hundred horses and oxen, and three thousand sheep. And since Berke was present, they were all slaughtered in accordance with the lawful ritual.[45]

In the midst of all this feasting, there arrived Qadan Oghul, his brother Melik Oghul, and Qara-Hülegü.[46] In accordance with their usual custom they performed the ceremonies of congratulations and joined in the revelry and merrymaking.

꘡ HISTORY OF HOW CERTAIN PRINCES OF THE family of Ögetei Qa'an meditated guile and treachery against Möngke Qa'an; how their plot was discovered by *Kesege*[47] Qushchi; how he brought the news; and how they were arrested

They were still awaiting the arrival of the other princes and continued to be excessive in their joy and revelry. None of them dreamt that the ancient *yasa* of Chingiz-Khan could be changed or altered and there had been no kind of quarrel or disagreement amongst his family. In their revelry, therefore, they had neglected to exercise precaution.

Meanwhile, Shiremün and Naqu, the grandsons of Ögetei Qa'an, and Totoq,[48] the son of Qarachar, having reached agreement among

[42] See Glossary.

[43] On Mengeser, the "great *yarghuchï*," or Grand Judge, see below, pp. 209 and 211; also *Campagnes*, pp. 368–69.

[44] Rubruck's Bulgai, "the grand secretary of the court," a Nestorian Christian.

[45] Berke being a convert to Islam. For a theory that he was the son of a Khwārazmī princess, the sister of Sultan Jalāl al-Dīn, see Richard 1967.

[46] See above, p. 204 and note 35.

[47] Verkhovsky's text has KSK and Blochet's KŠK. In *HWC*, p. 574 and note 75, I took the name to be identical with Mo. *kesig* (*keshig*), "guard." I now read *KSKH in accordance with the K'o-hsieh-chieh, that is, Kesege ("The Warner") of the *Yüan shih*. See Cleaves 1962–1963, p. 73 and note 65.

[48] He too was a grandson of Ögedei. See above, p. 22, where he is called Totaq. See also *Chapitre CVII*, p. 78. Juvainī does not mention his participation in the plot.

themselves, had drawn near with many wagons full of arms and meditating guile and treachery in their hearts. All of a sudden, by a lucky chance indicative of fortune, a falconer called *Kesege of the Qanqlï bone, one of Möngke Qa'an's *qushchïs*,[49] lost a camel. He was wandering about in search of it when he stumbled into the middle of Shiremün's and Naqu's forces. He beheld a great army and wagons without number heavily loaded, allegedly, with food and drink for a feast of congratulation. Ignorant of the secret purpose of all this, *Kesege continued to search for his stray camel. As he moved about he came upon a young lad seated beside a broken wagon. The lad, thinking he was one of their horsemen, asked for his assistance in mending the wagon. *Kesege dismounted in order to help him, and his glance fell upon the weapons and warlike equipment which they had stacked in the wagon. He asked the lad what the load was. "Arms," replied the lad, "the same as in the other wagons." *Kesege realized that their coming with wagons filled with arms was not devoid of guile and treachery, but he feigned indifference. When he had finished helping he entered a tent and became a guest; and having established friendly relations [with his host] he gradually discovered how matters lay. When he was apprised of the truth and knew for certain that the thoughts of these people were full of guile and hypocrisy and that they intended, in the course of the auspicious feast, when all were drunk, to step aside from the highway of decency and, stretching out the hand of oppression, to put into effect what they had planned ("*But the plotting of evil shall only enmesh those who make use of it*"),[50] *Kesege let go the reins of free will, bade farewell to his camel, and traveled 3 days' journey in one. All of a sudden, without permission and without fear, he entered the audience chamber and began to speak with a stout heart. "You are engaged," he said, "in sport and pleasure, and your enemies have risen against you, having bided their time and prepared the tools of war." And he related to them, by word of mouth, all that he had seen and urged them to deal with the situation with the utmost speed. But since the like machinations were unknown in the customs of Mongols, especially in the age of Chingiz-Khan and his family, they were quite unable to believe him. Again and again they

[49] That is, falconers.
[50] Koran, xxv, 41.

questioned him and he repeated what he had said without any varia-
tion. His words took no root in Möngke Qa'an's ear and he paid no
attention to them. *Kesege continued to speak with great urgency,
and it could be seen that he was distressed and anxious, but Möngke
Qa'an remained calm and self-possessed. The princes and *noyans*
who were present cried out against this firmness fearing lest it might
lead to some misfortune. And before the opportunity had passed each
of the princes wished to set his foot in the road of dealing with that
affair and go and investigate in person. In the end, they agreed that the
Emir Mengeser Noyan, who was the leader of the emirs of Court,
should go on in advance and investigate the matter. Following his
instructions he mounted horse with some two or three thousand men
and at dawn drew near to their encampment. With five hundred
brave horsemen he rode forward and approached their tents, while
the armies came up on either side. Previously, Shiremün had left his
army and heavy baggage in *Maski[51] and he was now advancing at
the head of five hundred horsemen. In Sari-Keher[52] the aforesaid
Emir Mengeser, Prince Moge, who was in command of the army,
and Choqbal Küregen[53] of the Kereit bone, with their armies had
surrounded Shiremün, Naqu, Totoq, and the other princes that were
with them. They then sent a messenger to them to say: "A tale has
been told concerning you and it has been brought to the Qa'an's
august ear that you are coming with evil intent. If those words are
false the proof thereof will be for you to present yourself without
hesitation at Court. Otherwise we are commanded to arrest you and
take you thither. Which do you choose of these two alternatives?"
When they heard this message, being like the point in the middle of
the circle and their friends and following far away, they were exceedingly perplexed and bewildered. Of necessity they resigned themselves to fate and, denying the accusation, said: "We are coming with

[51] Or *Baski. Unidentified.

[52] The Sa'ari-Ke'er of *SH*, which Pelliot (*Campagnes*, p. 26) interprets as meaning
"valley covered with rounded hillocks." He locates it (*Campagnes*, p. 27) to the west
of the southern part of the great bend of the Kerulen, "là où il y a les deux lacs
Qala'atu-nōr ('Lac Profond'), déjà connus sous ce nom à l'époque mongole." See
also *Polo I*, pp. 319 ff. Neither Sari-Keher nor *Maski/*Baski is mentioned by Juvainī.

[53] Juvainī (*HWC*, p. 578) makes no mention of Möge and the imperial son-in-law
(*küregen*) Choqbal as accompanying Mengeser.

good intent." And on the understanding that they should accompany each other to Möngke Qa'an, the aforesaid emirs went to Shiremün and the princes and held cups for one another. Then, accompanied only by a small number of horsemen, they set out for the Court of the Qa'an. When they drew near, the greater part of their *nökers* were detained and their arms taken from them. And it was commanded that some of the emirs who had accompanied the princes should stand outside. They were all detained, and then having made obeisance nine at a time they entered the *ordo*. For 3 days they feasted and no questions were asked of them. On the fourth day, when they came to the audience chamber and tried to enter, a messenger from Möngke Qa'an arrived and said: "Stay for today." And at once another messenger arrived and said: "Let every *nöker* and soldier that was with them go back to his own unit of a thousand, a hundred, or ten. If they remain here they will be put to death." In accordance with this command, they all went back and the princes were left alone, and a soldier was appointed to guard them.[54]

◆ HISTORY OF HOW MÖNGKE QA'AN WAS PRESENT in the *ordo* of Chingiz-Khan and tried the princes in person

The next day Möngke Qa'an went to the *ordo* of Chingiz-Khan, sat upon a chair, and tried Shiremün and the [other] princes in person. He questioned them in the following terms: "This is what has been related concerning you. Although it is incredible and inconceivable and cannot be heard or accepted by the ear of reason, nevertheless it is necessary and essential that this matter be examined and investigated in an open and friendly manner in order that the countenance may be cleansed of the dust of doubt and uncertainty. If this be nought but calumniation and slander, the liar and slanderer will receive his punishment so that it may be a warning to all mankind." The princes denied their guilt, saying that they had no knowledge of this matter. Then Möngke Qa'an ordered Shiremün's *atabeg*, *Qata-Kürin[55] by

[54] The account of the princes' detention is told here with rather more detail than in Juvainī (*HWC*, p. 579).

[55] The corrupt name is undoubtedly to be identified with the *Qata-Kürin of Juvainī and the Ho-ta Ch'ü-lin, that is, Qada-Kürin of the *Yüan shih*. In both sources

name, to be questioned with the bastinado, whereupon he confessed and said: "The princes knew nothing. We, the emirs, plotted and conspired, but the fortune of Möngke Qa'an foiled our scheme." And he struck himself with his sword and so died.

◈ HISTORY OF HOW MENGESER NOYAN EXAMINED the case of the emirs who had plotted treason along with the princes

The next day he ordered the detention of the group of *noyans* and emirs, men such as Elchitei the great *noyan*, Taunal, Jangi, Qankhitai, Sorghan, Taunal the Younger, Toghan, and Yasa'ur,[56] each of whom regarded himself as of such rank that the highest heaven had no power over him, and also a number of other *tümen* commanders and leaders, whom it would take too long to name. And he commanded the Emir Mengeser, the *yarghuchï*,[57] to sit and hold an inquiry along with a number of other emirs. They began their questioning and continued the trial for several days. They put the questions in an extremely subtle manner, so that in the end the contradictions in their words became apparent, no doubt remained as to their conspiracy, and they all together confessed and admitted their guilt, saying: "We had made such a conspiracy and plotted treason." Möngke Qa'an, following his laudable custom, wished to accord them the honor of pardon and forgiveness, but the *noyans* and emirs said: "To neglect and delay removal of an enemy when the opportunity presents itself is remote from the highway of rectitude.

Wherever thou oughtest to make a scar, when thou puttest a salve thereon, it availeth not.[58]

Realizing that their words were spoken out of sincerity and not from motives of self-interest or hypocrisy, he ordered them all to be bound and imprisoned, and for awhile he reflected about their fate.

---

he is included in the list of *noyans* detained and tried for their part in the conspiracy. See *HWC*, p. 580 and note 88. Juvainī too (*HWC*, p. 583) mentions Qada-Kürin's committing a kind of *hara-kiri*.

[56] These are the names given in Juvainī (*HWC*, p. 580) minus Qada-Kürin, whose name has however been arbitrarily inserted by Blochet (p. 293) on the basis of MSS of Juvainī.　　　　　　　　　　　　[57] See Glossary.

[58] According to Muḥammad Qazvīnī, a *bait* from the *Ḥadīqa* of Sanā'ī.

One day when he was seated in his Court on the throne of empire and sovereignty, he ordered each of the emirs and pillars of state to recite a *bilig* about the guilty men based upon what he had seen. Each of them said something within the limits of his understanding and to the extent of his knowledge, but none of this took root in his heart. Maḥmūd Yalavach was standing at the far end of the assembly. Said Möngke Qa'an: "Why does not this *ebügen*[59] say something?" They said to Yalavach: "Come forward and speak." He replied: "In the presence of kings it is better to be an ear than a tongue. However I remember one story which I will relate if I am so commanded." "Speak," said Möngke Qa'an. Yalavach related as follows: "When Alexander had conquered most of the countries of the world he wished to go to India, but his emirs and chief men set foot outside the high-way of obedience and loyalty and each of them breathed the breath of despotism and autocracy. Alexander was at a loss and sent a messenger to Rūm to Aristotle, his peerless vizier, to tell him of the refractoriness and arrogance of his emirs and to ask what measures he should take to deal with them. Aristotle went into a garden with the messenger and ordered the trees with large roots to be dug out and small, frail sap-lings to be planted in their stead. He gave no reply to the messenger, and when the latter grew tired [of waiting] he returned to Alexander and said: 'He gave me no answer.' 'What didst thou see him do?' asked Alexander. 'He went into a garden,' said the messenger, 'and pulled out the large trees and planted small branches in their stead.' 'He gave his answer' said Alexander, 'but thou didst not understand.' And he destroyed the despotic emirs who had been all-powerful and set up their sons in their stead."

Möngke Qa'an was extremely pleased with this story[60] and realized that these people must be done away with and others maintained in their place. He ordered the emirs that were imprisoned and those who had incited the princes to rebellion and cast them into the gulf of so great a crime to be put to the sword of public execution. There were seventy-seven persons, all of whom were put to death. Amongst them were two sons of Eljigitei, whose mouths were stuffed with stone

[59] Mo. *ebügen*, "old man."
[60] The story (not in Juvainī) is taken from the Muslim version of the Alexander Romance. See Budge, pp. xlix, 366–67 and 393–94.

until they died. As for their father, he was arrested in Bādghīs and taken to Batu to join his sons.[61]

❧ HISTORY OF THE ARRIVAL OF YESÜN-TO'A, THE grandson of Chaghatai, his wife Toqashi, and Büri, and what befell them

Yesün-To'a, his wife Toqashi, and Büri now arrived also, having left their troops in the road and coming themselves with [only] thirty horsemen. He sent Büri in the company of ambassadors to Batu, who put him to death after establishing his guilt. Toqashi Khatun was tried by Qara-Hülegü in the presence of Yesün-To'a. He ordered her limbs to be kicked to a pulp and so relieved his bosom filled with an ancient grudge.

At the time when Shiremün and Naqu set out, Qadaq realized that he was the instigator of that rebellion, that it was he who had stirred up the dust of that estrangement, and that it was not in his power to make amends; and he therefore held back. Suddenly the agents of the Court arrived like so many angels of death and said:

> All thy friends have gone; now 'tis thy turn.

He pretended to be ill and so they set him on a wagon and brought him thus. When he reached the Court, although his guilt was clearer and more notorious than the infidelity of Iblīs, nevertheless orders were given that he should be tried, and after he had confessed and admitted to his crime orders were given that he should be dispatched after his friends. Praise be to God and blessings and peace upon our Lord Muḥammad and all his good and holy family!

❧ HISTORY OF HOW MÖNGKE QA'AN SENT FOR Oghul-Qaimish and Khwāja, the son of Güyük; how Oghul-Qaimish was put to death; how he punished the *idi-qut*

Since some of the guilty men had not yet arrived and men's minds had not been cleansed of their wickedness, Möngke Qa'an sent

---

[61] See *HWC*, p. 590: Juvainī does not mention Eljigitei's sons.

*Bürilgitei[62] Noyan with an army consisting of 10 *tümens* of valorous Turks to the frontiers of Ulugh-Taq,[63] *Qanghai,[64] and *Qum-Sengir,[65] which lies between Besh-Balïq and Qara-Qorum, so that from thence his *nerge*[66] might join the *nerge* of Qonquran[67] Oghul, who was in the region of Qayalïq, and whose *nerge* stretched to the confines of Otrar. And he sent Möge Noyan[68] to the frontier of the Qïrqïz and the Kem-Kemchi'üt[69] with 2 *tümens* of troops. And to Oghul-Qaimish and Khwāja, who had not yet arrived, he sent Shilemün Bitikchi with the following message: "If you had no share with these men in this conspiracy it is essential for your happiness that you hasten to Court." When Shilemün had delivered his message, Khwāja Oghul was about to commit an abominable act upon him. But one of his wives, lower in rank than the rest but superior in wisdom and intelligence, prevented his intention and said: "It is the messenger's duty to deliver his message, and in no age have men molested the messengers [even] of rebels. How then can one make an attack upon an ambassador who has come from Möngke Qa'an? And by the killing of one person what harm can be done to his kingdom, especially as many evils will spring therefrom? A sea of unrest and commotion will rage; the peaceful world will be set in confusion; the flame of calamity will flare up; and then repentance will be of no avail. Möngke Qa'an is the *aqa* and in the position of a father. We must go to him and obey his command." Khwāja listened to her loving advice with the ear of consent and showed honor and respect to Shilemün. He set out for Court accompanied by his wife, and by his good fortune in hearkening to advice he did not fall into the whirlpool of endless troubles but alighted in the courtyard of security.

[62] The Pu-lin-chi-tai of the *Yüan shih*. See *HWC*, p. 246, note 9.

[63] The "Great Mountain," in the region of the present-day Kobdo.

[64] The Khangai mountain range. See *HWC*, p. 585, note 107 and p. 609, note 9.

[65] See above, Section 2, p. 121, note 95.

[66] On *nerge*, a variant form of *jerge*, see Doerfer, I, p. 293.

[67] This is the spelling of the name in Juvainī. Qonqïran was the fourth son of Orda. See *HWC*, p. 585 and note 109; also above, p. 105.

[68] Juvainī (*HWC*, p. 585) has Yeke Noyan.

[69] The country (strictly speaking, the *people*) between the Kem (the Upper Yenisei) and its left-bank affluent, the Kemchik. This was the region then inhabited by the Qïrqïz (Kirghiz) Turks. See *HWC*, p. 585, note 110, *Campagnes*, p. 317, Khetagurov, pp. 150–51, and Hambis 1956.

As for Oghul-Qaimish, Khwāja's mother, she sent back the messenger saying: "You princes promised and gave a written undertaking that the kingship would always remain in the family of Ögetei Qa'an and you would not rebel against his descendants. And how you have not kept your word." When this message was delivered Möngke Qa'an was exceedingly angry and wrote the following *yarligh*: "The wives of Jochi-Qasar, Otchigin, and Bilgütei Noyan, who were the brothers of Chingiz-Khan, attended the counsel for the *quriltai*, but Oghul-Qaimish did not. If the *qams* and Qadaq, Chinqai, and Bala,[70] who were the emirs of the *ordo* of Güyük Khan, should call or proclaim any one ruler or *khatun* and that person becomes ruler or *khatun* because of their words, they shall see what they shall see." And at once he sent a messenger to seize and bring her with her hands stitched together in raw hide. When she arrived she was sent with Qadaqach, the mother of Shiremün, to the *ordo* of Sorqoqtani Beki. Mengeser Yarghuchi stripped her naked, dragged her into court, and began to question her. She said: "How can others see a body which has been seen by none but a king?" Her guilt having been ascertained she was wrapped in felt and flung into the river.[71] Chinqai too arrived, and he was dealt with by Dānishmand Ḥājib in Ramaḍān of the year 650 [November–December, 1252].

In Besh-Balïq the *idï-qut*,[72] who was the leader of the idolaters, arranged with certain people to rise up on a Friday, when the Muslims were gathered together in the Friday mosque, and kill them all inside the mosque. A slave amongst them, who was informed of their plan, confessed Islam and, turning informer against them, demonstrated their guilt of this crime. The *idï-qut* was brought to the *ordo* and put on trial; and when he had confessed his guilt orders were given that he should be taken to Besh-Balïq and put to death on a Friday after prayers in the presence of the whole population.[73]

---

[70] These were the three secretaries who composed Güyük's letter to Innocent IV. See Rockhill, p. 28.

[71] Her trial and execution are not mentioned by Juvainī.

[72] The ruler of the Uighur, *idï-qut* (or rather *idhuq-qut*, "Holy Majesty") being a title which they took over from the earlier Basmïl. See *Turcs d'Asie Centrale*, p. 37.

[73] For a detailed account of these events, see *HWC*, pp. 48–53.

❧ HISTORY OF HOW MÖNGKE QA'AN DISPATCHED emirs in every direction to deal with the remainder of the rebels and how he pardoned their crime

Since some of the rebels were still left [hidden] in corners and it would have been difficult and would have taken a long time to bring them to Court, he sent Bala Yarghuchï with a group of *nökers* to the armies of Yesü-Möngke to inquire about these people and put to death all that had taken part in the conspiracy. And he sent another emir to Khitai charged with the same task.

And when the thought of those wicked men had been dismissed from his august mind the fair character of the fortunate Emperor required him to regard it as his first duty to respect the claims of kinship and consanguinity. He ordered Shiremün to accompany Qubilai Qa'an, Naqu, and Jaghan Noyan to Khitai. As for Khwāja, out of gratitude to his wife, who had spoken praiseworthy words, he exempted him from taking part in the campaign and fixed his *yurt* in the region of the Selenge, which is near Qara-Qorum.

It was from this time that discord first appeared amongst the Mongols. Chingiz-Khan used to urge his sons to concord and unity and say: "As long as you are in agreement with one another fortune and triumph will be your friends, and your opponents will never gain the victory." By reason of this quality it has been possible for Chingiz-Khan and his posterity to conquer the greater part of the world. It is said that one day at the time of his first rising to power he was giving advice to his sons, and by way of an example he drew an arrow from his quiver, gave it to them, and said: "Break it." It was broken with only a little effort. Then he gave them two, which were also easily broken. And he went on increasing the number up to ten, and even the athletes and *bahadurs* of the army were unable to break them. "So it is with you also," he said. "As long as you support one another none will gain the victory over you and you will enjoy kingship and empire for a long period of time."[74] Had the sultans of Islam followed the same path, their dynasty would not have been extirpated.

[74] Reproduced from Juvainī (*HWC*, p. 41 and note 7 and p. 594. The story, as Muḥammad Qazvīnī, the editor of Juvainī, points out, is told in Ṭabarī of the famous Umaiyad general Muhallab. It is, in fact, the fable of the husbandman and his

❧ HISTORY OF HOW THE PRINCES AND EMIRS
sought permission of Möngke Qa'an to return to their own homes and
how he dismissed them with the greatest honors and favors

When the august mind of Möngke Qa'an was relieved of all necessary
business, and the distraught empire had at last found rest, and the
kingship had by the unanimous resolve of all the princes been entrusted
to him, the princes and emirs besought permission to return to their
own *yurts*. He commanded them to break up and depart each to his
own dwelling place, having been favored with all manner of generosity
and every kind of benevolence. And since Berke and Toqa-Temür,
who came from Batu, had the greatest distance to go and had been the
longest absent, he dismissed them first, bestowing upon them all
manner of gifts without number and sending with them for Batu
presents worthy of such a king. As for the sons of Köten and Qadaghan
Oghul and Melik Oghul, he granted each of them an *ordo* from the
ordos and residences of Qa'an along with his wives. He next dismissed
Qara-Hülegü with great honor, bestowing upon him the place of his
grandfather which had been seized by his uncle. He returned triumphant, but when he reached the Altai he died without having
attained his desire. As for the other princes, emirs, and *noyans*, he
dismissed each of them in accordance with the dignity of his rank and
station. And as for *Kesege, he made him a *tarkhan*[75] and bestowed upon
him so much wealth that he became very rich and his rank exceedingly
high. And when the princes and emirs had departed and their business
had been dispatched, he turned his attention to the administration and
organization of the realm and caused the world to flourish with his
justice.

---

quarrelsome sons, of which the earliest version appears to be that of Babrius. The story
seems to have been popular amongst the 13th-century Mongols. It occurs in *SH*,
where it is related (§§19–20) not of Genghis Khan himself but of his mythical ancestress,
Alan Qo'a, and it was also known to Ricoldo da Monte Croce (Laurent, pp. 119–20)
and the Armenian Haithon (*Recueil*, pp. 154 and 288–89).

75 "*Tarkhan*," says Juvainī (*HWC*, pp. 37–38), "are those who are exempt from
compulsory contributions, and to whom the booty taken on every campaign is surrendered: whenever they so wish they may enter the royal presence without leave or
permission." On this ancient Altaic title, see Doerfer, II, No. 879 (pp. 460–74).

❧ HISTORY OF HOW MÖNGKE QA'AN ATTENDED TO
the affairs of the realm and instituted the administration and organization thereof; how he showed mercy to all classes of men; and how he
dismissed the governors of the various regions.

When Möngke Qa'an's royal resolve was directed toward favoring
the righteous and subduing rebels, and the reins of his auspicious mind
were turned toward the path of relieving the people and alleviating
all manner of compulsory labor, his perfect intellect preferred earnestness to jest, and, abandoning the constant quaffing of ancient wine,
he first dispatched armies to the uttermost parts of the East and West
and to the lands of the Arabs and non-Arabs. The eastern part of the
Empire he bestowed upon the Ṣāḥib Maḥmūd Yalavach, whose former
services had been rewarded with marks of favor and who had arrived
before his auspicious accession, and the country of the Uighur, Fargh-
āna, and Khwārazm [he bestowed] upon the Emir Mas'ūd Beg,
who had experienced much terror and danger because of his honesty
and devotion to the Emperor and who, like his father, had had the
honor of being received in audience before the rest. In token of his
gratitude he dismissed them first, and those who had accompanied
them from all parts were distinguished with every kind of favor.
Thereafter, the Emir Arghun Aqa, who because of the length of his
journey had arrived after the *quriltai* had broken up and who had
previously distinguished himself in service and devotion to the Emperor,
was singled out by the granting of his wishes and the attainment of his
desires; and there was entrusted to him authority over the countries
of Persia, such as Khurāsān, Māzandaran, 'Irāq, Fārs, Kirmān,
Ādharbāijān, Georgia, Lūr, Arrān, Armenia, Rūm, Diyār Bakr,
Mosul, and Aleppo. And those *maliks*, emirs, ministers, and *bitikchis*
who accompanied him were on his recommendation treated with
favor; and on the 20th of Ramaḍān 650 [24th of November, 1252]
he set out on the return journey. 'Alī Malik[76] was sent as his *nöker*,
and the region of Isfahan and Nishapur in particular was entrusted
to him. They were ordered to carry out a new census of the *ulus* and
the army, to introduce a fixed tax, and, when they had finished these

---

[76] Juvainī (*HWC*, pp. 513 and 518) gives his name as Nāṣir al-Dīn 'Alī Malik.

tasks, to return to Court. And he ordered each of them to investigate and inquire into the previous taxes because he was concerned with alleviating the lot of the people, not increasing the wealth in the treasury. And he issued a *yarligh* about reducing the people['s taxes]. And since after the death of Güyük Khan many of the *khatuns* and princes had issued *yarlighs* and *paizas* without number to the people, had dispatched ambassadors to all parts of the Empire, and had given protection to noble and base on the pretext of their being *ortaqs*, etc., he issued a *yarligh* instructing each one of them to conduct an inquiry in his own territory and call in all the *yarlighs* and *paizas* which the people had received from them and the other princes during the reigns of Chingiz-Khan, Ögetei Qa'an, and Güyük Khan. Henceforth the princes were not to write or issue instructions in any matter relating to the administration of the provinces without consulting the ministers of the Court. As for the great ambassadors, they were not to have the use of more than fourteen post horses: they should proceed from *yam* to *yam* and not seize the people's animals *en route*. In the reign of Qa'an it had been the custom for merchants to come to Mongolia on post horses. He denounced this practice, saying: "Merchants journey to and fro for the sake of gain. What is the point in their riding post horses?" And he commanded them to travel on their own animals.[77] He likewise commanded ambassadors not to enter any town or village in which they had no business and not to take more than the amount of provisions allotted to them. Furthermore, since injustice and oppression had gained the upper hand and the peasants in particular had been driven to despair by the quantity of troubles and requisitions and the collection of levies to such an extent that the produce of their crops did not amount to the half of the requisitions, he gave orders that noble and base, *ortaqs* and financial and administrative agents should tread the path of lenity and compassion with their subordinates. Each should pay in proportion to his circumstances and ability the amount due from him according to the assessment without excuses or delay, except those who were exempt from inconveniences and exactions, in accordance with the *yarligh* of Chingiz-Khan and Qa'an, that is, of the Muslims, the great *saiyids* and *shaikhs* and the excellent *imams*, of the

---

[77] The ban on the use of post horses by merchants is not mentioned by Juvainī.

Christians, the *erke'üns*,[78] priests, monks, and scholars (*aḥbār*), of the idolaters the famous *toyïns*,[79] and of every community those who were advanced in age and no longer capable of earning a living.[80] And in order that every agent might make a [new] distribution every day he instituted an annual scheme whereby in the countries of Khitai a man of great wealth paid 11 dinars and so on, in proportion down to a poor man who paid but one; and so it was in Transoxiana also; in Khurāsān and 'Irāq a rich man paid 7 dinars and a poor man 1 dinar. The governors and scribes were not to show favor or partiality or to take bribes. As for the levy on animals, which they call *qubchur*,[81] if a person had a hundred head of a particular kind of beast he was to give one, and if he had less, none. And whenever there were arrears of taxes and whoever owed them they were not to be exacted from the peasants.

And of all the peoples and religious communities he showed most honor and respect to the Muslims and bestowed the largest amount of gifts and alms upon them. A proof of this is the following: On the occasion of the *īd-i fiṭr* in the year 650 [5th of December, 1252] the Cadi Jalāl al-Dīn Khujandī and a group of Muslims were present at the gate of the *ordo*. The cadi delivered the sermon and led the prayers, adorning the *khuṭba* with the titles of the Caliph. He likewise prayed for Möngke Qa'an and uttered praises of him. [Möngke] ordered them to be given wagon-loads of gold and silver *bālish* and costly clothing as a present for the festival, and the greater part of mankind had their share thereof.

He issued a command for the release of all captives and prisoners throughout the Empire; and messengers proceeded to all parts upon this errand.

Now were one to begin describing the deeds which occur daily in that Court by reason of his justice and equity, whole volumes would be filled to overflowing and there would be no end to these tales. *A little of it is a guide to the greater part.*

And since the fame of his justice and equity had spread to all the

[78] On *erke'ün*, "Christian (Nestorian) priest," see Doerfer, I, No. 15 (pp. 123–25).
[79] T. *toyïn*, from Chinese *tao-jen*, "Buddhist priest."
[80] That these privileges were denied to the Jews (*HWC*, p. 599) is passed over in silence by Rashīd al-Dīn. Spuler (1939, p. 249) adduces this silence as one of the indications of the historian's Jewish origin.
[81] See above, Section 1, p. 55, note 217.

ends and corners of the lands, Turks and Tāzīks from far and near with a sincere desire sought refuge in allegiance to him. And the kings of countries that had not yet submitted sent gifts and presents.

As there has already been some brief mention of his praiseworthy qualities and character, we shall relate a story which comprehends many noble attributes in order that mankind may know of a certainty that this narration is unmarked with the brand of extravagance. Merchants used to come from all parts to the Court of Güyük Khan and conclude large deals with his ministers, receiving in payment drafts upon the various lands. However, on account of his death these sums were held up and did not reach them. His servants, sons, and nephews continued to conclude deals in this fashion and to write drafts upon the lands, and crowds of merchants arrived one after another and carried out further transactions for which they received drafts. When Möngke Qa'an was auspiciously seated upon the throne and the position of those people had changed from what it was, some merchants had not received a tenth part of [the payment on] their goods, some had not reached the stage of a transfer, some had not received a draft, some had not delivered their wares, and some had not fixed the prices. Being at their wits' end, they set out for Court and, by way of a test and in hope of [enjoying the benefit of] his justice and bounty, they entered the audience chamber and brought their case to the ears of Möngke Qa'an. The functionaries of the Court and the pillars of state protested on the grounds that it was not necessary to pay the amount due on this transaction from the Emperor's treasury and that no one could object [if payment was refused]. Nevertheless, because of his perfect compassion, he spread the wing of benevolence over them and issued a *yarligh* that the whole sum should be met from the finances of his Empire. It amounted to more than 500,000 gold and silver *bālish*, and had he withheld it none would have had cause to object. With such bounty he stole away the glory of Ḥātim-like kings. And in what work of history has it been heard that a king paid the debt of another king? This is a particular instance of his excellent practices and pleasing customs from which one can deduce his behavior in other matters.[82]

He commanded that whenever there was to be an inquiry into the

[82] Abridged from Juvainī (*HWC*, pp. 602–604).

affairs of people at large this task should be undertaken by Mengeser Noyan together with a body of experienced emirs, who should thus consolidate the foundations of justice. And Bulghai Aqa, who had acquired rights by reason of his past services, he commanded to be leader of the scribes and to write and copy the decrees and mandates. Of the Muslim *bitikchis*, he appointed 'Imād al-Mulk, who had occupied this position at the Courts of Ögetei Qa'an and Güyük Khan, and the Emir Fakhr al-Mulk, who was an ancient servant of the Court. They were not to issue *paizas* to merchants, so that a distinction might be made between them and those engaged in the affairs of the Divan. Some of these have brought goods to sell to the treasury. Some value jewelry, others furs, others cash money. He also appointed experienced well-informed and adroit persons to issue *yarlïghs*, strike *paizas*, [supervise] the arsenal, and deal with the affairs of every community and people. And it was commanded that all these officials should avoid the stain of usury and excessive covetousness. They were to arrest no one and were to bring each man's case promptly to the Emperor's attention. They are attended by scribes of every kind for Persian, Uighur, Khitayan, Tibetan, and Tangqut, so that [for] whatever place a decree has to be written it may be issued in the language and script of that people. When were there such organization and such customs in the days of ancient kings and the reigns of bygone sultans? Truly, if they were alive today, they would follow this path.

◅ HISTORY OF HOW MÖNGKE QA'AN DISPATCHED HIS brothers Qubilai Qa'an and Hülegü Khan with armies into the East and the West and how he himself set out to conquer the lands and countries of Khitai that had not yet submitted

When Möngke Qa'an had been auspiciously seated upon the throne of the empire and had brought victory to his friends and defeat to his enemies, he passed the whole of the winter in the *yurt* of Ögetei Qa'an, which is in the region of Qara-Qorum in a place called Ongqïn.[83] And when the second year came round after the great *qurïltai*, being now firmly established on the seat of fortune and no longer concerned with the affairs of friend and foe, he turned his august attention toward

[83] See above, Section 1, p. 64, note 281.

the subjugation of the farthest East and West of the world. And first, because a number of persons seeking justice against the Heretics had been brought to his most noble notice, he dispatched against them into the land of the Tājīks in the Year of the Ox[84] his youngest brother Hülegü Khan, upon whose forehead he had observed the signs of conquest, sovereignty, royal majesty, and fortune. And his middle brother, Qubilai Qa'an, he appointed and dispatched in the Year of the Panther[85] to defend and conquer the eastern countries, sending Muqali Guyang[86] of the Jalayir people to accompany him. (The details [of these campaigns] will be given in the histories of both princes when they became rulers.)[87] When Qubilai had already set out, he sent a messenger back from the road to say that no provisions were to be found along that route and it was impossible to travel by it. If the command was given, they could proceed to the province of Qara-Jang.[88] Permission was given and Qubilai Qa'an attacked and plundered that province, which is known as Qandahār,[89] and then returned to Möngke Qa'an. Thereafter, Möngke Qa'an held a *quriltai* in a place called Qorqonaq Jubur,[90] which lies in the middle of Mongolia. It was in this place that Qutula Qa'an, when he had gained a victory, danced under a tree with his *nökers* until the ground fell into a ditch.[91] When the *quriltai* was over, and the great crowd of people had dispersed, and each of the emirs and princes was uttering a *bilig*, in the midst of all this Derekei[92] Küregen of the Ikires[93] people, who was a son-in-law of Chingiz-Khan, said: "The kingdom of Nangiyas is so near and they are hostile to us. How can we neglect and delay [our

[84] 1253.

[85] 1254.

[86] On Muqali Guyang (*guyang* is the Chinese title *kuo-wang*, "prince of the kingdom") the famous general whom Genghis Khan left in command in China during his absence in western Asia, see *Campagnes*, pp. 360–72.

[87] For Qubilai's campaign in China, see below, pp. 246ff.; for Hülegü's campaign in the West, see Arends, pp. 20–47, and *CHI*, pp. 340 ff.

[88] Marco Polo's Caragian, the Mongol name for Yunnan. See Polo I, pp. 169–81.

[89] See below, p. 247 and note 23.

[90] Unidentified. A wooded region on the banks of the Onon. See *SH*, §§57, 115–17, 201, and 206. The *quriltai* here was held in the autumn of 1257.

[91] On the victory dance of Qutula, a great uncle of Genghis Khan, see *SH*, §57, Arends, p. 197 (where his name is wrongly given as Qubilai Qa'an), and *CHI*, p. 392,

[92] Or Dayirkei. He was a *küregen* ("imperial son-in-law"), being the husband of Genghis Khan's daughter Tümelün. See Khetagurov, p. 164.

[93] The Ikires were a branch of the Qonqirat. There is still an "Ikirat" clan amongst the Buryat Mongols. See *Campagnes*, pp. 31–32.

attack]?" Möngke Qa'an approved these words and said: "Our fathers and *aqas*, who were the former rulers, each of them wrought a deed and conquered a land and raised up his name amongst mankind. I too shall go to war in person and march against Nangiyas."[94] The princes replied with one voice: "One who is ruler of the face of the earth and has seven brothers, how shall he go to war against the enemy in his own person?" And he said: "As we have spoken finally, to oppose our words is remote from counsel and policy." And in the *taulai yïl*,[95] corresponding to Muḥarram of the year 653 [February–March, 1255], which was the sixth[96] year from his auspicious accession, he went to war against Jaugan,[97] the ruler of Khitai, leaving his youngest brother Arïq Böke in charge of the *ordos* and the Mongol army that had been left behind there. He likewise entrusted the *ulus* to [Arïq Böke] and left his own son Ürüng-Tash with him. As for the armies he took with him, he appointed to the command of them the following princes, *küregens*, and great emirs. The right[98] hand—Princes: [from the] branch of the house of Qa'an; Yeke-Qadan, and Totaq; [from the] branch of the house of Chaghatai; Qushiqai and other princes, Abishqa, Narin-Qadan and Qadaqchi-Sechen; [from the] branch of the sons of Tolui; Möge and Asutai; [and from the] branch of the cousins of Ja'utu and other princes, ———;[99] Emirs: Baiju of the house of Möngke Qa'an; [and] Qorchi Noyan. The left hand[100] —Princes: Taghachar, son of Otchi Noyan; [and] Yesüngge, son of Jochi-Qasar; Emirs: Chaqula, son of Elchitei Noyan; Qurumshi, son of Muqali Guyang;[101] Alchi Noyan[102] of the Qonqïrat; Nachin

---

[94] See above, p. 22 and note 43.

[95] The Year of the Hare: Mo. *taulai*, "hare." The campaign was actually launched early in 1258, a Year of the Horse. See also below, p. 225 and note 108 and p. 228 and note 123.

[96] The reference apparently is not to his official enthronement in 1251 but to the earlier ceremony held under the auspices of Batu in 1249.

[97] From the Chinese Chao kuan, "Chao official." This was the Mongols' contemptuous designation of the Sung Emperor, who bore the family name of Chao.

[98] That is, the West.   [99] Blank in Blochet's MSS.

[100] That is, the East.

[101] The name of Muqali's only son according to the Chinese sources and another passage in Rashīd al-Dīn (Khetagurov, p. 93) was not Qurumshi but Bo'ol. See *Campagnes*, p. 371.

[102] The brother-in-law of Genghis Khan. He had fought in the war against the Chin and had also apparently taken part in the Campaign in the West. See Boyle 1963, p. 238.

Küregen[103] of the Qonqïrat; Derekei Küregen of the Ikires people; Kehetei and Bujir[104] of the Uru'ut; [and] Möngke-Qalja and Chaghan Noyan of the Mangqut.

All these tribes, [which made up] the Mongol army, now set out upon the campaign. Those who belonged to the right hand, along with the Jauqut, accompanied Möngke Qa'an. The sum total of those two bodies was 60 *tümens*. The Jauqut consist of [the people of] Khitai, Tangqut, Jürche, and Solangqa, which regions are called Jauqut by the Mongols.[105] The armies of the left hand he dispatched, under the aforementioned Taghachar, by another route. Their sum total was 30 *tümens*, and their leader [was] the aforesaid Taghachar. In that council Bilgütei Noyan said: "Qubilai Qa'an has already carried out one campaign and performed his task. Now he is suffering from gout.[106] If it be so ordered, let him go home." Möngke Qa'an approved of this. Bilgütei Noyan was a hundred and ten years old, and he died that year.[107]

In the *lu yïl*,[108] corresponding to Muharram of the year 654 [January–February, 1256], they set out, Möngke Qa'an and Kökechü, the son of Sübetei Bahadur, being of the right flank, with 10 *tümens*. That summer Möngke Qa'an arrived on the frontiers of Tangqut and Nangiyas and he passed the summer in a place called Liu Pan Shan.[109] It was in this place that Chingiz-Khan was taken ill and died when he arrived there upon his way to Khitai. In the autumn he set out for Yesün Qahalqa,[110] which is on the frontier of Nangiyas, and captured twenty

---

[103] He was the son of Alchi Noyan. Neither he nor Derekei is mentioned in Verkhovsky's text.

[104] On Bujir, see *Campagnes*, pp. 5–7.

[105] On the term Jauqut, see *Polo I*, pp. 227–29.

[106] *Dard-i pāi.*

[107] Belgütei, Genghis Khan's half brother, born *ca.* 1172, would, in fact, have been only eighty-six years old in 1258. See *Campagnes*, p. 186.

[108] The Year of the Dragon: T. *lu*, "dragon." Apparently 1258 (a Year of the Horse) is meant.

[109] The Liupan or Lung Shan mountains in Kansu.

[110] In Mongol, "Nine Gates (Passes)." In a letter dated the 19th April, 1968, Dr. Igor de Rachewiltz writes: "This name is briefly mentioned by Pelliot, *Notes on Marco Polo*, I, 327, but no identification is suggested. We know that Möngke, after spending most of the month of May 1258 at Liu-p'an shan in Kansu, divided his forces into three armies which invaded Szechwan from different directions. The army

fortresses in that region. That province is called Khan Siman.[111]
He encamped around a great fortress called Do Li Shang[112] and laid
siege to it. He had sent Taghachar Noyan with 100,000 horsemen by way
of the great river Qa'an-Keng[113] to besiege and reduce the great towns
of Sang Yang Fu[114] and Fang Cheng.[115] When he arrived there, his
army besieged [these towns] for a week and, not being able to capture
them, withdrew and encamped in their own quarters. Möngke Qa'an
was angry at this and reprimanded them. He sent this message: "When
you return we shall order a suitable punishment." And Qorïqchï,[116]
the brother of Yesüngge, sent this message to Taghachar: "Qubilai
Qa'an took many towns and fortresses, but you have returned with
stolen battles, that is, you have been busy only with food and drink."

✺ HISTORY OF HOW QUBILAI QA'AN SET OUT FOR
Nangiyas in accordance with a *yarlïgh*; how he laid siege to the town
of Yauju;[117] and how he turned back and crossed the River Gang

---

led by Möngke passed through the San Pass, the other two armies crossed the Mi-
ts'ang Pass and the Yü Pass. See the *Yüan-shih* (Po-na ed.) 3, 8b–9a. Since Rashīd
speaks of Möngke's army, the place in question should be the San Pass. If so, Yisün
Qahalqa must be the Mongol name of this pass and/or of the mountainous area
around it."

[111] On this unidentified name, Dr. de Rachewiltz writes in the same letter: "I
would tentatively propose either Han-shui nan, that is, '[the region] south of the
Han-shui,' or more likely Han hsi-nan that is, '[the region] southwest of the Han
(= Han-shui).' This was, broadly speaking, the area in which Möngke's military
operations took place."

[112] Verkhovsky reads this name Dali Shank and identifies it with the Tiao-yü shan
mountains near Ho chou (Hochwan), the actual stronghold to which the Mongols
were laying siege.

[113] The Yangtse. Referred to elsewhere as Keng (Chinese *chiang* "large river")
or Keng Mören (Mo. *mören*, "river"), it is here called the "Emperor river." Cf.
Polo's Quian or Quiansui, on which see *Polo II*, pp. 817–20.

[114] Siangyang (Siangfan) in Hupeh: Polo's Saianfu, on the siege of which see
below, pp. 290–91.   [115] Fancheng in Hupeh.

[116] None of the sources mention a son of Jochi-Qasar bearing this name.

[117] Verkhovsky (p. 147, note 51) takes this to be O chou (Wuchang), spelt Oju
below, pp. 229 and 248. However, it would appear that in the present chapter the
earlier operations in Yunnan (see below, pp. 246–47) have been confused with the
campaign of 1258–1259; and Yauju may well be Yao chou, identified in the *Yüan
shih* with Ya-ch'ih (Polo's Iaci), that is, apparently, Yün-nan fu, the modern Kunming.
See *Polo II*, pp. 747–48.

Thereupon Möngke Qa'an gave this order: "Qubilai Qa'an, although he is ill, has again taken part in a campaign. Let him hand over this campaign to Taghachar, and let Taghachar take part in his stead." When the *yarlïgh* arrived, Qubilai Qa'an sent the following message: "My gout is better. How is it fitting that my *aqa* should go on a campaign and I should remain idle at home?" And he at once set out and made for Nangiyas. And because the road was extremely long and difficult, the country in rebellion, and the climate unhealthy, in order to save themselves they fought two or three times a day and went on until they came to the town of Yauju, which they besieged until of 10 *tümens* only 2 *tümens* were left. Then Qubilai Qa'an withdrew from the campaign,[118] leaving Uriyangqadai with Bahadur Noyan,[119] the son of Chila'un Guyang, the son of Muqali Guyang, and an army of 5 *tümens*. He built a bridge of boats over the River Keng Müren. An immense army now arrived from Nangiyas, and the Mongol army wished to cross the bridge, but [this] proved impossible, and many of them fell in the water or perished at the hands of the Nangiyas.[120] Some were left behind in those regions, and afterward, when Nangiyas had been conquered, those who survived came back. Qubilai Qa'an, leaving those parts, came to his *ordo* near the town of Jungdu[121] and alighted there. And during this time Möngke Qa'an was engaged in besieging the aforementioned town.

◈ HISTORY OF HOW MÖNGKE QA'AN WAS TAKEN ill and died; how his coffin was brought to the *ordos*; and how they mourned him

---

[118] Here the reference would seem to be to Qubilai's withdrawal from the Yunnan campaign after the fall of Tali. See Franke, V, p. 318.

[119] According to an inscription quoted by Pelliot (*Campagnes*, p. 371 Bahadur was a younger brother, not the son, of Chila'un, and their father was not Muqali but his son Bo'ol.

[120] Uriyangqadai, advancing northward through Kwangsi and Hunan after his victories in Annam, reached the Yangtse at the beginning of 1260. The bridge of boats was, on the orders of the Sung commander rammed by a flotilla of junks while his troops were crossing, but only 170 men were lost. See Franke, IV, p. 325.

[121] The Chinese Chung-tu "Middle Capital", that is, Peking. Qubilai arrived here at the beginning of 1260, not, as implied in the next sentence, whilst his brother was still laying siege to Hochwan.

When Möngke Qa'an was laying siege to the aforesaid fortress, the summer having come on and the heat being intense, the climate of the region gave rise to an epidemic of dysentery, and cholera too attacked the troops, so that many of them died. To ward off the cholera the World Emperor began to drink wine and persisted in doing so. All of a sudden he was seized with an indisposition, his illness[122] came to a crisis, and in the *mogha yïl*[123] corresponding to Muḥarram of the year 655 [January, 1257] he passed away beneath that ill-fated fortress. He was fifty-two years of age, and this year was the seventh from his accession to the throne of the Empire.[124]

Upon the occurrence of [Möngke Qa'an's] death, Asutai Oghul left Qundaqai Noyan in charge of the army, and, taking his father's coffin, brought it to the *ordos*. They mourned for him in the four *ordos*: on the first day in the *ordo* of Qutuqtai Khatun, on the second day in the *ordo* of Qotai[125] Khatun, on the third day in the *ordo* of Chabui Khatun,[126] who had accompanied him on that campaign, and on the fourth day in the *ordo* of Kisa Khatun.[127] Each day they placed the coffin on a throne in a [different] *ordo* and lamented over him with the greatest possible fervor. Then they buried him in Bulqan-Qaldun,[128] which they call Yeke-Qoruq,[129] alongside Chingiz-Khan and Tolui

---

[122] According to some reports, he died of an arrow-wound. See Franke, IV, p. 324, V, pp. 170–71.

[123] Year of the Snake: Mo. *moghai*, "snake." In point of fact his death occurred 2 years later, on the 11th August, 1259. Cf. above, p. 224 and note 95.

[124] Born on the 10th January, 1209, he was in his fifty-first year at the time of his death. If one reckons his reign from the ceremony of 1249 (see above, p. 224, note 96), 1257 was the eighth year; so too there were eight years between his enthronement in 1251 and the actual date of his death in 1259.

[125] Rubruck's Cota, Möngke's second wife, an "idol follower" (Rockhill, p. 190), whom the friar visited on her sick bed and who taught him a little Mongol (Rockhill, pp. 192–94).

[126] The chief wife of Qubilai. See below, p. 241.

[127] Presumably one of Möngke's wives; she is not mentioned elsewhere.

[128] For the normal Burqan-Qaldun, "Buddha Mountain" (cf. its other name Buda-Öndür, "Buddha Height," below, pp. 310 and 314) or, according to Rintchen, "Willow God, Holy Willow." The most recent support for its identification with Kentei Qan in the Great Kentei range in northeastern Mongolia comes from Professor Johannes Schubert. See *Polo I*, pp. 339–47, Schubert, pp. 72 and 95 ff., and Poppe 1956, pp. 33–35.

[129] The "Great Inviolable Sanctuary." On this secret cemetery of the Mongol Great Khans, see *Polo I*, pp. 335 ff. On T. *qoruq*, "inviolable sanctuary, taboo," see Doerfer, III, No 1462 (pp. 444–50).

Khan. May God Almighty make the Lord of Islam[130] during many years the heir to [countless] lives and may He grant him enjoyment of empire, power, and kingship, by His grace and the amplitude of His bounty!

❧ THE FURTHER HISTORY OF QUBILAI QA'AN during that campaign and how the news of Möngke Qa'an's death reached him

At that time, Qubilai Qa'an had departed from thence and had reached the great river of the Nangiyas country which they call Khui Kho.[131] When he heard the bad news about Möngke Qa'an he consulted Bahadur Noyan, the grandson[132] of Muqali Guyang, and said: "Let us pay no attention to this rumor." And he sent Erke Noyan, the son of Bulqan Qalcha of the Barulas people, ahead with the vanguard, and he himself followed. They captured and killed the scouts of the Nangiyas army and so prevented them from reporting that news. Then he crossed the River Keng, which is 2 parasangs wide, by boat and came to the town of Oju,[133] which he besieged and captured.[134] A force, which had returned from fighting against Möngke Qa'an, came to the aid of that town: the names of their commanders were Gia Dau[135] and Ulus Taifu.[136] When they arrived, Qubilai Qa'an had already taken the town. Immediately afterward there arrived messengers from Chabui Khatun and the emirs of her *ordo*, Taichi'utai Noyan and Yekü Noyan. The messengers, whose

130 That is, Ghazan.
131 The Hwai Ho. See also below, p. 248 and note 29.
132 This is correct. See above, p. 227 and note 119.
133 O chou, the modern Wuchang, in Hupeh. See above, p. 226, note 117.
134 In actual fact, Qubilai, upon receiving the news of his brother's death, raised the siege of Wuchang and withdrew northward, having first concluded some kind of peace with the Sung. See *Steppes*, pp. 351–52, and Franke, IV, pp. 324–25.
135 Reading KYA DAW with Blochet's MS. B. This was the infamous Chia Ssŭ-tao, to whose incompetence and cowardice the collapse of the Sung was largely due. See Franke, IV, pp. 322 ff., 330 ff., 336 ff.
136 According to the *Yüan shih* (quoted by Verkhovsky, p. 148, note 68), the second of the two commanders was Lü Wên-tê, the brother of Lü Wên-huan, the defender of Siangyang. His name, however, bears little resemblance to Rashīd al-Dīn's Ulus Taifu. On *taifu* (Chinese *t'ai-fu*) as a military title, see below, p. 278, *Polo I*, p. 222, and *Polo II*, pp. 851–52.

names were Toqan and Ebügen, brought the news of Möngke Qa'an's death. And when Qubilai Qa'an realized that the news was true, he left the army and mourned for his brother. He was now left alone in the Nangiyas country, and Hülegü Khan was in the West, in the Tāzīk country, both of them at a great distance from the capital. When, therefore, Arïq Böke heard the news of his brother's death, his glance fell upon the throne and the Empire, and the emirs and attendants encouraged him in this until he rose in rebellion against Qubilai Qa'an. The general and particular history of Arïq Böke [and] the sons of Möngke Qa'an, Asutai and Ürüng-Tash, will all be included in the history of Qubilai Qa'an, if God so wills.[137]

The history of Möngke Qa'an and the detailed account of the events of his reign are now complete, and we shall begin recording, briefly and concisely, if God Almighty so wills, the history of the Emperors of Khitai and Māchīn and the emirs, caliphs, sultans, *maliks*, and *atabegs* of the lands of Persia, Syria, Egypt, and the West that were contemporary with him, from the beginning of the *qaqa yïl*, corresponding to the year 648/1250 to the end of the *mogha yïl*, falling in Muḥarram of the year 655 [January–February, 1257].

☙ HISTORY OF THE EMPERORS OF KHITAI AND Māchīn and the emirs, caliphs, sultans, *maliks*, and *atabegs* of Persia and the countries of Syria, Egypt, and the West that were contemporary with Möngke Qa'an, from the beginning of the *qaqa yïl*, that is, the Year of the Pig, corresponding to the year 648/1250–1251, to the end of the *mogha yïl*, that is, the Year of the Snake, corresponding to the year 655/1257–1258; the strange and unusual occurrences that happened during this period

History of the emperors of Khitai and Māchīn

History of the emirs, caliphs, atabegs, sultans, and maliks

History of the emirs

The Emir Arghun Aqa, who was governor of most of the countries of Persia, set out for the Court of Möngke in Jumādā I of the year 649

[137] See below, pp. 252–65.

[July–August, 1251] to attend the *quriltai*. When he arrived there the *quriltai* had already been held and, the princes and emirs having dispersed, Möngke Qa'an, was busy arranging the affairs of the Empire. On the day after his arrival, he presented himself before the Emperor, it being the 1st Muḥarram of the year 650 [16th March, 1251], and reported on the confused conditions in Persia. He was distinguished with marks of favor, and inasmuch as the *qalan* of the people of these parts had previously been fixed at 7 dinars a year for a rich man and one dinar for a poor man, Möngke Qa'an commanded that no further demands should be made on them. He gave him a *yarlïgh* and charged him to follow the same course as previously, and he turned back, having obtained the office of *ṣāḥib-dīvān* for Bahā al-Dīn Juvainī and Sirāj al-Dīn, who was a *bitikchi* representing Beki, and having received a *yarlïgh* and *paiza* for them. They set out in the year 651/1253–1254, and when the Emir Arghun arrived in Khurāsān he caused the edicts to be read out and delivered the *yasas*. The people rejoiced and he commanded that no one should contravene [these *yasas*] or offer violence to the peasantry. And having put the affairs of Persia to rights, he then, in accordance with the command, set out together with Najm al-Dīn Gīlābādī for the Court of Batu by way of Darband. And having carried out a census of the countries of Persia and imposed a fixed tax, he remained in charge of the affairs of that country until the arrival of Hülegü Khan.[138]

History of the caliphs

In Baghdad the caliph was al-Mustaʿṣim billāh, a pious and ascetic man who never drank intoxicants or stretched out his hand to anything unlawful. During these years Ḥusām al-Dīn Khalīl Badr ibn Khurshīd al-Balūchī, who was one of the chiefs of the Kurds,[139] abandoned his allegiance to the caliphs and took refuge with the Mongols. He had previously worn the garb of the Ṣūfīs and considered himself a disciple

---

[138] Abridged from Juvainī (*HWC*, pp. 514–21).

[139] In fact, he belonged to a collateral branch of the *atabegs* of Lesser Lur and had recently overthrown and killed (1242) the then ruler, ʿIzz al-Dīn Garshāsf. His hostility toward Sulaimān-Shāh was due to the fact that ʿIzz al-Dīn's widow, who was Sulaimān-Shāh's sister, had sought asylum with her brother along with her three infant sons. See Qazvīnī's note on Sulaimān-Shāh, Juvainī, III, pp. 453–63 (457–59).

of Saiyidī Aḥmad.[140] At that time, having plotted with a party of Mongols, he went to Khulanjān,[141] in the neighborhood of Najaf, attacked some of Sulaimān-Shāh's followers, killing and plundering, and then departed from thence to the castle of Vahār,[142] which belonged to Sulaimān-Shāh, and laid siege to it. Sulaimān-Shāh received news of this and, having obtained the Caliph's permission, set out for that region in order to drive him off. When he reached Ḥulwān,[143] an immense army rallied around him, and a number of Muslims and Mongols gathered around Khalīl also. They met at a place called Sahr.[144] Sulaimān-Shāh had set an ambush, and when the fighting became fierce he turned in flight and Ḥusām al-Dīn Khalīl went in pursuit of him. When he had passed the ambush he turned back, and the soldiers broke ambush and caught [Khalīl and his army] between them, killing a great number. Khalīl was captured and put to death, and his brother, who had sought refuge in a mountain, asked for quarter and came down. Sulaimān-Shāh captured two castles in their country: Shīgān,[145] which is a strong fortress, and the castle of Dizbaz in the middle of the town of Shāpur-Khwāst.[146]

During these years a party of Mongols, nearly fifteen thousand horsemen, attacked the neighborhood of Baghdad from Hamadān, and one detachment of them attacked Khānaqīn, fell upon a detachment of Sulaimān-Shāh's men, and came ———.[147] Others again went toward Shahrazūr.[148] The Caliph ordered Sharaf al-Dīn Iqbal Sharābī, Mujāhid al-Dīn Ai-Beg, the Lesser Davāt-Dār, and 'Alā al-Dīn Altun-Bars, the Greater Davāt-Dār[149] to go out [of the city]

---

[140] Apparently the dervish-saint Aḥmad al-Badawī (d. 1276) who spent some time in Iraq *ca.* 1236. See *EI*[2] *s.v.*   [141] Unidentified.

[142] The present-day Bahār, 8 miles northwest of Hamadān. On Shihāb al-Dīn Sulaimān-Shāh, the ruler of the Ive Turcomans and afterward the unsuccessful defender of Baghdad against the Mongols, see Qazvini's note referred to above, note 139.

[143] Near the present-day Sar-Pul-i Zuhāb.

[144] Unidentified. According to Qazvini, (Juvaini, III, p. 458) the battle was fought in an equally unidentified place called Dihlīz.

[145] Unidentified.   [146] The later Khurramābād.

[147] Blank in two of Blochet's MSS.

[148] The present-day Halabja Plain in the Liwa of Sulaimaniya.

[149] On the Lesser Davāt-Dār, see above, p. 192, note 51. The Greater Davāt-Dār 'Alā al-Dīn Abū Shujā' Altun-Bars ibn 'Abdallāh al-Ẓāhirī had held the office of davāt-dār under the Caliph Ẓāhir (1225): he died in 650–1252–1253: See Qazvīnī in Juvaini, III, pp. 450–51, note 1.

at the head of a great army of slaves and Arabs and set up mangonels on the walls of Baghdad. News now came that the Mongols had reached the castle of ————.[150] Sulaimān-Shāh and this band of *nökers* prepared for battle, and the Mongols came up to Ja'farīya,[151] lit fires in the night, and then turned back. Suddenly there came news that the Mongols had plundered Dujail. Sharābī[152] set out at the head of an army to drive them off, and the Mongols withdrew.

History of the sultans

In Rūm, 'Izz al-Dīn Kai-Kā'us was sultan. His brother 'Alā al-Dīn rose in rebellion and went to Ankūrīya.[153] He brought him from thence and imprisoned him for 7 years in the castle of Hushyār.[154]

In Mosul, Badr al-Dīn Lu'lu' was sultan. During these years he equipped an army and sought the help of Tāj al-Dīn Muḥammad ibn Sallāba, the ruler[155] of Irbīl, who sent a thousand men. The Sultan of Mārdīn[156] also mustered an army and sought help from Aleppo. When the two sides met, the right wing of the Mārdīnīs was defeated and the army of Mosul went in pursuit of them and obtained a quantity of booty. Meanwhile, the son of Qaimarī,[157] the leader of the army of Aleppo, attacked and defeated the center of the army of Mosul. Sultan Badr al-Dīn fled and reached Mosul with only ten men. His treasury was plundered, and his soldiers fled and followed them back.

In Egypt, Malik Ṣāliḥ Najm al-Dīn Aiyūb ibn al-Kāmil was sultan. He died, and the emirs and people of Egypt sent for his son Malik Mu'aẓẓam Tūrān-Shāh, who was governor of Ḥiṣn Kaifā.[158] When he came to the town of Damascus he seized it and proceeded from

---

[150] Blank in all the MSS.

[151] A western suburb of Baghdad.

[152] See above, p. 190 and note 38. The Mongol attack here described took place in fact much earlier, in 1238. See Barhebraeus, p. 404.

[153] Angora, the modern Ankara.

[154] Spelt Minshār in Ibn Bībī (Duda, p. 61): it was somewhere in Malatya.

[155] *Za'īm*: actually the representative of the Caliph, to whom Muẓaffar al-Dīn Kök-Böri, the last (d. 1232) of the Begtiginids, had bequeathed his principality.

[156] Najm al-Dīn Ghāzī I (1239–1260).

[157] On Ḥusām al-Dīn al-Qaimarī, the son-in-law of Malik al-Ashraf, see above, p. 46 and note 163.

[158] In Jazīra or Upper Mesopotamia, now Hasankeyf in southern Turkey.

thence to Egypt. In the year 648/1250 the Sultanate of Egypt was settled upon him, and he gave battle to the army of Franks, who had seized Damietta and various regions of Egypt. He defeated them, nearly thirty thousand Franks being killed and Afrīdīs,[159] one of their rulers, being taken prisoner along with an immense number of others; and Damietta was liberated. The Baḥrī Turks[160] then conspired to kill the Sultan. Ai-Beg the Turcoman,[161] who was the leader of the emirs, presented himself to the Sultan at table. While he was addressing the Sultan, the latter spoke harshly to him. Ai-Beg stood up, drew his sword, and struck at the Sultan. The Sultan warded off the blow with his arm, but he received a severe wound and fled into a wooden house.[162] The Turks said to Ai-Beg: "Finish the work thou hast begun." They fetched a naphtha-thrower to discharge a pot of naphtha on to the house. [The house] caught fire and the Sultan went up on to the roof. Ai-Beg shot an arrow at him. He flung himself into the river and made for the bank. They went after him, caught him, kicked him to death, and threw him into the river. When the Frankish prisoners learnt of this, they broke the bonds on their feet and began to slaughter the Muslims. The Turcoman nökers came in and surrounded them; and, drawing their swords, in a single moment they killed thirteen thousand Franks. The Arabs now withdrew to their homes, and the Kurds returned to Cairo, while the Turks remained in Manṣūra and took possession of Damietta after completely freeing it from the hands of the Franks. They set a price of 200,000 dīnārs[163] on Afrīdīs, and, leaving his brother, son, and some of his kinsmen[164] as securities, he took a Muslim with him to hand the money over to him. And in the year 652/1254–1255 Ai-Beg the Turcoman made himself master of

[159] A corruption of the normal Raid Ifrans, "roi de France," that is, here Louis IX. See Blochet, p. 346, note k, and Mostaert-Cleaves, p. 471 and note 57.

[160] The Baḥrī Mamlūks, the baharis of Joinville, were so called (baḥrī "of the river") because of their barracks on the island of Rauḍa in the Nile.

[161] This was al-Muʻizz ʻIzz al-Dīn Ai-Beg, the second (1250–1257) of the Baḥrī line of the Mamlūk dynasty.

[162] Joinville (Hague, p. 110) describes this building as "a tower of firpoles covered with dyed cloth."

[163] Two hundred thousand livres (pounds), according to Joinville (Hague, pp. 122 and 280), the actual amount paid being £167,102 18s. 8d.

[164] Joinville (Hague, pp. 119 and 122) speaks only of Louis' brother, the Count of Poitiers, as being held by the Egyptians.

Egypt. None of the children of Malik Kāmil was left, and [Ai-Beg] suddenly put Aq-Tai the Jāma-Dār[165] to death. He then ordered the *khuṭba* to be read and coin to be struck in his own name and mounted the throne as sultan.

In Kirmān, Rukn al-Dīn was sultan. In the year 650/1252–1253 Quṭb al-Dīn came from Court, and Rukn al-Dīn fled at once and sought safety in the Seat of the Caliphate. For fear of the Mongols, he was not admitted. From thence he betook himself to Court, whither he was followed by Quṭb al-Dīn. He was brought to trial, and Rukn al-Dīn, after his guilt had been established, was handed over to Quṭb al-Dīn for execution. The latter was given the sultanate of Kirmān and mounted the throne of kingship.[166]

History of the maliks and atabegs

In Māzandarān ————.[167]
In Diyār Bakr ————.[168]
In the Maghrib ————.[169]
In Fārs the *atabeg* was Muẓaffar al-Dīn Abū Bakr ————.[170]
And in Sīstān ————.[171]

History of the strange and unusual occurrences that happened during this period[172]

[165] On Fāris al-Dīn Aq-Tai (Joinville's Faraquatay), the Mamlūk general, see Lane-Poole, pp. 257–60. The *jāma-dar*, or Master of the Wardrobe, was a high official in the Egyptian Sultan's household.

[166] For a fuller account, see *HWC*, pp. 481–82.

[167] Blank in the MSS.   [168] Blank in the MSS.
[169] Blank in the MSS.   [170] Blank in the MSS.
[171] Blank in the MSS.

[172] The text of this section is absent in all the MSS.

PART III

OF THE HISTORY OF MÖNGKE QA'AN

On his praiseworthy character and morals;
the excellent biligs, *parables, and pronouncements*
which he uttered and promulgated;
such events and happenings as occurred during his reign
but have not been included in the two previous parts,
the information having been acquired
on separate occasions and at irregular intervals
from various books and persons

There has been some brief mention of his noble character and actions in the foregoing histories and also a more detailed account. Nevertheless, by way of corroboration, a story, which is the meeting-place of justice and generosity, is here recorded in order that mankind may know of a certainty that this narration is unmarked with the brand of extravagance and innocent of the sin of boasting. That story is as follows. Merchants had hastened to the presence of Güyük Khan from all parts of the world and concluded very large deals. But since Güyük Khan did not live long, the greater part of that money remained unpaid and did not reach those merchants. And after his death, his wives, sons, and nephews concluded deals on a still greater scale than during his lifetime and wrote drafts on the Empire in the same way. When the position of those people changed and their cause was lost, there were some merchants who from former transfers had not obtained even a tenth of their due; some had not yet reached the stage of a transfer; some had delivered their wares but a price had not yet been fixed; and others had not yet received a draft. When Möngke was auspiciously seated upon the throne of kingship, those dealers approached him by way of a test partly hoping [to enjoy the benefit of] his justice and partly despairing of [achieving anything by] their petition for the money involved in this transaction; and they brought their case to his auspicious attention. All the functionaries of Court and the pillars of state [were of the opinion] that there was no obligation to pay the amount due on this transaction out of the Emperor's treasury and that no mortal would have cause to object [if payment was refused]. Nevertheless, the Emperor spread the wing of generosity over them all and gave orders for the whole sum to be met from the finances of his Empire. It amounted to more than 500,000 silver *bālish*, and had he withheld it none would have had cause to object. This is an example of his royal customs and practices, from which one can deduce his behavior in other matters.[173]

[173] This is simply a reproduction, almost *verbatim*, of p. 221.

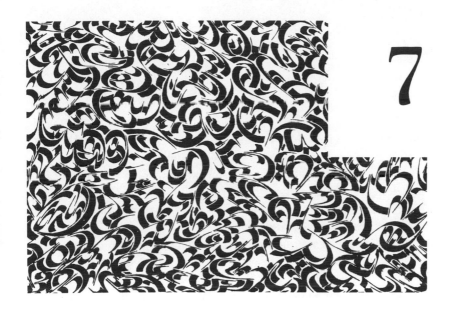

7

Beginning of the History of Qubilai Qa'an,

the Son of Tolui Khan, the Son of Chingiz-Khan:

History of Qubilai Qa'an

BEGINNING OF THE HISTORY OF
QUBILAI QA'AN,
THE SON OF TOLUI KHAN,
THE SON OF CHINGIZ-KHAN

History of Qubilai Qa'an

When Arïq Böke conceived the desire to be Qa'an, he rebelled against his elder brother Qubilai Qa'an and aided the sons of Möngke Qa'an, Asutai and Ürüng-Tash, and their sons and kinsmen. But in the end their design came to nought, and they submitted to Qubilai Qa'an; and the narrative of these events is therefore included in the present history, which consists of three parts:

❧ PART I. An account of his lineage, a detailed account of his wives and sons and the branches into which they have divided down to the present day; a picture of him; and a genealogical table of his descendants.

❧ PART II. The events preceeding his accession; a picture of him with his wives and the princes and emirs on the occasion of his mounting the throne of the Khanate; the events of his reign; the history of Arïq Böke and the princes allied with him; the battles which the Qa'an fought and the victories which he gained; an account of his emirs.

❧ PART III. His praiseworthy character and the excellent *biligs*, parables, and edicts which he made, uttered, and proclaimed; such events as occurred during his reign but have not been included in the two previous parts, having been ascertained at irregular intervals from various books and persons.

OF THE HISTORY OF QUBILAI QA'AN

An account of his lineage
and a detailed account of his wives and sons
in the branches into which they have divided down to the present day;
his picture;
and a genealogical table of his descendants

❧ AN ACCOUNT OF HIS ILLUSTRIOUS LINEAGE

Qubilai Qa'an was the fourth son of Tolui Khan by Sorqoqtani Beki. His nurse was the mother of Möge, a concubine of the Naiman people. It chanced that he was born 2 months before Möge, and when Chingiz-Khan's eye fell upon him he said: "All our children are of a ruddy complexion, but this child is swarthy like his maternal uncles. Tell Sorqoqtani Beki to give him to a good nurse to be reared." He was given to Möge's mother, Saruq by name. Two months later when Möge was born his mother gave him to a nurse of the Tangqut people to be reared, and [she] reared Qubilai Qa'an herself until he had grown up. She regarded him as her own child and cared for and protected him in every way. The Qa'an held her in the highest honor, and when she died he constantly remembered her and used to give alms for the sake of her soul.

❧ AN ACCOUNT OF HIS WIVES AND SONS

Qubilai Qa'an had many wives and concubines, of whom the most senior was Chabui Khatun, the daughter of Alchi Noyan of the family of the rulers of the Qonqïrat. She was extremely beautiful and charming and his favorite wife. She died before Qubilai Qa'an, in the *bichin yïl*, the Year of the Monkey, corresponding to 682/1283–1284.[1] Qubilai Qa'an had twelve chief sons, and just as Chingiz-Khan's four sons by his chief wife, Börte Fujin, enjoyed the highest rank, so of these twelve the four sons whose mother was Chabui Khatun ranked the highest. The names of the twelve sons are as follows.

First son of Qubilai Qa'an—Dorji

He was born of Chabui Khatun. He did not marry and had no issue. He was older than Abaqa Khan. He was always sickly and ill and died of that chronic illness.

Second son of Qubilai Qa'an—Jim-Gim[2]

He was originally called Gim-Jim. He was born of the senior wife, called Tai-Khu, who was of the Qonqïrat bone. The meaning of *tai-khu* is "mother of the Qa'an."[3] This Jim-Gim died young, leaving three excellent sons, as follows.

First son—Kamala

He had three sons: Yesün-Temür,[4] Jungshan, and Delger-Buqa.

Second son—Tarmabala

He too had three sons: Khaishang,[5] Amoga, and Ajur-Pariya-Batra.[6]

Third son—Temür Qa'an

He is the reigning Qa'an and is called Öljeitü Qa'an.[7] He has two sons: Tishi-Taishi and Maqabalin.

---

[1] Actually 1284.

[2] The name is Chinese: Chên-chin, "True Gold," Polo's Cinchim. See *Polo I*, pp. 278–80.

[3] *T'ai-hou* was, in fact, the title given to an empress dowager.

[4] Yüan Emperor 1323–1328.

[5] Yüan Emperor 1307–1311.

[6] The name is thus restored by Blochet. His MSS have a form NRMH, with which cf. Verkhovsky's Barma. This is the Emperor Buyantu (1311–1320).

[7] See below, pp. 320ff.

Third son of Qubilai Qa'an—Mangqala

He too was born of Chabui Khatun. His chief wife was called Qutui, which in the Indian language means "God-born."[8] She was the grand-daughter of Alchi Noyan of the Qonqïrat people. He had three sons, as follows.

First son—Arslan-Buqa

Second son—Altun-Buqa

Third son—Ananda

The reason for this name was that at the time of his birth they were near a rebellious tribe whose chief's name was Ananda, and they gave him the same name. He is a Muslim. The Qa'an has allotted him the land of the Tangqut. He has one son, Örüg-Temür, and a daughter whose name is unknown.[9]

Fourth son of Qubilai Qa'an—Nomoghan[10]

He was also born of Chabui Khatun. There are many tales about him, each of which will be told in the proper place. He had two chief daughters, but their names are not known.

Fifth son of Qubilai Qa'an—Qoridai

He was born of Qoruqchin Khatun of the Merkit bone. Qubilai Qa'an married her before any of his other wives, and she was also older than the others. In the end her rank was reduced. She was the daughter of Qutuqu, the brother of Toqta Beki, the ruler of the Merkit, who rose in rebellion during the reign of Chingiz-Khan and fought many battles against him but was finally forced to submit and surrender.

---

[8] Blochet suggests that Qutui is a corruption of either *putrī* or *kumārī* in the sense of "princess."

[9] On Ananda, see below, pp. 323–26.

[10] Polo's Nomogan, on whom see *Polo II*, pp. 795–96; also below, pp. 266–69. Of the "many tales about him," Rashīd al-Dīn recounts only that of his participation in the campaign against Qaidu and his subsequent captivity amongst the Golden Horde.

Sixth son of Qubilai Qa'an—Hügechi[11]

He was born of Dörbejin Khatun of the Dörben.[12] The Qa'an had allotted him the province of Qara-Jang. One day he took some water-fowl from a village in excess [of his needs]. When this reached the Qa'an's ears he commanded him to receive seventy blows with the rod so that his tender flesh was torn to pieces. He had a son called Esen-Temür, and after his death the Qa'an set this son over the province of Qara-Jang in his father's place. In the Indian language, Qara-Jang is called Kandar, that is, "great country."[13]

Seventh son of Qubilai Qa'an—Oqruqchï

He was born of Dörbejin Khatun. The Qa'an allotted him the province of Tibet. He had two sons.

First son—Temür-Buqa

He had a son called Shasgaba. When Oqruqchï died, the province of Tibet was given to this Temür-Buqa.

Second son—Ejil-Buqa

Eighth son of Qubilai Qa'an—Ayachi

His mother was Hüshijin, the daughter of Boroqul Noyan of the Hüshin[14] people. This son took a wife, and they lived together for awhile but she bore him no children.

Ninth son of Qubilai Qa'an—Kököchü

This son too was born of the mother of Ayachi, Hüshijin by name, of the Hüshin people. At the present time ———,[15] and previously he set out with Nomoghan and went to Deresü[16] to make war on Qaidu.

[11] Polo's Cogacin. See *Polo I*, p. 394.
[12] On the Dörben tribe, see *Campagnes*, pp. 400–402.
[13] See below, p. 247 and note 23.
[14] Or Üshin. See above, p. 247, note 57.
[15] Blank in the MSS. [16] See above, p. 103, note 25.

He was captured along with Nomoghan and after awhile sent [back] to the Qa'an.

Tenth son of Qubilai Qa'an—Qutluq-Temür

His mother's name is unknown. He was born in the year in which Arïq Böke rebelled against the Qa'an. He died when he was twenty years of age. He was married but had no children.

Eleventh son of Qubilai Qa'an—Toghan

He was born of Baya'ujin Khatun, the daughter of Boraqchin of the Baya'ut people. He was called Laujang. In the province of Manzi, which is called Māchīn, there is a great city called Jingju,[17] a province of nearly 10 tümens. The Qa'an allotted this to him.

Twelfth son of Qubilai Qa'an ———[18]

He was born of Nambui Khatun, the daughter of Nachin Küregen. The Qa'an married [her] a year after the death of Chabui Khatun. He brought her to his yurt and ordo, for she was Chabui Khatun's cousin.

The genealogical table of the above mentioned sons is as shown here.

[17] As Pelliot suggests, this must be the same as Yangju (see below, p. 282), that is, Yangchow in Kiangsu.
[18] Blank in the MSS.

PART II

OF THE HISTORY OF QUBILAI QA'AN

The events preceding his accession;
a picture of his throne with his wives and the princes and emirs
on the occasion of his mounting the throne of the Khanate;
the events of his reign; the history of Arïq Böke and the princes allied with him;
the battles which Qubilai Qa'an fought and the victories which he gained;
an account of the army commanders whom he set on every frontier;
an account of the princes at his Court
and the names of his emirs

↝ THE EVENTS PRECEDING HIS MOUNTING THE throne of the Empire

When the just monarch Möngke Qa'an ascended the throne of the Khanate, his residence being near to Qara-Qorum, in the region of Onan-Kelüren, he disposed of the affairs of the Empire and then dispatched his brother Qubilai Qa'an to the eastern countries and the empire of Khitai and sent his younger brother Hülegü Khan to the West and the Tāzïk countries.[19] And, as has been mentioned in the history of his reign, he commanded that 80 *tümens* of picked troops, Mongols and Jauqut,[20] should accompany Qubilai Qa'an to Khitai, establish themselves there, and subjugate the country of Nangiyas, which is adjacent to Khitai. Qubilai Qa'an set off but avoided the roads leading to Nangiyas. Because the ruler of those parts had cleared the places along the road of food, it was altogether impossible to proceed by that route. He sent a messenger to Möngke Qa'an to report the position and to seek permission first to conquer the provinces of Qara-Jang and Chaghan-Jang,[21] so that the troops might procure

---

[19] See above, p. 223, note 87.   [20] See above, p. 225, and note 105.
[21] The Mo-so region of Likiang in northwest Yunnan. See *Polo I*, p. 171. On the Mo-so people, see Marvazī, pp. 149–50.

246

provisions, and then to proceed against Nangiyas. Those two provinces are called, in the language of Khitai, Dai-Liu,[22] that is, "Great Empire;" in the Indian language, Qandar; and in the language of these parts, Qandahār.[23] They border on Tibet, Tangqut, some of the countries and mountains of India, and the countries of Khitai and Zar-Dandān.[24]

Möngke Qa'an approved these words and gave permission; and in the *lu yïl*,[25] corresponding to Muḥarram of the year 654 [January–February, 1256] Qubilai Qa'an slaughtered and pillaged throughout that province and, having captured their ruler, Mahārāz[26] by name, that is, "Great King," took him with him and left the army [behind]. Afterward, when Möngke Qa'an set out to conquer the country of Nangiyas, he decreed that since Qubilai had gout and had previously fought a campaign and subjugated a hostile country he should now repose at home. In accordance with this command, [Qubilai] rested in his own *ordos* in Qara'un-Jidun[27] in Mongolia. A year later, when Taghachar Noyan and the princes of the left hand who had gone to Nangiyas had returned without profit, Möngke Qa'an sent them a severe reprimand, and a *yarligh* was issued to the following effect: Qubilai had sent a message, saying: "My gout is better. How is it fitting that Möngke Qa'an should go on a campaign whilst I sit at home?" He should therefore take the troops which Taghachar Noyan had commanded and set out for Nangiyas. In obedience to this command, [Qubilai] set out with 1 *tümen* of his own troops and 10 *tümens* of Jauqut, which belonged to Taghachar Noyan and which he took from him. When he reached the frontiers of Nangiyas, he conquered many of the cities and provinces. At that time Möngke Qa'an was

---

[22] Pelliot (*Polo I*, p. 177) suggests that Dai-Liu is "a weakened pronunciation of *Dai-li-gu = Ta-li-kuo, 'Kingdom of Ta-li.'" Ta-li was the name of the non-Chinese kingdom which afterward became the province of Yunnan.

[23] On the application of these names to Yunnan, see *Polo I*, p. 177.

[24] In Persian, "Gold-Teeth," Polo's Çardandan, the Chinese Chin-Ch'ih. "The territory of the Chin-ch'ih proper lay to the west of the Salween, either on the Nam-ti and Ta-ping, or on the Shweli River, all of them tributaries of the Irawadi . . . ." See *Polo I*, pp. 603–606.

[25] Year of the Dragon: T. *lu*, "dragon."

[26] A variant of the Indian title *mahārāja*. See *Polo I*, pp. 177–78.

[27] Qara'un-Jidun is mentioned in *SH* (§§183 and 206) as a mountain ridge between the Onon and Lake Baljuna. It has not been identified.

laying siege to the fortress of Do Li Shang.[28] Because of the unhealthiness of the climate there was an epidemic of cholera, and Möngke Qa'an fell ill and died. News of his death reached Qubilai on the banks of the River Quiqa Mören.[29] He consulted with Bahadur Noyan, the grandson[30] of Muqali Guyang, the father of Hantum Noyan of the Jalayir bone, saying: "We have come hither with an army like ants or locusts: how can we turn back, our task undone, because of rumors?" He set out for Nangiyas and made a sudden attack upon their army, taking their scouts prisoner. Then he crossed the River Keng, which flows like a sea and is 2 parasangs in breadth, by means of a talisman which he had fashioned out of birch-bark[31] and laid siege to Oju,[32] which is a great city. Previous to this, Möngke Qa'an had sent against the other side of Nangiyas, an army amounting to 3 *tümens*, led by Uriyangqadai, the son of Sübedei Bahadur; with him he had sent Abishqa, a grandson of Chaghatai, and fifty of the princes of the left hand.[33] And since the roads were difficult and the places and castles hard to capture, they had repeatedly given battle, and entry and exit had been made difficult for them. Moreover, on account of the unhealthy climate, many of that army had fallen sick and died, so that of their total number more than five thousand had perished. Receiving news of Qubilai's arrival, they set out toward him and after 20 days suddenly joined him in the neighborhood of that town. The people of the town, in their impotence, sent envoys to him and tendered submission. Then, all of a sudden, the army which had been sent against Möngke Qa'an returned rejoicing at his death, and the townspeople were heartened by their arrival. Meantime the messengers of Chabui Khatun and the emirs of her *ordo*, Taichi'utai and Yekü, arrived and delivered the following message: "The great emirs Dorji and 'Alam-Dār have come from Arïq Böke and are raising *turqaqs* from the Mongols and Jauqut, and the reason for this is unknown.

---

[28] See above, p. 226 and note 112.   [29] The Mongol name of the Hwai Ho.
[30] This is correct. See above, p. 227, note 119.

[31] It is a pity that Rashīd al-Dīn provides no further details about this charm, the purpose of which was, apparently, to placate the water spirits. For the practices adopted in various parts of the world "to propitiate the fickle and dangerous spirits of the water at fords," see J. G. Frazer, *Folk-Lore in the Old Testament* (London, 1918), Vol. II, pp. 414 ff.

[32] See above, p. 229 and note 133.   [33] See above, p. 204, and note 34.

Shall we give them the troops or not?" And they spoke a parable [in the form of] a riddle: "The heads of the big fish and the little fish have been cut off. Who is left but thou and Arïq Böke? Is it possible for thee to return?" Two days later the messengers of Arïq Böke also reached Qubilai and [said] that they had been sent to inquire after his health and bring greetings. He asked them in what direction they were sending the *turqaqs* and *cherigs* they were raising. The messengers replied: "We slaves know nothing. Assuredly it is a lie." Since they kept the matter hidden, Qubilai became suspicious and reflected: "If thou needest *cherigs* for some area, why dost thou conceal this? Therefore it may be a matter of deceit and treachery." He consulted in secret with Bahadur Noyan and Uriyangqadai, saying: "It is some such case as this, and it is not known what Arïq Böke has in mind for us. Both of you remain here with some of the troops, whilst I go back to the Qara-Mörcn in the land of Khitai, where after ascertaining the state of affairs I will send you word." And so it was agreed.

Meanwhile, the princes Taghachar, Qadan, and Yesüngge each went out with the troops that were left, seizing and laying waste provinces and villages. As for Qubilai Qa'an, when he reached the town of Namgin,[34] which is on the Qara-Mören, he discovered that Dorji and 'Alam-Dār had come in search of soldiers and had greatly oppressed the Mongols and Jauqut. He sent a messenger to Arïq Böke to say: "No good will come of the *turqaqs* and *cherigs* that are being raised from Mongol households and the Jauqut country. As for the goods and animals that have been levied from the provinces, let him give them back to them and give them to us and the troops that were with me, Taghachar, Yesüngge, and Narin-Qadan and the troops of the left hand, and also to the troops of the right hand that accompanied Möngke Qa'an and are now with Möge, Qadan, Asutai and Ja'utu. [Give them to us] so that being provided with mounts, fodder, and arms we may deal with Nangiyas." He despatched a message to this effect.

At that time, 'Alam-Dār had departed from thence, while Dorji had remained in the town of Jungdu, which they call Khan-Balïq.[35]

---

[34] A variant of Namging, that is Nan-ching, the modern Kaifeng.

[35] On Khan-Balïq ("Khan Town"), Polo's Cambaluc, the Turkish name for Peking, see *Polo I*, pp. 140–43.

Qubilai Qa'an sent to him to say: "Thou too send a *nöker* with these messengers." Dorji secretly sent a message through his own *nöker* to Arïq Böke, saying: "It appears that Qubilai Qa'an has become aware of your intent. It would be opportune for thee to send a *noyan* from amongst the great emirs along with messengers with falcons and [hunting] animals so that Qubilai Qa'an may feel secure and grow careless." Arïq Böke approved these words and sent a *noyan* with five falcons as a present in the company of the messengers. And he said: "He is coming to bring back news of thy health." And he charged the man together with Dorji Noyan to speak sweet words to Qubilai Qa'an, so that from carelessness and a feeling of security he might quickly turn back. Speaking pleasant words in this strain, the messengers of Arïq Böke declared in one voice before him that he had cancelled the raising of *turqaqs* and *cherigs*. Qubilai replied: "As you have explained those unseemly words, everyone's mind is set at rest." And he dismissed them kindly and sent messengers to Bahadur Noyan and Uriyangqadai saying: "Abandon the siege of Oju at once and come back, for our mind, like the revolution of Fate, has changed." By the time the messengers arrived, Taghachar, Yesüngge, and Narin-Qadan had returned, and Bahadur and Uriyangqadai, descending (?) and turning back, came to Qubilai Qa'an.

And when Dorji and Toqan came to Arïq Böke and informed him of what had happened he said: "Since Qubilai has some inkling of our guile and treachery, it is expedient that we summon the princes and emirs, who are firmly established each in his own *yurt* and home, and settle the question of the Khanate, which has been [too long] deferred and neglected." Having consulted together, they dispatched messengers in every direction. Naimadai, the son of Taghachar, and Yesü, the younger brother of Jibik-Temür, both came to him, but the other princes each found an excuse to stay away. Since no great assembly was gathered, Arïq Böke again took counsel with the emirs [and said]: "It is expedient that once again we send messengers to Qubilai Qa'an and make him feel secure by deceiving him with false words." And he sent Dorji with two others from amongst the emirs and *bitikchis*, giving them the following message: "In order to mourn for Möngke Qa'an it has appeared necessary that Qubilai and all the [other] princes should come." (They intended when they came to seize them all.) When the messengers reached Qubilai Qa'an from that direction, the princes Taghachar, Yesüngge, Narin-Qadan, and the others and the *tümen* commanders had joined him in the town of Jungdu. The messengers delivered their message, and they all declared as one man: "These words are true, and it is the height of expedience. To go is both right and necessary. But we have not yet returned from the campaign. First let us go to our homes and then let us assemble and go together." Dorji said: "My *nökers* will return with this message and I will remain here until I may go in your company." He dispatched his *nökers* accordingly. Qubilai Qa'an then sent a messenger to the army which had invaded Nangiyas under Möngke Qa'an and also gave a message to Asutai, bidding him come quickly. As for Möge he had died during the campaign.

When the *nökers* of Dorji came to Arïq Böke and delivered their message, the princes who were present exclaimed as one man: "How long can we wait for them?" And some of those that were there reached an agreement among themselves and set Arïq Böke on the throne of the Khanate in the Altai summer residence.[36] That group consisted of Orghana Qïz,[37] the wife of Qara-Hülegü, Asutai and Ürüng-Tash, the sons of Möngke Qa'an, Alghu, the grandson of Chaghatai, Naimadai, the son of Taghachar, Yesü, the younger brother of Jibik-Temür, Durchi, the son of Qadan, Qurumshi, the son of Orda, Qarachar, and one son of Bilgütei Noyan. And since they had brought Asutai from the army, they sent 'Alam-Dār as commander and *shaḥna* over the army in order that by [gaining their] confidence he might protect them and show them kindness so that they might not disperse. They then dispatched to the *ordo* of Ögetei Qa'an, to the sons of Köten and Jibik-Temür, and to the countries of the Mongols, Tangqut, and Jauqut, and [they] sent *yarlïghs* and spread rumors to the following effect: "Hülegü, Berke, and the [other] princes had agreed together and raised me to the Khanate. You must pay no attention to the words of Qubilai, Taghachar, Yesüngge, Yeke-Qadan, and Narin-Qadan, nor must you listen to their commands." They composed false words to this effect and wrote and dispatched them. Jibik-Temür and the

---

[36] This was Arïq Böke's own residence. See below, p. 310.

[37] The corrupt form is so read by Blochet, who sees it as T. *qïz* "daughter," in the sense of "princess." On Orqïna (Orghana) Khatun, see above, pp. 149–51.

emirs of Khitai seized the messengers and sent them with the letters [they were carrying] to Qubilai Qa'an. Then he knew for certain that Arïq Böke had risen in rebellion. Hereupon, Taghachar, Yesüngge, Yeke-Qadan, Narin-Qadan, Jibik-Temür, Ja'utu, and the other princes; from amongst the emirs, the sons of Muqali Guyang, Qurum-shi, Nachin Küregen and Derekei Küregen; from amongst the emirs of the left hand, Borcha, the son of Sodun Noyan, and Ejil, the son of Borji, both *tarkhans*; and all the emirs of the right hand—all these gathered together [and] consulted with one another, saying: "Hülegü has gone to the Tāzīk country; the seed of Jochi Khan is exceedingly far away. Those who are at one with Arïq Böke acted in ignorance. Before Hülegü Khan and Berke could come, Orghana Qïz, on the word of the emirs, went to Arïq Böke from [the *ulus* of] Chaghatai. If we do not now set up someone as Qa'an, what can we do?" And having thus consulted together, they were all of one mind, and in the *bichin yïl*,[38] corresponding to the year 658/1259–1260, in the middle of the summer[39] in the town of Kai-Ming-Fu,[40] [they] set Qubilai Qa'an upon the throne of Empire. At that time he was forty-six years of age.[41] As is their wont and custom, all the princes and emirs gave written undertakings and knelt [before him].

❧ HISTORY OF HOW, AFTER HIS ENTHRONEMENT Qubilai Qa'an sent messengers to Arïq Böke; how [Arïq Böke], fought two or three battles against the Qa'an; and how in the end he was defeated.

Thereafter, a hundred messengers were appointed to represent the princes and sent to Arïq Böke, to whom they delivered the following

---

[38] The Year of the Monkey: T. *bichin*, "monkey." 1260.

[39] According to the *Yüan shih*, on the 5th May. See Franke, V, p. 171.

[40] Polo's Chemeinfu, that is, K'ai-p'ing fu, Qubilai's famous summer residence, the name of which was changed on the 16th June, 1263, to Shang-tu, "Upper Capital," familiar to English readers as Coleridge's Xanadu. The ruins of K'ai-p'ing fu "still exist north of the Luan river, in the region generally called by Europeans Dolōn-nōr (the "Seven Lakes"); but the locality called today Dolōn-nōr is actually south of the river." See *Polo I*, pp. 238–40 and 356–57.

[41] Born on the 23rd September, 1215, he was actually still in his forty-fifth year.

message: "We, the princes and emirs, having taken counsel together, have set up Qubilai Qa'an as Qa'an." They feasted all that day, and when night fell Durchi made off in flight. Learning of this they sent messengers after him: the yamchïs[42] seized him and brought him back. They questioned him, using threats, and he confessed the whole story from beginning to end of the rebellion and the thoughts they had harbored. They imprisoned him and, setting Abishqa, the son of Büri, the son of Mö'etüken, over his grandfather's ulus, dispatched him together with his younger brother Narin-Qadan. On the border of the Tangqut country they were met by the envoys of Arïq Böke with a large force of men, who seized them and brought them before him. They were imprisoned and kept in custody, while the messengers of Qubilai Qa'an were sent back.

During that summer they sent many messengers to each other, but agreement could not be achieved. Then they put out reports to the effect that Hülegü Khan, Berke, and the other princes had arrived and that Arïq Böke had become Qa'an upon their advice and with their support. They continued to spread such rumors until autumn came around, when Arïq Böke gave an army to Jumqur, the eldest son of Hülegü Khan, and Qarachar, the son of Udur, together with several other princes and sent them to make war on Qubilai Qa'an. The van of the Qa'an's army was led by Yesüngge and Narin-Qadan. They met and joined battle in the land of ———.[43] The army of Arïq Böke was defeated, and Jumqur and Qarachar with some few others escaped and got away. As for Arïq Böke and his army, they took fright and scattered in disorder, having first put to death the two princes that had been imprisoned and the hundred envoys.

They went into the Qïrqïz country.[44] It had been the custom to bring the food and drink for Qara-Qorum on wagons from Khitai. Qubilai Qa'an banned this traffic and there occurred a great dearth and famine in that region. Arïq Böke was at his wit's end and said: "The best thing is for Alghu, the son of Baidar, the son of Chaghatai, who has long been in attendance on the throne and has learnt the way

---

[42] See Glossary.

[43] BASYKY or BABBKY. Apparently identical with the place-name mentioned above, p. 209.

[44] See above, p. 214, note 69.

and *yosun* of every matter, to go and administer his grandfather's residence and *ulus* and so sent us assistance and provisions and arms and guard the frontier along the Oxus so that the army of Hülegü and the army of Berke cannot come to the aid of Qubilai Qa'an from that direction." With this idea in mind, he spoke kindly to him and sent him on his way. Alghu leapt forth like an arrow from a bow and took his own head. When he reached Kāshghar nearly 150,000 mounted warriors were gathered around him, and he rose in revolt and insurrection.

Meanwhile, the Qa'an had set out upon the campaign and proceeded at great speed until he came to Qanqï Daban,[45] where he heard how Arïq Böke had put to death Abishqa and the two princes that were with him and the hundred envoys. He was incensed and had Durchi Noyan, whom he was holding in custody, put to death. Before setting out on the campaign, he had sent the princes Yeke-Qadan and Qaral-ju, the son of Jochi-Qasar, with several other princes and Büri, from amongst the emirs, with a great army into the Tangqut country, because it had been reported that Arïq Böke had sent 'Alam-Dār and Qundaqai as emir and *shaḥna* respectively, at the head of the army which had been with Möngke Qa'an in Nangiyas and which, after his death, had been commanded by Asutai, who had come post-haste to join him; and they were now in the Tangqut region. When Yeke-Qadan and Qaralju came upon them, they joined battle and 'Alam-Dār was killed in that engagement; and part of the army was slain and part scattered, and the survivors fled to join Arïq Böke in the Qïrqïz country.

As for Qubilai Qa'an, having reached the neighborhood of Qara-Qorum, he found the four *ordos* of Arïq Böke and the *ordos* of Kölgen and restored them and then wintered on the River Ongqï Mören.[46] Meanwhile, Arïq Böke, distraught and bewildered, with a lean and hungry army, was on the borders of Kem-Kemchi'üt on the River *Yus.[47] Fearing the approach of the Qa'an, he sent messengers and

[45] *QNQY DYAN*. The second element of the name is Mo. *dabagh-a(n)*, "mountain pass." This is apparently the modern Khangin-Daba, 35 kilometers southwest of Ulan Bator. See Thiel, p. 113.

[46] The River Onqïn, the modern Ongin Gol, which rises in the Khangai and in wet years reaches and replenishes the Ulan Nur. See Thiel, pp. 39 and 409.

[47] So Hambis (1956, p. 300, note 69) suggests that this corrupt name should be

sought pardon, saying: "We *inis* committed a crime and transgressed out of ignorance. Thou art my *aqa*, and thou knowest thy power. I shall go whithersoever thou commandest and shall not deviate from the *aqa's* command. Having fattened and satisfied my animals I will present myself before thee. Berke, Hülegü, and Alghu are also coming: I will await their arrival." When the messengers came to the Qa'an and delivered their message, he said: "The princes that had gone astray are now awake, and in their right mind, and having come to their senses have confessed to their crime." And in reply he said: "When Hülegü, Berke, and Alghu arrive we shall determine where the meeting-place shall be. As for you, you must first keep your word, and if you come before their arrival it will be all the more praiseworthy." And sending the messengers back, he himself returned and took up abode in his own *ordos* in Qara'un-Jidun,[48] giving the *cherig* leave to break up and depart to their own *yurts*. And he dismissed the [occupants of] the *ordos* of Arïq Böke and Kölgen to their *yurts* and ordered them to remain there. And he placed Yesüngge, who was a cousin of the Qa'an, in command of the frontiers of the *ulus* with an army of 10 *tümens* and bade him stay there until Arïq Böke arrived and then [to] come with him.

Now at that time Hülegü and Alghu favored the Qa'an and were constantly sending messengers to each other. Hülegü sent messengers and reproached Arïq Böke for his activities and sought to restrain him. He also kept sending messengers to the Qa'an, as did Alghu. And when he learnt that Qaidu and Qutuqu were siding with Arïq Böke, he several times attacked and repelled them. It was at this time that the Qa'an sent a message to Hülegü Khan and Alghu, saying: "The lands are in revolt. From the banks of the Oxus to the gates of Egypt the Tāzīk lands must be administered and well guarded by

---

emended, the Yus (in Chinese transliteration, Yu-hsü) being, according to a passage in the *Yüan shih* quoted by Hambis (pp. 282 and 295), a tributary of the Yenisei. It could equally well be the Us (Wu-ssŭ), referred to in *Yüan shih* 63, 34b–35a (not 17a as stated by Hambis, p. 286), where mention is made of a district of this name "east of the Kirghiz and north of the Ch'ien River," that is, the Kem = the Yenisei; the text says that this locality "takes its name from the [homonymous] river," that is, the Us, one of the affluents of the Yenisei. I am indebted for this reference to Dr. Igor de Rachewiltz, who made it available to me in a letter dated the 29th May, 1968.   [48] See above, p. 247 and note 27.

thee, Hülegü; from the Altai on the far side to the Oxus *el* and *ulus* must be administered and maintained by Alghu; and from the Altai on this side to the shores of the Ocean-Sea [all lands] will be maintained by me." And Berke kept sending messengers to both sides and sought to reconcile them.

As for Arïq Böke, when he had fattened his horses in the summer and autumn, he did not keep his word but broke his promise and again went to war against the Qa'an. When he came to Yesüngge, who was stationed on the frontier of the region, he sent a messenger to say that he was coming to surrender. Having thus rendered him careless he fell upon him, routed and scattered him and his army, and restored the *ordos* of Chaghatai Khan and Kölgen as well as his own. Meanwhile, Yesüngge crossed the desert and made his way to the Qa'an, to whom he reported that a rebel was approaching. The Qa'an sent a messenger to Taghachar and gathered *cherigs*. He himself, Taghachar, Hulaqur, the son of Elchitei, and Narin-Qadan, with the armies they commanded, were the first [to be ready]. Hulaqur, Nachin Küregen, Derekei Küregen of the Ikires people, Oradai, and Qadan, each with his own *tümen*, proceeded in the van and fought well. As for Yesüngge, because his troops had been dispersed, he did not take part in this battle. The Qa'an, with the aforementioned armies, encountered Arïq Böke on the edge of the desert. They joined battle in a place called Abjiya-Köteger,[49] in front of a hill called Khucha-Boldaq[50] and a *na'ur* called Shimultai.[51] Arïq Böke's army was defeated, and many of the Oirat tribesmen were killed. And when Arïq Böke was defeated with his army and fled, the Qa'an said: "Do not pursue them, for they are ignorant children. They must realize what they have done and repent." (The picture of the battle is as shown.) Ten days later Asutai, the son of Möngke Qa'an, who led Arïq Böke's rearguard, came to

[49] The Abji'a-Köteger of *SH*, §§187 and 191. It was here that Genghis Khan passed the winter following his destruction of the Kereit. This mountainous area is located by Pelliot and Hambis (*Campagnes*, p. 409) somewhere near the sources of the Khalkha, in the Great Khingan.

[50] "Ram Hillock:" unidentified.

[51] Mo. *shimughultai*, "having midges." In the letter referred to in note 47, Dr. de Rachewiltz writes: "Although several identifications of this lake have been proposed (by Hung Chün, T'u Chi a. o.), none of them seems very convincing to me. It certainly is one of the small lakes of the Eastern Gobi—the region of the Upper Khalkha River—but at present I cannot offer a more definite identification."

[Arïq Böke] and heard that the army of Taghachar and the other armies of the Qa'an had turned back. Arïq Böke and Asutai consulted together again and gave battle after mid-day on the edge of the sand desert called Elet,[52] by Shirgen-Na'ur[53] and Shilügelig[54] hill. The Qa'an's army defeated the right wing of Arïq Böke's army, but the left wing and center stood firm till nightfall and in the night caused the Qa'an to withdraw. Both princes now retired with their armies and went to their own *ordos*, while most of their troops perished because of the great distance and their being on foot. In the winter both encamped in their own quarters and passed the spring and summer there. As for Arïq Böke, having several times asked Alghu to help him with arms and provisions and having received no response, he equipped an army and set out against him. *And God knows best what is right.*

THE REVOLT OF ALGHU AGAINST ARÏQ BÖKE and the reason thereof; how he fought the army of Arïq Böke [and] was defeated; how he recovered his strength; and [how] Arïq Böke's cause began to weaken

Alghu, the son of Baidar, the son of Chaghatai, had been appointed by Arïq Böke to rule over the *ulus* of Chaghatai. When he left him and arrived in the country of Turkistān, nearly 150,000 horsemen gathered around him. Orghana Khatun, who was the ruler of the *ulus* of Chaghatai, set out for the Court of Arïq Böke, and Alghu sent Negübci Oghul with five thousand horsemen, a man called Uchachar from amongst his emirs, Sulaimān Beg, the son of Ḥabash 'Amīd,[55] from amongst the *bitikchis*, and a man called Abishqa from amongst the

---

[52] Apparently identical with Qalaqaljit-Elet, "the Qalaqaljit Sands," the scene of the battle in 1203 between Genghis Khan and Ong-Khan, the ruler of the Kereit. See *Conquérant*, pp. 157–60.

[53] "The lake that dries up, evaporates (in the summer)." See *L'Empire Mongol*, p. 549.

[54] With Shilügelig Dr. de Rachewiltz, in the letter referred to above, note 47, compares Shilügeljit, the name of a river in this area (*SH* §§153 and 173). In his opinion, Qalaqaljit-Elet, Shirgen-Na'ur, and Shilügelig "must be found . . . east of modern Tamzag-Bulak, that is, between Tamzag-Bulak and the western slopes of the Khingan, in the easternmost part of the Mongolian People's Republic."

[55] See above, p. 156.

yarghuchis to Samarqand, Bukhārā, and the countries of Transoxiana to defend the frontiers in that direction and execute his orders. When they arrived in that region, they put to death all the dependants and *nökers* of Berke, even martyring the son of a *shaikh al-Islām*, Burhān al-Dīn, the son of the great shaikh Ṣaif al-Dīn Bakharzī, on this account. They carried off all the property of these people and sent some of the valuables to Negübei Oghul, [and] Uchachar then [went] to Khwārazm. At this juncture Arïq Böke's messengers arrived, headed by Büritei Bitikchi and Shādi, the son of Yoshmut and Erkegün, and delivered the *yarlïgh* ordering the levying of goods, horses, and arms. In a short time they had collected a great quantity of goods. Alghu coveted these and was seeking excuses and holding the messengers up until one day he was told that they had said: "We have collected these goods in accordance with the *yarlïgh* of Arïq Böke. What concern is this of Alghu?" He was offended and in his anger ordered them to be arrested and the goods seized. His emirs said: "Having committed such an act thou has lost Arïq Böke's favor, especially as Orghana Khatun has gone to complain to him. We [by ourselves] are unable to withstand his reproach and anger. Since we have become his enemies, it is advisable that we give support to the Qa'an." Having agreed upon this, they put the messengers to death and distributed the goods amongst the troops.

When Arïq Böke learnt of this he was extremely annoyed. He killed Alghu's messenger and said: "Let the people of Qara-Qorum assist us." But the *imāms*, *bakhshis*,[56] and Christians declared: "The *yasaq* is hard: how can we [help]?" And he said: "What army will these three groups defeat and of what use would they be in battle? Let them remain here and assist us, with prayer. And if the Qa'an arrives, let them hasten to join him." And he set out to make war on Alghu. Upon [Arïq Böke's] departure the Qa'an at once arrived before the town of Qara-Qorum at the head of a large army, which formed a *jerge* around the town. Some people from each community came out and reported on Arïq Böke. The Qa'an treated them kindly and made them *tarkhan*, as they had been previously in accordance with the decrees of Ögetei Qa'an and Möngke Qa'an. He intended to go in

[56] See Glossary.

pursuit of Arïq Böke, but messengers arrived and reported that because of his absence, madness and confusion had appeared in the land of Khitai. He therefore returned to his capital there.

Meanwhile, Qara-Buqa, who commanded Arïq Böke's vanguard, gave battle to Alghu near the town of Pulad[57] in a place called Süt-Köl.[58] Alghu was victorious, and Qara-Buqa was killed. Alghu, marveling and elated because he had defeated Arïq Böke's vanguard and killed Qara-Buqa, turned back in a careless fashion along the River Hïla[59] and alighted at his own *ordos* after dismissing the *cherigs*. Asutai, who with his army formed Arïq Böke's rearguard, now arrived and, passing through the hills which in that country are called Temür-Qahalqa,[60] attacked the Hïla Mören[61] and Almalïq with picked troops and captured Alghu's *ulus*.

Since his *cherigs* had been dispersed, Alghu took his wife and the army of the right hand, which Asutai had not yet reached, and fled in the direction of Khotan and Kāshghar. Arïq Böke now arrived in his pursuit and passed that winter on the Hïla Mören and in Almalïq, continually feasting and slaughtering and pillaging Alghu's army and *ulus*. After a month Alghu was joined by his fugitive troops and, setting out with his heavy baggage, he made for Samarqand. [In the] meantime, Jumqur, the son of Hülegü, having been affected with some slight ailment, asked Arïq Böke for permission to leave him, saying that he was going to Samarqand for medical treatment. He parted from him in the *qulquna yïl*, that is, the Year of the Rat, falling in Rabī' I of the year 662 [January, 1264]. And since Arïq Böke was ruthlessly slaughtering and injuring Alghu's army and *ulus* without their having committed any crime, the emirs conceived an aversion to him and each of them turned away on some pretext. "He is now," they said, "wantonly slaughtering the Mongol army that was gathered

---

[57] The Bolat of Rubruck (Rockhill, p. 137), where Büri's German prisoners were "digging for gold and manufacturing arms." Bretschneider (II, p. 42) suggests that the town was situated somewhere in the valley of the Borotala, which flows into the Ebi Nor.

[58] In Turkish "Milk Lake:" Lake Sairam.

[59] The Ili.

[60] "Iron Gate" (cf. above, Section 1, p. 61, note 260). Here the Talki Defile, north of Kulja. See Bretschneider, II, p. 34, note 804.

[61] That is, the River Ili: Mo. *mören*, "river."

together by Chingiz-Khan. How should we not rebel and turn against him?" And in that winter most of them departed. And when spring came around, dearth and famine appeared in Almalïq. The soldiers gave their horses wheat instead of barley, and as they did not eat their fill of grass, they all perished. Many of the people of Almalïq died of starvation, and the survivors sought refuge from the tyranny and oppression of the soldiers in the Court of God and raised their hands [in] supplication [and] prayer. One day Arïq Böke was carousing and making merry when a whirlwind suddenly sprang up, ripped the thousand-pegged audience tent, and broke the supporting pole, with the result that a number of people were hurt and wounded. The ministers and emirs of his court took this occurrence as an omen predicting the decline of his fortune. They abandoned him altogether and dispersed on all sides, so that Arïq Böke and Asutai were left alone with only a small force and knew for certain that their condition of distress was due to the curses of the destitute people who had lost their lives in that dearth and famine. And what doubt can there be of this, seeing that many great houses have been destroyed by the sighs of the oppressed?

Truly the sigh of an oppressed person in the morning is worse than an arrow or a quarrel or a javelin.

At that time Ürüng-Tash, the son of Möngke Qa'an, was in Mongolia near the Altai on the river which they call Jabqan Mören.[62] When the commanders of thousands arrived in that region they sent a message to him, saying: "We are going with our armies to the Qa'an. What doest thou advise in this matter?" Ürüng-Tash approved and joined them. And he sent a messenger to Arïq Böke and asked for his father's great jade *tamgha*,[63] which he had in his possession. Arïq Böke sent it to him, and he departed with the commanders of thousands to wait upon the Qa'an.

As for Alghu, when he learnt of Arïq Böke's weakened position he set out to attack him. Learning of his intention and knowing he was close at hand, Arïq Böke dismissed Orghana Khatun, together with Mas'ūd Beg, and sent her to Alghu, in order that his violence might be abated. [Alghu] married her and, in order to set her mind

---

[62] The modern Dzabkhan.   [63] See Glossary.

at rest, showed favor to Mas'ūd Beg, making him ṣāḥib-dīvān of his realm and sending him to Samarqand and Bukhārā to administer those places. He proceeded thither, and began to collect taxes continuously from the population and despatch them to Alghu as they came in. As a result, the affairs of Alghu recovered. He gathered his scattered forces together, fought a battle with Berke's army, and defeated them and plundered Otrar. A year later he died, and Orghana Khatun, in agreement with the emirs and viziers, set her son Mubārak-Shāh in his place, as has been related in the history of Chaghatai.[64] *O Lord, give aid and a good end!*

❧ HOW ARÏQ BÖKE FROM WEAKNESS WAS COMPELLED to go to the Court of the Qa'an and confess his crime; his latter end

When the army and the emirs turned away from him and the princes each went his own way, Arïq Böke was at his wit's end and from weakness was compelled to betake himself to the Qa'an in the *qulquna yïl*, that is, the Year of the Rat, corresponding to the year 662/1263–1264.[65] When he arrived at the Court of the Qa'an orders were given for a large body of troops to be stationed there, and the Qa'an ordered him to make his submission. Now it is their custom in such cases to cast the door of the tent over the shoulders of the evildoer. He made submission covered in this manner and after awhile was given permission and entered. He took his stand amongst the *bitikchis*. The Qa'an looked at him for a time and was moved with brotherly feeling and sorrow. Arïq Böke wept and tears came to the Qa'an's eyes also. He wiped them and asked: "Dear brother, in this strife and contention were we in the right or you?" Arïq Böke answered: "We were then and you are today." Now at that time a messenger called Chingqur had come from Hülegü Khan and was present on this occasion. When he returned he reported to Hülegü what had occurred. Hülegü Khan sent a message to the Qa'an to say: "How is it in keeping with the *yasa* that our family should be allowed to make submission in this manner and that *aqa* and *ini* should be thus humiliated?" Qa'an

[64] See above p. 151.
[65] Actually 1264.

listened to these words and approved of them; and he sent the following reply: "Hülegü is right. I acted out of ignorance." And after that he did not admit Arïq Böke to his presence for a whole year.

On that occasion Ajïqï, the brother of Abishqa, who had been put to death by Asutai, said to the last named: "It was thou who killed my brother." He replied: "I killed him by the command of the then ruler, Arïq Böke. Moreover I did not wish a member of our family to be killed by a *qarachu*. Today Qubilai Qa'an is ruler of the face of the earth. If he so commands, I will kill thee too." The Qa'an said to Ajïqï: "This is not the time for such words; there is violent anger in them." In the midst of this exchange Taghachar Noyan stood up and said: "It is the Qa'an's command that today we should not inquire about bygone matters but should concern ourselves with feasting and merrymaking." The Qa'an approved of this and that day they occupied themselves with drinking. Taghachar then said: "Arïq Böke is standing. Let the Emperor assign a place for him to sit in." The Qa'an indicated that he should sit with the princes, and they spent the rest of the day feasting and carousing.

The next morning the princes and great emirs, Taghachar, the son of Otchi Noyan, Yesüngge, the son of Jochi Qasar, Hulaqur, Yeke-Qadan, Jibik-Temür, the son of Ajïqï, Ja'utu, the son of Shiremün, the son of Shingqur, and Ajïqï, the son of Büri and grandson of Chaghatai, assembled in the audience chamber. The Qa'an ordered the emirs to seize Arïq Böke and bind him. He then gave orders that, of the princes, Shiregi, Taqai, Charaqu, and Bai-Temür, and, of the emirs, Hantum Noyan, Dörbetei, and Bolad Chingsang, who had been in this country, should sit down, examine Arïq Böke and his emirs, and make a report. Arïq Böke said: "It is I who am the author of this crime which has spread so far and wide. These men have committed no crime." His words were not listened to, and the Qa'an ordered the guilty emirs to be told as follows: "In the days of Möngke Qa'an the emirs of the time did not string a single bow against him, and there was no great revolt, only a little discord which they harbored in their hearts. All the world knows how they were punished and chastised.[66] How then shall it be with you who have stirred up all these troubles, and cast so much confusion and tumult amongst all mankind, and destroyed so

[66] See above, pp. 210 ff.

many princes, emirs, and soldiers?" They were all silent. Then Tümen
Noyan who was the senior amongst them and belonged to the great
bone,[67] said: "O emirs, why do you not answer? Have your eloquent
tongues become mute? That day when we set Arïq Böke upon the
throne we promised each other that we should die in front of that
throne. Today is that day of dying. Let us keep our word." Said the
Qa'an: "It is a fine promise of thine, and thou has kept thy word."
Then he asked Arïq Böke: "Who incited thee to rebellion and insurrection?" He replied: "Bulgha and 'Alam-Dār said to me: 'Both
Qubilai Qa'an and Hülegü have gone on campaigns and the great
ulus has been entrusted by the Qa'an to thee. What hast thou in mind?
Wilt thou let them cut our throats like sheep?' I said: 'Have you
consulted Dorji?' They said: 'Not yet.' I said: 'Consult Tümen,
Toquz, Alichar, and Khoja.' They all agreed in their advice. Since
Dorji was not present on account of illness, I said: 'Send for him so
that we may finish our talking.' He too presented himself and agreed
in his advice. This act was carried out and completed by all of them
together. Tümen [alone] of them did not turn against my words and
performed what I had ordered. It was Jibik-Temür who did harm,
that is, he uttered words about the Qa'an that did not befit his like."

The emirs all said with one voice: "The facts of the case are as
Arïq Böke says, and his words are all true." But Jibik-Temür said:
"Arïq Böke instructed me to do everything which he now attributes
to me, and Bulgha Aqa is witness to this and knows [that it is so]."
The Qa'an then ordered Jibik-Temür to be confronted with Arïq
Böke. He repeated those same words to his face. Arïq Böke was dis-
pleased and said: "If it is so, then thou must remain alive whilst I die."
These words were reported to the Qa'an, and he thus knew that
Jibik-Temür had spoken the truth. He released him and, having
consulted all the princes, aqa and ini, declared as follows: "Bulgha
Bitikchi has listened to the words of Ögetei Qa'an and Möngke Qa'an.
We will release him alive and he will bear witness to their conduct
in this matter to Hülegü and the other princes." And with the agreement of all the princes, [he] released him.

When Asutai learnt of his release he said: "How is it fitting that
Bulgha should remain alive? I will confront him and expose his crimes."

[67] See above, p. 197, note 3.

And he said to him: "Thou citedst a Mongol proverb, the meaning of which was that we had done something and must not now abandon it or fail in it. That was thy great crime for which thou must die." Bulgha Noyan did not deny this but confirmed to him that it was so. And when those words of his were reported to the Qa'an he said: "Since it is so let him be executed."

As for Elchitei, his guilt was greater than the others' since he had made false accusations against Qurumshi, the son of Qadan, so that they put him to death. Toquz's guilt was heavy also, for he had striven to put many members of the Qa'an's *ulus* to death. All the above-mentioned emirs were executed. As for Hoqu, the son of Güyük Khan, Chabat, the son of Naqu, and Totoq, the son of Qarachar, they were sent by the Qa'an along with some other princes to Turkistān. Then he wished to examine Arïq Böke, for which purpose he was awaiting the arrival of Hülegü Khan, Berke, and Alghu. However, since they were exceedingly far away and time was passing, the princes in that region, viz. Taghachar, Yesüngge, Yeke-Qadan, Hulaqur, Jibik-Temür, and the other Mongol and Khitayan princes and emirs gathered together and examined Arïq Böke and Asutai.

And when ten of Arïq Böke's emirs had been put to death and he himself had been examined, a royal *yarlïgh* was dispatched to all parts of the Empire [telling of these matters]. And the emirs all consulted together, saying: "How shall we look at the crime of Arïq Böke and Asutai? Shall we spare their lives for the Qa'an's sake?" And they sent messengers to Hülegü, Berke, and Alghu, saying: "Since your presence was not possible because of the distance of the road and the multiplicity of your preoccupations, and since to wait longer might have introduced into the affairs of the Empire such weakness and confusion as might not be put to rights, we have therefore executed their emirs and have examined them both. We now consult you on this matter. We, that is all the *aqa* and *ini*, are agreed that we should spare Arïq Böke's life and release Asutai. What do you say to this?" The messengers came first to Alghu and delivered their message. He replied: "I too succeeded Chaghatai without consulting the Qa'an and Hülegü Aqa. When all the *aqa* and *ini* are assembled and question me as to whether I am right or wrong, if they approve of me, I shall say whether I think well or ill of it." The messengers then came

to Hülegü Khan and made their report. He said: "Howsoever it may
be decided when all the *aqa* and *ini* assemble and consult with one
another, so let it be. When Berke sets out for the *quriltai*, we too
will quickly start on our way." And he sent his own messengers with
them to Berke in order that they might fix a meeting place and go
[together] to the Qa'an [and] the *quriltai*. When they came to Berke
and reported all the circumstances he said: "Whatever the Qa'an
and Hülegü Khan and all the *aqa* and *ini* agree upon, so it shall be.
We for our part shall set out in the *hüker yïl*;[68] we shall travel throughout the *bars yïl*;[69] and we shall arrive at the *quriltai*, along with Hülegü,
in the *taulai yïl*."[70] When the messengers reached the Qa'an and made
their report, Arïq Böke and Asutai were permitted to do homage and
were admitted into the *ordo*. In the autumn of that year, which was
the Year of the Panther, corresponding to 664/1265–1266, Arïq
Böke was taken ill and died. As for Hülegü Khan and Berke, hostilities
broke out between them, as has been mentioned in their history, and
shortly afterward both died. May the Lord of Islam, Ghazan Khan
(*God cause him to reign forever!*), be the heir to [other men's] lives during
many years and countless ages! May he enjoy his life and fortune!
And when the news of their deaths reached the Qa'an he set Abaqa,
the eldest son of Hülegü Khan, over the Mongols and Tāzīks of
Persia and granted the *ulus* of Jochi to Möngke-Temür. As for Alghu,
he was at that time afflicted with a long illness and so could not go
to the *quriltai*; and then he too died. Orghana Khatun, with the agreement of her emirs, set her son Mubārak-Shāh in his place. Baraq,
the son of Yesün-To'a, the son of Mö'etüken, the son of Chaghatai,
stated in the presence of the Qa'an: "Why has Mubārak-Shāh succeeded my uncle Alghu? If it is commanded that I take my uncle's
place, my loins are girded in service and obedience." The Qa'an
gave him a *yarlïgh* to the effect that he should rule the *ulus* until Mubārak-Shāh came of age. He came and took his place; and Chübei and
Qaban, the sons of Alghu, and their *aqa* and *ini* separated from
Baraq and went with their armies to the Qa'an.

[68] Year of the Ox: 1265.
[69] Year of the Panther: 1266.
[70] Year of the Hare: 1267.

ᴇᴧ HOW THE QA'AN SENT HIS SONS NOMOGHAN AND Kököchü with the other princes to make war on Qaidu; and how the princes plotted treason against them both

When the Qa'an had set his mind at rest regarding the rebellion of Arïq Böke, all the princes had girded the belt of obedience to him except Qaidu, the son of Qashi, the son of Ögedei Qa'an, and some of the descendants of Chaghatai. Qubilai Qa'an sent messengers to them, seeking to win them over, and said: "The other princes have all presented themselves here: why have you not come? It is my heart's desire that we should brighten our eyes with the sight of one another. Then, having consulted together on every matter, you will receive all manner of favors and return home." Qaidu had no mind to submit and gave the following excuse: "Our animals are lean. When they are fat we will obey the command." He delayed on this pretext for 3 years. Then, together with Qonichi Noyan, he drove off Narin, who was attached to Ürüng-Tash, the son of Möngke Qa'an, and was stationed with them, slaughtered and pillaged, and rose in rebellion and insurrection. To put down this rebellion the Qa'an dispatched his son Nomoghan with the following princes of the right and left hands: of the sons of Möngke Qa'an, Shiregi, of the sons of Arïq Böke, Yobuqur and Melik-Temür, of the nephews of the Qa'an, Toq-Temür, the son of Sögedei and Urughtai, and of his cousins, Charaqu, the grandson of Otchigin, along with emirs and troops without limit or measure, the emirs being headed by Hantum Noyan.[71]

They passed the summer on the banks of the river and for some days went on hunting expeditions. Toq-Temür and Shiregi became separated from the rest and met each other on the hunting field. They consulted together and said: "Let us between us seize Nomoghan and Hantum Noyan and hand them over to the enemy." And Toq-Temür tempted Shiregi, saying: "Thou art worthy of the rulership and the Qa'an has done us and our brothers much wrong." In the night they seized them both and sent Nomoghan and his brother Kököchü to Möngke-Temür and Hantum Noyan to Qaidu. And they said: "We are under

[71] His Chinese name was An-t'ung. He was a descendant of Genghis Khan's general, Muqali. See *Polo II*, p. 796.

many obligations to you. We have not forgotten this and have sent you Qubilai Qa'an's sons and his emirs, who were on their way to attack you. We must not think ill of each other but unite to drive off the enemy." The messengers came back bringing this message: "We are grateful to you, and it is what we expected of you. Since there is good water and grass in that region, stay where you are."

Toq-Temür went on an expedition against the *ordos* of Ögetei and Chaghatai and seized Sarban and the brother of Minqa-Temür, who were in charge of those *ordos*. He put about the rumor that the sons of Batu and Qaidu and the princes had formed an alliance and were following behind. They all set out and went away with Toq-Temür. Then, all of a sudden, the Qa'an's army, led by Beklemish, arrived and it became clear to the *ordos* that the story about the approach of the sons of Batu and Qaidu was false. Meanwhile, Toq-Temür and Sarban had joined Shiregi, and together they fought a battle with the Qa'an's troops. Toq-Temür, Shiregi, and Sarban were put to flight and made for the *el* of the Bārin[72] on the bank of the River Erdish, where they each of them busied himself with preparations. From thence Toq-Temür set out to attack the Qïrqïz country. The Qa'an's troops came up and plundered his heavy baggage. He came back in search of it and asked Shiregi for help, which he refused. Toq-Temür was offended with him and, having suddenly come upon Sarban upon the return journey, in order to spite Shiregi, he tempted him also with the promise of the rulership. At that time there was a great distance between them and Shiregi. However, It-Buqa of the ———[73] people was present. He was connected with Shiregi and hurried and informed Melik-Temür and the other princes of what had happened. Shiregi and Melik-Temür gathered their forces and stationed themselves on the ———[74] steppe. And they sent a messenger to Toq-Temür to say: "Why do we cause unrest and confusion in the *ulus*?" He replied: "There is no boldness or dash in Shiregi. I wish Sarban, who is worthy of it, to be the ruler." Having no choice, Shiregi sent to Sarban to say: "If thou must have the rulership ask me for it. Why dost thou ask Toq-Temür?" In reply Toq-Temür said: "Why should

---

[72] Not in Verkhovsky. This was the territory given by Genghis Khan to the Bārin Qorchi: it extended as far as the forest peoples along the Irtysh. See *Campagnes*, p. 300.
[73] Blank in the MSS.   [74] Blank in the MSS.

we ask thee for the rulership and go to thee? Thou must come to us.''
Shiregi realized that he could not resist them and that if he fought
many troops would be uselessly destroyed; and so he went to them.
In the meanwhile, Toq-Temür sent for It-Buqa. He fled and they
pursued him; and when they caught up with him he stabbed himself
with a knife and so died.

They then agreed among themselves that Sarban should sit in the
first place, and they charged Shiregi as follows: "If thou hast come
with a sincere heart send messengers this very instant to the sons of
Batu and Qaidu to announce that we of our own free will made Sarban
our chief and leader.'' He sent the messengers immediately. Then they
said to him: "Go back to thy own *ordo* and let Melik-Temür remain
here until the arrival of Yobuqur.'' Shiregi informed Yobuqur but
he refused and would not go to Sarban. Toq-Temür led an army
against him and when he drew near sent a messenger to say: "We
have reached this decision. If thou agreest, well and good; otherwise
prepare for battle.'' Yobuqur sent this answer: "I shall not fight.
I ask only for 5 days' grace to prepare my submission.'' And he
busied himself with equipping his army and on the fifth day came out
with it and drew up in line to give battle. Toq-Temür charged, and
his army at once turned round and went over to Yobuqur. Toq-
Temür fled with twelve *nökers* and after 3 days came to the Mongols'
tents covered with black felt. He asked for water. They recognized
him and brought curds. Immediately behind him came a party [of his
pursuers]; they found his trail and set out after him. All at once he
came to a stream of muddy water, and he said to his *nökers*: "It is
better if we fight and die with a good name.'' They answered: "Thou
art of the family; they will not hurt thee. But it would be bad for us.''
Despairing of the *nökers* he threw away his arms and was captured
by his enemies. He was taken before Yobuqur. Shiregi asked Yobuqur
to give him to him, and Yobuqur said: "If thou wilt protect him,
thou art my greatest enemy.'' Shiregi replied: "If he has done one
evil thing ten good things will not avail him.'' And he put Toq-Temür
to death. Sarban now came to Shiregi and said: "It was Toq-Temür
who made me do what I did.'' Shiregi took his troops from him, and
he wandered about with two or three *nökers*. After awhile they began
to desert in small groups and make their way to the Qa'an. Shiregi
wished to go after the fugitives and bring them back. He was afraid

Sarban might stir up unrest and he sent him with fifty *nökers* to Qonichi, the grandson of Jochi. It so happened that in the region of Jand and Özkend their route passed by a private estate (*khail-khāna*) of Sarban. His dependents gathered around, seized the fifty *nökers*, and released him. Sarban again set out at the head of an army, seized Shiregi's baggage train, and ordered it to be sent to the Qa'an, sending on a messenger in advance to report on his own position. Shiregi learnt of this and came to give him battle. His army at once went over to Sarban and he was left alone. Sarban ordered him to be guarded by five hundred horsemen. Hearing of this, Yobuqur led his army to give battle to Sarban, but his troops also went over to Sarban, and he too was captured and handed over to five hundred horsemen. They now set out to go to the Qa'an. Yobuqur feigned illness and asked for 2 or 3 days' grace, during which time he secretly sent a large sum in money and jewels to Otchigin, the nephew of Chingiz-Khan, whose *yurt* was in that region, and asked him to save him from that dreadful gulf. Prince Otchigin gathered together his army and suddenly drove off their horses and surrounded the soldiers. Sarban made off with his wife with only one mount. One of Otchigin's *bahadurs* saw his wife escaping and tried to seize her. She cried out. Sarban turned back, shot the man with a single arrow and set out with his wife to join the Qa'an. Shiregi had arrived there before him, and the Qa'an had not admitted him and had ordered him to reside on an island with a very unhealthy climate, where he remained all his life and finally died. As for Sarban, the Qa'an showed him favor and gave him lands and troops; and after awhile he too passed away.

As for Yobuqur, he took the *ordos* of Shiregi and Sarban and joined the following (*khail*) of Qonichi. Melik-Temür and Qurbaqa went to Qaidu, and Ulus-Buqa, the son of Shiregi, joined the following of Qonichi and remained there awhile. Yobuqur grew tired of serving Qaidu and fled to join the Qa'an, as did Ulus-Buqa with his mother and the *ordos*. And when Möngke-Temür, the grandson of Jochi, died, Töde-Möngke was set up in his stead, and Noqai, Töde-Möngke, and Qonichi consulted together and sent Nomoghan to the Qa'an, saying: "We have all submitted and will attend the *quriltai*." And Qaidu likewise sent back Hantum Noyan but did not go to the *quriltai*. They too revoked their intention, and Nomoghan died a year later. *And God knows best what is right.*

◆ HOW THE QA'AN SENT AN ARMY INTO THE LAND
of Nangiyas and subjugated those countries[75]

When the Qa'an had given the Mongol army several years of rest from campaigning, he reflected that since the land of Khitai had been completely subjugated Nangiyas also must be taken. During the reign of Möngke Qa'an the ruler of those parts had been very friendly with him and messengers were always passing to and fro between them, for the rulers of Nangiyas were of noble stock and high repute and in former time had held the countries of Khitai. Altan-Khan belonged to the race of the Jürchen people who rose up and seized those countries, whereupon the former rulers departed to Nangiyas, as shall be described in the history of that people which is appended to this book.[76] Because of their enmity toward the rulers of Khitai they rendered assistance when Chingiz-Khan was conquering those countries, and in particular, during the reign of Ögetei Qa'an they sent a great army and gave their aid until the ruler of Khitai was completely defeated, as has been related in the history [of Ögetei Qa'an].[77]

Möngke Qa'an was the first to have the intention of conquering Nangiyas, and Qubilai Qa'an had the same intention, especially as his capital was in Khitai and therefore near to their countries. However, whenever he sent an army to their frontiers little progress was made until the date ———[78] a man called Bayan,[79] the son of Kökechü[80] of the Bārin bone, whose grandfather, Alaq,[81] had been executed for a great crime. This Bayan fell to the lot and share of Qubilai Qa'an, and since he was in Persia in the service of Abaqa Khan, Qubilai Qa'an sent Sartaq Noyan, the son of Sodun Noyan, as a messenger

---

[75] On the campaign against the Sung, see Franke, IV, pp. 334–50.

[76] That is, in Rashīd al-Dīn's (as yet unpublished) *History of China*.

[77] See above, pp. 39–41.

[78] Blank in all the MSS.

[79] Polo's Baian Cingsan, "Bayan of the Hundred Eyes," on whom see *Polo I*, pp. 67–68; also Cleaves 1956.

[80] Or He'ügütei. See *Polo I*, p. 68, and Cleaves 1956, p. 204 and note 12.

[81] In the Campaign in the West he had taken part in the operations along the Syr Darya. See *HWC*, p. 91. The nature of his crime is not known.

together with 'Abd al-Raḥmān[82] and asked for Bayan. In the Year of the Ox,[83] in which Hülegü Khan died, [Bayan] was sent to the Qa'an along with Sartaq Noyan, while 'Abd al-Raḥmān remained behind in those countries to settle the accounts. When he arrived there the Qa'an fitted out 30 tümens of Mongol and 80 tümens of Khitayan troops. Over the latter he appointed Semeke Bahadur,[84] a Khitayan emir from the town of Balghasun,[85] who had submitted during the reign of Möngke Qa'an and had given aid with a sincere heart. Over the Mongol troops he placed the Emir Aju,[86] the grandson of Sübedei Noyan, of the Uriyangqat people. He ordered Semeke Bahadur to be the commander-in-chief, because his yasaq was severe and he had always performed his tasks well, [and] he sent them toward Nangiyas. Semeke remained behind en route because of illness, and Bayan and Aju became the commanders of both armies. Since the extent of the countries of Nangiyas is extremely vast and their troops innumerable and immeasureable, it was difficult to conquer them and took a long time. They strove and endeavored for 4 years[87] and subjugated some parts and then sent messengers to the Qa'an to say their troops were not sufficient. Being unable to procure troops quickly, the Qa'an issued a yarlïgh that all the prisoners in the kingdom of Khitai should be brought before him. They were nearly twenty thousand men. He spoke to them as follows: "You are all destined to die and be killed. For your heads' sake I have set you free and I will give you horses, arms, and clothing and send you to the army. If you exert yourselves you will become emirs and men of standing." And he trained them, made the more skilful amongst them commanders of a thousand, a hundred, and ten, and sent them to join the main army. Then he sent a messenger and summoned Bayan and Aju to him by post relays. They came with seven relays and he instructed them how they were

[82] Apparently the same man that Princess Töregene appointed governor of northern China in place of Maḥmūd Yalavach. See above, p. 177, also HWC, p. 243.

[83] 1265.

[84] Apparently a title given to Shih T'ien-tsê, who had been in command at Chengting. His native place was actually Yung-ch'ing near Peking. See Franke, V, p. 166, and Cleaves 1956, pp. 207–208 and note 33.

[85] For Chaghan-Balghasun, the Mongol name for Chengting, see above, p. 165 and note 16.

[86] A variant of Ajul (Polo's Aguil). See Polo I, pp. 14–15.

[87] See below, p. 272, note 89.

to fight.[88] Then they returned, and in the seventh year[89] from their first approaching those lands they gave battle on the banks of the River Keng Mören and beat a Nangiyas army of 80 *tümens*.[90] They captured that kingdom, killed the ruler, whose name was ———,[91] and also conquered the countries of Kandar,[92] Ikibüze,[93] ———,[94] ———,[95] ———,[96] Kafje-Guh,[97] etc.

The Solangqas, who had submitted in the reign of Möngke Qa'an and had then risen in rebellion again, came to Court and submitted a second time when Qubilai Qa'an ascended the throne.[98] As for the province of Java, one of the countries of India, he sent an army to take it by war.[99] And he sent ambassadors by sea to most of the countries of India [to call on them] to submit. They were compelled to promise this and up to the present time ambassadors pass to and fro discussing the terms of submission.[100]

[88] All of this is in complete contradiction of the facts as given by the Chinese authorities. Far from being involved in difficulties and requiring reinforcements, Bayan and Aju were advancing rapidly down the Yangtse valley capturing city after city when the former was recalled by Qubilai because of the threat from Qaidu (see above, pp. 266–69). Having convinced the Great Khan that the war against the Sung should receive priority, Bayan returned to the scene of operations to resume his advance. See Franke, IV, p. 337.

[89] Presumably in the seventh year from Aju's having laid siege to Siangyang in 1268. The final campaign against the Sung was not launched until August, 1274. The "four years" referred to above, p. 271, must also refer to the siege of Siangyang, on which see below, pp. 290–91.

[90] This is conceivably a reference to the desperate stand at Ch'ang chou, the present-day Wutsin, in Kiangsu. See Franke, IV, p. 338.

[91] Blank in all the MSS. Neither the then Emperor, Kung-tsung (1274–1276), nor his brothers Tsuan-tsung (1276–1278) and Ti-ping (1278–1279) were killed by the Mongols. The reference is perhaps to Ti-ping's death by drowning after the defeat of his fleet in a sea-battle off Macao. See Franke, IV, pp. 348–49.

[92] Yunnan. See above, p. 247 and note 23.

[93] AYKY BWRH in the MSS: the I-ch'i-pu-hsieh of the Chinese sources, the name of a tribe in southern China. Blochet's emendation—ANKR PWRH, that is, Angkor in Cambodia—is, of course, to be rejected. See Pelliot 1920, p. 151.

[94] MQWMAN.   [95] KLNK.

[96] KYAY.

[97] Polo's Caugigu, the Chiao-chih kuo of the *Yüan shih*, "Kingdom of Chiao-chih," that is, Tonking. Chiao-chih survives as the first element of Cochin China. See *Polo I*, pp. 233–34.   [98] See Franke, IV, p. 303.

[99] For the details of this expedition, see Franke, IV, pp. 463–64.

[100] On Qubilai's relations with the kingdoms of Malabar (the Coromandel Coast) and Quilon (in Travancore), see Franke, IV, pp. 461–63.

He divided the countries of Nangiyas amongst the princes and set a regular army upon each of the frontiers. The Emir Bolad Chingsang,[101] who is fully informed on the conditions of those countries, states that although it is the custom of the Nangiyas to include in the census only persons of standing, who are the leaders of that people and possessed of a following, the number of people in the census there is 99 *tümens*. And no country is vaster than this, for it is written in books that the beginning of the five climes is from that country. Nevertheless the buildings in that country all adjoin one another. Those Mongol and Jauqut troops settled there and never left the country: every commander of a *tümen* is stationed with a force of men in a specified area, the governorship of which has been entrusted to him. And when the taxes of that country are exacted, the Qa'an's *yarligh* is sent to that commander, and in accordance with the command he arranges [the collection of the tax] from all the towns belonging to that area and sends it [to the Qa'an]; and none of them has any connection with any other employment. As for those prisoners, they have all become important emirs and have provided themselves with summer and winter residences. *And God knows best what is right, and it is to Him that we return.*

The events of Qubilai Qa'an's life from his birth until the time when he ascended the throne of sovereignty and completely subjugated the countries of Khitai and Māchīn have been related in detail. We shall now record some other stories relating to his Empire, to the regulations which he introduced, and to the armies which he assigned to every area and frontier in those countries, *if Almighty God so wills, the One and Only.*

◄ OF THE BUILDINGS WHICH THE QA'AN BUILT IN the land of Khitai and of the regulations, rules, administration, and organization observed in that country[102]

---

[101] Bolad Aqa or Bolad Chingsang, "Bolad the *ch'eng-hsiang* or Minister," was the representative of the Great Khan at the Persian Court. It was he who interpreted to Rashīd al-Dīn the *Altan Debter*, or "Golden Book," the official Mongol chronicle. He belonged to the Dörben tribe. See *Turkestan*, pp. 44–45, and Khetagurov, p. 187.

[102] Yule's translation of this and the following two chapters (*Cathay*, pp. 113–33) is based on earlier versions by Klaproth (*JA*, 1833) and d'Ohsson (in the appendix to Vol. II of the *Histoire des Mongols*).

The land of Khitai is an exceedingly broad and vast country and very thickly populated. Reliable authorities declare that in the whole of the inhabitable quarter there is in no other country such populousness or multitude of people as here. A gulf[103] of the Ocean-Sea, not very large, goes out from the southeast on the borders and coasts between Manzi and Goli[104] and comes into the middle of Khitai up to 4[105] parasangs from Khan-Balïq, to which people come by ship. Because of the proximity of the sea there is a heavy rainfall, and some of those provinces have a hot and some a cold climate. During his reign, Chingiz-Khan conquered the greater part of those countries and they were all of them taken during the reign of Ögetei Qa'an. Chingiz-Khan and his sons had no capital in Khitai, as has been mentioned in every history, but because Möngke Qa'an had given that kingdom to Qubilai Qa'an, and he with a farsighted view had seen in it an exceedingly prosperous kingdom with many important provinces and countries adjacent to it, he had chosen it [as the site of] his capital. He established his summer residence in the town of Khan-Balïq, which in Khitayan is called Jungdu[106] and which had been one of the capitals of the rulers of Khitai. It was built in ancient times under the direction of astrologers and learned men with a very auspicious horoscope and had always been regarded as extremely fortunate and prosperous. As it had been destroyed by Chingiz-Khan, Qubilai Qa'an wished to rebuild it, and for his own fame and renown he built another town called Daidu[107] alongside it so that they adjoin each other. The wall of the town has seventeen towers and there is a distance of 1 parasang from tower to tower. So populous is the town that buildings without number have been constructed outside [the walls].

All sorts of fruit trees have been brought from every land and planted in the gardens and orchards there; and most of them bear fruit. And in the middle of the town he has built as his *ordo* an exceedingly large palace to which he has given the name of Qarshi. The pillars and

[103] The Po Hai.

[104] Chinese Kao-li, Korea.

[105] Klaproth (*Cathay*, p. 113, note 2) supposes that the text must originally have had *twenty-four*, the real distance between Peking and the coast of the gulf.

[106] See above, p. 227 and note 121.

[107] Polo's Taidu, Chinese Ta-tu, "Great Capital," on which see *Polo II*, pp. 843–45.

floors are all of marble, extremely beautiful and clean. He has surrounded it with four walls, between each of which there is the distance of a bowshot. The outside wall is for the tethering of horses, the inside one for the emirs to sit in when they assemble every morning, the third for the guards, and the fourth for the courtiers. The Qa'an resides in this palace in the winter. A model of it has been engraved by artists in history books; it is as engraved [in the picture].

In Khan-Balïq and Daidu there is a great river[108] which flows from a northerly direction, from the region of Chamchiyal,[109] which is the route to the summer residence. There are other rivers also, and outside the town they have constructed an extremely large *na'ur* like a lake and have built a dam for it so that they can launch boats in it and sail for pleasure. The water of that river used to flow in a different channel and empty itself into the gulf that comes from the Ocean-Sea to the neighborhood of Khan-Balïq. But because the gulf was narrow in that vicinity vessels could not approach, and the cargoes used to be loaded on to pack animals and carried to Khan-Balïq. The engineers and learned men of Khitai, having carried out a careful inquiry, declared that it was possible for ships to come to Khan-Balïq from most parts of Khitai, from the capital of Māchïn, from Khingsang and Zaitun, and from other places also. The Qa'an ordered a great canal to be cut and the water of that river and several other rivers to be diverted into that canal. It is a 40 days' voyage to Zaitun, which is the port of India and the capital of Māchïn. On these rivers many sluices have been built for [the provision of] water to the provinces. When a ship comes to one of these sluices it is raised up by means of a winch together with its cargo, no matter how large and heavy it is, and set down in the water on the other side of the dam so that it can proceed. The width of the canal is more than 30 ells. Qubilai Qa'an ordered it to be walled with stone so that no earth should fall into it.[110] Alongside the canal is a great highway which leads to Māchïn, a distance of 40 days. The whole of that road is paved with stone so that, when there is a heavy rainfall, the beasts of burden may not get stuck

---

[108] The Sankan or Yungting.

[109] The Mongol name for the Nankow pass some 30 miles northwest of Peking.

[110] On Qubilai's lengthening of the Grand Canal to link Peking and Hangchow, see Franke, IV, pp. 569 ff.

in the mud. On either side of the road willows and other trees have been planted so that the shadow of the trees falls upon the whole length of the road. And no one, soldier or other, dares to break a branch from the trees or give a leaf to his animals. Villages, shops, and temples have been built on either side so that the whole of the 40-day route is fully populated.

The walls of the town of Daidu were made of earth, for it is the custom of that country to put down two planks, pour damp earth inbetween, and beat it with a large stick until it is firm. Then they remove the planks and there is a wall. And because there is a great deal of rain and the earth of that country has little strength, the wall is thus rendered firmer. At the end of his life the Qa'an ordered stones to be brought and intended to dress the wall with stone, but he passed away. God willing, Temür Qa'an[111] will succeed in completing the work.

The Qa'an decided to build a similar palace in his summer residence at Kemin-Fu, which is 50 parasangs from Daidu. There are three roads from the winter residence: one road which is reserved for hunting and along which no one may travel except couriers; another road by way of Joju,[112] to which one travels along the banks of the River Sangin,[113] where there is [an] abundance of grapes and other fruit and near which is another small town called Sinali,[114] the people of which are mostly from Samarqand and have laid out gardens in the Samarqand fashion; and there is another road, by way of a low hill, which they call Sing-Ling,[115] and when one passes over that hill the steppe is all grassland and [suitable for] summer pasturage up to the town of Kemin-Fu. On the eastern side of the town he laid the foundations of a *qarshi* called Lang-Ten,[116] but one night he had a dream and abandoned it. He then consulted the scholars and engineers

---

[111] Qubilai's grandson and successor, Temür Öljeitü (1294–1307).

[112] Polo's Giogiu, Cho chou, the modern Chohsien. On the other hand, Pelliot *Polo II*, p. 736, thinks that "both mentions of 'J̌oju' in the text where Rašīd praises the vines of that region . . . are altered from . . . Fuju, which the Persian writer gives elsewhere, and apply to . . . Fu-chou outside the Great Wall."

[113] The Sankan. Cf. Polo's Pulisanghin, which is Persian for either "Bridge over the Sankan" or, by popular etymology, "Stone Bridge." See *Polo II*, p. 812.

[114] Unidentified.   [115] Unidentified.

[116] Chinese Liang-Tien, "Cool Pavilion."

as to where the foundations of another *qarshi* might be laid, and they all agreed that the most suitable site was a *na'ur* beside the town of Kemin-Fu in the middle of meadows. They decided to drain it. Now in that country there is a stone which they use instead of firewood;[117] they collected a great quantity of this and also of charcoal. Then they filled the *na'ur*, and the spring which fed it, with pebbles and broken bricks and melted a quantity of tin and lead over it until it was firm. They raised it up to a man's height from the ground and built a platform on it. And since the water was imprisoned in the bowels of the earth, it came out in the course of time in other places in meadows some distance away, where it flowed forth as so many springs. And on the platform they built a *qarshi* in the Khitayan style. The meadow they surrounded with a wall of marble, and between that wall and the *qarshi* they set a wooden barricade so that no one could enter or leave the meadow. They collected all kinds of game animals in the meadow and by generation and increase their numbers have multiplied. They also built a smaller palace and *qarshi* in the center of the town and have constructed a road from the exterior *qarshi* to that interior one so that he can enter the *qarshi* by that private thoroughfare. And as a tethering-place for horses, a wall has been drawn around that *qarshi* at the distance of a bowshot. The Qa'an is mostly in the *qarshi* outside the town.

There are many large towns in those countries, and each has been given a name which has a special meaning in its derivation. The ranks of the governors are known from the titles of the towns, so that there is no need whatsoever to state in *yarlïghs*, or have any dispute about, the greater importance of the governor of a particular town, nor is there any discussion in public assemblies about [precedence] in sitting. The rank [of the town] itself specifies which governor must go out to meet the other and kneel in front of him. Those ranks and titles are as follows: first rank, *ging*;[118] second rank, *du*;[119] third rank, *fu*;[120]

[117] Coal was unfamiliar to Marco Polo also: "You must know that all over the province of Cathay there is a kind of black stone, which is dug out of the mountains like any other kind of stone, and burns like wood" (Benedetto, p. 160).

[118] *Ching*, "capital."

[119] *Tu*, "residence."

[120] *Fu*, "prefecture, prefectural city."

fourth rank, *jo*;[121] fifth rank, —————;[122] sixth rank, *gün*;[123] seventh rank, *hin*;[124] eighth rank, *jen*;[125] [and] ninth rank, *sun*.[126]

The first rank they give to a large country like Rūm, Fārs, or Baghdad, the second to a place which is the residence of the ruler, and so on downward, the seventh rank being given to small towns, the eighth to boroughs, and the ninth to villages and farmsteads. Villages and farmsteads are also called *mazim*.[127] Coastal harbors they call *matau*.[128]

This procedure and organization does not exist in other lands. Most of the affairs of the country are administered in this way. *And God knows best.*

❦ ACCOUNT OF THE EMIRS, VIZIERS, AND *BITIKCHIS* of the land of Khitai; details of their ranks; the laws and regulations observed amongst them; the nomenclature of that people

The great emirs who have the qualifications to be ministers and viziers are called *chingsang*,[129] army commanders *taifu*,[130] commanders of *tümens vangshai*,[131] and emirs, viziers, and ministers of the Divan, who are Tāzīks, Khitayans, and Uighurs, *finjan*.[132] It is the custom in the Great Divan to have four *chingsangs* from amongst the great emirs and four *finjans* from amongst the great emirs of the various peoples, Tāzīks, Khitayans, Uighurs, and Christians. These too have ministers in the Divan, and the offices of the emirs and governors

---

[121] *Chou*, "district." This was an administrative area of two kinds: one subject to, and the other independent of, a *fu*. The *hsien* was a sub-division of the latter kind of *chou*.　　　　　[122] Blank in the MSS.

[123] *Chün*, "chief military garrison."　　　　[124] *Hsien*, "township."

[125] *Chên*, "district" (sub-division of a *hsien*).

[126] *Ts'un*, "village."

[127] Verkhovsky adopts Blochet's suggestion that this represents a form *mo-hsien* instead of the normal *hsien-mo*, "paths dividing fields," and so "cultivated fields."

[128] *Ma-t'ou*, "quay." See *Polo II*, p. 834.

[129] *Ch'êng-hsiang*. See *Polo I*, p. 365.

[130] Apparently *t'ai-fu*, "in principle a civilian title." See *Polo II*, pp. 851–52.

[131] *Yüan-shuai*, "commander of an army." The first element of the term has nothing to do with *wan*, "ten thousand." See *Polo II*, p. 858.

[132] *P'ing-chang*. See *Polo II*, p. 803.

there are in accordance with their rank. Their ranks are as shown in detail below.

First rank—*chingsang* (he is qualified to be a vizier or minister).

Second rank—*taifu* (he is an army commander and, however senior, must defer to the chingsang).

Third rank—*finjan* (these are ministers and viziers from the various nationalities).

Fourth rank—*yu-ching*.[133]

Fifth rank—*zo-ching*.[134]

Sixth rank—*sam-jing*.[135]

Seventh rank—*sami*.[136]

Eighth rank—*lanjun*.[137]

Ninth rank—(not known; all the secretaries are under him).

In the reign of Qubilai Qa'an, the *chingsangs* were the following emirs: Hantum Noyan, Uchachar, Öljei, Tarkhan, and Dashman. Hantum Noyan is now dead, but the rest are still the *chingsangs* of Temür Qa'an along with one other. Formerly the office of *finjan* was given to Khitayans, but now it is given to Mongols, Täniks, and Uighurs also. The chief of the *finjans* is called *sufinjan*, that is, "cream of the *finjans*."[138] At the present time, in the reign of Temür Qa'an, the leader of them all is Bayan Finjan, the son of Saiyid Nāṣir al-Dīn and the grandson of Saiyid Ajall:[139] he too now is called Saiyid Ajall. The second is 'Umar Finjan, a Mongol, and the third Teke Finjan, an Uighur. Formerly it was Lachïn Finjan, the nephew of the Emir Sunchaq, and now it is his son, called Kermane. The fourth is Yïghmïsh Finjan, who takes the place of Temür Finjan, and he too is an Uighur.

Since the Qa'an resides mostly in the town of Daidu, a place has been made for the Great Divan, which they call *shing*,[140] where they

---

[133] *Yu-ch'êng*. See Doerfer, I, No. 407 (pp. 554–55).

[134] *Tso-ch'êng*. See Doerfer, III, No. 1201 (pp. 215–16).

[135] *Ts'an-chêng*. See Doerfer, I, No. 215 (p. 342).

[136] *Ts'an-i*. See Doerfer, I, No. 216 (p. 342).

[137] *Lang-chung*. See Doerfer, I, No. 358 (pp. 492–93).

[138] Cf. below, p. 289, the title of Aḥmad Fanākatī. The etymology of *su* or *shu* is not clear. See Doerfer, III, No. 1330, (p. 327).

[139] On Saiyid Ajall and his son Nāṣir al-Dīn, see below, pp. 287–88.

[140] *Shêng*, Polo's *scieng*. This was the Chung-shu shêng, or Grand Secretariat, which "worked at the capital, but had provincial delegations called 'moving' (. . . *hsing*) Chung-shu-shêng, or simply *hsing-shêng*, and even *shêng* alone; the areas under the

hold the Divan. And it is the custom for there to be a minister, who has charge of the gates: the memorials[141] that are received are taken to that minister and he makes inquiries about them. The name of this Divan is *lais*.[142] And when the inquiries are finished the facts of the case are written down and the report sent, along with the memorial, to the Divan called *lusa*,[143] which is higher than the other Divan. From thence it is sent to a third Divan, which they call *chubivan*,[144] and then to a fourth Divan, the name of which is *tunjinvan*,[145] and matters relating to *yams* and couriers are under the charge of that Divan. It is taken from thence to a fifth Divan, which they call *zhushitai*[146] and which deals with military affairs. Then it is taken to the sixth Divan, the name of which is *sanvisha*.[147] All ambassadors, merchants, and travelers are there, and *yarlīghs* and *paizas* are the concern of that Divan. This office belongs exclusively to the Emir Dashman. And after it has been taken to all these Divans it is then taken to the Great Divan, which they call *shing*, and inquiries are made there. They take the fingerprints of the persons that are questioned. And the meaning of fingerprint is as follows. It has been discovered and confirmed by experience that the finger joints of all people are different. And so whenever they take a deposition from anyone, they place the paper between his fingers and on the back of the document mark the place where his finger joints touched, so that should he at some time deny his statement they can confront him with

---

control of each *hsing-chêng* soon came to be themselves named *shêng* colloquially, and this is the origin of the modern use of *shêng* in the sense of 'province.'" See *Polo II*, pp. 727–28.

[141] Such seems to be the natural translation of a word (*bularghui*, or the like) which in other contexts means "lost property." See *Iranica*, pp. 82–84, Doerfer, I, No. 93 (pp. 213–15).

[142] LYS. Blochet reads LYŠH, in which he sees *li-ssŭ* "chambre qui s'occupe des fonctionnaires civils" or "chambre des rites."

[143] LWSH. Blochet reads LWSH, which he thinks may represent *lu-ssŭ*, "la chambre qui s'occupe des voies et communications."

[144] *Ch'u-mi yüan*. This was the central organization for military affairs. See Doerfer, III, No. 1060 (pp. 45–46).

[145] Explained by Blochet as probably the *t'ung-chêng yüan*, which directed the post.

[146] The *yü-shih t'ai*, the function of which was to sort out good and bad officials. See Doerfer, III, No. 1202 (p. 216).

[147] The *hsüan-wei ssê*, which was concerned with the care of the military, particularly in the frontier areas. See Franke, IV, p. 561.

the marks of his fingers, and since these are correct, he can no longer deny it.[148] And having taken this precaution in all the Divans, they make their report and take action in accordance with the order then given.

It is the custom for the above-mentioned emirs to go to the *shing* every day and interrogate people. The affairs of the country are numerous, and when these four *chingsangs* are sitting, the other officials also, each with their *bitikchis*, are seated in due order according to their office. In front of each of them is placed a stand like a chair with a pen-case on it. They are always there, and each emir has a special seal and *tamgha*. And several *bitikchis* are appointed, whose duty it is to write down the names of the persons who came to the Divan every day, so that if they do not attend for several days their wages are deducted. And if someone fails to attend without a valid excuse he is dismissed. It is these four *chingsangs* that report to the Qa'an.

The *shing* of Khan-Balïq is extremely large, and the Divan archives for several thousand years are housed there. They record [everything] accurately in them and they contain excellent precepts. The employees in that *shing* number nearly two thousand. There is not a *shing* in every town, only in [those] places that provide a capital for many towns and provinces, such as Baghdad, Shiraz, and Qoniya in Rūm. In the Qa'an's empire there are twelve *shings*. In all the *shings*, except that of Khan-Balïq, there is no *chingsang*; at the head of each is an emir, in the capacities of both *shaḥna* and emir, and four *finjans*; and there are also the other Divans and offices. The locations of the twelve *shings* and their ranks are such as shall be recorded in this place, with the help of God Almighty.

First—the *shing* of Khan-Balïq and Daidu.

Second—the *shing* of the province of Jürche and Solangqa. This Divan is situated in the town of Chunju,[149] which is the largest town in

---

[148] Rashïd al-Dïn clearly had only a vague idea of what the process of taking fingerprints involved. On the antiquity of the practice in China and Japan, see *Cathay*, pp. 123–24, note 2.

[149] This would appear to be Chŏngju, in the extreme northwest of Korea. On the other hand, Rashïd al-Dïn is far more likely to have heard of Ch'ungju, in the South, attacked by the Mongols in 1253 and again in 1256. See Henthorn, pp. 113, 127, and 129. Actually the capital of the Yüan province to which Rashïd al-Dïn here refers was Liaoyang in Manchuria.

Solangqa. 'Alā al-Dīn Finjan, the son of Ḥusām al-Dīn Sam-Jing of Almalïq, and Ḥasan Zo-Ching are stationed there.

Third—the *shing* of Goli and ———,[150] which is a separate kingdom. The ruler is called *yang*.[151] Qubilai Qa'an gave him his daughter in marriage. His son is one of the Qa'an's intimates, but he is not *yang* there.[152]

Fourth—the *shing* of the town of Namging.[153] This is a large town in the kingdom of Khitai on the bank of the River Qara-Mören: it is one of the ancient capitals of Khitai.

Fifth—the *shing* of the town of Yangju,[154] which is on the frontier of Khitai. Toghan, the son of ———,[155] is stationed there.

Sixth—the *shing* of the town of Khingsai,[156] which is the capital of Manzi. 'Alā al-Dīn Finjan, the son of Saif al-Dīn Taghachar Noyan, is stationed there together with a Khitayan *nöker* called Suching, 'Umar Finjan Manzitai, and Beg Khocha Finjan Ṭūsī.

Seventh—the *shing* of the town of Fu-Ju,[157] one of the towns of Manzi. Formerly the *shing* was here and then it was transferred to Zaitun,[158] but now it has been brought back. The governor at one time was Zhen, the brother of Dashman, and is now the Emir 'Umar. Zaitun is the port, of which the governor is Bahā al-Dīn of Qunduz.

[150] Blochet corrects the corrupt form to read Kokuli, that is, Kao-chü-li/Koguryŏ, an old name for Korea. See *Polo I*, pp. 234–35, and Ledyard, p. 17.

[151] Chinese *wang*, "prince." The then ruler was Ch'ungnyol (1275–1308).

[152] His name was Wŏn, afterwards King Ch'ungsŏn (1309–1313). See Henthorn, p. 183.

[153] The present-day Kaifeng in Honan.

[154] Polo's Yangiu, Yangchow in Kiangsu. It was this city that Polo claimed to have governed for 3 years "by order of the Great Kaan" (Benedetto, p. 225). In point of fact, as suggested by Pelliot (*Polo II*, p. 834), he probably held an office in the salt administration.

[155] There is a blank in all the MSS, but, as Pelliot has shown (*Polo II*, pp. 875–76), this Toghan must be Qubilai's eleventh son, on whom see below, p. 285 and note 176. As a consequence of his failure in Indo-China, he was banished from the Court and governed Yangchow from 1291 until his death in 1301.

[156] Hangchow. Khingsai, Polo's Quinsai, represents the Chinese expression *hsing-tsai*, a shortened form of *hsing-tsai so*, meaning "Emperor's temporary residence." See Moule 1957, pp. 8–11.

[157] Polo's Fugiu, Foochow in Fukien.

[158] Chuanchow, on the coast of Fukien, Polo's Çaiton. On this famous seaport, see *Polo I*, pp. 583–97.

Eighth—the *shing* of the town of Lukin-Fu.[159] It is a town in the province of Manzi, one side of which belongs to Tangqut.[160] Ḥasan Finjan, the brother of Bayan Finjan, and the brother of Lachïn Finjan, whose name is also Ḥasan, are governors there.

Ninth—the *shing* of *Kongi,[161] which the Tāzīks call Chīn-Kalān.[162] It is an extremely large town on the seashore below Zaitun and is a great port. A man called Noqai and Rukn al-Dīn ————[163] Finjan are governors there.

Tenth—the *shing* of Qara-Jang, which is a separate country. There is a large town there called Yachi,[164] and the *shing* is in that town, the population of which are Muslims, the governors being Yaghan Tegin and Ya'qūb Beg, the son of 'Alī Beg, of the race of Yalavach.

Eleventh—the *shing* of Kinjanfu,[165] which is a town in the Tangqut country. Ananda,[166] the son of Mangqala is in that country. The governors are ————,[167] the brother of Dashman Finjan, and 'Umar Khitā'ī. Ananda's *yurt* is in a place called Chaghan-Na'ur,[168] where he has built a *qarshi*.

Twelfth—the *shing* of Qamju,[169] which is also one of the towns of the Tangqut country. It is a very large kingdom with countless dependent territories. Ajïqï is stationed there, and an emir called Khojo is there in the capacity of governor.

Since these countries are far apart from each other, a prince or emir is resident in each of them along with an army. He is responsible for the people of that province and its concerns and interests; he administers and protects it. The *shing* of each country is in the largest town of that country and each *shing* is the size of a village, for they have

---

[159] Lung-hsing fu, the modern Nanchang, in Kiangsi. See *Polo I*, p. 590.

[160] The reference to Tangqut, that is, to the Ordos Region, is clearly due to some mistake on the part of Rashīd al-Dīn.

[161] Canton. Pelliot (*Polo I*, p. 276) sees in *Kongi a corrupt form of *Konfu or *Kongfu, that is, Kuang fu, a popular short form of Kuang-chou fu, that is, Canton.

[162] Or Chīn-i Kalān, "Great China," the Persian name for Canton. See *Polo I*, p. 276. [163] Blank in the MSS.

[164] Polo's Iaci, "either the present Yün-nan-fu [Kunming in Yunnan], or a town quite near to it and also on the banks of the lake." See *Polo I*, pp. 745–48.

[165] Polo's Quengianfu, that is, Sian, the capital of Shensi province. See *Polo II*, pp. 813–14. [166] See below, pp. 323–26.

[167] Blank in the MSS. [168] See below, p. 286 and note 183.

[169] Polo's Campcio, that is, Kanchow (Changyeh), in Kansu. See *Polo I*, pp. 150–53.

built many houses and rooms with their various appurtenances, and there are many slaves and servants in attendance on them.

The details of the arrangement and organization of those Divans are extremely fine and subtle. It is their custom to put some criminals and offenders to death and to separate others from their homes, goods, and property and send them to dig clay, pull wagons, and carry stones, so that the people seeing emirs and important persons in such a position may take warning therefrom. Their *yasaq* and organization is of many kinds, and there are all sorts of stories about those countries, but since the history of those regions will be given separately in the appendix to this book,[170] we have limited ourselves here to what is stated above.

❧ THE BORDERLANDS OF THE QA'AN'S EMPIRE: AN account of the princes and emirs who are stationed with armies on the frontiers to defend the realm

The Qa'an has no enemies in the Southeast, for all the countries lying in that direction are included in his Empire as far as the Ocean-Sea, except that near the coast of Jürche and Goli in the middle of the Ocean-Sea there is a large island called Jimingu,[171] which is nearly 400 parasangs in circumference. There are many towns and villages there; it has its own ruler and is still now, as before, in rebellion. The people are short in stature with short necks and large bellies. There are many mines there.

From the East to the shores of the Ocean and the borders of the Qïrqïz country he has no enemies.

In the southwest of Manzi, between the provinces of *Kongi[172] and Zaitun,[173] there is a very large forest. A son of the ruler of Manzi has fled thither and although he has no strength or power he passes his time in brigandage and knavery.

---

[170] That is, in the *History of China.*

[171] That is, Japan, Jimingu, like Polo's Cipingu, representing the Chinese Jih-pên kuo. See *Polo I*, pp. 608–609. Curiously enough, Rashīd al-Dīn makes no mention of Qubilai's attempt at an invasion of Japan, on which see Franke, IV, pp. 432 ff., and *Steppes*, pp. 356–57.

[172] See above, p. 283, note 161.

[173] See above, p. 282, note 158.

In the West there is a province called Kafje-Guh,[174] in which there are forests and other places of difficult access. It adjoins Qara-Jang and parts of India and the coast. There are two towns there, Lochak and Khainam[175] and it has its own ruler, who is in rebellion against the Qa'an. Toghan, the son[176] of the Qa'an, who is stationed with an army in Lukinfu[177] in the country of Manzi, is defending Manzi and also keeping an eye on those rebels. On one occasion, he penetrated with an army to those towns on the coast, captured them, and sat for a week upon the throne there. Then all at once their army sprang out from ambush in the sea[shore], the forest, and the mountains and attacked Toghan's army while they were busy plundering. Toghan got away safely and is still in the Lukinfu area.[178]

In the Northwest, where the frontier with Tibet and the Zar-Dandān is, the Qa'an has no enemies, except in the direction of Qutlugh-Khwāja's army,[179] but there are difficult mountains between them and no enemy can enter. Nevertheless, certain troops have been stationed there to defend that area.

The Northeast in its whole extent adjoins [the territories] of Qaidu and Du'a. Between their frontiers and those of the Qa'an is a 40 days' journey through the desert. The armies and scouts of both sides are stationed on the frontiers, defending their territory and keeping a look-out; and sometimes there is also fighting. The Qa'an's frontier in that direction extends eastward for a month's journey, and there are armies and scouts in most of the vital places. Beginning in the East, princes and emirs have been stationed with armies [all along the frontier]. In the extreme East, Prince Kambala,[180] the great-uncle of the Qa'an on the father's side, is stationed with an army. Next to him

---

[174] That is, Tonking. See above, p. 272 and note 97.

[175] Apparently the Leichow Peninsula and Hainan Island are meant, though these identifications are not altogether satisfactory. See *Polo I*, pp. 242–44, and *Cathay*, p. 130 and note 3.

[176] He was Qubilai's eleventh son. See above, p. 245.

[177] See above, p. 283 and note 159.

[178] On Toghan's two expeditions into Indo-China (1285 and 1287–1288), see Franke, IV, pp. 452–55, and *Steppes*, pp. 357–58.

[179] That is, the Qaraunas in the Ghazna area of Afghanistan. See above, p. 144.

[180] Apparently, a brother of Genghis Khan, but there must be some mistake since none of his brothers bore this name.

is Körgüz Küregen,[181] the son-in-law of the Qa'an; next to him, Jungqur, the son of Toqtaq, who was one of Qubilai Qa'an's great emirs; next to him, Nangiyadai, the son of Nayan Küyükchi, who also was a great emir; next to him, Kököchü, the uncle of Temür Qa'an. Then comes the Tangqut country, which is administered by Prince Ananda,[182] the son of Mangqala, who is stationed there with his army in the neighborhood of Chaghan-Na'ur.[183] Next to him is the frontier of Qara-Khocho, which is a town of the Uighurs. There is good wine there. It is between the frontiers of the Qa'an and Qaidu, and the people are on good terms with them both and render service to both sides. Next to them are stationed the princes Ajïqï, the grandson of Chaghatai, and Chübei, the son of Alghu. Then come the difficult mountains of Tibet, already mentioned. It is impossible to travel along the roads of this country in summer because of the lack of water; it is possible in winter only if one drinks snow water. *And God knows best what is right.*

❧ OF THE PRINCES AND GREAT EMIRS IN ATTENdance on the Qa'an and dependent on him

Of the princes, Toqta Kö'ün,[184] the son-in-law of the Emir Öljei Chingsang, administers the *uruq* of Taghachar[185] in place of Nayan. When the latter was put to death, a *yarlïgh* was issued that all their slaves and prisoners that they had taken should be released; they all gathered around him. Another, ———,[186] the son of Tögüz, one of the wive's of ———,[187] lives in the *yurts* on the Onan and Kelüren. Khai-

---

[181] This is Polo's Prince George of the Nestorian tribe of the Öngüt, who was converted to Roman Catholicism by Giovanni da Montecorvino. See *Polo II*, p. 737.

[182] See below, pp. 323–26.

[183] In Mongol, "White Lake." According to Pelliot (*Polo I*, p. 247), it was situated "inside the great bend of the Yellow River, somewhat west of Yü-lin and north of the district of Huai-yüan (now Heng-shan). . . ."

[184] That is, *Prince* Toqta, Mo. *kö'ün*, "son," like T. *oghul*, being a title applied to princes of the blood. Toqta was Nayan's son.

[185] Nayan's grandfather and the grandson of Genghis Khan's brother Temüge-Otchigin. See *Polo II*, p. 788. On Nayan's revolt, see below, p. 298.

[186] Blank in the text.   [187] Blank in the text.

shang,[188] the son of Taiki,[189] one of the wives of Asutai, who is extremely beautiful and is married to the Qa'an, is a prince: Töre Oghul and Yasa'ur are brothers.[190] Söse, the son of Köchü of the *uruq* of Ögetei, is a great prince. Of the *uruq* of Chaghatai [there] is Ajïqï,[191] the son of Büri, the son of Mö'etüken: he is the oldest of all the princes and today [is] a very great and important person.

As for the sons-in-law of the Qa'an, those whose names are known are as follows. One is the son of the ruler of Solangqa.[192] Another is Manzitai of the Qonqïrat tribe: he is married to a daughter whose name is *Ünegejin.[193] Another is the son of the ruler of Manzi, who in former times was their ruler but [who] has now been deposed and resides with the Qa'an in the capacities of son-in-law and emir.[194] *And God knows best what is right, and it is to Him that we return.*

OF THE SON OF SAIYID AJALL BUKHĀRĪ, THE vizier of the Qa'an, and his grandson, Bayan Finjan

The grandson of Saiyid Ajall Bukhārī[195] was vizier at the Court of Qubilai Qa'an after [the death of] Yalavach, and the Qa'an entrusted the province of Qara-Jang to him. When Qubilai Qa'an entered that country on the orders of Möngke Qa'an, and his army was left hungry and naked, [the grandson of Saiyid Ajall Bukhārī] came forward and duly performed the ceremonies of service. Qubilai Qa'an agreed to have him trained in the service of Möngke Qa'an, and so he did. Möngke Qa'an treated him kindly and showed him many favors, and when the turn came for Qubilai Qa'an to reign he too showed him favor and bestowed upon him the office of vizier, sending his son,

[188] Not to be confused with the future Great Khan (1307–1311), a great-grandson of Qubilai.   [189] See below, p. 327.

[190] Neither can be identified.

[191] He was prince of Wei-yüan, a town in Yunan. See *Chapitre CVII*, p. 57.

[192] See above, p. 33 and note 99.

[193] "Vixen." Blochet's text has AWTKČYN, Verkhovsky's ANKHYN.

[194] This was the child Emperor Kung-tsung (1274–1276) brought to Shang-tu after the fall of Hangchow. He received the title of "Duke of Ying kuo." In 1288 he is said to have gone to Tibet to study Buddhism and in 1296 to have become a monk. See Franke, IV, p. 342.

[195] This was the Saiyid Ajall, Shams al-Dīn 'Umar, born *ca.* 1210, died in 1279, on whom see *Steppes*, p. 365, note 2, and Franke, IV, p. 47, V, pp. 224–25.

Nāṣir al-Dīn,[196] to take his place as governor of Qara-Jang. He was vizier for 25 years, and no informer ever appeared against him and no misfortune ever befell him. He died a natural death; and this was a great marvel. Nāṣir al-Dīn remained governor of Qara-Jang and came to make submission to the Qa'an. He died during the last 5 years and was buried in his own garden in Khan-Balïq. Previously, Nāṣir al-Dīn's son, Abū Bakr by name, now called Bayan Finjan, had been sent as governor to the town of Zaitun.

When Saiyid Ajall died, the Emir Aḥmad Fanākatī[197] became the Qa'an's vizier, and the loosening and binding of affairs was in his hands. When Chabui Khatun was still in her father's house, the Emir Aḥmad had some close connection with them. Therefore, when she became the Qa'an's wife, he was in attendance at her *ordo*. He acquired authority, became one of the great emirs, and obtained control of the Empire. The Khitayan emirs, out of envy, were ill disposed toward him. Jim-Gim too had a dislike for him, to such an extent that one day he struck him on the head with a bow and split his face open. When he came before the Qa'an, the latter asked: "What has happened to thy face?" He replied that he had been kicked by a horse. Jim-Gim, who was present, was offended and said: "Art thou ashamed to say that Jim-Gim hit thee?" And he punched him a number of times with his fist in the Qa'an's presence. Aḥmad was always afraid of him.

In the summer of that year, when the Qa'an was leaving the town of Daidu for his summer residence, he put Aḥmad and an emir called Tergen of the Qïpchaq people in charge of the Divan and treasuries to guard the *qarshi*. The Khitayan emirs who were present in attendance, moved by feelings of long-standing envy and hatred, began to plot against his life.

☙ OF THE EMIR AḤMAD FANĀKATĪ, WHO WAS THE vizier of the Qa'an; how he was killed by Gau Finjan; and how Manzi was conquered by Gau Finjan[198]

[196] Polo's Nescradin. See *Polo II*, pp. 793–94. Polo's spelling, like the Chinese transcription Na-su-la-ting, indicates a form Naṣr al-Dīn, but Rashīd al-Dīn—*pace* Pelliot, p. 794—has only Nāṣir al-Dīn.

[197] Polo's Acmat. See *Polo I*, pp. 10–11.

[198] For a translation of this chapter by the late Professor Reuben Levy, see Moule 1957, pp. 70–72 and 79–80.

During the reign of Qubilai Qa'an, when the Emir Aḥmad Fanākatī was vizier, a Khitayan called Gau Finjan was also vizier.[199] Now since the Emir Aḥmad possessed great authority, he was called *su-finjan*, that is, "alert vizier," *su* being the title of the great *finjans*.[200] Gau Finjan had many followers and was jealous of the Emir Aḥmad. In the aforementioned summer, when the Qa'an had put him in charge of the *qarshi* and Divan of Khan-Balïq and Daidu, Gau Finjan plotted with a group of Khitayans to make an attempt on [Aḥmad's] life. A slave, one of the Emir Aḥmad's attendants, learnt of their intention and informed him. He took forty choice horses from the Qa'an's own geldings, which had been put to barley, and made off in the night. The Khitayans learnt of his departure. By daylight he had reached a village 5 parasangs off, which they call ———,[201] and the Tāzīks call Chula Village or Saiyid Ajall's *yam*. The Khitayans, having already traveled along these roads, did not allow him to cross the bridge. He tried to enter the river and cross it, but the Khitayans blocked the way and prevented him. In the midst of his exchanges with them, Gau Finjan arrived in his pursuit, seized his halter and said: "The Qa'an has placed us here to see to the affairs of the Divan. Why art thou going away without consulting us?" He replied: "The Qa'an has sent for me and I am going to him." But Gau Finjan would not let him pass, and in the midst of their argument four messengers arrived from the Qa'an on matters of business. Seeing them the Emir Aḥmad cried out: "I am going to the Qa'an and they will not let me pass." The messengers said: "The Qa'an has sent us to fetch the Emir Aḥmad." Gau Finjan said: "He has put us here to attend to the affairs of the Divan, and we have business with this man." The messengers insisted and they released him. He went and joined the Qa'an in his summer residence. Procuring a black tray, he poured all kinds of pearls on to it, placed a knife on it, and, covering it with red

---

[199] In the Chinese sources he appears as Kao Ho-chang, that is, "Kao the Buddhist monk;" there is no question of his holding the office of *p'ing-chang*, let alone "vizier." Moreover, he is mentioned only as a participant in the plot against Aḥmad Fanākatī and not at all in connection with the siege of Siangyang. For a discussion of the problems involved, see Moule 1957, pp. 86–87, and *Polo I*, pp. 10–11.

[200] See above, p. 278 and note 132.

[201] Blochet's text has ŠNDAY, whence Levy's Shandai (Moule 1957, p. 71). Verkhovsky's text has ŠZAY.

torghu,[202] brought it before the Qa'an, who asked: "What is this and what is the meaning of it?" He replied: "Formerly, when I [first] entered the Qa'an's service, my beard was as black as this tray; in serving it has become as white as these pearls. Gau Finjan wishes to take a knife and make my beard as red as this *torghu*." And he told what had happened and the messengers who had witnessed it testified that he was speaking the truth. The Qa'an ordered them to go and arrest Gau Finjan.

Learning that the matter had been reported, Gau Finjan fled to the town of Sayan-Fu on the border of Manzi on the banks of the Qara-Mören,[203] half on one side and half on the other. In the olden days, one half paid taxes to the rulers of Khitai and one half to the rulers of Manzi, there being peace between them. But when Khitai came under the control of the Mongols the whole of the town was seized by the ruler of Manzi. There is a strong castle, a stout wall, and a deep moat on this side of the town, and although the Mongol army went [and laid siege to it] it was impossible to take it. When Gau Finjan went thither the people were encouraged by his arrival since he was an important and celebrated emir. They placed their trust in him, and he became one of the chief emirs there also.

The Qa'an ordered Bayan to go in pursuit of him at the head of an army. Formerly there had been no Frankish mangonels in Khitai, but Ṭālib,[204] a mangonel-maker, had come thither from Baalbek and

---

[202] T. "fine silk." See Doerfer, II, No. 884 (pp. 478–80).

[203] Siangyang stands, of course, not on the Hwang Ho but on the Han.

[204] This was apparently I-ssŭ-ma-yin, (Ismā'īl), one of the two "makers of catapults," the other being A-lao-wa-ting ('Alā al-Dīn), sent to Qubilai by the Il-Khan Abaqa. Ismā'īl's native place is given as Hsü-lieh, which has been variously identified as Shiraz, Herat, and Hilla but is almost certainly Aleppo. See Moule 1957, pp. 76–77, and *Polo I*, pp. 4–5. We read in the *Travels of Marco Polo* that the mangonels used at Siangyang were constructed by an Alan and a Nestorian Christian under the instructions of Polo's father, uncle, and himself. It has however been demonstrated by Moule, (1957, p. 74) that "the siege was over about two years before Marco himself entered China, while it had not formally begun when Nicolo and Maffeo left China after their first visit." "For the story of the participation of Nicolo, Maffeo, and Marco in the siege no defence seems to be possible, it cannot be true, and it can hardly be due to failure of memory. We can only guess that Rustichello or some later editor felt that a good story would be made better by the substitution of the familiar names of his heroes for the strange uncouth names of unknown foreigners; and it is to be specially noted that this embarrassing statement is not found in the abbreviated texts of the MSS" (Moule 1957, p. 77).

Damascus, and his sons, Abū Bakr, Ibrāhīm, and Muḥammad, and his dependants had constructed seven large mangonels and set out to capture the town. Gau Finjan sent a spy to the commanders of the army to say: "I have committed no crime, but there was enmity between me and the Emir Aḥmad, and we used to attack each other, and now I have fled hither in fear. But if the Qa'an will spare my life I shall deliver the town into your hands, and the foundation of the kingdom of Manzi is laid upon this town, and when it is taken, the whole of the country will be conquered." They sent Gau Finjan's messenger to the Qa'an to report this message to him. The Qa'an received him with favor and sent a letter of safe-conduct and a sword for Gau Finjan. He was encouraged by this. The army now trained the mangonels on the castle and destroyed the towers; and Gau Finjan made a hole from the inside and came out. And when the ruler of Manzi learnt of the destruction of the towers and Gau Finjan's treachery he abandoned the castle and departed with a large following to the far side of the river. And when Bayan had captured the castle on this side and massacred and looted, he fled with his forces from the far side also and was unable to make a stand in any place and face the army of the Qa'an; and so the whole of Manzi was subdued and conquered. As for Gau Finjan, he joined the Qa'an's army, and when he arrived in Court was distinguished with all manner of favors, being reinstated as *finjan* and becoming the associate of the Emir Aḥmad.

The Emir Aḥmad held the vizierate with honor for nearly 25 years, and Gau Finjan was associated with him for 9 years more with his customary rancor and envy; and after another 9 years he made another attempt on his life. It happened as follows. A certain Khitayan laid claim to properties of holiness and chastity and had made himself known in the *ordos* for his asceticism and piety. One day he pretended to be ill and sent some of his disciples to the emirs to say: "I shall die and come to life again after 40 days." They went and said this, and some people were sent to investigate. He was lying in his house in the manner of the dead and his children were mourning and lamenting over him. They thought that he was really dead, but after 40 days he came out and put about the story that he had come to life again. The Khitayans rallied around him and his affairs prospered greatly. Gau Finjan and the people of Daidu now went to him and consulted him about getting rid of the Emir Aḥmad. As he was extremely cautious and alert, always having guards with him and his sleeping-place not being known, they decided to send two thousand men to a valley known as Chamchiyal,[205] 4 parasangs from Daidu, in order to hold it, whilst a thousand men should go and spread the rumor that Jim-Gim was coming, so that the Emir Aḥmad might come out to meet him and they might kill him.

Gau Finjan seated himself in a palanquin, for it is a custom of the rulers of those parts sometimes to sit in a palanquin and they often travel this way by night. And from that valley relays of heralds and messengers were dispatched to announce that Jim-Gim was coming. Aḥmad was afraid of him. And all the men he sent in advance they killed. In the night they entered [the town] with torches and candles as is the custom of their rulers. When they drew near to the *qarshi*, the Emir Aḥmad came out to take a cup, and they seized him and put him to death. As for the Emir Tergen, who was his *nöker*, he had acted with caution and had guessed that something was wrong. Standing at a distance with his *nökers* he took an arrow and shot Gau Finjan dead in the palanquin.[206] The Khitayans fled and Tergen occupied the *qarshi*. There was a great deal of slaughter and tumult in the night, and the Khitayans went out [and hid themselves] in corners.

When this was reported to the Qa'an, he dispatched the Emir Bolad Aqa[207] and Hantum Noyan at the head of an army to execute all of the Khitayans who had caused this disturbance. And he ordered 4,000 *bālish* to be paid for the Emir Aḥmad's funeral expenses and sent the great men and emirs to bury him with full honors.

[205] See above, p. 275 and note 109.

[206] According to Polo (Benedetto, p. 128), the man shot in the palanquin was the conspirator he calls Vanchu, that is, the title *wan-hu*, "commander of ten thousand," used as a name; and both Moule (1957, p. 87) and Pelliot (*Polo I*, p. 11) conclude that Vanchu and Kao must be one and the same person. Vanchu's assailant was, according to Polo, not Tergen (whom he does not mention) but "a Tartar called Cogatai" (Benedetto, p. 127), whom Pelliot (*Polo I*, pp. 395–96) is inclined to identify with the official Kao Hsi.

[207] Referred to in the *Yüan shih* (Moule 1957, p. 84) as "the *shu-mi fu shih* Po-lo." A translation of this passage by Charignon "was used to revive the belief that the Po-lo of the Chinese texts is Marco Polo, which Pelliot had long ago shown to be impossible" (Moule 1957, p. 84).

Forty days later, the Qa'an sent for a large stone to set in his crown. It could not be found. Two merchants, who were there, came and said: "Previously we had brought a large stone for the Qa'an and [had] given it to the Emir Aḥmad." The Qa'an said: "He did not bring it to me." And he sent to have it fetched from his house. It was found on his wife Injü Khatun[208] and brought to the Qa'an. He was extremely annoyed and asked the merchants what should be the punishment of a slave who committed such a crime. They replied: "If alive he should be put to death, and if dead he should be taken out of his grave and publicly exposed as a warning to others." And the Khitayans for their part said to Jim-Gim: "He was thy enemy, and it was for that reason that we killed him." For that reason they had planted enmity toward him in the Qa'an's heart. Therefore, he ordered his body to be taken out of the grave and hanged in the market place by a rope tied to the feet, whilst wagons were driven over his head. Injü, his wife, was also put to death, and the forty other wives and four hundred concubines that he had were given away, whilst his possessions and effects were expropriated for the treasury. As for his sons, the Emir Ḥasan and the Emir Ḥusain, they were beaten until the skin came off, while his other children were given away. After [Aḥmad's] death, the vizierate was conferred upon an Uighur called Senge, whose history is as now follows.

◈ OF SENGE THE UIGHUR, WHO BECAME THE Qa'an's vizier after the Emir Aḥmad; his latter end

During the vizierate of Senge, a group of Muslim merchants came to the Qa'an's Court from the country of the Qori,[209] Barqu,[210] and Qïrqïz and brought as their audience-offering white-footed, red-beaked gerfalcons and a white eagle. The Qa'an showed them favor and gave them food from his table, but they would not eat it. He asked: "Why will you not eat?" They replied: "This food is unclean to us."

[208] The *Yüan shih* (Moule 1957, p. 84) refers to her as one of his concubines called Yin-chu.

[209] On the Qori, who along with the Barghut, the Tö'eles, and the Tumat inhabited the Barghujin-Tögum to the east of Lake Baikal, see *Campagnes*, pp. 63–64.

[210] That is, the Barghut, on whom see *Polo I*, pp. 76–79.

The Qa'an was offended and commanded: "Henceforth Muslims and People of the Book[211] shall not slaughter sheep but shall split open the breast and side in the Mongol fashion. And whoever slaughters sheep shall be slaughtered likewise and his wife, children, house, and property given to the informer."[212]

'Isā Tarsā Kelemechi,[213] Ibn Ma'ālī, and Baidaq, some of the mischievous, wicked, and corrupt men of their age, availed themselves of this decree to obtain a *yarlïgh* that whoever slaughtered a sheep in his house should be executed. On this pretext they extorted much wealth from the people and tempted the slaves of Muslims, saying: "If you inform against your master we will set you free." And for the sake of their freedom they calumniated their masters and accused them of crimes. 'Isā Kelemechi and his accursed followers brought matters to such a pass that for 4 years Muslims could not circumcise their children. They also brought false charges against Maulānā Burhān al-Dīn Bukhārī, a disciple of the godly Shaikh al-Islām Saif al-Dīn Bākharzī (*may God have mercy on him!*), and he was sent to Manzi, where he died. Conditions became such that most Muslims left the country of Khitai. Thereupon most of the chief Muslims of those parts —Bahā al-Dīn Qunduzī, Shādi Zo-Cheng, 'Umar Qirqizī, Nāṣir al-Dīn Malik Kāshgharī, Hindū Zo-Cheng and other notables— jointly offered many presents to the vizier, so that he made the following representation [to the Qa'an]: "All the Muslim merchants have departed from hence and no merchants are coming from the Muslim countries; the *tamghas* are inadequate and they do not bring *tangsuqs*;[214] and all this because for the past 7 years they have not slaughtered sheep. If it be so commanded, the merchants will come and go and the *tamgha* will be collected in full." Permission was given for the issue of a *yarlïgh* to this effect.

Again, the Christians in the Qa'an's reign showed great fanaticism against the Muslims and sought to attack them by representing to the

---

[211] That is, Christians and Jews.

[212] According to the *Yüan shih*, the edict forbidding ritual slaughter was issued on the 27th January, 1280. See *Polo I*, pp. 77–78.

[213] That is, Jesus the Christian, the Interpreter, the Ai-hsieh of the Chinese texts. On this Arabic-speaking Christian, who passed the whole of his life in the service of the Mongols and who took part in an embassy to the Pope, see Moule 1930, pp. 228–29.   [214] See Glossary.

Qa'an that there was a verse in the Qur'ān which ran: "*Kill the polytheists, all of them.*"[215] The Qa'an was annoyed and asked: "From whence do they know this?" He was told that a letter on this subject had arrived from Abaqa Khan. He sent for the letter and, summoning the *dānishmands*,[216] asked the senior amongst them, Bahā al-Dīn Bahā'ī. "Is there such a verse in your Qur'ān?" "Yes," he replied. "Do you regard the Qur'ān," asked the Qa'an, "as the word of God?" "We do," he said. "Since then," the Qa'an went on, "you have been commanded by God to kill the infidels, why do you not kill them?" He replied: "The time has not yet come, and we have not the means." The Qa'an fell into a rage and said: "I at least have the means." And he ordered him to be put to death. However, the Emir Aḥmad the vizier, the Cadi Bahā al-Dīn, who also had the rank of vizier, and the Emir Dashman prevented this on the pretext that they would ask others also. They sent for Maulānā Ḥamīd al-Dīn, formerly of Samarqand, and the same question was put to him. He said that there was such a verse. "Why then," said the Qa'an, "do you not kill [these people]?" He answered: "God Almighty has said, 'Kill the polytheists', but if the Qa'an will so instruct me, I will tell him what a polytheist is." "Speak," said the Qa'an. "Thou art not a polytheist," said Ḥamīd al-Dīn, "since thou writest the name of the Great God at the head of thy *yarlïghs*. Such a one is a polytheist who does not recognize God, and attributes companions to Him, and rejects the Great God." The Qa'an was extremely pleased and these words took firm root in his heart. He honored Ḥamīd al-Dīn and showed favor to him; and at his suggestion the others were released.

Senge was vizier for 7 years. It so happened that one day the Qa'an asked him for several pearls and he said that he had none. There was at the Qa'an's Court a native of Dāmghān called Mubārak-Shāh who was a favorite courtier. He was awaiting an opportunity to attack Senge, and he now spoke as follows: "Senge has a *kharvār* of pearls and jewelry in his house, and I have seen them. Let the Qa'an keep him occupied while I go and fetch them from his house." The Qa'an

[215] Apparently a contamination of Koran, ix, 5 ("... kill those who join other gods with God ...") and 36 ("... attack those who join other gods with God in all ..."). The reference is of course, in both cases, not to polytheists in general but to the heathen opponents of the Prophet.

[216] See Glossary.

kept him occupied in his presence, and Mubārak-Shāh fetched a pair of caskets from his house. They were opened, and in them were fine pearls and matchless jewelry. The Qa'an showed them to Senge and said: "How is it that thou hast so many pearls and, when I asked thee for two or three, thou didst not give them to me?" Senge was filled with shame and said: "The aforementioned Tāzīk dignitaries gave them to me." (These were each of them the governor of a special province.) "Why," asked the Qa'an, "did they not bring pearls and jewelry for me also? Thou bringest coarse and bad fabrics for me and takest money and matchless necklaces for thyself." Senge replied: "It was they who gave them. Let the Qa'an issue a *yarlïgh* that I am to give them back." His words being rude and impolite, the Qa'an ordered him to be seized and filth to be placed in his mouth; and he and such of the Tāzīk emirs as were present were put to death. As for the others, who were in Manzi, he sent to have them arrested. And when Bahā al-Dīn Qunduzī, Malik Nāṣir al-Dīn Kāshgharī, 'Umar Qirqizī, and Shādi Zo-Cheng were brought, he ordered them also to be executed. Then he said: "I obtained Bahā al-Dīn Qunduzī from his father." He shouted at him, struck him on the face several times with his own hand, and then had him placed in a cangue and thrown down a well. Of Nāṣir al-Dīn he said: "I summoned him from Kāshghar. Give him back his property." Having been pardoned, he had no sooner mounted horse than a number of people joined him on horseback, for he was a generous and bountiful man and had many friends. On his way he came upon the Emir Kerei Ba'urchi, who, because of his age, was traveling in a wagon. Malik Nāṣir al-Dīn could not see him because of the crowd of people and so did not greet him or pay him any attention. He was offended, and Pahlavān, the *malik* of Badakhshān, who had once come to those parts, said to him: "This is Malik Nāṣir al-Dīn, who was going to be put to death, and now his head is filled with all this pride and arrogance and he is accompanied by all these horsemen. And every year he sends more than a thousand *tenges*[217] for Qaidu's army." Being offended with him, Kerei made a charge against him when he came to the Qa'an, and a *yarlïgh* was issued for him to be

[217] On the *tenge*, a small silver coin which formed the main currency of the Mongol world from the end of the 14th to the beginning of the 16th century, see Doerfer, II, No. 946 (pp. 587–92).

brought back and put to death. As for 'Umar Qirqizī and Shādī Zo-Cheng, Prince Ajïqï interceded on their behalf and the Qa'an spared their lives: he liberated Bahā al-Dīn Qunduzī also and set up Öljei Chingsang in place of Senge.

~ OF THE QA'AN'S GREAT EMIRS; THE NAMES OF their chief men; the function of each one of them

Of the Qa'an's great emirs, one was Bayan Noyan of the Bārin people, who was brought from those parts and died 8 months after the Qa'an: he had sons and daughters. Another was Hantun Chingsang,[218] who was taken prisoner with Nomoghan and who died a year before the Qa'an. Another is Uchachar Noyan, who is still in power and holding office at the Court of Temür Qa'an, as is Öljei Chingsang. Dashman too is still a person of authority: he is in charge of *yarlïghs*, *paizas*, *ortaqs*, and incomings and outgoings. As for Tarkhan Chingsang, he enjoys greater authority than before: he is in the Divan. Nalïqu, Jirqalan, and Chirtaqu are three brothers at the head of the *qush-chïs*[219] and in charge of the Divans of the *totqa'ul*[220] and *getüsün*:[221] they have to report whatever they know and make arrests. Nalïqu died 2 years after the Qa'an. Badam Noyan was the chief *qushchï* and the brother of Sunchaq Aqa [the chief] *bitikchi*. When the latter died, his son Lachïn Finjan became Great Emir of the *bitikchis*. He too died, and his son Teke Finjan has now succeeded him: he administers many divans and *yams*. Kerei Ba'urchi died after the Qa'an. Of the great emirs of the army, Ambai was at the head of all the armies: he still occupies this post. Muqbil Finjan was *büke'ül*[222] of the army and still is. Hoqotai was the commander of the four *keziks* and is so still. The commanders of the *shükürchis*[223] are Ismā'īl, Muḥammad Shāh,

---

[218] The Hantum Noyan of above, p. 266 and note 71.

[219] T. *qushchï*, "falconer," on which see Doerfer, III, No. 1564 (pp. 548–49).

[220] On M. *todqa'ul*, "inspector of post relays," see Mostaert-Cleaves, pp. 436–37; also Doerfer, I, No. 124 (pp. 251–53).

[221] On M. *getüsün*, "spy, state police," see Doerfer, I, No. 353 (pp. 488–89).

[222] On T. *büke'ül*, "food-taster, commissary," see Doerfer, II, No. 755 (pp. 301–307).

[223] On M. *shükürchi*, "umbrella holder at the Imperial court," see Doerfer, I, No. 235 (pp. 257–58).

Akhtachi, Mubārak, Turmïsh, and Yïghmïsh. This Yïghmïsh was brought up by Temür Qa'an and he is recording the Qa'an's words, as is their custom.

⁊ OF THE BATTLE BETWEEN THE QA'AN AND Nayan Noyan of the *uruq* of Taghachar Noyan[224] and the princes allied with him; the appointment of Jim-Gim as heir-apparent

It is related that in the *qaqa yïl*, corresponding to the year 688/1289–1290,[225] Nayan Noyan of the *uruq* of Taghachar Noyan, the grandson of Otchi Noyan, along with certain descendants of Yesüngge Aqa[226] and other princes had had a difference with the Qa'an and had set out to join Qaidu and Du'a. The Qa'an's army had gone in pursuit of them, a battle had been fought, and they had defeated the army. News of this was brought to the Qa'an, and although he was suffering from rheumatism and had grown old and weak he set out in a palanquin on the back of an elephant.[227] The Qa'an's army was nearly put to flight. The elephant with the palanquin was then driven up on to a hill and the kettledrum beaten, whereupon Nayan Noyan and the princes fled with all their troops and the Qa'an's army went in pursuit of them. They were seized by their own fellow officers and brought before the Qa'an. He had them all put to death and divided up and scattered their forces.[228] Thereafter, the Qa'an could move but little

---

[224] See above, p. 204 and note 32.

[225] This is wrong; the Year of the Pig in question corresponded to 1287. Cf. *Polo II*, p. 789: "Nayan revolted between May 14 and June 12, 1287 .... Qubilai left Shang-tu on the 24th or 25th of June, the main battle took place about the 16th of July; Nayan was taken prisoner and executed. The fighting went on against his associates, and Qubilai returned to Shang-tu on the 15th of September, 1287."

[226] Yesüngge was the son of Genghis Khan's brother Jochi-Qasar.

[227] "The fabrication of the first 'elephant-litters' (... *hsiang-chiao*), evidently for Imperial use, is noted in the Annals toward the end of 1280 ...." (*Polo II*, p. 789.) According to Polo (Benedetto, p. 106), Qubilai was mounted "upon a bartizan borne by four elephants, full of crossbow-men and archers, with his flag above him, bearing the figures of the sun and the moon, and so high that it could be seen from all sides. The four elephants were all covered with very stout boiled hides, overlaid with cloths of silk and gold."

[228] Polo describes Nayan's execution: as a royal prince he was beaten to death in such a manner as not to shed his blood. See Benedetto, p. 108, and Boyle 1961, p. 150, note 5.

because of his rheumatism, and the armies remained on the frontiers of Du'a and Qaidu.

In previous years, when Nomoghan had not yet been carried off by Qaidu's army, there had been some talk of his being heir-apparent, and the wish had been present in the Qa'an's mind. Afterward, perceiving Jim-Gim to be extremely intelligent and able, he became very fond of him, and when Töde-Möngke sent Nomoghan back the Qa'an decreed that Jim-Gim was to be set up as Qa'an.[229] Nomoghan was displeased and said: "When he becomes Qa'an what will they call thee?" The Qa'an was annoyed and, after reprimanding him, dismissed him from his presence. He gave orders that [Nomoghan] was not to be admitted before him again, and he died within the next few days. The Qa'an then set up Jim-Gim as Emperor. He was Emperor for 3 days and then died, and his throne was sealed. His wife, Kökejin by name, was very intelligent and the Qa'an was on very good terms with her and did whatever she commanded.

Toward the end of the Qa'an's reign there was a rebellion in a province called Lukin[230] on the sea-coast below the province of Sayan Fu in Manzi. To quell the rebellion he sent, of the Mongol emirs, Yïghmïsh and Tarkhan, of the Khitayan emirs, Suching, and of the Tāzīks, Ghulām Sam-Jing and 'Umar Yu-Ching, the brother of Saiyid Ajall, at the head of an army. They defeated the rebels and plundered [their territory].

On the frontier with Qaidu and Du'a the scouts came in contact with each other but there was no war. At the end of the Qa'an's reign, Du'a once set out on a campaign and came to that [part of the] frontier and *sübe*,[231] where Chübei is stationed guarding the frontier with twelve thousand men. Du'a wished to make a night attack on him, but [Chübei] learnt of his intention and attacked the van of

---

[229] That is, Great Khan elect.

[230] This cannot be Lung-hsing (see above, p. 283, note 159), which is nowhere near the seacoast. On the whole, it would seem that we have to do with a garbled account of the expedition to Java in 1292, to which Rashīd al-Dīn has already briefly referred (p. 272). At any rate, Yïghmïsh (who appears in the Chinese sources as I-hei-mi-shih and is described as an Uighur) was one of the commanders of that expedition. See Franke, IV, pp. 463 and 465, V, p. 232.

[231] Mo. *sübe*, "eye of a needle ... narrow passage, defile; strategic point" (Lessing, s.v.).

Du'a's army by night, killing four thousand men. Du'a received news of this during that same night. He set out with all his forces; the two armies met at dawn, and many were killed on either side. Chübei had set out without notifying Ajïqï and Ananda, proceeding at high speed. It followed that he was unable to withstand the attack and [so] fled. When Ajïqï received the news he sent word to Ananda and set out. But by the time they had collected their forces and started, Du'a had turned back and their forces could not overtake him. This was one of the reasons for Du'a's bold attitude toward the Qa'an's army. When the Qa'an learnt of it he blamed Ajïqï and had him beaten nine blows with a stick but then restored him to favor and sent him once again at the head of the army; he is still there now in charge of that frontier. As for Qaban, the elder brother of Chübei, he had died some while before this battle.

It is well known that the countries of Turkistān were first laid waste by Alghu and afterward by Qaban, Chübei, Baraq, and Bayan, the son of Qonichi, who were princes of the right hand. Qaban and Chübei were at first with Qaidu but afterward submitted to the Qa'an.

❦ OF THE SAIYID AJALL, THE QA'AN'S VIZIER, who has been given the title of Bayan Finjan

One of the grandsons of the late Saiyid Ajall was called Abū Bakr. The Qa'an gave him the title of Bayan Finjan, made him the *nöker* of Öljei, and conferred on him the office of *finjan*, that is, *ṣāḥib-dīvān*. He was vizier for 2 years during the reign of the Qa'an, during which time informers arose against him from the Qa'an's Divans and stated that he had wasted 600 *tümens* of *bālish*. The Qa'an called him to reckoning, and he replied: "I left this amount [of tax] with the people, because for 3 years there had been a drought and no crops had come up, and the people had grown poor. Now, if the Qa'an so command, I will sell their wives and children and deliver the money to the treasury; but the country will be ruined." The Qa'an was pleased with his compassion for the people and said: "All the [other] ministers and emirs are concerned for themselves [only], but Bayan Finjan is concerned for the realm and the people." He showed him great favor, had him dressed in jewel-studded clothing, and entrusted all affairs to him.

That very day Kökejin, the mother of Temür Qa'an, sent for him and said: "Since thou hast found such favor and the Qa'an has settled the affairs of the realm upon thee, go and ask this question: 'Nine years have passed since Jim Gim's throne was scaled: what is thy command concerning it?'" (At this time Temür Qa'an had set off on a campaign against Qaidu and Du'a.) Bayan Finjan reported these words, and the Qa'an, from excess of joy, sprang up from his sick bed, summoned the emirs, and said: "You said that this *Sarta'ul*[232] was a wicked man, and yet it was he in his compassion who spoke for the people, it is he who speaks for the throne and the succession, and is he who concerns himself about my children, lest strife and discord should arise amongst them after my death." And again he showed favor to Bayan Finjan and called him by the great name of his grandfather, the Saiyid Ajall. He gave robes of honor, *yarlīghs*, and *paizas* both to him and to his seven brothers, who were all present, and he said. "Set out this very instant after my grandson Temur, who has left with the army proceeding against Qaidu. Bring him back, set him upon his father's throne as Qa'an, hold a feast for 3 days, and settle the succession upon him so that after the 3 days have passed he may set out and rejoin the army." In accordance with the Qa'an's command, the Saiyid Ajall went and fetched Temür Qa'an back and set him on Jim-Gim's throne in the town of Kemin-Fu. After 3 days he set out for the army and the Saiyid Ajall returned to the Qa'an.

Temür Qa'an was extremely fond of wine. However much the Qa'an advised and rebuked him, it was of no avail. He even on three occasions beat him with a stick, and he set several guards over him to keep him from drinking wine. Now in attendance on him was a *dānishmand*[233] from Bukhārā with the title of Radī, who laid claim to a knowledge of alchemy, magic, and talismans and by sleight of hand and deceit had endeared himself to Temür Qa'an. He used to drink wine with him in secret, and the Qa'an was annoyed with him on this account, but despite all the efforts to remove him from Temür Qa'an's service it proved impossible, for he was a sociable man and pleasant of speech. When the keepers and guards forbade the drinking of wine, Radī

---

[232] That is, Muslim.   [233] See Glossary.

suggested to him that they should go to the bath and tell the bath-attendant secretly to pour wine instead of water into the conduit, so that it passed through the pipe into the basin of the bath, where they used to drink it. The *keziktens* learnt of this and reported it to the Qa'an. He ordered Raḍī to be separated from him by force and sent upon some pretext to the town of ———;[234] and he was secretly put to death *en route*.

Now that he has become Qa'an, Temür Qa'an has abandoned [drink] of his own accord and drinks seldom and little. God Almighty, when he became a great lord, removed the love of wine from his heart, whereas Qubilai had been unable to prevent his drinking either by pleas or by compulsion. Despite his youth—and he is only twenty-five years old—his august feet are always in pain, and he used to sit in a palanquin on an elephant, but now does so less often because of suspicions and rumors amongst the people.

❧ OF THE *BAKHSHIS*[235] WHO HAVE BEEN AND ARE in attendance on the Qa'an; the authority they enjoy

At the end of Qubilai Qa'an's reign, there were two Tibetan *bakhshis*, one called Tanba and the other Kanba. The two front teeth of Tanba Bakhshi were exceedingly long, so that his lips would not close. They used to sit in the Qa'an's private temple, which the Nangiyas call ———.[236] They were related to each other and were of great authority and importance in the Qa'an's eyes. They were descended from the rulers of Tibet, and although there have been and are many Khitayan and Indian *bakhshis*, the Tibetans enjoy the greatest authority. There is also another *bakhshi*, a Kashmiri, called Qarantās Bakhshi. He too is a person of authority. Temür Qa'an also continues to believe in them, and those two *bakhshis* are all powerful. They have made their *nökers*, who have a knowledge of medicine, attendants on the Qa'an in order to prevent Temür Qa'an from taking too much food or drink. They have two sticks bound together, and when the occasion arises they beat them on themselves, and the sticks produce a noise, whereupon Temür Qa'an takes warning and reduces his eating and drinking. Great auth-

[234] Blank in the MSS.   [235] See Glossary.
[236] Blank in the MSS.

ority is attached to their words, and we shall, if God the One and Mighty so wills, adjoin to the history of Temür Qa'an one of the stories illustrating the authority enjoyed by Tanba Bakhshi.

❧ OF THE DEATH OF QUBILAI QA'AN

After reigning for 35 years and having reached the age of eighty-three, Qubilai Qa'an passed away in the *morin yïl*, that is, the Year of the Horse, corresponding to the year 693/1293–1294,[237] and left this transient world to his grandson, the Qa'an of the Age, the Illustrious Monarch, Temür Qa'an. May God grant many years of happiness and good fortune to his noble *uruq* and in particular to the Emperor of Islam, the Supreme Sultan Ghiyāth al-Dunyā wa'l-Dīn Öljeitü Muḥammad (*may God cause him to reign forever!*)[238]

❧ HISTORY OF THE RULERS OF MĀCHĪN AND THE

sultans, *maliks*, and *atabegs* of Persia, Syria, Egypt, the Maghrib, etc., who were contemporary with Qubilai Qa'an from the beginning of the *bichin yïl*, the Year of the Monkey, corresponding to the year 658/1259–1260,[239] to the end of the *morin yïl*, the Year of the Horse, corresponding to the year 693/1293–1294;[240] history of the strange and unusual occurrences that happened during this period—briefly and succinctly related

History of the rulers of Māchīn during this period

Lizun, 41 years, then 26 years past 15 years.[241]

Tuzon,[242] 10 years, and after the said Tuzon a man called Shuju[243] became ruler of that kingdom. When 2 years of his reign had passed, the army of Qubilai Qa'an seized the whole of that kingdom.

[237] Actually 1294. Born on the 23rd September, 1215, Qubilai, at the time of his death on the 18th February, 1294, was in his eightieth (not his eighty-fourth) year. Rashīd al-Dīn is more correct about the length of his reign—35 *lunar* years.

[238] The mention of Ghazan's brother and successor, Öljeitü (1304–1316), shows that this part of the work was written during his reign.

[239] Actually 1260.   [240] Actually 1264.

[241] Li-tsung reigned from 1224 to 1264, that is, approximately 41 lunar years. The meaning of the other figures, which add up to the years of his reign, is not clear.

[242] Tu-tsung (1264–1274).

[243] Tu-tsung was succeeded by his four-year-old son Hsien, usually referred to as

History of the sultans, atabegs, *and* maliks

In Rūm, 'Izz al-Dīn Kai-Kā'ūs, the son of Sultan Ghiyāth al-Dīn Kai-Khusrau, was Sultan. He was defeated at Köse-Dagh[244] by a Mongol army commanded by Baiju Noyan. He ruled jointly with his brother Rukn al-Dīn. Mu'īn al-Dīn Parvāna was the administrator of Rukn al-Dīn's kingdom and had brought him up. A dispute arose between them, and Sultan 'Izz al-Dīn ceded his Sultanate to his brother, made for the region of Niqīya,[245] and went from thence to the *takfūr*[246] of Constantinople.[247] When Berke's army came to Constantinople, ['Izz al-Dīn] was taken to Berke and given the sultanate of the town of Qïrïm, where he died.[248] His brother, Rukn al-Dīn, was martyred by the infidels,[249] and his son, Ghiyāth al-Dīn Kai-Khusrau ibn Qïlïj-Arslan, succeeded to the Sultanate. He was martyred[250] in Arzinjān, and the Sultanate was settled upon Ghiyāth al-Dīn Mas-'ūd ibn Kai-Kā'ūs, who is Sultan now.[251]

In Diyār Bakr and Mosul, Badr al-Dīn Lu'lu' was Sultan ———.[252]

In Egypt and Syria, a Turcoman[253] had conquered Egypt and had

---

Ying-kuo kung. See Franke, IV, p. 336, V, pp. 176–77. Shuju (Verkhovsky has Shundzhou) is perhaps some kind of nickname.

[244] The Battle of Köse-Dagh was fought on the 26th June or the 1st July, 1243, the Battle of Aksaray (with which Rashīd al-Dīn evidently confuses it) on the 14th October, 1256. See Duda, pp. 227 and 335. Even the latter battle ought, of course, to have been mentioned under Möngke's reign. Rashīd al-Dīn repeats his mistake elsewhere (Arends, p. 31), representing the Battle of Köse-Dagh as having taken place after Baiju's interview with Hülegü at Hamadan in the late spring or early summer of 1257.

[245] Nicaea, now Iznik.

[246] A title, apparently derived from the Armenian *t'agawor*, "king," applied by Muslim writers to the Byzantine Emperors.

[247] 'Izz al-Dīn sought refuge with the Emperor Michael Palaeologus in April 1261. See Spuler 1939, p. 54.

[248] In 1278 or 1279. See Spuler 1939, p. 54, and Duda, pp. 284–85 and 322.

[249] He was murdered by his minister Mu'īn al-Dīn Parvāna in 1267 or 1268; whether this was on the orders of the Il-Khan Abaqa is not quite certain. See Spuler 1939, pp. 54–55.

[250] Murdered in 1282 or 1283 or later with the connivance of the then Il-Khan. See Spuler 1939, p. 84.

[251] The last of the Seljuqs, he died in 1304 or 1305.

[252] Blank in all the MSS.

[253] Mu'izz 'Izz al-Dīn Ai-Beg, on whom see above, p. 234 and note 161, must be meant.

had several disputes with the Lord of Aleppo and Damascus, but in the end they had made peace. Quduz rose in rebellion against the Turcoman, killed him, and made himself master of Egypt and Syria.[254] After Hülegü Khan had captured Aleppo and Damascus and turned back, Quduz together with the emirs of Syria and Egypt and the khans of Khwārazm, who were the remnants of Sultan Jalāl al-Dīn's army, fought a battle with Ket-Buqa Noyan.[255] Malik Nāṣir Ṣalāḥ al-Dīn Yūsuf was the Lord of Syria: he had gone to Hülegü Khan and had been put to death on the plain of Mūsh.[256] When Quduz returned after the battle with Ket-Buqa, he was put to death by Bunduq-Dār,[257] who seized the throne. Bunduq-Dar died after returning from Rūm, where he had fought a battle[258] with Toqu and Töden. Alfī[259] became the ruler, and after Alfī's death his son Ashraf[260] succeeded his father.

In Kirmān, Quṭb al-Dīn was Sultan. When he died he left two sons: Muẓaffar al-Dīn Ḥajjāj and Jalāl al-Dīn Soyurghatmïsh. Sultan Ḥajjāj was nominally the Sultan, but the real power was in the hands of Terken Khatun. Since Terken's daughter, Pādshāh Khatun, had been given in marriage to Abaqa Khan, she used to go to Court every 2 or 3 years and to return loaded with honors. On one occasion she went thither and when she returned Sultan Ḥajjāj had gone out to welcome her, but before they met he became alarmed, went back to Kirmān and made his way to India, where he sought refuge with Sultan Shams al-Dīn of Delhi. He remained there nearly 15 years and finally died there. Terken Khatun was extremely just, and the affairs of the kingdom of Kirmān were kept in perfect order by her justice

---

[254] It was not Quduz (Muẓaffar Saif al-Dīn Qutuz) but Ai-Beg's own wife, Queen Shajar al-Durr, the first of the Mamlūk rulers, who was responsible for his death. See Lane-Poole, p. 260.

[255] This was the famous Battle of 'Ain Jālūt, in which the Mongol invaders of Syria were decisively defeated. See CHI, pp. 251–52.

[256] See CHI, p. 352.

[257] On Ẓāhir Rukn al-Dīn Bai-Bars al-Bunduqdārī al-Ṣāliḥī (1260–1277), see Lane-Poole, pp. 262 ff. He is the Bondocdaire of Marco Polo.

[258] The Battle of Abulustān, fought on the 15th April, 1277, on which see CHI, p. 361.

[259] On Manṣūr Saif al-Dīn Qïla'un al-Alfī al-Ṣāliḥī (1279–1290), see Lane-Poole, pp. 278–84.

[260] Ashraf Ṣalāḥ al-Dīn Khalīl (1290–1293), the conqueror of Acre. See Lane-Poole, pp. 284–88.

and equity. During the reign of Sultan Aḥmad, she came to the *ordo* and died near Tabriz.[261] Her body was brought back to Kirmān, and the Sultanate was entrusted to Jalāl al-Dīn Soyurghatmïsh. It is true to say that he was a very intelligent and perfect ruler. During the reign of Geikhatu Khan,[262] Pādshāh Khatun, who was his wife, came to Kirmān, seized her brother Soyurghatmïsh, and imprisoned him in a castle. He escaped from the castle, betook himself secretly to Geikhatu and asked for asylum. Geikhatu sent him to Pādshāh Khatun, who held him in custody for several days and then put him to death.[263] When Baidu,[264] who was married to Soyurghatmïsh's daughter Shāh 'Ālam, rose in rebellion, they sent a messenger, and Kürdünjin, the daughter of Prince Möngke-Temür, who was the wife of Soyurghatmïsh, seized Pādshāh Khatun and was bringing her to the *ordo*. Between Shiraz and Isfahan she was put to death as an act of vengeance.[265] *And God knows best what is right.*

History of the maliks and atabegs

In Māzandarān ———.[266]

In the Maghrib ———.[267]

In Fārs, Muẓaffar al-Dīn Abū Bakr was *atabeg*. When he died, his son the *atabeg* Sa'd had been to Court and was returning in poor health. The news of his father's death reached him in Tūrāqū,[268] a dependency of Parāhān. He too died 12 days[269] later. When the news of his death was brought to Shiraz, his twelve year-old son, the *atabeg* Muḥammad, was set on the throne and called Sultan 'Aḍud al-Dīn, the affairs of the kingdom being administered by his mother, Terken Khatun, the daughter of the *atabeg* Quṭb al-Dīn Maḥmūd Shāh.

---

[261] In June or July, 1282. See Spuler 1939, p. 154.

[262] 1291–1295.

[263] On the 21st August, 1294. See Spuler 1939, p. 154.

[264] Geikhatu's successor as Il-Khan, whose short reign (April–October, 1295) is not recognized by Rashīd al-Dīn.

[265] In June or July, 1295. See Spuler 1939, p. 154.

[266] Blank in all the MSS.   [267] Blank in all the MSS.

[268] Perhaps identical with the Sārūk mentioned by le Strange, p. 198, as a town in the district of Farāhān (Parāhān) between Hamadān and Burūjird.

[269] Or 18 days. See Spuler 1939, p. 142.

That son too died shortly afterward[270] and his mother became ruler. Muḥammad Shāh, the nephew of the *atabeg* Abū Bakr, who had married [Terken Khatun's] daughter, Salghum, picked a quarrel with his mother-in-law, and, in the end, he was put to death.[271] Terken Khatun had betrothed her youngest daughter, Abish Khatun, to Prince Möngke-Temür.

Terken Khatun now became the wife of Saljuq-Shāh, who after a time put her to death and imprisoned her two daughters in the Qal'a-yi Sapīd. This was reported to Court, and the Emir Altachu was sent at the head of an army to proceed [to Fārs] and seize Saljuq-Shāh, with the assistance of Rukn al-Dīn 'Alā al-Daula of Yezd, who was the brother of Terken Khatun, the *maliks* of Shabānkāra,[272] and the Tāzīk *cherig* of that country. When the army reached Abarqūh, they were met by six thousand Shirazi horsemen. 'Alā al-Daula attacked them with five hundred horsemen and drove them back to the gates of Shiraz. Saljuq-Shāh took refuge in Kāzarūn. The army proceeded thither and fought a battle. They captured the town, looting and massacring; and Saljuq-Shāh was dragged out and killed, and his head was sent to Shiraz. The *atabeg* 'Alā al-Daula received a wound there and died several days later. The daughters were taken out of the castle and brought to Court by their grandmother, Yāqūt Terken, who was the daughter of Qutlugh-Sultan Baraq Ḥājib, the ruler of Kirmān. Abish Khatun was given in marriage to Prince Möngke-Temür, and she was in effect the *atabeg* of Shiraz. The other sister, Bībī Salghum, was given in marriage to the *atabeg* Yūsuf-Shāh of Yezd, who was her cousin. Abish Khatun died[273] during the reign of Arghun Khan. Her body was taken to Shiraz and buried in the Madrasa-yi 'Aḍudīya, which her mother had built in honor of the aforementioned 'Aḍud al-Dīn Muḥammad. Princess Kürdünjin became her heir, and although the office of *malik* of Shiraz is now performed by *ortaqs* and merchants, the drums are still beaten at the gates of the *atabegs'* palace and the Great Divan is still held there.

---

[270] In October or November, 1262. See Spuler 1939, p. 143.

[271] As a reprisal for Saljuq-Shāh's revolt. See Spuler 1939, p. 144.

[272] The easternmost part of Fārs, which under the Mongols was treated as a separate province: it is Polo's Soncara, the seventh of the "eight kingdoms" of Persia.

[273] In 1286 or 1287. See Spuler 1939, p. 145.

In Sīstān, Malik Shams al-Dīn Muḥammad Kart had, in accordance with a *yarlīgh* of Möngke Qa'an, put to death Malik Shams al-Dīn of Sīstān and become ruler [of the country]. Subsequently, Malik Nuṣrat al-Dīn,[274] the nephew of the deceased *malik*, brought a messenger from Hülegü Khan, recovered Sīstān from Shams al-Dīn Kart, and took possession of that country, of which he is still the ruler and *malik*.

History of the strange and unusual occurrences that happened during this period

In the year 659/1260–1261, Badr al-Dīn Lu'lu' died in Mosul.

On the 17th Rajab of the year 644 [5th May, 1266] there died Mu'aiyid al-Daula 'Urḍi,[275] who was a learned philosopher and without a peer in the mathematical sciences.

During the morning of the 19th of Ṣafar of the year 699 [8th September, 1270] there was an earthquake of such violence that it was thought that stone would not remain upon stone in the mountains and that every clod of earth on the plains would be scattered in the atmosphere.

In the heart of winter in the year 671/1272–1273, there occurred a great earthquake in the capital city of Tabrīz such that there were tremors every hour for a space of 15 days.

On Monday the 17th Dhul-Ḥijja of the year 672 [25th June, 1274] the death of Khwāja Naṣīr[276] took place in Baghdad, at sunset. In his will he had asked to be buried in the shrine of Mūsā and Jawād.[277] A vacant place was found at the foot of Mūsā's grave and [the earth] dug up. There was revealed a ready-made grave complete with tiles. Inquiries having been made, [it was ascertained that] the Caliph al-

[274] Or Nāṣir al-Dīn. See Spuler 1939, pp. 119 and 157.

[275] On this famous scientist, one of Naṣir al-Dīn Ṭūsī's collaborators, see Sarton, *Introduction to the History of Science*, Vol. II, Part II, pp. 1013–1014. His description of the instruments in the Marāgha observatory is available in the translations of J. Jourdain (Paris, 1809) and H. J. Seeman (Erlangen, 1928).

[276] That is, Naṣir al-Dīn Ṭūsī. On his scientific work at Marāgha, see now *CHI*, pp. 668 ff.

[277] The famous Shrine of the Two Kāẓims (Kāẓimain), so called after the two Shī'a Imāms whom he buried there: Mūsā, grandson of the grandson of Ḥusain, the son of the Ḳaliph 'Alī, and Mūsā's grandson, Muḥammad al-Jawād. They were, respectively, the seventh and ninth Imāms, Mūsā having been put to death by Hārūn al-Rashīd in 802, while Muḥammad died, of poison, it is said, in 834 during the reign of Mu'taṣim. See *Baghdad*, pp. 160–61.

Nāṣir li-Dīn Allāh[278] had had it dug for his own resting-place and that his son, Ẓāhir,[279] acting contrary to the terms of his will, had buried him in Ruṣāfa[280] amongst his forefathers. Now it is one of the marvels of Time that the birth of Khwāja Naṣīr took place on the very day on which this chamber was completed, Saturday, the 11th Jumādā I, 597 [18th February, 1201]. He lived for 77 years, 7 months and 7 days.

On the 25th Dhul-Ḥijja, 673 [22nd June, 1275] Arghun Aqa[281] died in the meadows of Rādkān, near Ṭūs.

[278] 1180–1225. [279] 1225–1226.
[280] On the tombs of the Caliphs in Ruṣāfa in eastern Baghdad, see *Baghdad*, pp. 193–94. [281] See above, pp. 230–31.

PART
III
OF THE HISTORY OF QUBILAI QA'AN

*His praiseworthy character
and the excellent biligs, edicts, and parables
which he uttered and proclaimed;
such events as occurred during his reign but have not
been included in the two previous parts,
having been ascertained at irregular intervals
from various books and persons*

——————282

◆ OF THE WIVES AND CHILDREN OF ARÏQ BÖKE
after his death; how the Qa'an divided his *ordos* amongst his children;
of the emirs of Melik-Temür

When, after the extinction of the flames of revolt, Arïq Böke had
gone to his brother Qubilai Qa'an and had stood in the attitude of
seeking forgiveness and making apologies, he had brought all his
wives with him but had left his four sons, Yobuqur, Melik-Temür,
Naira'u-Buqa, and Tamachi, in his *yurt*. His summer residence was in
the Altai and his winter quarters on the Ürünge[283] and ————,[284]
the distance between the two places being a journey of 2 or 3 days.
Sorqoqtani Beki was there.

Arïq Böke was a month and 6 days with the Qa'an and then died.
His body was taken to Buda-Öndür,[285] which is the great *ghoruq* of
Chingiz-Khan near the River Selenge.[286] Sorqoqtani Beki and the

---

[282] This section is absent from all the MSS.

[283] The modern Urungu, the Ürünggü of *SH*, §§158 and 177. See *Polo I*, p. 342.

[284] Both Blochet and Verkhovsky have Qïrqïz (Kirghiz), which, as Pelliot (*Polo I*
p. 342) remarks, "seems improbable here."

[285] "Buddha Height." See above, p. 228 and note 128.

[286] Pelliot (*Polo I*, p. 342) points out that if Buda-Öndür and Burqan-Qaldun
are identical, the mention of the Selenga, which is in a quite different region, is "a
bad slip" on the part of Rashīd al-Dīn.

other princes and princesses are all buried there except Qubilai Qa'an.

Of Arïq Böke's wives, one was El-Chïqmïsh of the Oirat people. The second was Qutuqta Khatun of the Küchügür people, who are a group of the Naiman.[287] By her he had two daughters. The elder was Chaluqan Aqa, who was given in marriage to Nayanqa Küregen of the Baya'ut. The daughter of this Chaluqan is married to Melik-Temür, and her name is Negüder. She lives in the *yurt* and residence of Sorqoqtani Beki. He has another daughter by her, called Qamtai, who is not yet married. The other daughter [of Qutuqta Noyan] is called Nomoghan; she was given in marriage to Choban Küregen of the Oirat. The third wife was Qutlu Khatun of the Qonqïrat people. She too lives in the *yurt* of Sorqoqtani Beki and has no children.

He had a concubine called Iraghui of the Barulas people, the sister of Qadan, who came to these parts as ambassador. By this concubine he had a son called Nairaqu-Buqa. He had another concubine who is still alive, called Eshitei, of the Qonqïrat tribe. She was in the *ordo* of Qutuqta Khatun; he had a son by her called Tamachi.

When Arïq Böke died, his wives went back to their *yurts*. Three years later the Qa'an commanded: "Let the sons of Arïq Böke come and see me." When they were honored with an audience he said: "Let the great *yurt*, in which Yesüder Khatun lived, be administered by Yobuqur, and let Yobuqur marry Yesüder." They lived together for 3 years, but she bore no children and died. In her place he married ————[288] Khatun of the Üshin, by whom he had two sons: Öljei-Temür and Hulachu. Hulachu is in attendance on his father in Arïqan-Chaidan,[289] which belongs to ————,[290] while Öljei-Temür is in attendance on Temür Qa'an. He has another son, older than these two, by Chalun Khatun of the Qaranut, who are a branch of the Qonqïrat and Qorulas. He has yet another son, called Ödege, by Oghul-Tegin of the Naiman, a niece of Küshlüg Khan.[291]

[287] The Küchügür were the dominant Naiman clan at the time of the campaigns of Genghis Khan. See *Campagnes*, pp. 306–307.

[288] AZTHMH, in which Blochet, pp. 564–65, note *i*, sees a Tibetan name.

[289] Unidentified. The second element seems to be Mo. *chaidam*, "salt marsh."

[290] YSKY. Cf. the corrupt place-names above, p. 209 and note 51 and p. 253 and note 43.

[291] That is, Küchlüg, the Naiman prince who seized the Qara-Khitai throne. See *Conquérant*, pp. 262–66.

He had also one of Tolui's wives, called Nayan Khatun, of the Qonqïrat people, and that *yurt* had been transmitted by [Sorqoqtani Beki] to Arïq Böke. When Qutui Khatun[292] came to these parts,[293] she left Jumqur and Taraqai in that *ordo*. None of Hülegü's people being left there, they said: "How can we leave such an *ordo* empty?" And they placed Oghul-Tegin Khatun there. At the present time that *ordo* belongs to Ödege, who is now eighteen years old: he is in attendance on Melik-Temür and has a wife called Baiqa, the daughter of Ja'utu Noyan of the Süldüs people, a grandson of Sodun Noyan.

Arïq Böke's second son was ordered by the Qa'an to administer the *ordo* of Lingqun Khatun,[294] the daughter of Küshlüg Khan, a wise and able woman, who was the mother of Prince Qutuqtu. Qutuqtu had a son, called Tükel-Buqa, by a concubine, called Buta Egechi,[295] of the Qïpchaq people. This Tükel-Buqa died upon reaching puberty. [Qutuqtu] also had two daughters. His elder daughter, Kelmish Aqa, was given in marriage to Salji'utai Küregen of the Qonqïrat people. His younger daughter, Shirin Aqa, born of Qunduz Egechi of the Baya'ut people, was married to Tuqchi Küregen of the Üshin people. When Lingqun Khatun died, she left a daughter, called El-Temür, who was married to Bars-Buqa Küregen. In place of her, Melik-Temür married the daughter of Taran Noyan, the grandson of Olduqur Noyan of the Jalayir, called Gilte Khatun, and placed her in this great *yurt*. That *yurt* had fallen to the lot of Hülegü Khan, but on account of the distance and the absence of members of his *uruq* Melik-Temür has taken possession of it. By this Gilte he has no children. He has also another wife called Töre,[296] the daughter of Shiregi of the Dörbet, one of the great emirs of the *jasa'ul*.[297] By her he has two sons: one called Oiratai, who is in attendance on his father,

---

[292] The wife of Hülegü and the mother of the Il-Khan Tegüder (Aḥmad).

[293] That is, Persia, where she arrived during the reign of Abaqa. See Arends, pp. 69–70.

[294] Or Linqum Khatun. She was one of Tolui's widows. See above, p. 160. On her name, derived from a Chinese title, see *Campagnes*, p. 221; also Doerfer, I, No. 359 (pp. 493–94).

[295] Verkhovsky has Tuba-Ikachi. The Mongol word *egechi*, "elder sister," is used here in the sense of "concubine." See Doerfer, I, No. 67 (p. 101). Cf. immediately below, Qunduz Egechi.

[296] Verkhovsky has Bura, that is, Bora.

[297] Apparently to be understood as a plural: the *yasa'ul* (of which *jasa'ul* is a variant form) was, in Timurid times, an officer concerned with discipline and the enforcement

and the other Maḥmūd, also there. By her he also has two daughters: one called Emegen, who is married to Toq-Temür Küregen, the grandson of Bars-Buqa of the Oirat, who is grandson of Törelchi Küregen; and the other called Il-Qutluq, who is married to the son of Köbek of the Süldüs people, who is in command of the emirs under Du'a and is stationed on this side of the Oxus. Melik-Temür also has a concubine called Tuqluq-Öljei, the daughter of Baighara of ———,[298] the commander of a hundred. Melik-Temür's sons are as follows: Mingqan, Ajïqï, Yesün-To'a, and Baritai, [all] by Emegen Khatun, the daughter of Bars-Buqa of the Oirat people.

As for the *ordo* of El-Chïqmïsh Khatun of the Oirat people, the senior wife of Arïq Böke, Qubilai Qa'an gave it to his son Nairaqu-Buqa, who, at the time of Arïq Böke's death, made an attempt on his life; he was prevented and [afterward] died of grief. In this *yurt* he had a daughter called Ashïqtai. Afterward, when he went to the Qa'an, he left that *yurt* to Melik-Temür; it is now held by Ajïqï, the son of Melik-Temür.

To Tamachi the Qa'an gave the *yurt* of Qutuqta Khatun, but she died before they came together. In place of her [Tomachi] married Er-Tegin, the daughter of Sorqadu Ba'urchi of the Naiman, the nephew of Sartaq and Burunduq, who are resident in these parts. And when he took this wife with him to the Qa'an, that *yurt* was left unoccupied.

Nairaqu-Buqa has five sons, as follows: Qurbaqa, Bachin, Samghar, Bayan Ebügen, and Ara-Temür. Ara-Temür's mother is Ujin Egechi of the Olqunut, and the mother of the other four is Ashïqtai Khatun of the Qonqïrat, the niece of Chabui, the senior wife of Qubilai Qa'an.

Tamachi has two sons: one called Bayan and the other Dörben.

◆ THE GREAT EMIRS OF PRINCE MELIK-TEMÜR, the son of Arïq Böke, who are now with Qaidu

The first is the Emir Ja'utu of the Süldüs people, the grandson of Sodun Noyan, the son of Sunchaq Noyan, a commander of a *tümen*

---

of nomad law. See *Four Studies*, II, 118 and 126, and, on the post at the Ṣafavid Court, Minorsky 1943, p. 133.

[298] The text has ANAQLYQ, which could be either Almalïq or Qayalïq.

on the left hand. He has one son, called Qadan. He disposes of one guard and weapon, and has married the daughter of Melik-Temür.

Another is Qïpchaq, the grandson of Menglik Echige of the Qong-qotan[299] people. His father, Kökechü, was the commander of a thousand and a *chaqurchi*[300] of the right hand. He disposes of one guard and weapon.

Another is Alaqa, the commander of a thousand of the Qataqïn,[301] the son of Chilge Bahadur, who came to these parts.

Another is Jangqï Küregen of the Jalayir, the commander of a thousand. This thousand was previously under a commander called Oqai, who with a thousand-unit of Oirats used, in accordance with a *yarlïgh*, to guard Buda-Öndür,[302] which is the great *ghoruq*, where the bones of the princes are laid to rest. When the princes who accompanied Nomoghan rebelled and the armies joined battle, most of this thousand joined Qaidu's army, where some of them remained; the unit now belongs to the sons of Oqai.

Another is Kereidei, the senior *bitikchi*, of the Süldüs people.

Another is Kehetei, the foster-brother of Melik-Temür, also of the Süldüs. He is responsible for the business of the *ordo*, such as [the provision of] food, etc.

Another is Qadaqa of the Merkit, who is a great emir and in command of the *büke'üls*: the affairs of the *cherig* are in his hands.

Another is Saqtai of the Qongqotan, commander of the *kezik*.

Another is Batuqa, the son of Qutuqu Noyan, the commander of a thousand.

Another is Esen-Temür Ba'urchi, the son of Tümen Ba'urchi.

Another is Besütei Bahadur, the commander of the *ordo*.

Another is Arïq Böke Noyan of the Naiman.

Another is Cha'uldar, the son of Borghuchi Yarghuchï of the Arulat people.

Another is Ebügen, the son of Bughra Yarghuchï of the Jalayir.

---

[299] The Qongqotan were a branch of the Orona'ut, the Oronar of *SH*. See *Campagnes*, pp. 73–74.

[300] On the strength of a dubious etymology supplied by Blochet (p. 576, note *i*), Verkhovsky (p. 203) translates this word as "falconer." It is perhaps a corruption of *ghajarchi*, "guide," on which see Doerfer, I, No. 253 (pp. 376–77).

[301] On the Qataqïn, see *Campagnes*, pp. 393–97.

[302] See above, p. 228 and note 128.

Another is Toqan Akhtachi of the *uruq* of Jebe Noyan of the Besüt people.

Another is Toghrïl, the son of Burtaq, of the Süldüs.

Another is Qundaqai *Khizānechi,[303] the son of Abaqai, of the Qara-Khitai.

Another is Abishqa Shükürchi of the Qorulat.

Another is Malikī Tdechi,[304] of the Tāzīks.

[303] "The Treasurer."
[304] "The Butler." Or perhaps *E'üdechi "the Doorkeeper."

Beginning of the History of Temür Qa'an,

the Son of Jim-Gim, the Son of Qubilai Qa'an,
the Son of Tolui Khan, the Son of Chingiz-Khan:

History of Temür Qa'an,

which History is in Three Parts

BEGINNING OF THE HISTORY OF TEMÜR QA'AN,

THE SON OF JIM-GIM, THE SON OF QUBILAI QA'AN, THE SON OF TOLUI KHAN, THE SON OF CHINGIZ-KHAN

History of Temür Qa'an, which History is in Three Parts

◆ PART I. Account of his august lineage, a detailed account of his wives and of the branches into which they have divided down to the present day; his august portrait; and a genealogical table of his children.

◆ PART II. The events preceding his august accession; a picture of the throne; his wives and the princes and emirs on the occasion of his mounting the throne of the Khanate; some events which have occurred from the commencement of his auspicious reign (may it be God-aided!) up to the present time; some of his wars and victories about which knowledge is available.

◆ PART III. His praiseworthy character and the parables, *biligs*, and edicts which he uttered and promulgated; some events which occurred during his reign but have not been included in the two previous parts, having been ascertained at irregular intervals from various books and persons.

PART I

OF THE HISTORY OF TEMÜR QA'AN
THE GRANDSON OF QUBILAI QA'AN

Account of his lineage;
a detailed account of his wives and the branches into which
his sons have divided down to the present day;
his august portrait;
and a genealogical table of his descendants

Temür Qa'an, who is called Öljeitü Qa'an (may the shadow of his justice and equity extend for many years over the heads of all creation!), is the son of Jim-Gim, the son of Qubilai Qa'an, the son of Tolui Qa'an, the son of Chingiz-Khan. He was born of Jim-Gim's senior wife. Kökejin, in the *hüker yïl*, that is, the Year of the Ox, corresponding to the year 663/1264–1265.[1] There are many wives and concubines in his *ordos*, but on account of the great distance and the closure of the roads the names of all of them have not so far been ascertained. His senior wife is called Bulughan Khatun. She is of the Bay'aut bone, and by her he has a son called Tishi-Taishi. He has another son, called Maqabalin, by another wife.

The genealogical table of his sons and grandsons is as shown.

[1] Actually 1265.

319

PART

II
OF THE HISTORY OF TEMÜR QA'AN

The events preceding his accession;
a picture of the throne, his wives, and the princes and emirs
on the occasion of his mounting the throne of the Khanate;
some events and occurrences which have happened
from the commencement of his auspicious reign
(may it be God-aided and everlasting!)
up to the present time;
his victories and wars
as far as knowledge is available about them

ᵔ THE EVENTS PRECEDING HIS AUGUST ACCESSION

When Qubilai Qa'an passed away in the *morin yïl*, that is, the Year
of the Horse, corresponding to the year 693/1293–1294,[2] the senior
wife of Jim-Gim, who was the mother of Temür Qa'an, despatched
Bayan that very same day along with the great emirs in search of
Temür Qa'an to inform him of the Qa'an's death and bring him back
so that he might sit on the throne of Empire. For the space of a year
before his return, Kökejin administered the affairs and business
of the realm. Upon his auspicious arrival a great *quriltai* was held, which
was attended by his uncles Kököchü and Toghan; his brothers Kamala
and Yesün-Temür; his cousin Ananda Oghul, the son of Mangqala;
the sons of Oqruqchï, Temür-Buqa and Ejil-Buqa; the great emirs,
such as Bayan Chingsang, Uchachar Noyan, Toqtaq, Ölüg, Öljei
Chingsang, Altun Chingsang, Dashman Aqa, Jirqalan, Nalïqu,
Ambai of the Tangqut, Badraqa of the *uruq* of Eshige, Qutuqu
Chingsang of the Tatar people, and Arqasun Tarkhan Chingsang
of the *uruq* of Badai;[3] princesses, such as Nambui Khatun and her

---

[2] Actually 1294.

[3] Badai was one of the two herdsmen who warned Genghis Khan of Ong-Khan's

daughter Bekchin Khatun, Manzitai and Kökejin Khatun; and other princes, emirs, and princesses, such that it would be impossible to enumerate them all.

There was a dispute about the throne and the succession between Temür Qa'an and his brother Kamala. Kökejin Khatun, who was an extremely intelligent and able woman, said to them: "Chechen-Qa'an[4] (that is, Qubilai Qa'an) said that whoever knew the *biligs* of Chingiz-Khan best should ascend the throne. Now, therefore, let each of you recite his *biligs* so that the great men who are present may see which knows them better." Being extremely eloquent and [a good] reciter, Temür Qa'an declaimed the *biligs* well and with a pure accent, while Kamala, having something of a stammer and not being so well gifted in this respect, was unable to match him in the contest. All cried out with one voice: "Temür Qa'an knows them better and recites them better also. It is he that is worthy of crown and throne."[5] And in the town of Kemin-Fu in the ———— *yïl*, corresponding to the year ————,[6] he was seated, auspiciously and under a favorable horoscope, upon the throne of the Khanate, and the customs and practices that are usual with them were duly performed, as here shown.

❧ HOW THE QA'AN ORGANIZED THE AFFAIRS OF the realm

When they had done with feasting and merrymaking and had observed all the usages of congratulation, the Qa'an turned the face of his august counsel toward organizing the affairs of army and state: he assigned princes and emirs to the various provinces and regions and appointed the viziers and officials of the Divans.

To his elder brother Kamala he gave a full share of the property

---

intended treachery and as a reward received the hereditary title of *tarkhan*. See *HWC*, pp. 36–38, and *Conquérant*, pp. 155–56.

4 "The Wise Khan," apparently a posthumous title. See above, p. 159 and note 2. On *chechen*, a variant form of *sechen*, "wise," see Doerfer, I, No. 207 (pp. 332–34).

5 The *Yüan shih* makes no mention of this dispute but represents Kamala as standing down in favor of Temür on the ground of having been charged by Qubilai with the defense of the northern frontiers. See Franke, IV, p. 491.

6 The blanks are in all the MSS. In fact, Temür ascended the throne in the year of his grandfather's death, the Year of the Horse corresponding to 1294.

inherited from their father, and he sent him to Qara-Qorum, which is the region of the *yurts* and *ordos* of Chingiz-Khan. He placed the armies of that region under his command, and he administers all the countries of Qara-Qorum, the Chinas,[7] the Shiba'uchi,[8] the Onan and Kelüren, the Kem-Kemchi'üt,[9] the Selenge and Qayalïq as far as the region of the Qïrqïz, and the great *ghoruq* of Chingiz-Khan, which they call Burqan-Qaldun and where the great *ordos* of Chingiz-Khan are still situated. These latter are guarded by Kamala. There are four great *ordos* and five others there, nine in all, and no one is admitted to them. They have made portraits of them there and constantly burn perfumes and incense.[10] Kamala too has built himself a temple there.

Prince Ananda was sent by the Qa'an to the country of the Tangqut at the head of his army and *ulus*. Prince Kököchü and Körgüz, who is the Qa'an's son-in-law, were sent to the frontier with Qaidu and Du'a. He dispatched Toghan with an army to Manzi to guard that country. The Emir Ajïqï he sent at the head of an army to the frontier at Qara-Qocha.[11] He retained Bayan Finjan in the office of *ṣāḥib-dīvān*; and since the title of Saiyid Ajall was highly thought of by the Tāzīks, and since the Mongols too had observed that the grand vizier was called by that title and it was in consequence the highest of names and titles in their eyes also, therefore the Qa'an, in order to increase his importance and authority, called him Saiyid Ajall. Today he is an extremely great and powerful vizier and dispenses the business of the Great Divan and administers the affairs of the Empire together with Öljei-Tarkhan, Teke Finjan, Toina, 'Abdallāh Finjan, the Emir Khwāja Sami, Quṭb al-Dīn Samjing, and Mas'ūd Lanjun.

---

[7] On the tribe known as the Chinas ("Wolves"), see *Campagnes*, pp. 131–35.

[8] Presumably "the country of the falconers" (Mo. *sibaghuchi*), a reference perhaps to a northern area from which the Mongol Emperors obtained their gerfalcons. See *Polo I*, pp. 78–79.   [9] See above, p. 214 and note 69.

[10] Presumably this is the passage which Barthold had in mind when he quotes Rashīd al-Dīn as speaking of "stone statues (*kamennyya baby*) erected at the tombs of Chingiz-khan and of the lineage of Tolui, in front of which sweet-smelling substances were constantly burnt." See *Polo I*, p. 349. In point of fact, as Pelliot remarks (*Polo I*, p. 350), "the 'portraits' must have been the images which are often mentioned by mediaeval travellers and by Chinese sources; at first they hung in the tents of the *ordos*; at a later period of the Mongol dynasty, when Chinese influences became predominant, these portraits, woven with brocade, were placed in various temples in or near the capital . . . ."

[11] The Qara-Khocho of above, pp. 94 and 286.

❧ HISTORY OF PRINCE ANANDA, THE SON OF Mangqala, the son of Qubilai Qa'an, who is ruler of the Tangqut country and has become a Muslim; an account of some of the circumstances in that country and a description of his kingdom

Prince Ananda is the son of Mangqala, the third son of Qubilai Qa'an and the elder brother of Nomoghan. (It was this latter who was betrayed by the princes who accompanied him on a campaign against Qaidu. They seized him and sent him to the *uruq* of Jochi, and when Töde-Möngke became the ruler of that *ulus* he sent him back to Qubilai Qa'an proffering excuses. He died shortly afterward.) Temür Qa'an bestowed upon Ananda the army which Qubilai Qa'an had given to Mangqala and the Tangqut country which belonged to him. Tangqut is a large kingdom of [great] length and breadth and in the Khitayan language is called Kho-Si, that is, the great river in the West:[12] it has received this name amongst them because the country is situated to the west of Khitai. The large towns there, which are the residences of their rulers, are as follows: Kīnjanfu,[13] Qamjiu,[14] Irqai,[15] Khalajan[16] and Aq-Balıq.[17] There are twenty-four large towns in that kingdom, and most of the inhabitants are Muslims, but the cultivators and peasants are idolaters. In appearance they resemble the Khitayans. Formerly they used to pay tribute to the rulers of Khitai, and their towns have been given Khitayan names, and their customs and practices, *yasaq* and *yosun*, are similar.

Because Nomoghan left no issue, Ananda was confided to a Turkistānī Muslim called Mihtar Ḥasan Aqtachi to be brought up, and he was suckled by this man's wife, whose name was Zulaikhā. On that account

[12] In fact, Ho-hsi, from *ho*, "river," and *hsi*, "west," means "the country west of the river (the Hwang Ho)." See also, above, p. 22 and note 45.

[13] Sian, the capital of Shensi. See above, p. 283 and note 165.

[14] Kanchow (Yangyeh) in Kansu. See above, p. 283 and note 169.

[15] Pelliot (*Polo II*, p. 641) hesitates between Irqai, the native name of Ningsia (Yinchwan) in Kansu, Polo's Egrigaia, and Uraqai, another place in Tangut.

[16] Polo's Calacian, on which see Pelliot, *Polo I*, pp. 132–37, where he identifies it with the "temporary residence" built by Li Yüan-hao in 1047 in the Ho-lan shan or Ala Shan mountains and also with the Alashai or Alashai Nuntuq "Camp of Alashai," of *SH*, §265.

[17] In Turkish, "White Town," Polo's Acbalec Mangi, identified by Pelliot (*Polo I*, pp. 7–8) with Hanchung (Nancheng) in southern Shensi.

Islam took firm root in his heart. He learnt the Qur'ān and writes the Tāzīk script extremely well, and his time is always devoted to acts of devotion and worship. There are nearly 150,000 Mongol troops subordinate to him, and he has converted the majority of them to Islam. One of his emirs, called Sartaq, who was opposed to Islam, went to the Qa'an and complained that Ananda was always in the mosque, praying, fasting, and reading the Qur'ān; that he had circumcised the children of most of the Mongols; and that he had converted the greater part of the army to Islam. The Qa'an was extremely annoyed at this report and he sent Jirghalang and Chirtaqu, who are brothers and in charge of the *qushchïs*, to forbid his performing acts of devotion and worship, to withdraw the Muslims from his Court, and to encourage him to worship idols and burn incense in idol temples. He refused to do so and would not listen to them, saying: "An idol is a man-made thing—how can I worship it? The sun was created by the Great God and is the soul of the corporeal world and the cause of the life and growth of animal and vegetable, and yet I do not think it right to worship it. How then should I worship a material form made by man? I worship Him Who created the Qa'an and me." The Qa'an was extremely angry at these words and ordered Ananda to be imprisoned. But he remained constant in his faith and Islam and continued to affirm his belief, saying: "Our fathers were all monotheists and knew and worshipped God alone. Therefore, thanks to that sincere belief, the Ancient God bestowed upon them the whole face of the earth so that they held their heads high in pride and never bowed to any idol." The Qa'an sent for him and asked: "If thou hast dreamt a dream, or heard a voice, or something has appeared to thee, or someone has guided thee to Islam, tell me so, that he may guide me too." Ananda replied: "The Great God guided me through knowledge of Him." Said the Qa'an: "It was a devil that guided thee." He replied: "If it was a devil that guided me, who was it who guided Ghazan Khan, who is my *aqa*?" The Qa'an was silent and reflected for awhile. Kökejin Khatun said to him by way of advice: "It is 2 years since thou mountedst the throne and the realm is not yet settled. Ananda has a large army, and all those troops and the people of the Tangqut country are Muslims and opposed to this state of affairs; moreover they are close to enemy territory. Heaven forbid that they should change their allegiance! It is not advisable to use force on him. He knows best about his belief and religion." The Qa'an realized that this advice was given out of compassion. He freed Ananda, consoled and soothed him, and conferred honors upon him, sending him back at the head of the Tangqut army and bestowing the kingdom of Tangqut upon him.

Although Ananda had believed in and practised Islam from his childhood, he went to extremes in this when he heard that the Lord of Islam (*may God cause him to reign forever!*) had become a Muslim, a monotheist, and a man of pure faith, and that all the Mongols in Persia had become Muslims, breaking all the idols and destroying all the idol-temples. Then he too, in imitation of him, strove to strengthen the faith of Islam. Now the case of Ananda and his army may be deduced from the fact that within a short space of time the cause of Islam has attained to perfection in those countries, and, in accordance with the words of the Qur'ān—"*entering the religion of God by troops*"[18]— they arrive in a throng to become believers, monotheists, Muslims, and men of pure faith. And the sons and grandsons of the aforesaid Mihtār Ḥasan, Hindu, Daulat-Shah, Ḥamid, Jamāl Aqa, and Muḥammad A'qtachi are all men of standing and importance. Some of them are attached to the mother of Temür Qa'an and strive to strengthen the faith of Islam.

Afterward, in recent years, Ananda went to the Qa'an on the occasion of a *quriltai* and was treated with honor and respect. He openly paraded his Islam, and the Qa'an, having heard of the conversion of the Lord of Islam, expressed his approval and said: "In becoming a Muslim Ananda has followed Ghazan. Let him practice Islam as his heart desires, for I have reflected [and found] that Islam is a good way and religion." On this account, Ananda went to even greater extremes in [the propagation of] Islam. He returned again as head of the Tangqut state and the army, and although the ministers and *bitikchis* of the Qa'an are in charge of the *tamghas* there, most of the revenue is expended on the army and not much of it reaches the Divan. And today even Sartaq, who was opposed to Islam and denounced Ananda, has become a Muslim and is one of his great emirs. Another is a man called Mengli, who is also a Muslim. Ananda, at the present time, is certainly thirty years old. He is swarthy with a black beard,

[18] Koran, cx, 2.

tall and corpulent. He has a son called Örüg-Temür, who, in his own *ulus*, is firmly established on the throne of sovereignty. He has built mosques and places of worship in his own *ordos* and *yurts* and is always employed in reading the Qur'ān and performing acts of worship.

Four years after the august accession of Temür Qa'an, Du'a, the son of Baraq, set out at the head of an army to attack the aforementioned princes and emirs who control the frontier of Temür Qa'an's Empire. As is the custom of the army, there is a patrol stationed in every *sübe*[19] and from the *sübe* of Ajïqï and Chübei, who are in the extreme West, to the *sübe* of Muqali, who is in the East, *yams* have been set up and couriers stationed in them. On this occasion they reported to one another that a large army had made its appearance. It so happened that the princes Kököchü, Jungqur, and Nangiyadai[20] had gathered together and held a feast and were drinking and making merry. At night, when the news arrived, they were drunk and had fallen unconscious, incapable of mounting horse. Körgüz Küregen,[21] the son-in-law of Temür Qa'an, set out at the head of his army, and at once the enemy arrived. Since they were unaware of the situation, and some of the armies of the right and left hand were without news, and the distance between them great, they were unable to join one another, and Du'a, the son of Baraq, and his army fell upon Körgüz, who had not more than six thousand men with him. He was unable to stand up to Du'a and [so] fled, making in the direction of a mountain. The enemy pursued and captured him and were about to kill him. He said: "I am Körgüz, the son-in-law of the Qa'an." Du'a's commander gave orders that he was not to be killed but held [prisoner]. The fleeing troops went to the Qa'an. Now Kököchü, the Qa'an's uncle, having failed to join the army because of neglect, was afraid and lay skulking in a corner. He was sent for several times but did not appear. In the end the Qa'an sent Ajïqï to coax him out [of his hiding-place]. And when the routed army reached the Qa'an's presence, he was displeased with its commanders: Jungqur and Nangiyadai were seized and bound, and

[19] See above, p. 299 and note 231.
[20] Only the first of the three would appear to be a prince of the blood: Kököchü, a son of Qubilai and uncle of the Great Khan. Jungqur and Nangiyadai are apparently the commanders referred to above, p. 286.
[21] On Körgüz, "Prince George," see above, p. 286 and note 181.

he said to them: "How could you be so neglectful and allow such waste of time?"

At the very time when the routed army and Du'a were in that area, the princes Yobuqur and Ulus-Buqa and the Emir Dorduqa, who had fled to Qaidu in the time of Qubilai Qa'an and had been sent by Qaidu to Du'a, consulted together and then deserted Du'a and set out to join Temür Qa'an with an army of twelve thousand men. When the Qa'an heard of their approach he did not trust them, for Dorduqa had come back once during the reign of Qubilai Qa'an and had taken the above-mentioned princes away with him. Therefore he dispatched Chirtaqu, Mubārak-Shāh Dāmghāni, and Satuq, along with Ajïqï, to bring them to him. Yobuqur and Dorduqa both came but left Ulus-Buqa with the tents in the region of Qara-Qorum with instructions to follow them slowly. He plundered Qara-Qorum and looted the market and granaries. When he arrived, the Qa'an accused him, saying: "How didst thou dare to commit such an act in the resting-place of Chingiz-Khan?" And he had him bound and imprisoned. He excused himself by saying: "I came hither as a fugitive. Du'a's army was pursuing us; they joined battle with us and plundered [the town]." His excuse was not accepted. Taiki, the wife of Asutai, and Khaishang, his son, toward whom the Qa'an was very well disposed, interceded on behalf of Ulus-Buqa, who was Asutai's brother. He was set free, but the Qa'an did not trust him and did not send him on any other campaign, ordering him to remain in attendance on the throne. As for Yobuqur, he treated him kindly and said: "He has committed no crime." However he was angry with the Emir Dorduqa and said: "Put him to death, for he deserted on two occasions." Dorduqa wept and said: "I was afraid of Qubilai Qa'an and ran away, but as long as I was there I never attacked or fought the Qa'an's army. And when Temür became Qa'an, I took advantage of this opportunity and, after consulting with these princes, I came back bringing more troops than I had taken with me, my intention being to render service. If the Qa'an will show me favor I will set out with the troops I have brought and whatever other troops he gives me, and pursue Du'a and punish him for what he has done. Perhaps I may be able to rescue Körgüz." The emirs reported these words and interceded on his behalf, whereupon the Qa'an pardoned his crime and dispatched him at the head of a fully equipped army. But he ordered Yobuqur not to go. He interceded on his behalf and said: "We have come to render service. Let our dependents remain here and let us go, for we are familiar with the conditions of that country and army. It may be that, thanks to the Qa'an's fortune, we shall avenge that incident." The Qa'an honored Yobuqur also and spoke kindly to him; and they all set out together.

Meanwhile, Du'a, his mind set at rest with the defeat of the [Qa'an's] army, was moving at a slow pace, intending to proceed to his own *ordos* and then to send troops to the posts and areas of Ananda, Ajïqï, and Chübei, who are in the region of Qara-Qocha, and whom he hoped to attack, defeat, and put to flight. At the time when the army was spread out on the banks of a large river, which they were about to cross, Yobuqur, Ulus-Buqa, and Dorduqa suddenly appeared and attacked Du'a and his army. They killed many, and many were drowned. Although they tried, they were unable to get hold of Körgüz, but they captured Du'a's son-in-law, called ————,[22] and returned victorious and triumphant. The Qa'an received them kindly and showed them favor. The emirs then thought of releasing Du'a's son-in-law in the hope that he for his part might send back the Qa'an's son-in-law. In those same few days ambassadors arrived from Du'a bearing the following message: "We have done something and have been punished for it. Now Körgüz is with us and Du'a's son-in-law is with you." Körgüz too had sent a *nöker* along with them with this message: "I am safe but have no *nökers* and am without food and sustenance. Send two or three *nökers* and something for me." They dispatched four of his emirs with an abundant supply of goods in the company of Du'a's son-in-law. Before they arrived they had killed Körgüz. They excused themselves by saying that they were sending him to Qaidu and that he died on the way.

❧ HOW THE QA'AN'S ARMY FOUGHT TWO ENGAGEments with the army of Qaidu and Du'a and how Qaidu was wounded in battle and died of his wound

[22] Blank in all the MSS.

Thereafter Bayan, the son of Qonichi, who is of the *uruq* of Orda and is now ruler of that *ulus*, sent an ambassador to the Qa'an to report on his cousin Küilük, who had risen in rebellion, sought refuge with Qaidu and Du'a, and fought several battles with him—as has been recorded in the history of Jochi. The ambassador's message was as follows: "Let your army set out at once from that direction and the army of Badakhshān, which is constantly being harrassed by them, from the East. The army of the Lord of Islam (*may God cause him to reign forever!*) will assuredly render assistance from the West, and we shall surround Qaidu and Du'a from every side and at once make an end of them." When this proposal was discussed in private, Kökejin Khatun, the mother of the Qa'an, said: "In the lands of Khitai and Nangiyas our *ulus* is large, and the country of Qaidu and Du'a is far away. If thou goest to war, it will require a year or two before that business is settled. Heaven forbid that in the meantime some disturbance may occur which it may take a long time to put down. We must be patient now and send a reply to this effect: 'We agree with what you say. Wait for a communication.'" On this account there was some delay, and it was 2 or 3 years later, in the year —— ,[23] that the Qa'an's army set out for this purpose against Qaidu and Du'a. They made for an area that was nearer to Qaidu['s territory]. The two armies met and there was a fierce battle: Qaidu was wounded and they put his army to flight. Du'a, being some distance away, did not arrive till several days later. Again they gave battle and fought fiercely, and Du'a too was wounded. As for Qaidu, he died of the wound he had received.[24]

◆ THE FRAUDULENT BEHAVIOR OF THE EMIRS AND viziers of the Qa'an with respect to jewels and ornaments which they had bought from merchants; and how Tanba Bakhshi interceded for them by means of a trick and so obtained their release

Tanba Bakhshi the Tibetan, of whom an account was given in the history of Qubilai Qa'an,[25] was a man of great influence with Temür

[23] Blank in all the MSS.
[24] On the contradictory accounts of Qaidu's death, see *Four Studies*, pp. 128–29.
[25] See above, pp. 302–303.

Qa'an also. The following is one of the many stories illustrating that influence. On one occasion some merchants had brought a large quantity of jewelry and precious stones and were selling them to the Qa'an. The emirs, viziers, and brokers who were present valued it all at a sum of 60 *tümens* of *bālish*. This amount was brought from the treasury and the merchants dispensed nearly 15 *tümens* of this amongst the emirs and viziers. Now there was an emir called Muqbil Finjan, against whom the other emirs had presented a petition. He had in consequence been dismissed and the Qa'an had appointed him in the capacity of a *totqa'ul*, which in Khitayan is called *leng-qish*.[26] There were two brokers who were not allowed by the other brokers to take part in their transactions. These brokers said to that emir: "That jewelry is not worth more than 30 *tümens*." Muqbil reported these words and orders were given for the jewelry to be valued again. Shihāb al-Dīn Qunduzī, who had been *chingsang* of the town of Khingsai and had been dismissed, was present at Court and valued it at 30 *tümens*. The Qa'an then ordered the merchants and brokers to be arrested. They confessed as to how much they had given to each emir, and in consequence the emirs and viziers were arrested also. There were twelve of them: Dashman Chingsang, Toina, Sarban, Yïghmïsh, Teke Finjan, 'Īsā Kelemechi, Bayanchar, the brother of Bayan Finjan, Shams al-Dīn Qunduzī, and three other *finjans*. They were all of them imprisoned in the Divan building in the *shing*, and orders were given that they were all to be put to death. Their wives and dependents went to Kökejin Khatun to intercede for them. She tried to obtain their release but in vain. They then resorted to Tanba Bakhshi. Now it so happened that a comet had appeared that day. Accordingly, Tanba Bakhshi sent to the Qa'an suggesting that he should worship the comet. The Qa'an came and the *bakhshi* said: "Forty prisoners must be freed." Then he said: "One hundred more prisoners must be pardoned." And so they were saved. He then represented to the Qa'an that a royal *yarlïgh* ought to be issued. The Qa'an prayed in the temple for 7 days. Then he came out and sent those people back to their posts; and all their followers rejoiced. However the 30 *tümens* of *bālish* in excess of the [true] value of the jewelry were taken back from them.

[26] On this form, see Blochet, p. 614, note *i*.

Appendix

BIBLIOGRAPHICAL
ABBREVIATIONS

Allen	W. E. D. Allen: *A History of the Georgian People*. London, 1932.
Altan Tobchi	*The Mongol Chronicle Altan Tobči*. Ed. and trans. C. R. Bawden. Wiesbaden, 1955.
AO	*Acta Orientalia.*
Arends	Rashīd al-Dīn: *Dzhami-at-Tavarikh* (*Sbornik letopisei*), Vol. III. Trans. A. K. Arends. Baku, 1957.
Baghdad	G. le Strange: *Baghdad during the Abbasid Caliphate*. Oxford, 1924.
Barhebraeus	*The Chronography of Gregory Abû'l Faraj . . . Barhebraeus.* Trans. and ed. E. A. Wallis Budge. Oxford and London, 1932.
Becquet-Hambis	Jean de Plan Carpin: *Histoire des Mongols*. Ed. and trans. J. Becquet and L. Hambis. Paris, 1965.
Benedetto	*The Travels of Marco Polo*. Ed. L. F. Benedetto; trans. A. Ricci. London, 1931.
Blochet	Rashīd al-Dīn: *Djami el-Tévarikh*, Vol. II. Ed. E. Blochet. Leiden and London, 1911.
Boyle 1956	J. A. Boyle: "On the Titles Given in Juvainī to Certain Mongolian Princes." *HJAS* 19/3-4 (1956), pp. 146–54.
Boyle 1961	J. A. Boyle: "The Death of the Last 'Abbāsid Caliph: a Contemporary Muslim Account." *JSS* VI/2 (1961), pp. 145–61.
Boyle 1962	J. A. Boyle: "Juvaynī and Rashīd al-Dīn as Sources on the History of the Mongols." *Historians of the Middle East*. Ed. B. Lewis and P. M. Holt. London, 1962, pp. 133–37.
Boyle 1963	J. A. Boyle: "The Mongol Commanders in Afghanistan and India according to the *Ṭabaqāt-i-Nāṣirī* of Jūzjānī." *Islamic Studies*, II/2 (1963), pp. 235–47.
Boyle 1964	J. A. Boyle: "The Journey of Het'um I, King of Little Armenia, to the Court of the Great Khan Möngke." *CAJ* IX/3 (1964), pp. 175–89.
Boyle 1965	J. A. Boyle: "A Form of Horse Sacrifice amongst the 13th- and 14th-century Mongols." *CAJ* X/3-4 (1965), pp. 145–50.

Boyle 1968   J. A. Boyle: "The Burial Place of the Great Khan Ögedei." *AO* XXXII (1968), pp. 45–50.

Boyle 1969   J. A. Boyle: "Batu's Title of Sayin-Khan." *Annali (R.) Istituto Orientale di Napoli* (1969), pp. 67–70.

Boyle 1970   J. A. Boyle: "The Seasonal Residences of the Great Khan Ögedei." *Wissenschaftliche Zeitschrift der Humboldt-Universität zu Berlin* (1970).

Bretschneider   E. Bretschneider: *Medieval Researches from Eastern Asiatic Sources.* 2 vols. London, 1888.

Browne   E. G. Browne: *A Literary History of Persia*, Vol. III. Cambridge, 1928.

BSOAS   *Bulletin of the School of Oriental and African Studies.*

Budge   *The Life and Exploits of Alexander the Great.* Trans. E. A. W. Budge. London, 1896.

CAJ   *Central Asiatic Journal.*

Cammann   Schuyler Cammann: "Mongol Costume—Historical and Recent." *Aspects of Altaic Civilization.* Ed. Denis Sinor. Bloomington, 1963, pp. 157–66.

Campagnes   *Histoire des campagnes de Gengis Khan: Cheng-wou ts'in-tcheng lou*, Vol. I. Ed. and trans. P. Pelliot and L. Hambis. Leiden, 1951.

Cathay   *Cathay and the Way Thither*, Vol. III. Ed. and trans. Sir Henry Yule. (New edition revised by Henri Cordier.) London, 1914.

Caucasian History   V. Minorsky: *Studies in Caucasian History.* London, 1953.

CHI   *Cambridge History of Iran*, Vol. V (the Mongol and Saljuq Periods). Ed. J. A. Boyle. Cambridge, 1968.

Chapitre CVII   *Le Chapitre CVII du Yuan che.* Ed. and trans. L. Hambis. Leiden, 1945.

Cleaves 1952   F. W. Cleaves: "The Sino-Mongolian Inscription of 1346." *HJAS* 15/1–2 (1952), pp. 1–123.

Cleaves 1956   F. W. Cleaves: "The Biography of Bayan of the Bārin in the *Yüan shih*." *HJAS* 19/3–4 (1956), pp. 185–301.

Cleaves 1962–3   F. W. Cleaves: "*Aqa Minu.*" *HJAS* 24 (1962–1963), pp. 64–81.

Conquérant   R. Grousset: *Le Conquérant du monde.* Paris, 1944.

Dawson   Christopher Dawson: *The Mongol Mission.* London, 1955.

Doerfer   G. Doerfer: *Türkische und mongolische Elemente im Neupersischen*, Vols. I, II, and III. Wiesbaden, 1963, 1965, and 1967.

Duda   *Die Seltschukengeschichte des Ibn Bībī.* Trans. Herbert W. Duda. Copenhagen, 1959.

*EI*²   *Encyclopaedia of Islam.* 2d ed. Leiden and London, 1960–.

Fischel 1953   W. J. Fischel: "Azarbaijan in Jewish History." *Proceedings of the American Academy for Jewish Research,* XXII (1953), pp. 1–21.

Four Studies   V. V. Barthold: *Four Studies on the History of Central Asia,* Vols. I. and II. Trans. V. and T. Minorsky. Leiden, 1956 and 1958.

Franke   O. Franke: *Geschichte des chinesischen Reiches,* Vols. IV and V. Berlin, 1948 and 1952.

Gibb II   *The Travels of Ibn Battūta.* Trans. H. A. R. Gibb. Vol. II. Cambridge, 1962.

Gottschalk   H. L. Gottschalk: *Al-Malik al-Kāmil von Egypten und seine Zeit.* Wiesbaden, 1958.

Grigor   Grigor of Akner: *History of the Nation of the Archers.* Ed. and trans. R. P. Blake and R. N. Frye. Cambridge, Mass., 1954.

Hague   John of Joinville: *The Life of St. Louis.* Trans. R. Hague. London, 1955.

Haenisch   *Die Geheime Geschichte der Mongolen.* 2nd ed. Trans. E. Haenisch. Leipzig, 1948.

Hambis 1956   L. Hambis: "Notes sur Käm, nom de l'Yénissei supérieur." *JA* (1956), pp. 281–300.

Harva   U. Harva: *Die religiösen Vorstellungen der altaischen Völker.* Helsinki, 1938.

Henthorn   W. E. Henthorn: *Korea: the Mongol Invasions.* Leiden, 1963.

Hinz   W. Hinz: "Islamische Masse und Gewichte" in *Handbuch der Orientalistik.* Leiden, 1955.

HJAS   *Harvard Journal of Asiatic Studies.*

Hodgson   M. G. S. Hodgson: *Order of Assassins.* The Hague, 1955.

Horde d'Or   P. Pelliot: *Notes sur l'histoire de la Horde d'Or.* Paris, 1950.

Houdas   Nasawī: *Histoire du Sultan Djelal ed-Din Mankobirti.* Trans. O. Houdas. Paris, 1895.

Ḥudūd   *Ḥudūd al-'Ālam.* Ed. and trans. V. Minorsky. London, 1937.

HWC   'Alā-al Dīn 'Aṭā-Malik Juvainī: *The History of the World-Conqueror.* Trans. J. A. Boyle. 2 vols. Manchester, 1958.

Ibn Ḥajar	Ibn Ḥajar: *Al-Durar al-Kāmina fī A'yān al-Mi'a al-Thāmina*, Vol. III. Hyderabad, 1349/1930–1931.
Iranica	V. Minorsky: *Iranica*. Tehran, 1964.
JA	*Journal Asiatique.*
Jahn 1956	K. Jahn: "A Note on Kashmīr and the Mongols." *CAJ* II/3 (1956), pp. 176–80.
Jahn 1963	K. Jahn: "Study on Supplementary Persian Sources for the Mongol History of Iran." *Aspects of Altaic Civilization*. Ed. Denis Sinor. Bloomington, 1963, pp. 197–204.
Jahn 1964	K. Jahn, "The Still Missing Works of Rashīd al-Dīn." *CAJ* IX/2, pp. 113–22.
Jahn 1965	K. Jahn: *Rashīd al-Dīn's History of India*. The Hague, 1965.
Jahn 1969	K. Jahn: *Die Geschichte der Oğuzen des Rašīd ad-Dīn*. Vienna, 1969.
JSS	*Journal of Semitic Studies.*
Juvainī	*Ta'ríkh-i-Jahán-Gushay of Juwayní*. Ed. Muhammad Qazvīnī. 3 vols. London and Leiden, 1912, 1916, and 1937.
Kāshgharī	Maḥmūd Kāshgharī: *Divanü Luğat-it-Türk*. Trans. B. Atalay. 3 vols. Ankara, 1939–1941.
Khetagurov	Rashīd al-Dīn: *Sbornik letopisei*, Vol. I, Part 1. Trans. L. A. Khetagurov. Moscow–Leningrad, 1952.
Koran	*The Koran*. Trans. J. M. Rodwell. London (Everyman's Library), 1909.
Krause	F. E. A. Krause: *Cingis Han*. Heidelberg, 1922.
Lane-Poole	S. Lane-Poole: *A History of Egypt in the Middle Ages*. London, 1901.
Laurent	J. C. M. Laurent: *Peregrinatores Medii Aevi quattuor*. Leipzig, 1864.
Ledyard	G. Ledyard: "The Mongol campaigns in Korea and the Dating of *The Secret History of the Mongols*." *CAJ* IX/I (1964), pp. 1–22.
Lessing	F. D. Lessing: *Mongolian-English Dictionary*. Berkeley and Los Angeles, 1960.
Le Strange	G. le Strange: *Lands of the Eastern Caliphate*. Cambridge, 1905.
Macartney	C. A. Macartney: "Where was 'Black Wallachia' in the thirteenth century?" *JRAS* (1940), pp. 198–200.
Minorsky 1942	*Sharaf al-Zamān Ṭāhir Marvazī on China, the Turks and India*. Trans. and ed. V. Minorsky. London, 1942.

APPENDIX

Minorsky 1943   *Tadhkirat al-Mulūk*. Trans. and ed. V. Minorsky. London, 1943.

Minorsky 1952   V. Minorsky: "Caucasica III: The Alān capital *Magas and the Mongol campaigns." *BSOAS* XIV/2 (1952), pp. 221–38.

Mostaert-Cleaves   A. Mostaert and F. W. Cleaves: "Trois documents mongols des Archives secrètes vaticanes." *HJAS* XV/3–4 (1952), pp. 419–506.

Moule 1930   A. C. Moule: *Christians in China before the Year 1550*. London, 1930.

Moule 1957   A. C. Moule: *Quinsai with Other Notes on Marco Polo*. Cambridge, 1957.

Mustaufī   Ḥamd Allāh Mustaufī Qazvīnī: *The Geographical Part of the Nuzhat-al-Qulūb*. Trans. G. le Strange. Leiden and London, 1919.

Olbricht   Peter Olbricht: *Das Postwesen in China unter der Mongolenherrschaft im 13. und 14. Jahrhundert*. Wiesbaden, 1954.

Olschki   L. Olschki: *Guillaume Boucher*. Baltimore, 1946.

Papauté   P. Pelliot: "Les Mongols et la Papauté." *Revue de l'Orient Chrétien*, XXIII (1922), pp. 3–30; XXIV (1924), pp. 225–335; and XXVIII (1931), pp. 3–84.

Pelliot 1920   P. Pelliot "A propos des Comans." *JA* (1920), pp. 125–85.

Petrushevsky 1967   I. P. Petrushevsky: "Rashīd al-Dīn in Persian Historiography of the Middle Ages." XXVII. International Congress of Orientalists: Papers Presented by the U.S.S.R. Delegation Moscow, 1967.

Polo I, II   P. Pelliot: *Notes on Marco Polo*. 2 vols. Paris, 1959 and 1963.

Poppe 1956   Nicholas Poppe: "On Some Geographic Names in the *Jamiʿ al-Tawārīx*." *HJAS* 19/1–2 (1956), pp. 33–41.

Poucha 1962   P. Poucha: "Mongolische Miszellen." *CAJ* VII/3–4 (1962), pp. 192–204.

Quatremère   *Histoire des Mongols de la Perse écrite en persan par Raschid-eldin*. Ed. and trans. M. Quatremère. Paris, 1836.

Recueil   Haithon: "*Flos Historiarum Terre Orientis*" in *Recueil des Historiens des Croisades, Documents arméniens*. Paris, 1906.

337

APPENDIX

Richard 1967	J. Richard: "La Conversion de Berke et les débuts de l'islamisation de la Horde d'Or." *Revue des Etudes Islamiques*, 1967, pp. 173–84.
Rintchen	Y. Rintchen: "L'explication du nom *Burqan Qaldun*." *AO* I (1950–1951), pp. 189–90.
Rockhill	*The Journey of William of Rubruck to the Eastern Parts of the World*. Trans. W. W. Rockhill. London, 1900.
Schmidt	L. J. Schmidt: *Geschichte der Ost-Mongolen und ihres Fürstenhauses*. St. Petersburg, 1829.
Schubert	J. Schubert: *Ritt zum Burchan-chaldun*. Leipzig, 1963.
SH	*The Secret History of the Mongols*. See Haenisch.
Smirnova	Rashīd al-Dīn: *Sbornik letopisei*, Vol. I, Part 2. Trans. O. I. Smirnova. Moscow–Leningrad, 1952.
Spooner 1965	B. Spooner: "Arghiyān. The Area of Jājarm in Western Khurāsān." *Iran* III (1965), pp. 97–107.
Spuler 1939	B. Spuler: *Die Mongolen in Iran*. Leipzig, 1939.
Spuler 1943	B. Spuler: *Die Goldene Horde*. Leipzig, 1943.
Steppes	R. Grousset: *L'Empire des Steppes*. Paris, 1939.
Strakosch-Grassmann	G. Strakosch-Grassmann: *Der Einfall der Mongolen in Mitteleuropa in den Jahren 1241 und 1242*. Innsbruck, 1893.
Thiel	E. Thiel: *Die Mongolei*. Munich, 1958.
Togan 1962	A. Z. V. Togan: "The Composition of the History of the Mongols by Rashīd al-Dīn." *CAJ* VII/1–2, pp. 60–72.
Turcs de l'Asie Centrale	W. Barthold: *Histoire des Turcs de l'Asie Centrale*. Paris, 1945.
Turkestan	W. Barthold: *Turkestan down to the Mongol Invasion*. London, 1928.
Verkhovsky	Rashīd al-Dīn: *Sbornik letopisei*, Vol. II. Trans. Y. P. Verkhovsky. Moscow–Leningrad, 1960.
Vernadsky	G. Vernadsky: *The Mongols and Russia*. New Haven, 1953.
Vullers	Firdausī: *Firdusii Liber Regum qui inscribitur Schahname*. Ed. J. A. Vullers. 3 vols. Leiden, 1877–1884.

Mo.	Written Mongolian.
T.	Turkish.

Aiqaq	Informer.
Al-tamgha	A vermilion seal attached by the Mongols to their documents. Cf. tamgha.
Anda	"Brother by oath," the relationship that existed between Genghis Khan's father and Ong-Khan and Genghis Khan himself and his later rival Jamuqa.
Aqa	In Mongol, "elder brother" used in the sense of "senior prince," as compared with *ini* (q.v.).
Atabeg	A Turkish title, originally given to the guardians of Seljuq princes, borne by the rulers of Fars and Azerbaijan.
Bahadur	Hero; brave warrior.
Bakhshi	Buddhist priest.
Bālish	The Persian word for "pillow," applied to an ingot of gold or silver.
Basqaq	Mongol governor of a conquered territory.
Ba'urchi	Cook, steward.
Bilig	Maxim; wise saying.
Bitikchi	Secretary.
Büke'ül	Taster; officer responsible for commisariat.
Cherig	Auxiliary troops.
Dānishmand	Muslim divine.
Divan (Dīvān)	Government department; secretariat; chancery.
El (Il)	Subject territory.
Ev-Oghlan	Page.
Fatwā	Ruling on a disputed point of Muslim law.
Fidā'ī	Ismāʿīlī assassin.
Hazāra	Military unit of one thousand men.
Ini	Younger brother. The *aqa* and *ini*, that is, the senior and junior Mongol princes.
Injü	Crown land(s).
Ispahbad	Title of local rulers in the Caspian region.
Jerge	See *nerge*.
Kezik, Kezikten	Guard.
Khan	In Mongol times the ruler of an *ulus* (q.v.).
Khaqan	An old Turkish title of sovereignty, applied by Rashīd al-Dīn to the Emperors of China.

Kharvār	"Donkey load" = 100 Tabriz maunds, under Ghazan equivalent to 83.3 kg.
Khatun	Title applied to Turkish and Mongol princesses.
Khuṭba	Friday sermon in the mosque.
Madrasa	A school for Muslim learning.
Malik	Title of Muslim local rulers, inferior to sultan.
Nasīj	A kind of brocade.
Na'ur	Lake.
Nerge	Ring of hunters in a *battue*; similar formation in battle.
Nöker	Follower; assistant.
Noyan	Commander.
Oghul	The Turkish for "son," applied as a title to Mongol princes of the blood.
Ordo	Camp of a Mongol prince, under the management of one of his wives.
Ortaq	Merchant in partnership with a prince or high official and operating with the latter's money.
Pahlavān	Wrestler.
Paiza	Chinese *p'ai tzŭ*, a kind of *laissez-passer*, Polo's "tablet of authority."
Qa'an	A variant of *khaqan* (q.v.), always applied by Rashīd al-Dīn to the Mongol Emperor, the Great Khan.
Qalan	Tax collected by the Mongols from the sedentary population.
Qalandar	Wandering dervish.
Qam	Shaman; witch-doctor.
Qarachu	Man of the people; commoner.
Qarshi	Palace.
Qorchi	Bodyguard.
Quriltai	Assembly or diet of the Mongol princes.
Qushchï	Falconer.
Ribāṭ	Blockhouse on the frontiers of Islam.
Ṣāḥib-Dīvān	Minister, especially minister of finance.
Shaḥna	The Arabo-Persian equivalent of *basqaq* (q.v.).
Tamgha	Seal; octroi at the gates of a town.
Tangsuq	Rare or precious object brought as a gift.
Tarkhan	Person enjoying certain hereditary privileges, such as exemption from taxes.
Tikishmishī	Action of presenting gifts to a ruler.
Tümen	Ten thousand; also an army unit of ten thousand.

APPENDIX

Turqaq	Day guard.
Tuzghu	Offering of food to a traveler.
Ulus	The subjects of a Mongol prince.
Uruq	Family; posterity.
Yam	Post station.
Yamchï	Official in charge of a post station.
Yarghuchï	Judge.
Yarlïgh	Decree; rescript.
Yasa(q)	The code of Genghis Khan.
Yosun	Mongol customary law, as distinct from the *yasa* of Genghis Khan.
Yurt	Apanage of a Mongol prince.
Zunnār	Kind of belt worn by eastern Christians and Jews.

TABLE I. THE GREAT KHANS AND THE YÜAN DYNASTY OF CHINA

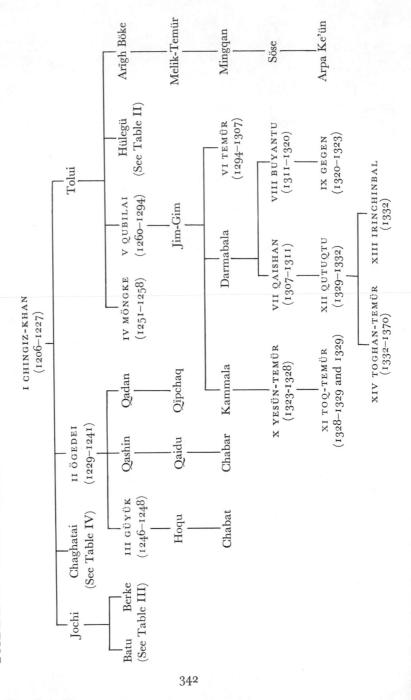

TABLE II. THE IL-KHANS OF PERSIA

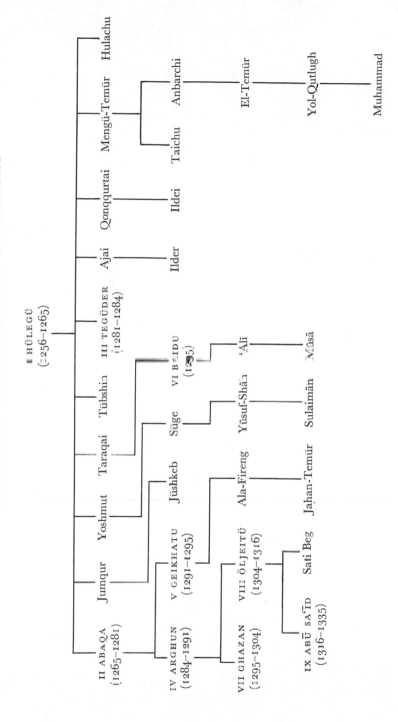

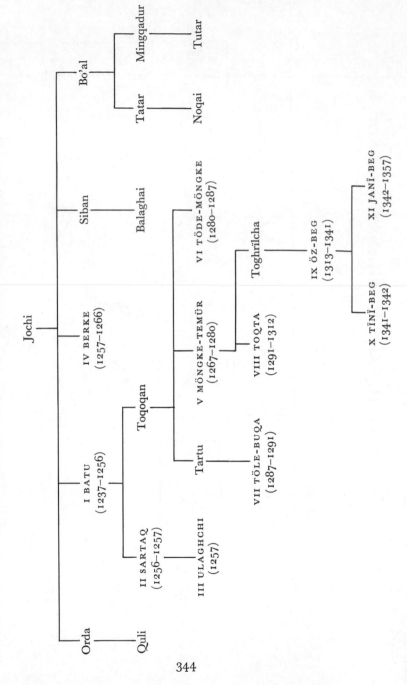

TABLE III. THE KHANS OF THE GOLDEN HORDE, 1237–1357

Jochi

Orda — Quli

Siban — Balaghai

Bo'al

Tatar — Mingqadur

Noqai — Tutar

I BATU
(1237–1256)

IV BERKE
(1257–1266)

II SARTAQ
(1256–1257)

Toqoqan

III ULAGHCHI
(1257)

Tartu — V MÖNGKE-TEMÜR
(1267–1280)

VII TÖLE-BUQA
(1287–1291)

VI TÖDE-MÖNGKE
(1280–1287)

VIII TOQTA
(1291–1312)

Toghrïlcha

IX ÖZ-BEG
(1313–1341)

X TÏNÏ-BEG
(1341–1342)

XI JANÏ-BEG
(1342–1357)

344

TABLE IV.   THE CHAGHAṬAI KHANATE, 1227–1338

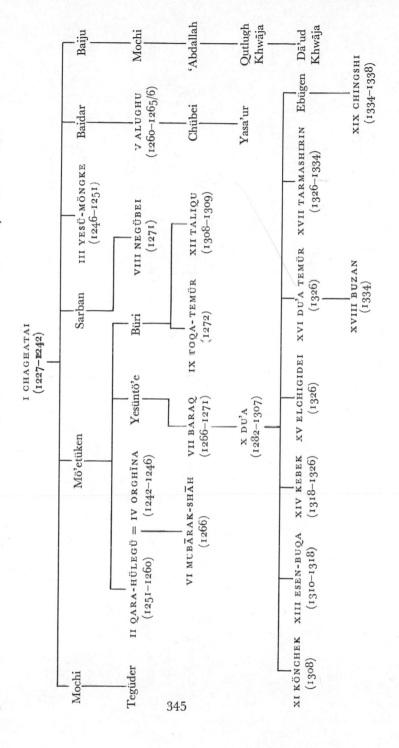

345

TABLE V. YEARS ACCORDING TO THE ANIMAL CYCLE, 1168–1371

RAT	1168	1180	1192	1204	1216	1228	1240	1252	1264	1276	1288	1300	1312	1324	1336	1348	1360
OX	1169	1181	1193	1205	1217	1229	1241	1253	1265	1277	1289	1301	1313	1325	1337	1349	1361
TIGER	1170	1182	1194	1206	1218	1230	1242	1254	1266	1278	1290	1302	1314	1326	1338	1350	1362
HARE	1171	1183	1195	1207	1219	1231	1243	1255	1267	1279	1291	1303	1315	1327	1339	1351	1363
DRAGON	1172	1184	1196	1208	1220	1232	1244	1256	1268	1280	1292	1304	1316	1328	1340	1352	1364
SNAKE	1173	1185	1197	1209	1221	1233	1245	1257	1269	1281	1293	1305	1317	1329	1341	1353	1365
HORSE	1174	1186	1198	1210	1222	1234	1246	1258	1270	1282	1294	1306	1318	1330	1342	1354	1366
SHEEP	1175	1187	1199	1211	1223	1235	1247	1259	1271	1283	1295	1307	1319	1331	1343	1355	1367
MONKEY	1176	1188	1200	1212	1224	1236	1248	1260	1272	1284	1296	1308	1320	1332	1344	1356	1368
HEN	1177	1189	1201	1213	1225	1237	1249	1261	1273	1285	1297	1309	1321	1333	1345	1357	1369
DOG	1178	1190	1202	1214	1226	1238	1250	1262	1274	1286	1298	1310	1322	1334	1346	1358	1370
PIG	1179	1191	1203	1215	1227	1239	1251	1263	1275	1287	1299	1311	1323	1335	1347	1359	1371

Index

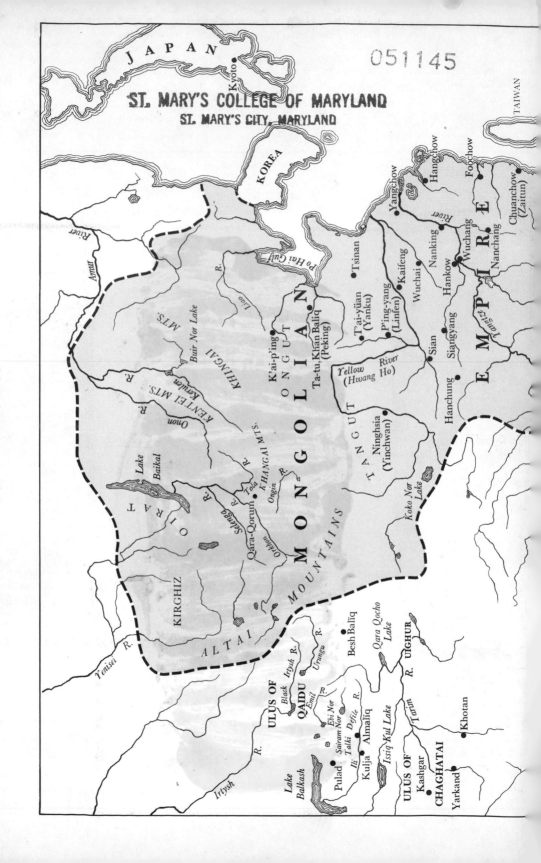

JAPAN

Kyoto

051145

ST. MARY'S COLLEGE OF MARYLAND
ST. MARY'S CITY, MARYLAND

KOREA

TAIWAN

Amur *River*

Chuanchow
(Zaitun)

Hangchow

Foochow

Yangchow

Nanchang

Po Hai Gulf

Nanking

Wuchang

Hankow

Liao R.

Tsinan

Kaifeng

KHINGAI MTS.

Buir Nor Lake

K'ai-p'ing

Wuchai

Ta-tu, Khan Baliq
(Peking)

T'ai-yüan
(Yanku)

P'ing-yang
(Linfen)

Sian

Siangyang

ONGUT

Kerulen R.

Onon R.

Yellow *River*
(Hwang Ho)

Hanchung

KENTEI MTS.

MONGOLIAN

*Lake
Baikal*

Ninghsia
(Yinchwan)

TANGUT

KHANGAI MTS.

Qara-Qorum

Tola R.

Ongin R.

Orkhon R.

Selenga R.

OIRAT

Koko Nor
Lake

E M P I R E

Yangtze R.

ALTAI

MOUNTAINS

KIRGHIZ

Qara Qocho
Lake

Besh Baliq

Yenisei R.

ULUS OF
QAIDU

Black Irtysh R.

Emil R.

Urungu R.

UIGHUR

Tarim R.

Khotan

Ebi Nor

Qara Qocho

Sairam Nor

Ili R.

Talki Defile

Almaliq

Issiq Kul Lake

*Lake
Balkash*

Pulad

Kulja

ULUS OF
CHAGHATAI

Kashgar

Yarkand

Irtysh